Meeting the Challenges of Data Quality Management

Meeting the Challenges of Data Quality Management

Laura Sebastian-Coleman

ELSEVIER

ACADEMIC PRESS
An imprint of Elsevier

Academic Press is an imprint of Elsevier
125 London Wall, London EC2Y 5AS, United Kingdom
525 B Street, Suite 1650, San Diego, CA 92101, United States
50 Hampshire Street, 5th Floor, Cambridge, MA 02139, United States
The Boulevard, Langford Lane, Kidlington, Oxford OX5 1GB, United Kingdom

Notices
Knowledge and best practice in this field are constantly changing. As new research and experience broaden our
understanding, changes in research methods, professional practices, or medical treatment may become necessary.

Practitioners and researchers must always rely on their own experience and knowledge in evaluating and using any
information, methods, compounds, or experiments described herein. In using such information or methods they
should be mindful of their own safety and the safety of others, including parties for whom they have a professional
responsibility.

To the fullest extent of the law, neither the Publisher nor the authors, contributors, or editors, assume any liability
for any injury and/or damage to persons or property as a matter of products liability, negligence or otherwise, or
from any use or operation of any methods, products, instructions, or ideas contained in the material herein.

British Library Cataloguing-in-Publication Data
A catalogue record for this book is available from the British Library

Library of Congress Cataloging-in-Publication Data
A catalog record for this book is available from the Library of Congress

ISBN: 978-0-12-821737-5

For Information on all Academic Press publications
visit our website at https://www.elsevier.com/books-and-journals

The cover image comes from a 12th century English manuscript (currently housed at The Walters Art Museum,
Baltimore) that served as a scientific textbook for monks. This diagram presents a geocentric view of the universe,
describing the movement of the seven planetary bodies (the Sun, the Moon, and the five known planets — listed on
the vertical axis) around the earth. The zodiacal names are listed on the top horizontal. The path of each planetary
body through the zodiac moves from left to right. The bottom of the diagram lists the distances of planetary bodies
using musical values (tone, semitone, three semitones).

©ISO. This material is adapted from ISO 8000-16:2016, with permission of the American National Standards
Institute (ANSI) on behalf of the International Organization for Standardization. All rights reserved.

Publisher: Mara Conner
Editorial Project Manager: Mariana L. Kuhl
Production Project Manager: Punithavathy Govindaradjane
Cover Designer: Vicky Pearson

Typeset by MPS Limited, Chennai, India

Working together
to grow libraries in
developing countries

www.elsevier.com • www.bookaid.org

In Memoriam

In words, like weeds, I'll wrap me o'er,
Like coarsest clothes against the cold:
But that large grief which these enfold
Is given in outline and no more.
—Alfred, Lord Tennyson.

Mr. J.J. O'Brien, 1933−2015
Ryan O. Sebastian, 1988−2017
Mr. C.M. Sidlo, 1928−2018
Professor Joe Voelker, 1947−2020

In praise of *Meeting the Challenges of Data Quality Management*

"*Meeting the Challenges of Data Quality Management* is likely the most comprehensive and well-researched treatise on data quality produced to-date. The book details how to achieve alignment of people, processes and technology toward data quality, positions data quality in the overall context of data management and the business, and includes a most-excellent chapter on data literacy. I highly recommend it for any current or aspiring chief data officer."

—Douglas B. Laney, West Monroe Innovation Fellow and author of *Infonomics: How to Monetize, Manage, and Measure Information as an Asset for Competitive Advantage*, Chicago, IL, USA

"*Meeting the Challenges of Data Quality Management* covers the hard stuff, from in-depth discussion on why data quality matters, setting strategy, why managing data quality at scale is so difficult, to the brutal politics associated with data. And it is aimed specifically at PROFESSIONAL DATA QUALITY MANAGERS. So, if you are one of those, or hope to become one, start here."

—Tom Redman, the Data Doc, Data Quality Solutions, Rumson, NJ, USA

"If you are concerned about poor-quality, untrustworthy data and its impact on your organization (and the world), then Laura Sebastian-Coleman's latest book, *Meeting the Challenges of Data Quality Management*, is for you. Readers will appreciate her ability to think deeply about the problems, combine research with her years of experience, and come to well-thought-out conclusions. She clearly expresses the challenges and solutions in a way that speaks to those who create and manage data, as well as to those leaders who are promoting better use of data to help their organizations. Read it, use it, share it!"

—Danette McGilvray, President, Granite Falls Consulting, Clinton, UT, USA, and author of *Executing Data Quality Projects: Ten Steps to Quality Data and Trusted Information*,™ 2nd ed.

"Laura Sebastian-Coleman has done it again with another incisive and insight-filled book exploring the challenges and opportunities in data management. Whether it is the global financial crisis of over a decade ago or the global Covid crisis of today, robust and rigorous thinking is needed in data management to mitigate and prevent the social and societal problems we face. This is all too often lacking. This book seeks to counterbalance that, and Laura delivers with aplomb."

—Daragh O Brien, Managing Director, Castlebridge, Wexford, Ireland

"It is irrefutable that data, information and knowledge constitute a strategic business asset without which no business activity, no business process, and no business decision can be conducted or made. It is the only business asset that cannot be replaced if lost, destroyed, or stolen. It is the source and enabler of business value, benefit, and service provision. It carries and mitigates organisational and personal risk. Yet, globally, it is managed badly. How often to Boards ask to see

the Financial Reports? Every single Board meeting. And how often do they ask to see the Information Asset Reports? Never; they don't even know what they are. Laura Sebastian-Coleman is one of the world's leading thinkers and practitioners in the management of these critical data assets. Her latest book, *Meeting the Challenges of Data Quality Management*, is a comprehensive, pragmatic guide to managing data well. I commend it to anyone interested in improving service delivery, driving business value, mitigating risk, or just going home on time."
—James Price, Author and keynote presenter, Founder and Managing Director, Experience Matters, Adelaide, Australia

"It has been a long time since the topic of data quality was given a sound analysis from the standpoint of the role and nature of data in organizations. A lot has changed since Larry English's book. Laura Sebastian-Coleman's new book brings the discipline of data quality into the 21st century, clarifying its role in new views and uses of data. Laura has written a thorough, and more importantly, a useful survey of the topic of data quality. There is something in here for CxOs, managers, and stewards of organizational data. She brings together ideas from across the data field and provides a valuable resource for any data stakeholder in any organization."
—John Ladley, Principal, Sonrai Solutions, O'Fallon, MO, USA, author of *Data Governance: How to Design, Deploy, and Sustain a Data Governance Program*

"Laura Sebastian-Coleman has forgotten more about data quality management than most of us have ever known. To call her an "expert" does not do justice to her expertise. And her latest book, *Meeting the Challenges of Data Quality Management*, proves this statement.

In this book, Laura explores in-depth the meaning of data and why we should care about it in today's corporate environment. She delves into how to manage it effectively in an enterprise. But this is no simple how-to manual. It is instead a comprehensive look at all things data from the five key challenges faced in managing data quality today to how data quality is best governed and explained to the processes that keep us from fully realizing data quality. The book is replete with examples, statistics, and anecdotes that help support her views and give substance to the solutions proposed. Laura is a wonderful writer and some of the best parts of the book go into the background of data. There is a fascinating view of the history of data that will enlighten even the most knowledgeable data practitioners.

This book is a MUST READ for anyone who is attempting to manage data in any size company, for executives who need to understand the lifeblood of their organizations, and for those who on a daily basis lament the quality of their data."
—Theresa Kushner, Consultant, Data and Analytics, NTT DATA, Dallas, TX, USA

"Laura Sebastian-Coleman recognizes that data is a representation of the activities of an organization and that to improve the business' data quality is also to improve the organization, its people and technology as such. Those who might claim that a Data Governance program, or AI, or a better system, or coercive management, or other quick fixes will "straighten out our data" suffer from lack of insight, insight that this book depicts. This book is a must read for anyone attempting data quality improvements. Laura provides the fundamental and in-depth knowledge needed to accomplish changes that work and last; this is the improvement hiker's comprehensible guide to the data galaxy."

—Håkan Edvinsson, Author, consultant, and founder of the Diplomatic Data Governance concept, Helsingborg, Sweden

"Every organization, regardless of industry or size, faces issues with data quality. These issues create challenges that can result in lost revenue, increased costs, poor productivity, regulatory and legal concerns, etc. Yes, data quality can be improved, if professionals in all fields know how to analyze, improve, and sustain data quality—and how to address the challenges inherent in the use of data in any organization. Laura Sebastian-Coleman's fantastic book provides insight into all the components of data quality management, including the need for enterprise data management programs and the value of a data literate organization. If you read one book on data quality, this is the one to choose!"

—Anne Marie Smith, Ph.D., Data management and data governance expert, author, and consultant, Philadelphia, PA, USA

"Dr. Sebastian-Coleman's new book, *Meeting the Challenges of Data Quality Management*, is a great sequel to her book *Measuring Data Quality for Ongoing Improvement*. Our Information Quality Graduate Program has been using *Measuring Data Quality for Ongoing Improvement* as a standard textbook for the program's Principles of Information Quality course since its publication in 2013. While *Measuring Data Quality for Ongoing Improvement* provides a very clear and effective guide for "how" to systematically measure data quality, her new book, *Meeting the Challenges of Data Quality Management*, expands this perspective to include the broader context of "why" an organization should incorporate data quality management best practices into its strategic plan. It provides a clear roadmap for bringing together data, processes, technology, and people into systems that maximize the value of an organization's data assets. It also describes how data quality management practices must be adapted to meet the challenges of big data, data literacy, data governance, and data protection. I highly recommend this book for any organization trying to build and improve its data strategy, and as a textbook for data management, data science, and information science programs."

—John R. Talburt, PhD, IQCP, CDMP, Acxiom Chair of Information Quality, University of Arkansas at Little Rock, and Lead Consultant for Data Quality and Data Governance, Noetic Partners, Little Rock, AK, USA

"Most Data Governance (DG) programs are not successful primarily because Boards, Executives and Management fail to truly understand and buy into the importance of data or they fail to effectively implement Data Quality frameworks that deliver measurable uplift through incremental transformative business improvements. Data Governance Programs fail because they are not able to effectively articulate a road map that makes sense from a pragmatic perspective. Laura's new book goes well beyond the world's best Data Quality practice. I thoroughly commend it as essential reading for students and professionals within the Data Management Community and even more so by captains of Industry, Government and Social Enterprises."

—Andrew Andrews, Vice President, DAMA Australia, Adelaide, Australia

Contents

Section 3 Data Quality Management Practices

About the Author

Laura Sebastian-Coleman, Data Quality Director at Prudential, has been a data quality practitioner since 2003. She has implemented data quality metrics and reporting, launched and facilitated working stewardship groups, contributed to data consumer training programs, and led efforts to establish data standards and manage metadata. In 2009, she led a group of analysts in developing the Data Quality Assessment Framework (DQAF), which is the basis for her 2013 book, *Measuring Data Quality for Ongoing Improvement*. An active professional, Laura has delivered papers, tutorials, and keynotes at data-focused conferences, such as MIT's Information Quality Program, Data Governance and Information Quality (DGIQ), Enterprise Data World (EDW), Data Modeling Zone, and Data Management Association (DAMA)-sponsored events. From 2009 to 2010, she served as IAIDQ's Director of Member Services. In 2015, she received the IAIDQ Distinguished Member Award. DAMA Publications Officer (2015 to 2018) and production editor for the *DAMA-DMBOK2* (2017), she is also author of *Navigating the Labyrinth: An Executive Guide to Data Management* (2018). In 2018, she received the DAMA award for excellence in the data management profession. She holds an IQCP (Information Quality Certified Professional) from IAIDQ, a Certificate in Information Quality from MIT, a B.A. in English and History from Franklin & Marshall College, and a Ph.D. in English Literature from the University of Rochester.

Foreword

Why PROFESSIONAL Data Quality Management Is so Important

Have you ever wondered if finance professionals actually like finance? I can't figure it out. On the one hand, it seems like a cool profession. On the other hand, heads of finance groups report that their teams spend three-quarters of their time on mundane data tasks, not finance. So maybe not.

Have you ever wondered if data scientists like to see their clever, new AI-driven models succeed in helping solve some of their companies' most difficult problems? On the one hand, *Harvard Business Review* advises that data science is the sexiest job of the 21st century, and solving tough problems seems pretty sexy to me. On the other hand, data scientists are well aware of "garbage in, garbage out" and that poor data quality keeps their models in the lab.[1] So maybe not.

Have you ever wondered if senior managers enjoy making timely, inspired decisions? That seems like their job. But most agree that they must do so in the face of numbers that are clearly wrong and disparate reports. That seems miserable to me, yet they don't take steps to resolve the issues. So maybe not.

Note that I would get the same answers if I asked equivalent questions about practically any profession. It seems as if everyone's job has two components: Their job and dealing with the mundane data issues that slow them down and make them less effective.

We all experience the impact of poor data quality. And most of us have grown way too tolerant of the problem and the little indignities it adds to our lives.

In a similar vein, have you ever wondered if companies really want to make money? Everyone I talk to insists that this is the case. Yet poor data means all employees must spend/waste incredible amounts of time dealing with data issues. People do their best, but plenty of errors leak through to customers, causing all sorts of problems. Bad data breeds mistrust among teams, departments and customers. It makes it more difficult to unleash data's transformative powers—at today's levels of data quality, AI is downright scary! A good first estimate is the associated costs come to 20% of revenue.[2] Attacking data quality issues may be the single best step a company can take to improve profits and build its future. So maybe companies aren't all that interested in making money.

On the broad canvass, poor-quality data threatens democracies, gets people killed, and throttles much innovation.

Owing to the impact, scope, and ubiquity of data quality issues, we're all going to have to get involved in making improvements. And if the general indifference to the issues isn't enough, other factors complicate matters still further. Consider the following scenario. You receive a phone call on your commute home. It's the principal of your teenager's school. They were involved in a fight and being suspended for the next week.

You arrive home and ask your teenager, "How was your day?"

"Great," they reply. "I got an A— on my Chinese test."

---

[1] Nithya Sambasivan, Shivani Kapania, Hannah Highfill, Diana Akrong, Praveen Kumar Paritosh, Lora Mois Aroyo. SIGCHI, ACM (2021). "Everyone wants to do the model work, not the data work: Data Cascades in High-Stakes AI." https://research.google/pubs/pub49953/.

[2] Redman, T.C. (2017). Seizing Opportunity in Data Quality. MIT Sloan Management Review. November 27, 2017. https://sloanreview.mit.edu/article/seizing-opportunity-in-data-quality/

Presumably, your kid told the truth. But clearly, they did not provide the high-quality data you sought. Data quality, it seems, is more than just "correctness."

The second complication is that many people make addressing data quality seem easier than it is. Throughout my career, I've heard hundreds of versions of the following, all promising an easy solution: "We all know you do data quality as you move the data to the warehouse." "In the age of big data, the sheer quantities of data mean you don't have to worry about quality." "Our data catalog will solve all your data quality problems." "Data governance will solve data quality woes." "The problems will all melt away when we start using AI." Yet here we are!

Dealing with all this requires the leadership of PROFESSIONAL data quality managers; skilled and experienced in the approaches and techniques needed to attack the issues properly; savvy enough to build needed political support and get everyone involved; wise enough to know the effort will take a long time; impatient enough to get on with it; courageous enough to rebut the nonsense promoted by amateurs.

There is much to do and much to learn. My top-shelf features works by AT&T, Beer, Covey, Brown and Duguid, Davenport, Deming, Drucker, English, Goldratt, Hay, Juran, Kent, Kotter, Ladley, Laney, McGilvray, Porter, the early work of my group at Bell Labs, Roberts, Silver, Tufte, the early work of Wang's group at MIT, Zachman, and others. I am adding Laura Sebastian-Coleman to that shelf. This book covers the hard stuff, from in-depth discussion on why data quality matters, setting strategy, why managing data quality at scale is so difficult, to the brutal politics associated with data. It is the only one aimed specifically at PROFESSIONAL DATA QUALITY MANAGERS. So, if you are one of those, or hope to become one, start here.

Professional data quality manager is a big job. It is most certainly not the "sexiest job of the 21st century," but it is quite possibly the "most needed and important job of the 21st century."

Thomas C. Redman
"the Data Doc", Rumson, NJ, United States

June 2021

Acknowledgments

"Treat people as if they were what they ought to be, and you help them to become what they are capable of becoming."

Goethe

While working on this book, I was fortunate to receive support and encouragement from many people. Thanks, first, to the team at Elsevier: Mara Conner, Gabriela Capille, Punitha Govindaradjane, and Joanne Gosnell, for the opportunity to publish my ideas and for their work to make a high-quality product. My manager at Aetna/CVS Health, Dawn Shane, and my teammates on the Finance Data Repository (FDR) and Enterprise Data Catalog projects have helped me stretch my ideas related to data governance, data quality management, and metadata management. Special thanks to Bob Furce for insight into the section on the Systems Development Life Cycle in Chapter 11 and for researching the use of data as documented in the *Project Management Body of Knowledge*. And to Az Rahman for feedback on the data literacy chapter and for his passionate commitment to improving data management. And, of course, I appreciate Aetna/CVS Health's support of my attendance at conferences.

I am indebted to Tony Shaw of Dataversity for giving me the opportunity to deliver a keynote presentation at Enterprise Data World in 2019, through which I began to solidify the ideas in this book, and for all of the work he and his team do to support data management education. Likewise, I am indebted to Marilu Lopez of DAMA Mexico for inviting me to speak on data and society, a topic that progressed my ideas further and for the wonderful hospitality of the DAMA Mexico chapter. Through the Certified Data Management Professional (CDMP) study group, my colleagues at DAMA New England have helped me relearn and gain insight into aspects of the DAMA data management framework. Thanks Agnes Vega, Karen Sheridan, Lynn Noel, Mary Lynn Early, and Nupur Gandhi.

Special thanks to DAMA New England president, Sandi Perillo-Simmons, for feedback on the data literacy chapter and Tony Mazzarella for feedback on the overall manuscript. Chris Heien generously allowed me to adapt his work on data products and the value chain for use in Chapter 11. Peter van Nederpelt, Peter Vieveen, and Andrew Black shared with me the work they were doing on data quality dimensions for DAMA Netherlands, which provided additional insight into Chapter 10. Ben Hu, by sending thought-provoking emails and articles, helped me keep the gears turning.

During 2019, Danette McGilvray asked me to participate in the Leaders Data Organization (LDO), a group from which I have benefited immensely. Danette and other members of the group provided extremely valuable input on the manuscript as well as ongoing conversation that informed it overall. Andrew Andrews, Peter de Haan, Theresa Kushner, John Ladley (especially for sharing his insights on the history of data governance and for his review of the data management framework in Chapter 9), Doug Laney, Marc Nolte, Daragh O Brien, and the incomparable James Price: Thank you all very much.

While working on this book, I had the opportunity to review the manuscript of the second edition of Danette's *Executing Data Quality Projects: Ten Steps to Quality Data and Trusted*

Information. Doing so refreshed my knowledge of the foundational concepts of data quality management and reminded me of how important it is to share knowledge around the processes we are trying to improve. Danette, your friendship over the past decade and a half has been invaluable.

As has the friendship of Anne Marie Smith, who read every word of the manuscript, including the parts that ended up on the cutting room floor, and provided unwavering support.

I owe a huge debt to Tom Redman, who has provided guidance throughout the writing process and has been a sounding board, mentor, and friend. When I started working in data quality in the early 2000s, it never occurred to me that I would spend Friday lunchtimes having in-depth conversations with the person whose work laid the foundations of data quality management. Thank you, Tom.

My family has been great through the whole process, even if they are not really sure what I do. Thanks, and much, much love, Mom and Dad, Karen and David, Virginia, Dick, and Nancy. To my kids, Richard and Janet, and my wonderful husband, George: thank you for being you.

Introduction: The Challenges of Managing Data Quality

"Not everything that is faced can be changed. But nothing can be changed until it is faced."

James Baldwin

Why Focus on Data Quality Management?

The purpose of this book is to help data management professionals meet the challenges of managing the quality of organizational data (data that represents the activities and stakeholders of the organization). This group includes data quality practitioners, data governance professionals, information technology (IT) teams, and others who help their organizations create and use data. It also extends to people higher up the organizational ladder (chief data officers, data strategists, analytics leaders) and in different parts of the organization (finance professionals, operations managers, IT leaders) who want to leverage their data and their organizational capabilities (people, processes, technology) to drive value and gain competitive advantage.

Given these goals, it is appropriate to start with two simple questions:

- Why is it important to manage the quality of data?
- Why is managing the quality of data challenging?

The short answer to the first question is easy: managing the quality of data is important because failure to do so is costly and dangerous to individuals and organizations. It is hard to get people to act on this insight, however, for three reasons connected to the second question:

- The complexities uncovered when one seriously engages the process of managing the quality of data—that is, when one recognizes that the challenges of managing data quality are deeply connected to the overall challenge of effectively managing the organization's people, processes, and technology.
- The recognition that many of the structures proposed to help organizations get more value from data are not working as promised.
- The fact that, in many organizations, poor-quality data and the costs associated with poor-quality data are tolerated to a degree that poor-quality products or services are not.

Poor-quality data may be tolerated because there is so much data, because organizations struggle to define the value of data, or because data is easy to copy, share, and manipulate. For many organizations, it has become normal to accept quality issues, encourage workarounds, and integrate stopgap measures into business processes. Whatever the reasons, many organizations choose to ignore poor-quality data, rather than take advantage of the opportunities presented by improving data quality.

It is commonplace to say that data is an "asset," but most organizations do not treat data as they treat their other assets. They do not know how much data they have or what condition the data is in. They create data for their immediate purposes and do not consider the potential for broader use. Many do not differentiate between data that is likely to bring value and data that is of little importance. Few provide guidance for employees about how to get value from data. They do not recognize the costs of low-quality data or the benefits of high-quality data, so no one is held accountable for ensuring that data is well managed. In short, they do not manage their data and information the way they manage financial and physical assets. The failure to do so can prevent organizations from taking advantage of the knowledge and insight they could gain from their data and the ways that they can derive value from their data. In many organizations, lack of understanding of their own data is a huge blind spot. It is also a terrible waste of resources.

Data Quality Management Goals

Data quality management is a way to address this blind spot. At its simplest, data quality management, the application of product quality management methodologies to data, aims to improve the quality of data and to sustain the levels of data quality that an organization needs to deliver on its mission and serve its customers. Regardless of how an organization defines its mission and customers, data quality practitioners must help the organization answer and act on the findings from three fundamental questions:

- What do we mean by high-quality data?
- How do we detect low-quality or poor-quality data?
- What action will we take when data does not meet quality standards?

To answer these questions, data quality practitioners must help the organization do the following:

- **Define expectations for quality:** Define what the organization means by "high-quality data" by identifying or setting standards and expectations for data quality. This process can begin with determining how parties who create, consume, or manage data identify and capture expectations for the quality of data. Some standards may exist, though they are not always recognized as such. For example, they may be embedded in data models or process expectations. Others may be implied by the requirements of data consumers. Organizations will greatly benefit from explicitly defining and documenting data quality standards and expectations.
- **Assess data quality:** Enable the organization to determine whether its data meets required standards for quality. This entails measuring the quality of data against standards and expectations. Assessment can take place in multiple ways: as part of formal data analysis for project work, as part of data quality improvement projects, or through data use, as when a data consumer reports an issue, and the impact of that issue must be determined. Monitoring data quality is another form of data quality assessment. Business processes and systems evolve. This evolution is reflected in changes in organizational data. Monitoring data can detect unexpected

changes in data so their causes can be investigated. Monitoring is not an end in itself. The most important reason to monitor data is to keep data consumers informed about its condition (through data quality reporting and issue management) so they can provide feedback about whether data meets their requirements and take action to improve data if it does not meet the requirements.

- **Take action:** Help the organization take appropriate action in response to situations in which data does not meet expectations. Monitoring, ongoing assessment, and the use of data by data consumers may uncover issues with data (obstacles to data use). Any of these may also identify new requirements for data.

  - For data that is critical to the organization's goals, taking action entails determining the root causes of problems, defining the costs and benefits of remediating issues, and then advocating for the process and technical changes necessary to reduce the risks associated with poor-quality data and remove the obstacles to the organization's ability to get value from its data. This may include fixing data and/or implementing controls to prevent future issues.

  - For data that is not critical to the organization's goals, taking action may mean deciding not to take action and instead choosing to live with identified issues and their associated risks. Not all data is equally valuable. The focus of data quality efforts should be on data that contributes to the organization's goals.

Asking these questions and helping the organization answer them is necessary to identify opportunities for improvement. As importantly the activities necessary to answer the three questions (setting standards, assessing data, taking action), which form the core of data quality management, will have numerous other benefits. Not the least of these is raising awareness of the ways data works in organizations, and consequently, the ways people in different parts of the organization depend on each other to produce reliable data. Done well, data quality management provides a means of developing organizational self-knowledge through data knowledge. This is one of the many reasons why metadata management, the discipline by which we capture knowledge of the data in the context of the business, is so critical to data quality management.

Data Quality and the Context of the Organization

Because data is a representation of the activities of an organization, data quality management should be understood in relation to the goals and overall strategy of an organization, its management and culture, its business processes, and its technical architecture. Strict focus on puzzling data issues, technical mechanisms, or worse yet, on checklisted activities like "data profiling for the sake of data profiling" will prevent data quality practitioners from seeing the larger context—the overall system that is the enterprise that produces, obtains, and uses data. Knowledge of the enterprise and its goals will prompt practitioners to ask better questions about context and better understand the size and shape of any given data-related challenge in context. This perspective also helps practitioners apply a range of tools and methodologies as they address challenges of different shapes and sizes.

An organization is like the human body: it is a cohesive overall entity comprising a set of systems and processes that turn inputs into outputs, bring about growth, and enable the enterprise to perpetuate itself and meet its goals. Bodies and enterprises are both complex systems, with subsystems that interact in ways that are largely predictable. (In organizations, these processes are rarely optimal under normal circumstances.) Bodily processes can be improved (through exercise and practice) or can deteriorate (through illness or neglect). To understand the body, we view it through the lens of subsystems: the respiratory system, the digestive system, the circulatory system, the muscular system, and so on. Each of these body systems can be understood as a thing in itself, with tissues, organs, and distinct functions. Each can also be understood in relation to the other systems of the body.

In biology textbooks, the systems of the body are usually depicted through a set of drawings, each with details of the body system superimposed on an outline of the body (Fig. 1). The skeletal system shows the bones; the circulatory system shows the heart, arteries, and veins; the nervous system shows the brain, spinal cord, and nerves; and so on. When conceptualizing data quality management, it is helpful to keep this idea of the body in mind because it allows us to envision how the different pieces of an enterprise can be both things in themselves and parts of a greater whole, the processes of

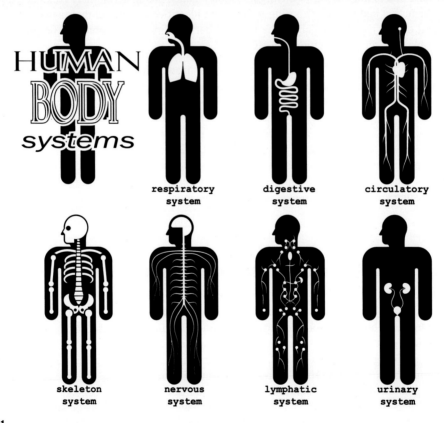

FIGURE 1

The human body as a system of systems.

which interact with each other. Within an organization, data is not only a thing itself; it is also the means by which different parts of the organization interact. Recognition of the role data plays is likely the origin of assertions that data is the "life blood" of the organization (DAMA, 2009). This assertion has been used so often that we tend to forget how well this metaphor works in describing data's role in connecting different parts of the organization: blood carries materials for all vital functions (oxygen, waste, immune response) among the various systems, just as different pieces of an organization exchange data to allow the other pieces to function.

The Five Challenges

Throughout the book, I will refer to the five challenges of managing data quality. These challenges involve data itself, the people, processes, and technology connected to data, as well as the organization's cultural practices and behaviors toward data (Fig. 2). It is critical for any organization to

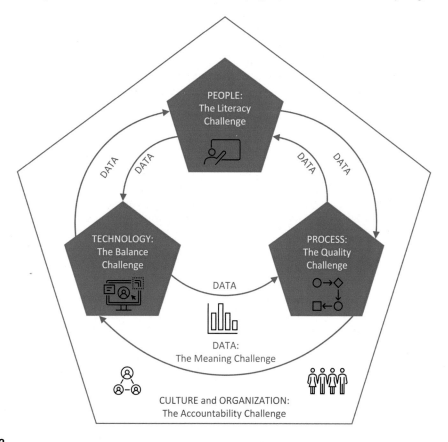

FIGURE 2

The five challenges of managing data quality.

manage people, processes, and technology. Data presents specific challenges for each and for the interactions among them. I refer to these challenges as:

- **Data: The meaning challenge:** Understanding the nature of data: how data works as a symbolic system that operates using defined conventions to represent real-world objects, events, and people; and recognizing the limits of this system.[1] Recognizing and adapting to both the human-created and "organic" properties of data. Knowledge about data-as-data is critical to two of the most important facets of data use:
  - **Interpretation:** Because data is a system of signs, using data always involves interpreting these signs.
  - **Quality:** Helping people in the organization define what they mean by high-quality data and how to recognize low-quality data.

  Knowledge about how data works is also critical to taking advantage of data opportunities: what can be learned from data, how data may be used to improve operations, and how data may drive value either directly, through monetization, or indirectly, through insights into customers, products, and partnerships.
- **Process: The quality challenge:** Helping people within the organization see the connection between process quality and data quality, that is, recognizing data as both an input to and an output from (i.e., a product of) organizational processes. Defining and managing processes so they result in higher-quality, more reliable data; ensuring that data producers understand how their choices affect the ability of data consumers to use data.
- **Technology: The balance challenge:** Understanding the role of technology in creating and managing data; recognizing the ways data is dependent on and independent from technology; acknowledging how choices related to technology affect the creation, accessibility, and use of data as well as its quality; and, ultimately, taking a data perspective on choices about technology.
- **People: The literacy challenge:** Ensuring that data producers and data consumers build the knowledge, develop the skills, and have access to the information they need to use and interpret data in general and their organization's data in particular; building organizational capability to communicate around data.
- **Culture and organization: The accountability challenge:** Establishing leadership accountability for data and leadership commitment to quality in order to get value from data. Changing the culture to live out that commitment. Establishing responsibility along the data supply chain. Reducing obstacles to data use. Implementing enterprise oversight of data via formal data governance practices. Actively cultivating desired behaviors around data through policy and incentives.

These challenges are interconnected. Knowledge of data-as-data—that is, understanding the processes and technologies through which data is created and understood—is fundamental to both data literacy and collaboration. The processes and technologies an organization uses to get its work

---

[1] In seminars and tutorials, I have referred to this as "the semiotic challenge." Semiotics is the study of signs and their interpretation. But I have found most people do not respond to the word *semiotic*—it is too abstract. Most do understand, however, the idea that they want to learn (e.g., gain insights, identify trends) from data and that this learning depends on the ability to "de-code" (interpret) data. See also Chisholm (2010 and 2012).

done reflect and represent its culture. Changing them to produce better data requires changing the culture. Defining accountability for data and desired behaviors around data requires understanding how data works in general as well as how it is created and used by people and integrated into processes via technology. So, while we will look at each of these challenges individually, we will also discuss their interactions and how they influence each other.

It is critical to understand that success in meeting the other four challenges is directly dependent on addressing the accountability challenge. People in organizations will not change their behaviors, increase their understanding of data, make process improvements, or adopt technologies to support high-quality data unless leadership not only recognizes data as a valuable asset but also treats it as such.

The Structure of This Book

This book will do three things:

- Describe the importance of high-quality data to organizations wanting to leverage their data and, more generally, to people living in today's digitally interconnected world
- Propose approaches to meeting the five challenges of data quality management
- Describe core data quality management capabilities, both as stand-alone processes and as integral components of projects and operations

Not surprisingly, content is organized into three sections, each focusing on one of these topics.

Section 1: Data in Today's Organizations

The purpose of Section 1 is to present the high-level context of data quality management. Data plays a critical role in organizational success. Over the past several decades, our ability to generate and capture data has grown exponentially, but our ability to manage it has not kept up. This section will start with an analysis of the current state of data evolution and the role of data quality management in response to this evolution. It will discuss the costs and risk of poor-quality data, describe the five challenges in data quality management (data, process, technology, people, and culture/organization), and propose that organizations that want to get more value and insight from their data should take a strategic approach to data quality management.

Chapter 1: The Importance of Data Quality Management discusses the current state of data quality management in the context of the evolution of data, technology, and digital connectedness. It argues that data quality management reduces the costs and risks of poor-quality data and enables the benefits and opportunities of high-quality data. Poor-quality data has been tolerated for decades. But as data grows bigger and organizations attempt to transform digitally, the costs and risks associated with poor-quality data have increased. Many organizations will need to ask themselves whether they can transform digitally if they do not have reliable data. As importantly, if organizations are to get more value from their data, they will need to take a strategic approach to managing its quality. Today's organizations are complex systems that are interconnected through the exchange of data and information. Quality data is integral to their success. It cannot be an afterthought.

Chapter 2: Organizational Data and the Five Challenges of Managing Data Quality summarizes the challenges within the context of an organization as a complex system. The chapter provides the context for the in-depth discussion in Section 2 (Chapters 4 to 8) and also introduces definitions of critical terms that will be used throughout the book.

Chapter 3: Data Quality and Strategy provides perspective on how to think strategically about data. It explores how concepts about strategy apply to planning and decisions that organizations make about their data, how data strategy is connected to overall business strategy, and how to account for the challenges particular to managing the quality of data. There is no simple answer to the challenge of producing high-quality data. However, there are ways to align people, processes, and technology with organizational strategy in order to build the skills and cultivate the behaviors that people and organizations must have, if they are to derive more value from their data and use it to gain competitive advantage. Such an approach reduces the risks related to data. A strategic approach to data quality management aligns priorities for data and information management with organizational goals and builds accountability for data into processes, system design, and individual performance.

Section 2: The Five Challenges in Depth

The purpose of Section 2 is to present a fuller analysis of each of the five challenges in data quality management (data, process, technology, people, culture/organization). Each chapter in this section will go into depth on one of the challenges, connect it to the other challenges, and propose ways of addressing the challenge under discussion.

Chapter 4: The Data Challenge: The Mechanics of Meaning defines the nature of the thing that we are trying to manage the quality of: data. Data is a means of encoding and sharing knowledge and information about the real world. Data is valuable to organizations because of what it can teach them about their products, customers, employees, and other stakeholders. Using data always involves interpreting data. But what we mean by *data* and how we create and use data have changed over time. Many assumptions about data quality are rooted in this evolution. A better understanding of what data is and how data works (how it encodes meaning through a series of choices about how people represent people, concepts, and events) helps us define and manage specific expectations related to data quality. This knowledge not only enables better data quality management, but it also improves data literacy—the ability of individuals and, collectively, organizations to understand, use, interpret, and thus learn from data. In describing how data works, This chapter will also argue for the criticality of metadata in the overall management of data quality.

Chapter 5: The Process Challenge: Managing for Quality presents basic principles of quality management as defined in the manufacture of physical products and applies these principles to data. Data is a product of organizational processes and an organizational asset. However, data differs from other products and assets, especially with respect to its life cycle and the ways in which organizations can derive value from it. Understanding these differences provides perspective on data quality management, allowing us to see the connections among the other challenges at different points in the life cycle. For example, the process challenges of data creation, the technical challenges of data management, the challenges associated with people (data creation, use, and interpretation), and the cultural challenges of ensuring that people take accountability for data within the organization.

Chapter 6: The Technical Challenge: Data/Technology Balance discusses the deep connection between the data we produce and the instruments and technologies used to create, collect, manage, access, and use it. Data brings value only when it is used. Without reliable technical management of data, people cannot access and use data. However, technology is not an end in itself, and, unfortunately, incorrect assumptions about the relationship between technology and data often result in poor-quality data. Because technology enables the creation and use of new forms of data, organizations must manage their technology to support their data strategy, while avoiding the risk of being sucked into technology hype. This chapter focuses on the need to put data and technology in the right relationship with each other. Both data and technology must serve organizational goals.

Chapter 7: The People Challenge: Building Data Literacy addresses a key component in any organization's ability to get value from data: the skills, knowledge, and experience of the people who use and interpret data. Despite fantasies about machine learning and artificial intelligence, data does not speak for itself—at least not without a lot of help and insight from people. Data literacy is a skill set that includes the ability to read, understand, interpret, and learn from data in different contexts and to communicate about data with other people. The people challenge is a knowledge challenge. No single individual can know everything about an organization's data. However, people can solve more problems in better ways if they understand data as a construct, recognize the risks associated with data production and use, cultivate a level of skepticism about data, and develop skills in visualizing and interpreting data.

Chapter 8: The Culture Challenge: Organizational Accountability for Data addresses questions related to people and data in order to meet the cultural challenges of data quality management: how to build accountability and responsibility for data, how to develop organizational commitment to quality, and how to execute on that commitment. People must behave differently toward data to do the work associated with making better data and making data better. Many organizations have tried to address the cultural challenges by implementing data governance and stewardship programs or by hiring a chief data officer, but these have met with limited or mixed success. Better data quality management demands a reexamination of data governance and stewardship. These programs have not delivered on their initial promise of improved data quality. Many have lost their way, due to lack of vision, conflicting demands, and unclear priorities. Consequently, the problems of accountability and oversight for data have not been solved. There is a need to focus their goals. There is also a need to return to the roots of quality management and establish the discipline required to get value from robust data quality management practices.

Section 3: Data Quality Management Practices

The purpose of Section 3 is to describe the capabilities an organization must develop to better manage its data and to show how these capabilities can be integrated into project and operational processes. Many organizational processes can have an impact on the quality of organizational data. Heightened awareness of these potential impacts can help an organization produce higher-quality, more reliable data. Core data quality management capabilities can help an organization raise awareness of these impacts, identify and mitigate risks associated with data, and improve its processes so these create higher-quality data. Data quality management is also necessary to sustain high levels of data quality.

Chapter 9: Core Data Quality Management Capabilities describes the functions required to build organizational capacity to manage data for quality over time. They include the following:

- **Data quality standards:** Describe what is meant by high-quality data; set standards and requirements for data quality.
- **Data quality assessment:** Observe and analyze characteristics of particular data to identify errors, risks, and obstacles to use, and quantify data quality levels.
- **Data quality monitoring:** Track quality levels within a system or process to detect unexpected conditions and to take action in response to them.
- **Data quality reporting:** Communicate information about the condition of data to data consumers and other stakeholders.
- **Data quality issue management:** Identify, quantify, prioritize, and facilitate the remediation of root causes of data issues (obstacles to data consumers' uses of data).
- **Data quality improvement:** Identify and facilitate the implementation of process and technical changes to prevent data issues, enforce data quality standards, and improve the overall trustworthiness of organizational data.

These activities are likely to be executed more consistently and with greater impact if there is a data quality team specifically responsible for defining them and facilitating their adoption within the organization.

Chapter 10: Dimensions of Data Quality provides an in-depth discussion about a core concept in data quality management: data quality dimensions. Dimensions provide a framework through which we can understand the core capabilities. As the foundation for data quality rules and requirements, they play a critical role in helping answer the first and second fundamental questions about data quality: "What do we mean by high-quality data?" and "How do we detect low-quality data?" They also provide a basis for assessment, issue management, data quality monitoring and reporting, and quantifying data quality improvement opportunities. As such, dimensions help accountable people in the organization answer the third question: "What action will we take when data does not meet quality standards?"

Chapter 11: Data Life Cycle Processes describes four processes that provide different perspectives on managing the quality of data: the data life cycle, the data supply chain, the data value chain, and the systems development life cycle. These cycles help put the core data quality management capabilities in the context of other work carried out within the enterprise. Each model offers a variation on how we can think about executing data quality management activities. In combination, they provide data quality practitioners, data producers, data consumers, as well as data stewards, data modelers, application developers, process improvement teams, and other stakeholders a means of understanding their work in the context of the wider enterprise. They also show the intersection of processes that can influence the condition of data. These models also help practitioners communicate across the enterprise because they depend on analogous processes that are executed by various business and technical teams (e.g., product management, supply chain management, value creation, project and program management).

Chapter 12: Tying It Together summarizes the arguments in the book as a whole and strongly encourages readers to apply the ideas and work to change their organizations for the better.

The book also contains a glossary and an extensive bibliography.

Why I Wrote This Book

When I began working on this book, I envisioned clarifying and simplifying the Data Quality Assessment Framework (DQAF) published in my 2013 book, *Measuring Data Quality for Ongoing Improvement*, and sharing new insights I had gained through another half decade working in the data quality management space. Between 2013 and 2019, I had edited the second edition of *The DAMA Data Management Body of Knowledge* (DMBOK2), published *Navigating the Labyrinth: An Executive Guide to Data Management*, and changed jobs twice, moving from UnitedHealth Group/Optum to Cigna and then to Aetna/CVS Health. Work on the DMBOK2 deepened my understanding of the complexity involved in trying to ensure that organizations have usable, accessible, high-quality data and, especially, the collaboration required to meet this goal. Working in different environments gave me a deeper appreciation for the ways organizations differ from each other, even as they attempt to solve common problems, and in the ways they get caught in similar traps, such as thinking that just the right tool will solve their data problems.

These experiences also helped me see what I had intuited from attending conferences and talking with people who are trying to improve data quality, implement data governance, and coordinate data management in their organizations: many of the structures that have been proposed to help organizations get more value from data are not working as promised. Organizations are floundering in their data governance efforts. Ideas about what data stewards are supposed to do are all over the map, and the expectations for and responsibilities of chief data officers morph each time an industry survey is published. It is not that these ideas are wrong. It is more that organizations struggle to implement them in ways that bring value to the organizations themselves. Not only that, but as ideas around data governance and data stewardship have emerged, the vision of a data quality management function based on successful practices of product and service quality management faded. The data quality function in many organizations is not about improving processes that create and use data but about "correcting" data and managing exception records—a losing, unsustainable proposition.

My engagement with the Leaders Data Organization (dataleaders.org) has stretched my thinking about these issues and given me a sense of urgency about the need to change behaviors and organizational structures around data if we are to truly benefit from the insights to be gained from data.

Beginning this work shortly before the outbreak of the Covid-19 pandemic and finishing it as the vaccine is being distributed across the world has also influenced my perspective. At the very time we need people to be smart about data and basic science, we find ourselves surrounded by misinformation (false information spread unintentionally), disinformation (false information spread with the intent to deceive), and a growing distrust in big tech and, by extension, in data itself (Kite-Powell, 2020; Lanata and Miller, 2021; Brumfiel, 2021). When we lose trust in data as a means of building and conveying knowledge about the world, we lose a lot. This response to the pandemic, combined with the swamp of deliberate lies about the 2020 US presidential election and the incitement to violence based on those lies, has driven home to me the importance of helping educate people about data.

Educating people about data goes beyond the skills they need to use data—beyond data literacy itself—to a recognition of what can be accomplished with data. Well-managed data has incredible potential to help organizations succeed and to enable individuals to lead better lives.

My original intention was to write a book aimed at data quality practitioners and focused on how to execute core data quality management capabilities. But this is not a how-to book. It does not contain detailed instructions on how to execute processes or templates for doing so (though I include references and recommendations for books that do present this information). The intended audience still includes data quality practitioners, who work to build core data quality management capabilities in their organization, and it includes the data management profession more widely, especially those who work in data governance, data strategy, and information technology and who can speak to the risks of managing data badly and the benefits of managing it well. My hope is that it will also include decision makers, upper management, and even boards. My purpose is to share my perspective on the issues we face, provoke thought, and, most importantly, contribute to the conversation that everyone who cares about data must engage in if we are to make better data and use it to improve the human condition.

Data in Today's Organizations

Section 1 will present the high-level context of data quality management. Data plays a critical role in organizational success. Over the past several decades, our ability to generate and capture data has grown exponentially, but our ability to manage it has not kept up.

Chapter 1: The Importance of Data Quality Management presents an analysis of the current state of data evolution and the role of data quality management in response to this evolution. It discusses the impact of poor-quality data on organizations, focusing on the costs and risks associated with poorly managed data. In many organizations, poor-quality data is tolerated to a degree that poor-quality products would not be. Data quality management reduces the costs and risks of poor-quality data and enables the benefits and opportunities of high-quality data, especially in an age of Big Data, digital transformation, and artificial intelligence.

Chapter 2: Organizational Data and the Five Challenges of Managing Data Quality describes the five challenges in data quality management (data, process, technology, people, culture/organization) and proposes that organizations that want to get more value and insight from their data should take a strategic approach to data quality management. Because quality is not an *accident, it cannot be an afterthought, especially in today's complex organizations. This chapter provides the context for Section 2 and introduces critical terminology used throughout the book.*

Chapter 3: Data Quality and Strategy *explores how concepts about strategy apply to data. Data strategy should be connected to overall business strategy while accounting for the challenges particular to managing the quality of data. A strategic approach to data quality management aligns priorities for data and information management with organizational goals and builds accountability for data into processes, system design, and individual performance.*

The Importance of Data Quality Management

"There is no medicine better than a good diagnosis."

Gabriel Garcia Marquez

Introduction

Data quality management is important because data is important. Organizations depend on data for basic operations, and they look to data as a source of competitive advantage. When data is of poor quality, it is difficult to run an organization and even more difficult to innovate and to take advantage of opportunities presented by innovations in technology. Time, money, and work effort are wasted dealing with errors and inconsistencies — lots of time, money, and work effort. Conservative estimates put this at 15%−25% of revenues for most organizations (Redman, 2017). Waste leads to dissatisfaction within the organization. Bad data can also lead to customer dissatisfaction. When customers are exposed to errors in data about themselves, they often cease to be customers. As new uses of data evolve, such as machine learning (ML) and artificial intelligence (AI), and as organizations collect more data about the personal lives of individuals, the risks associated with bad data increase.

And yet, despite the obvious importance of data and the potential value that can be derived from data, few organizations manage data for quality. They do not document the meaning of their data or pay close attention to the processes through which they create data. They fail to account for the impact of technology on data when managing their technology assets. They do not help their employees improve their data literacy. They do not support the basic need to manage metadata. They do not define accountability for data or create a culture focused on quality.

Managing data quality is an investment. It requires building organizational capabilities in metadata management, data assessment, data monitoring, and issue management. It requires addressing the root causes of data issues. It also requires changing how work gets done. Organizational change is hard, but it is necessary. The investment in data quality management is positioned to pay off; 15%−25% of revenues are sitting on the table. As we become more data dependent, this number is likely to increase.

This chapter will present a wide-angle view of the evolving role of data in organizational life and connect this state to challenges in managing data quality. The chapter provides a backdrop to the book as a whole. In the past several decades, there has been significant evolution in the types of data produced in the world and the potential uses of that data. However, the diminished focus on ensuring the quality of data has made this data more uncertain and therefore potentially less valuable than data produced in less voluminous times.

Meeting the Challenges of Data Quality Management. DOI: https://doi.org/10.1016/B978-0-12-821737-5.00001-8

Data and Value

Ask almost anyone if data is valuable, and you will get a resounding, "Yes!" Yet, we do not have standard ways of assessing that value. Data is an asset, but organizations struggle to say how much it is worth because they do not measure the costs and benefits of data and other information assets. In addition, data is not only abstract, it has other properties that physical assets and cash do not have (e.g., can be used multiple times, does not get used up). Because people understand the value of money, associating data with monetary value helps leadership understand the value of data management activities. But there are not consistent ways to do this, so it is difficult to convince leadership to invest in capabilities to manage data assets properly.

Organizational data is valuable because it reflects knowledge about the organization itself. Each organization's data is unique to itself. But this characteristic also makes it difficult to put a monetary value on data. Organizations realize value from their data in two interconnected ways: (1) by using their data to meet their operational goals and (2) by learning from their data and identifying new opportunities, such as finding ways to improve their products, operations, customer service, and thereby their competitive position. In some cases, organizations directly monetize their data. Poor-quality data affects both of these approaches and creates additional risks related to privacy, compliance, and ethics. These costs negatively affect the value equation, but they are hidden or unacknowledged in many organizations because they are difficult to measure and easy to ignore.

The process is made more complex because people recognize that data value depends, in part, on context. Although certain types of data, such as customer data, are likely to be consistently valuable, data asset valuation must recognize that the value of data depends on specific uses. What is valuable in one context may not be valuable in another (a map of New York City is more valuable when you are in New York City than it is when you are in Stockholm). What is valuable at one point in time may not be valuable after that point in time (e.g., information about stock prices when you are ready to make a trade).

If context makes data valuation too messy, then the value of data can also be understood in relation to the costs of production. It costs an organization time and effort to collect data about its customers. However, because these costs are embedded in the processes of transacting business, they may also be difficult to measure. Then, there are the costs associated with managing data. The risk here is that these costs are often expressed in terms of hardware, software, and storage, rather than the value that comes from the data itself. Finally, data value can also be viewed in terms of risk. What would it cost the organization if something went wrong with its data? How much would it cost to replace its customer data if the data were lost?

Despite these potential complexities, applying general cost and benefit categories to data provides a starting point for determining the value of data. For example:

- Cost of creating, collecting, or obtaining data
- Cost of storing and maintaining data
- Impact on the organization if data were missing
- Cost of replacing data if it were lost
- Potential impact of risks associated with data
- Cost of risk management
- Cost of improving data

- Benefits of higher-quality data
- What competitors would pay for data
- What the data could be sold for
- Expected revenue from innovative uses of the data

Douglas Laney's *Infonomics* (2018), a full-length study on managing information as an asset, presents case studies from across industries, activities, and products to demonstrate how organizations leverage their information assets to create value. Two core approaches emerge from this array of case study evidence:

- Exchanging information for goods, services, or cash
- Using information to increase revenue, reduce expenses, or manage risk

Although many associate "getting value from data" with direct monetization, selling data is not the only way to realize value from it. Laney presents the following fundamental business drivers for monetizing data:

- Use organizational data more effectively to retain existing customers, enter new markets, and create new products.
- Improve organizational efficiency by enabling a company to reduce maintenance costs, negotiate for better terms and conditions, detect fraud and waste, or defray the costs of managing data.

Some organizations have broken through on both of these counts, with operational improvements as well as direct monetization. But many have not even come close to the promise of getting value from their data. If they took data value as seriously as they should, they would see that their data is a significant liability. Case studies show that better data management, including data quality management, not only reduces costs, but also supports innovative uses of data. The first step to realizing value from data is to manage the data well.

The failure to put monetary value on data has another consequence that presents an obstacle to data quality management: in failing to put a monetary value on data, organizations also fail to comprehend the costs of poor-quality data. Indeed, Gartner's 2018 Data Quality Tools Magic Quadrant Survey reported that 57% of the respondents do not measure the financial impact of poor-quality data (Chien, 2019). They do not know either the quality of their data or the costs associated with poor quality. Keep in mind that these respondents are from organizations that have already implemented data quality tools and are providing feedback on those tools that other organizations rely on to make their tooling decisions. Yikes!

We live in a world in which people extol the potential value of data and downplay the difficulty of managing it in ways that enable its use. A simple Google search will tell us that data is not only the "new oil," but also "the lifeblood" of "the digital economy," "commercial success," "global capitalism," "the organization," and "every business."[1] Yet a 2015 report from PricewaterhouseCoopers (PwC) found that the confidence many organizations have in their ability

---

[1]This comes from a simple google search for "data is the lifeblood" and includes only a few samples from the 4,180,000 results returned on April 5, 2020. https://www.google.com/search?q=data+is+the+lifeblood+of+business&rlz=1C1SQJL_enUS854United States854&oq=data+is+the+lif&aqs=chrome.0.0j69i57j0l6.3076j0j4&sourceid=chrome&ie=UTF-8.

to extract commercial and operational advantage from their data and information is largely misplaced. Other studies over the past two decades back up this observation (PwC, 2015).[2]

Very few organizations use their data to its full potential. Very few manage data as an asset, despite lip service to doing so. Most organizations struggle to implement and then fail to establish data governance and data management behaviors and practices that will allow them to reap the beneficial insights they expect to get from their data.[3] As Evans and Price have shown, if a typical organization were to manage its money as it manages its information, "it would not survive." In addition to hidden value and significant risks, lack of focus on managing information as an asset "results in foregone revenue, in avoidable cost, in unrealized profit, in lost productivity, in unmitigated risk and in suboptimal staff morale" (Evans & Price, 2018).

There is a stark contrast between the potential value of data and the actual value people are able to get from data. This contrast is probably the source of the other set of metaphors for data: pollution. Data quality practitioners are very familiar with the idea that "a database is like a lake" (Redman, 2001); if people dump garbage into it upstream, that garbage will float downstream. The best way to clean it up is to eliminate the sources of pollution and prevent people from polluting it again. References to *data pollution* are becoming more common. Although we talk of data as "life blood" or "the new oil," we also recognize that some forms of data are seen as harmful contaminants within the information environment, "the exhaust of the Information Age" (Schneier, 2015). There is even a new form of hacking called *data poisoning*, which involves corrupting data used in ML and AI applications. The process can involve hiding data, adding incorrect data, or changing metadata such as labels of file names. When corrupted data is used in training AI models, the repercussions range from undermining a single model to reducing overall trust in AI in general (De Saulles, 2020). It is bad enough to envision bad actors "poisoning" an organization's data. But when organizations fail to manage the quality of their data, are they not poisoning themselves?

The More Things Change, the More They Stay the Same

The 2015 PwC report focuses on the cultural characteristics required to realize value from data: the skills, knowledge, experience, and perspective needed to leverage data and the technology that supports its use. PwC notes that the organizations that know how to exploit information have a strong governance component, treat data as an asset, protect sensitive information with robust controls, and employ data analysts who understand the role of data and information in executing business strategy (PwC, 2015). The PwC report rightly associates good data management practices with reliable and robust risk management and with the ability to share information across an organization. But the report also has a big gap: it does not acknowledge the risks associated with poor-quality data. This is a strange omission because PwC has known for a long time that poor-quality data is a big problem.

---

[2]See English (1999), Eckerson (2002), Marsh (2005), Thomas (2008), Redman (2018).

[3]See also Evans and Price (2012, 2020) and Moody and Walsh (1999) for discussions about the organizational obstacles to treating data as an asset as well as a model for improved management of information assets.

In 2001, PwC published a frequently cited assessment, the Global Data Management Survey, which reported that global businesses lost $1.4 billion per year as a result of poor data management practices that resulted in faulty data. Seventy-five percent of the 600 firms PwC interviewed had experienced significant problems, costs, and losses because of poor-quality data. These included the following:

- Costs in preparing reconciliations
- Delays in implementing new systems
- Failure to bill or collect receivables
- Lost sales or inability to deliver orders because of incorrect stock records
- Failure to meet contractual requirements or service-level agreements

At that time, only 15% of companies expressed high confidence in the data they received from other organizations. Only 40% expressed high confidence in their own data, even though they said they were responsible for the quality of their own data (PwC, 2001).

Some things have changed since 2001. The role of data within organizations has intensified. Big Data has emerged, and organizations are trying to take advantage of it. Technologies for ML and AI are being adopted and integrated into the work of many organizations. However, the drive to improve the quality of data has lost momentum, and organizational responsibility for data remains a hot potato that is quickly passed off to someone else. Many pay lip service to the importance of data, but few want to "own" its quality or commit to the kinds of organizational and cultural changes that would enable the production of more reliable data.

Every Organization Is Data-Dependent

PwC organized its 2001 findings around the distinction between *traditional* and *e-commerce* enterprises. Now this distinction seems quaint. Almost every organization, regardless of size, uses the Internet to conduct business. The term *e-commerce* itself has largely dropped out of the lexicon because the distinction between "e" and "brick and mortar" hardly matters any more. Still, the report clearly recognized the emergence of greater dependence on data as an economic force and the concomitant need to develop data management as a core business competency. Although every organization is now data-dependent, only a small minority, unfortunately, are yet data-driven (NewVantage Partners, 2020).[4]

Despite not yet making the leap to being data-driven, organizations also are spending a lot of money in the effort to achieve "digital transformation" (International Data Group, 2018, 2020). Digital transformation is the process of improving organizational success by implementing digital capabilities that enable a better customer experience across all channels, improve internal efficiency, and extend the organization's reach. These capabilities depend on the creation of a "digital

[4]McGilvray (2021) defines the concept of data dependency: "Societies, families, individuals, and organizations (whether for-profit in any industry, nonprofit, government, education, healthcare, science, research, social services, medicine, etc.) all depend on information to succeed—whether they consciously recognize it or not." Data dependence refers to the need for data. Redman (2008) defines being data-driven in relation to how data is used, especially in decision making. Evidence-based (i.e., data-driven) decision making reduces risks and helps identify opportunities. It provides a firmer foundation than intuition for creating a competitive advantage.

ecosystem" and "leadership capabilities that enable them to get the most out of their digital activities" (Westerman et al., 2014). In other words, they get more value from their investments in technology because they take a strategic approach and are willing to change their business models to succeed. *Digital* refers to the adoption of new technologies. *Transformation* refers to cultural change needed to take advantage of the opportunities presented by new technologies.

Although many talk about digital transformation as if it were dependent on technology alone, some have drawn attention to the thing that technology enables: innovative uses of data. According to *Forbes*, data must be tamed:

> Business leaders intent on digital transformation must first look at their data and how they will quickly cleanse, review and blend business-critical data from different systems across the enterprise. In addition, the harmonized and cleansed data must be able to be easily migrated into new systems error-free to accommodate the reinvention of the business. Neglecting the flow, quality and governance of data will inevitably negate any return on investment in technology and undermine digital transformation initiatives (Ahlstrom, 2019).

These are pretty strong words, and they seem to put data first. Unfortunately, this "taming" sounds remarkably like what was said about data warehousing. The initial promise of data warehousing was to bring disparate or heterogenous data together in one environment where it could be cleansed, transformed, stored, and then combined with other data to produce insights not available through the individual data sets. Organizations quickly learned that this combination did not happen by magic. It takes a lot of work to integrate or even "harmonize" data, especially if it is expected to be "error-free." Given what we know about the challenges with traditional data, *Forbes's* suggestions about the route to digital transformation come across as naïve or perhaps ill-informed.

Forbes recommends governance as a means for keeping data in check, but then asserts that data quality management and governance can be "effectively automated" using a "crowdsourced approach" in which errors will automatically be detected and corrected (but apparently not prevented in the first place). This mixing and matching (automatic detection of errors through crowdsourcing) further obscures the risks that digital transformation will be slowed down by poor-quality data. To top it off, this automagical approach is presented as making data quality and governance the "cornerstone" of digital transformation. In short, the hype around digital transformation sounds a lot like the hype around data warehousing (several decades ago), data lakes, and Big Data (more recently). Even as it celebrates the opportunities presented by technology, this kind of talk minimizes the challenges of getting the data right. By implying that high-quality data can quickly be harvested like mana from heaven, it ignores the knowledge required to manage data and the work involved in cultivating reliable, trustworthy data. Hype around ML and AI works similarly. ML will generate genuine stupidity if the data is bad.

As consultant James Price of Experience Matters puts it:

> There is no software in the world that can run around the organization, understand what products and services it delivers, who does what, what Information Assets they use, the relative value and sensitivity of those assets to whom, where to put and find those information assets and how and when to discard them. This is a human problem, demanding human judgement. And that requires corporate discipline. And discipline requires responsibility. And responsibility requires accountability (Price, 2021).

Big Data Is Here

Although the 2001 PwC report asked directly about the expansion of electronic data, the growth of automated decision making, and the need for trust among organizations who depend on each other for data, it did not quite anticipate the phenomenon we refer to as *Big Data* — the exponential increase in the variety and volume of electronic data brought about by the velocity at which we can create and use it.

Data as an idea and ways of creating data have been evolving since at least the 17th century, but recent changes in our technical capacity to create, store, process, and analyze data have created new opportunities related to the concept of Big Data. These changes have widened the range of information that we now refer to as *data* and, with this, the uses to which we may put this data. Indeed, it is not only organizations that create data, but individuals, through the daily use of electronic devices to carry out routine tasks, and machines, connected through the Internet of Things (IoT).

These changes have increased the excitement about data's potential and about the potential "disruption" that can be brought about by applications like ML and AI (Mayer-Schönberger & Cukier, 2014). These changes have a real impact (the information we now call *data* is different from what it was, even in the late 20th century), but they have also been surrounded by hype about the ease with which we will make breakthroughs with data. Unfortunately, they have done little to improve the quality of data. Some people even say that the quality of this information is not important (Myer, 2016). Others, thankfully, recognize that data is the "crucial factor that separates successful from unsuccessful AI projects.... AI requires data, usually a great deal of data, and ideally a great deal of high-quality data" (Ogbuji, 2017a). Given its pervasiveness and the risks associated with its collection and use, especially if we are to rely on it for applications like ML and AI, we would be foolish to ignore the implications of low-quality Big Data.

The Dream of Fully Integrated Data

Ignoring the impact or poor-quality data is basically ignoring lessons from the history of data management. The same things that are currently being said about Big Data were also said about data warehousing at the turn of the 21st century. The initial promise of data warehousing was to bring disparate data into a common environment to get value from it. A data warehouse is "an integrated decision support database and the related software programs used to collect, cleanse, transform, and store data from a variety of operational and external sources" (DAMA, 2011). By implementing a data warehouse, an organization is expected to reduce data redundancy, improve consistency, and enable itself to make better decisions (DAMA, 2017). The route to value was through the knowledge and insight the organization gained about itself, its performance, understood through "business intelligence," as well as its products and customers. Both warehouses and data lakes presuppose the availability of high-quality data: data will be complete, it will accurately reflect organizational activities, it can be integrated effectively, and analysts will be able to access it and learn from it.

Many organizations found that this work was not easy because their data did not fit together in the ways they expected. They learned that it took work and knowledge to extract, transform, and load (ETL) data from disparate sources and to create and maintain an enterprise data model that reflected how the pieces fit together in the warehouse (including knowledge that technical staff do not have about the data and cannot get without talking to data creators). It also took work and knowledge (in the form of documented specifications, lineage, and other metadata) to use data stored in data marts and other applications downstream from the data warehouses (Fig. 3).

A *data lake* is a "massive, easily accessible, centralized repository of large volumes of structured and unstructured data" (Technopedia.com). Data lakes make the same promise as data warehouses, that is, to bring all organizational data together in one place and then some. Because storing data in a data lake is significantly cheaper than storing it in a warehouse, data lakes are essential to setting up some forms of Big Data. They promise to allow an organization to combine its data with external data, perform analytics in real time, and scale everything at a lower cost and more quickly than a warehouse so that (it is asserted) data consumers can leverage data immediately. Indeed, some can, but not for free and not without knowledge and not without risk. It is argued that data can be brought into a data lake more quickly than it can be brought into a data warehouse because it is simply extracted and loaded (EL) to a data lake. Data modeling and transformation are not required to bring the data in (Fig. 4).

However, the organization also does not get the benefits of the metadata produced when building a warehouse. These include the specifications, standards, models, definitions, and other forms of explicit knowledge documented as part of the development process. In addition, the work, cost,

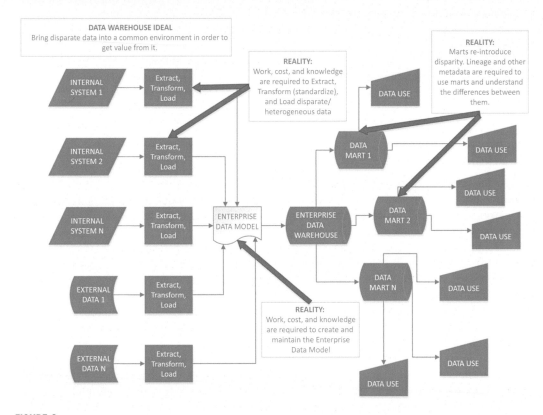

FIGURE 3

Data warehouse ideal versus data warehouse reality.

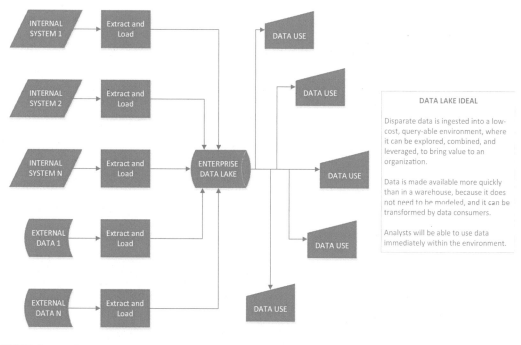

FIGURE 4

Data lake ideal.

and knowledge required to transform data from disparate sources is displaced from a project team, which would be required to capture this information in a sharable form to individuals or small groups of users who have no need to capture it outside of their own uses and may not document it at all. This knowledge disappears into the proverbial ether (e.g., someone's hard drive, a SharePoint site, or Teams channel). The problems associated with not managing knowledge around data are well-known.[5] They are intensified as data speeds up. The process of preparing data for different uses can create additional disparity within organizational data sets, and with this disparity, additional risks related to how data is understood and used (Fig. 5).

According to Gartner (2014), those who advocate for data lakes assume that data consumers do the following:

- Recognize and understand the contextual bias of how data is captured
- Know how to merge and reconcile data from different sources without *a priori* knowledge
- Understand the incomplete nature of data sets, regardless of structure

---

[5]See Aiken (2000) and Loshin (2001). Aiken explores the idea of "data reverse engineering," which amounts to working backwards from data to the meaning of that data and from there to questions of quality and use. Similarly, Loshin explores knowledge management from the perspective of information embedded in choices about how to organize data. Neither of these insightful books would have been needed if organizations managed their metadata (i.e., explicit knowledge about data).

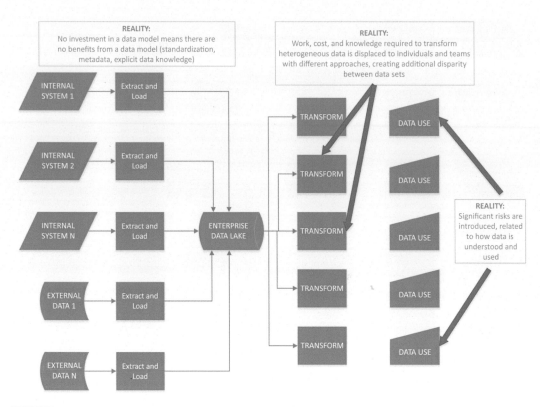

FIGURE 5

Data lake reality.

In other words, Gartner recognizes the risks posed by both the variety and the volume of Big Data. *Velocity* means these risks may affect an organization sooner rather than later. Organizations that fail to manage these risks are putting themselves and their stakeholders at risk.

This is not to say that there is no hope of getting value from data. I tell this cautionary tale because I truly believe in the value of data. People said the same things about data warehouses that they are saying about Big Data. Many organizations got less value from their warehouses than they could have gotten because they did not manage data quality, including the quality of the metadata, required to use data in the warehouse.

Perhaps because of vendor hype about data or perhaps because of the desire to quickly realize value from data, few organizations admit the following basic facts:

- Even very smart people need help to use data. At the very least, they need basic information about the data: what it represents, where it came from, and what limitations it may have.
- Data in its "raw" form is not always usable.
- If the work of making data usable is done inconsistently, then the results of analyses will be inconsistent.

Thus, managing Big Data represents the same challenges as managing traditional data:

- **The data challenge:** Knowing what the data represents, the conventions used in its representation, how it was created, and what its limitations are; defining what is meant by high-quality data and how to recognize low-quality data.
- **The quality and process challenge:** Ensuring that processes support the creation of high-quality data and that data producers understand how their choices affect the ability of data consumers to use and get value from data.
- **The technology challenge:** Understanding how particular technical choices affect the creation, accessibility, use, and quality of data.
- **The people challenge:** Ensuring that data consumers have the information and skills they need to access, understand, and interpret data.
- **The cultural and organizational challenge:** Ensuring that there is oversight of data within the organization and accountability for data along the data supply chain so the organization can generate expected value from its data.

As with managing traditional data, metadata plays a critical role in managing Big Data. Many would argue that it plays an even more critical role given the variety of Big Data sources and the differences in how data is captured and stored. If organizations do not manage the metadata needed to support their Big Data environments, then they cannot use that data effectively. It is also likely that more data will be redundant, obsolete, and trivial (ROT) (Aiken & Billings, 2013). Even if it costs less money to store this data in a lake than it does in a data warehouse, there is little value in doing so because the data will not be used.

These risks can be mitigated if, as part of Big Data projects, organizations commit to managing metadata and data quality as part of initial data ingestion. Such a process includes the following:

- Inspecting data, through profiling or other means, so people understand the condition of data before use
- Capturing at least the foundational information people require to find and use data (names, definitions)
- Using this information to standardize data where possible and prepare data for multiple uses

These actions reduce risks and inefficiencies. They reflect a basic awareness of the following needs of data consumers:

- Foundational metadata required for data use is harvested as part of the process. This basic information is likely to be created through a combination of automated data cataloging and associating data with existing data dictionaries and glossaries.
- Data consumers trust that data will be of high quality until they discover it is not. Being up front about the condition of data sets, even if it means showing their limitations, is better than having data consumers discover that they do not trust the data they are working with.
- Setting standards for data is one route to higher-quality data. Standards reflect and explicitly state expectations. Standardizing reduces disparity among data sets.
- Preparing data for use once is more cost effective and less risky than preparing it multiple times.

The Focus on Volume Distracts from Value

The contrast between a lack of focus on data quality and an enthusiastic focus on data volume is instructive. Tech reporters and vendors can hardly contain their excitement about the amount of data produced every year (90% of the world's data was created in the past 2 years!), every day (2.5 quintillion bytes per day!), and even every second (1.7 MB for every person on earth!). In such statistics, among the items counted as "data" created "every minute of every day" are:

- 3,877,140 Google searches
- 750,000 songs streamed by Spotify
- 120 professionals joining LinkedIn
- 49,380 photos posted to Instagram
- 18,055,555 forecast requests received by The Weather Channel
- 1,111 packages shipped by Amazon[6]

Next week, these statistics and the "data" they focus on will change again. Organizations collect and produce enormous amounts of electronic data during daily operations. They store this data for known operational and analytic uses and in hopes of getting more value from it in the future. Although the costs of data storage have gone down dramatically in recent years, the amount of data we store electronically has increased exponentially because we execute so much of our daily activity electronically, and we refer to virtually every molecule of the electronic exhaust from these interactions as *data*.

Larger amounts of data are more difficult to keep track of and to prepare for use (i.e., manage), never mind actually use, in ways that bring value. Studies about the productivity of data scientists show that they spend a large portion of their time simply trying to find and prepare the data they want to use (Dodds, 2020; Lohr, 2014; Press, 2016). The idea that somehow more data is always good stems from the potential all of the data represents. However, giddiness about volume seems to have caused a collective amnesia about purpose.

More data is just more stuff to keep track of. It brings value only if it is used. It has been argued that "data which is not used cannot be correct for very long," based on the logic that if an organization is not using data, then there is no feedback loop between the data and the real-world entities it represents. Over time, errors in capturing real-world changes will be ignored, and the data will essentially atrophy (Orr, 1996). Some would argue that the velocity of Big Data maintains the connection between data and the real world. Velocity can solve the problem of currency, but not of value. The organization just more quickly accumulates data that it does not use and about which it has little knowledge.

With the emergence of Big Data, what is included under the heading of *data* has evolved. Commerce-based organizational data no longer consists of just the output from transactional systems and electronic commerce, though it still includes these. It also includes anything that can be captured digitally. Many things beyond transactions are being captured digitally, and *data* now

---

[6]These numbers are from the report "Data Never Sleeps 6.0" (2018) by the Cloud vendor Domo (https://www.domo.com/solution/data-never-sleeps-6). Domo does not appear to be saying that the packages themselves are data, but data is created through the process of selecting, ordering, shipping, and delivering each package shipped by Amazon. Sadly missing from such enthusiastic forays are the remarkable advances in science brought about by the ability to collect and analyze data, such as insight into the size of black holes (Temming, 2021). In later chapters, we will discuss how these statistics relate to *data* in the traditional sense of the word.

includes all kinds of stuff we did not even imagine a decade ago: petabytes of sensor information from home appliances, images on phone cameras, streaming video, social media posts, email, and more social media posts, not to mention SharePoint sites and instant messages.

Many people get excited about the potential of this "unstructured" data (data that is not relational, not presented in rows and columns) because it seems to offer something substantively different from traditional data. Big Data does pile up more quickly (velocity), there is more of it (volume), and it comes in lots of different forms (variety), but that does not mean that it is all useful, usable, or even truthful (veracity). The hype around Big Data implies that it will magically reveal its secrets. But that is not how data works. People still must understand what it represents and how it was created to interpret what it may mean. They often must do so without the knowledge embedded when data is organized into columns and rows.

New Data Opportunities Conflict with Each Other

In addition to the hype surrounding the possibilities presented by new forms of data, there is also the recognition of risk; hence the increasing regulation of data usage, data responsibility, and data quality (e.g., Basel, the Health Insurance Portability and Accountability Act [HIPAA], the General Data Protection Regulation [GDPR], and the California Consumer Privacy Act [CCPA]). Unfortunately, there is limited effort to resolve the contradictory drivers for regulating data. These drivers can be understood in relation to the following different concepts of ownership:

- **Data as an organizational asset:** Organizations that want to generate value from their data most often express the desire to "treat data as an asset," even if they struggle to do so. Data is recognized as a knowledge asset. This is because organizational data reflects the activities of the organization and its customers in ways that no other information does, and organizations can leverage this knowledge to understand their customers, improve their products, and gain a competitive advantage. Organizations may find out in a painful way how much of an asset their data is if bad actors take over their computer systems and ransom their data (Shear et al., 2021).
- **Data protection:** Data privacy and security focus on the idea that data must be protected. If data is left unprotected, individuals may be harmed because information about them is available to organizations that may want to influence their behavior or to criminals and other bad actors who want to use data for their own advantage and in ways that harm others. The European Union concept of data protection goes beyond protecting the data and includes protecting the individuals who are represented in the data. In addition, the idea of data privacy implies that individuals should have some level of control over data that represents them. But if data about individuals "belongs" to individuals that it represents and they have a right to control it, then how can it also be an asset that belongs to an organization with a profit motive?
- **Data monetization:** The most direct way to leverage data as an asset is to make money from it by selling it or incorporating it into other products. However, the concept of data monetization quickly comes into conflict with the need for data privacy and the ethical questions that privacy raises about data ownership. Is it okay to make money from something that "belongs" to someone else? And if an organization creates data about a person (a data subject), then does the data not belong also to the organization that creates it? If it is not clear who "owns" data about individuals (the individuals the data represents or the organizations that create the data), then it is not clear who gets to make money from this data.

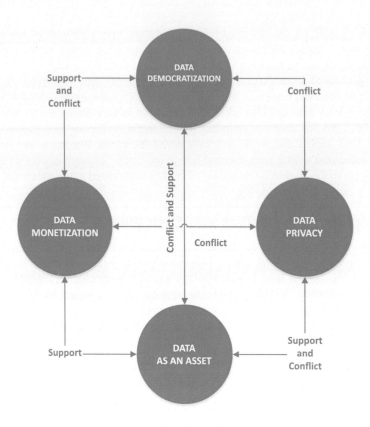

FIGURE 6

Conflicting drivers of data opportunity.

- **Data democratization:** Data democratization is the idea that if more people have wider access to more data, they will get better insight from it.[7] Because data brings value only when it is used, the idea is that the more people use a data asset, the more potential value can be derived from it. This, of course, assumes that all of these people are using the data in ways that create value and not in ways that diminish value or introduce risk. When data use does create value, data democratization supports the idea of data as an asset. But democratization comes into direct conflict with the idea of data privacy, and privacy risks will need to be managed (as will a host of other ethical considerations) by any organization that democratizes its data.

These ideas are usually talked about separately; few people point to the connections among them. But when we put them next to each other, the tensions seem clear (Fig. 6). Individuals cannot

---

[7] I find this assumption itself questionable, especially given the acknowledgment of a growing need for "data literacy" and the recognition that many bad decisions about data have been made by people who should know better. From the perspective of data quality, I think it is pretty risky to assume that anyone is going to get better insight from poor-quality data.

"own" their own data if organizations that collect it are democratizing it at the same time. We cannot democratize or monetize other people's data without their acknowledgment or consent. At least we should not, and, in some parts of the world, anyone who does is legally responsible for the consequences (the European Union under the GDPR; Australia under the CDR [Consumer Data Rights]; California under the CCPA).

The Drive to Improve Data Quality Has Faded

PwC's 2001 analysis makes little distinction between *data management* and *data quality*. The two are seen as essentially the same thing. The purpose of managing data is to ensure that an organization has reliable, high-quality data, with few obstacles to its use. In the past two decades, this perspective has changed. Now, many people think of data quality management only as a subcomponent of data governance rather than a set of practices that can stand on its own. The data quality management function is lumped together with data stewardship (e.g., one of the functions of stewardship is "data quality") to the detriment of both sets of responsibilities.[8]

This is unfortunate because managing and improving the quality of data requires a skill set that does not always exist in data governance organizations and that differs from many of the skills associated with generalized data stewardship (as discussed in Chapter 8). In some organizations, the data quality team's role is perceived simply as *data profiling*, and the data quality management function is seen as an add-on (i.e., when it is not being confused with quality assurance [QA], which, unfortunately, also has a history of being seen as an add-on). This means that the data quality management function is not seen for the value it should bring: enabling an organization to get more value from its data by helping improve the processes through which data is created, managed, and used within an organization.

Not only have there been significant changes in the perceived role of data quality practitioners, but the hopeful desire that data governance could bring about meaningful change has also waned. Many data governance programs have been relegated to the status of ensuring compliance or providing amorphously defined "stewardship" rather than providing the kind of oversight that will enable the enterprise to have higher confidence in the trustworthiness of its data. Data governance should define and encourage the kinds of behaviors that will enable this confidence by describing the enterprise perspective on data, creating awareness of the organizational data supply chain, focusing on the need to design quality into processes that produce data, and integrating metadata management into processes that create and use data. However, few such programs do. Many data governance programs would benefit from a renewed focus on data quality management because when executed with skill and purpose, the tools and techniques of data quality management result

---

[8]For example, the International Association for Information and Data Quality (IAIDQ; later renamed Information Quality International [IQ Int]) was founded in the early 2000s to support the evolution of the profession of data quality management. The organization's work included the development of a Code of Ethics and an Information Quality Certified Professional (IQCP) credential that focused on six knowledge areas that are critical to information and quality management: strategy and governance; environment and culture; value and business impact; architecture quality; measurement and improvement; and sustaining information quality. Much of this work has been absorbed under the general umbrella of *data management* as defined by DAMA, but a considerable amount of important detail was lost in the course of this shift, including the connection to the pioneers of quality in manufacturing. The discipline described in the IAIDQ's approach has been replaced by a set of general ideas about the need for data stewardship.

in organizational improvements related to both data and the business processes that produce it and provide insight into the best ways to increase the value the organization gets from data.

Data management's shift away from data quality has been, in part, a shift toward data protection. Given the risk associated with data, this is not surprising. Data requires protection. The kinds of data we can now store; the ways data is stored, accessed, and analyzed; and the regulations now in place to safeguard data have all made data protection a necessity. Despite this change, the need for high-quality data has not gone away. If anything, it has increased as organizations have become more data-dependent. Diminished focus on quality is doubly unfortunate because it is easier to protect high-quality, well-defined, well-managed data than it is to protect poorly managed, low-quality data. Indeed, the accuracy and accountability principles of the European Union's GDPR acknowledge the direct connection between the quality of data and the ability to protect data (European Commission, 2016).

Organizational Responsibility for the Quality of Data Remains Ambiguous

When PwC conducted the 2001 survey, the CIO (chief information officer, the executive responsible for information technology [IT]) was perceived as the "owner" of data quality (also known as *data management*), and IT departments were perceived as responsible for data management issues.[9] The conclusions from the survey argued that accountability for data quality should rest squarely on the business side of the house rather than the technology side.[10] Not only did the PwC authors recognize that "responsibility for data management is in the wrong place" (p. 9), they also emphasized that data management is integral to the business management of any organization: "If a company is not in control of its data, then not only is its control of its business in doubt, but also its ability to report the realities of that business to the marketplace. In short, a company without an explicit data strategy will find it hard to gain credibility with investors and access to capital markets" (PwC, 2001, p. 5).[11]

Most people would agree with the 2001 conclusion. However, organizations have not made the change. According to the NewVantage Partners' 2020 Big Data and IA Executive Survey, the question of organizational responsibility for data has still not been settled: "Many organizations continue to point to no single point of accountability for data within their firms, with 26.8% pointing to no single owner, and only 40.2% identifying the [chief data officer/chief data analytics officer] as primary executive with data responsibility."

IT picked up on the message that they do not "own" the data. Ask anyone in an IT role, "Who owns the data?" and you will get a consistent answer: "The business." Unfortunately, IT has also taken this to an extreme, drawing the conclusion that IT has no responsibility for data. Ask "the business" who is responsible for data, and they will more than likely give a knee-jerk reaction and

---

[9]Moody and Walsh (1999) made a similar point in their discussion about the relationship between IT investment and financial performance: "To be most effective, IT strategies should be focused on enhancing and sustaining the value of the information (the product) rather than on the systems and technology (the production equipment)" (p. 3).

[10]An argument that numerous thought leaders in data management continue to put forward: See Ladley (2010, 2019), Redman (2008), English (2009), and Aiken and Gorman (2013).

[11]PwC (2004), a follow up to the 2001 report, shows that little or no progress was made in 3 years. For other discussions about the impact of poor-quality data around the turn of the century, see Redman (1997), English (1999), and Eckerson (2002). Evans and Price (2020) make a similar point about the connection between managing information assets and basic management of a business.

say, "IT." After all, IT manages the systems in which data is created, stored, and accessed. If they take the question seriously, however, businesspeople may ask: "What do you mean by 'own the data'? If data is an organizational asset, then doesn't it belong to the organization, not a single team or individual?" Just the way the question is posed, "Who owns the data?" can get in the way of solving the problem the question implies.[12]

Assertions about ownership are really questions of accountability and responsibility. How does the organization ensure that people are acting in appropriate ways around data and taking care of it in ways that enable the organization to realize value from it? Before one can determine who is accountable, it is necessary to define what it means to be accountable for data. How does one act accountably toward data? Is accountability about the individual, the process, the function, the enterprise, or a combination? The concept of *data governance* was proposed to answer these questions.

The definition of data governance, formulated by Gwen Thomas of the Data Governance Institute, is that "Data Governance is a system of decision rights and accountabilities for information-related processes, executed according to agreed-upon models which describe who can take what actions with what information, and when, under what circumstances, using what methods." Data governance is a system. This implies that organizations are "governing" their data; there are de facto (and sometimes de jure) ways to make decisions. However, they may not be governing it effectively if existing practices are inconsistent or lead to organizational conflict.

This formulation recognizes complexity: multiple people and teams in an organization will have different kinds of responsibility toward data and will be authorized to make different types of decisions. Because responsibility is therefore shared and because data plays multiple roles in the complex system that is an organization, the system will benefit from oversight (governance) to reduce the chances of conflict and inconsistency. Unfortunately, few data governance programs have successfully applied this insight. Few have developed and gotten consensus on the models and methods through which the organization as a whole can build responsibility for data. Governance programs have also often found themselves saddled with overall accountability for data (which was not the intent) without the authority to exercise this power. The solution to this conundrum was to envision executive accountability for data (the chief data officer or CDO) (see Chapter 8).

Most organizations do not have a clear definition of either *data accountability, data responsibility*, or *data ownership*. Some think the goal of data governance is to assign owners to data. But among data management experts, ideas about "data ownership" are neither clear nor consistent.

- English (1999) is very clear about a basic premise: individuals do not "own" data; the enterprise owns data. But enterprises do not make decisions or take actions; people within enterprises do. So, how do you get people to "be accountable" if not through ownership? The idea of *data stewardship* was intended to help people understand how they should take care of data as an enterprise asset. But stewardship is specifically not ownership. A steward takes care of property that belongs to other people.
- The *DAMA Dictionary of Data Management* defines a data owner as, "An individual responsible for definitions, policy, and practice decisions about data within their area of responsibility. For business data, the individual may be called a business owner of the data" (DAMA, 2011). This definition sounds like stewardship in ownership clothing.

---

[12]See Laney (2018) Chapter 10 for an in-depth discussion about data ownership in a legal context.

- In the *DAMA Data Management Body of Knowledge* (DMBOK2), ownership and stewardship are conflated in many instances as are the concepts of ownership and accountability. For example, "A Data owner is a business data steward who has approval authority for decisions about data within their domain" (p. 77); a business data owner is accountable for stewardship of data quality while the steward takes appropriate corrective action (p. 488).
- Ladley (2019) also refers to "ownership/stewardship/custodianship" as a combined concept and uses *ownership* and *accountability* essentially as synonyms.

The idea of stewardship was introduced because it was recognized that individual people and teams do not own data. But in the effort to define data ownership, the concepts of ownership and stewardship have been fused, and very unrealistic ideas about ownership have emerged. In one organization I am familiar with, there was an effort to name the executive who was responsible for claim adjudication to be the "owner" of claim data across the entire organization. This meant being accountable not only for the claim data that was produced through the adjudication process, but also for claim data as it was set up in the data warehouse and used in analytics — long after it left the adjudication engine. Asking someone to be "accountable" in areas over which they have no control and no direct involvement is a losing proposition.

To solve this problem, we must step back and reframe it. Instead of asking who owns the data, we can ask, "What are people and teams actually and already responsible for, and how do their existing responsibilities connect with data?" The answer, in most cases, is that teams are responsible for executing processes. These processes produce data. Process owners can and should be accountable for the data that their teams produce. Being accountable includes at least three elements:

- **Making quality requirements clear to the people who supply the inputs to the process**. In the case of claim adjudication, this means providing instruction on how data is to be packaged and delivered for adjudication. Claims with data that is complete, accurate, and in the correct format can be adjudicated with fewer problems than claims with missing or incorrect data.
- **Ensuring that the outputs of the process meet the quality requirements of that process**. In the case of claim adjudication, this means adjudicating claims accurately and in a timely manner while reducing the incidence of claims that require rework.
- **Knowing the requirements of the people and processes that use the outputs**. In the case of claim adjudication, this means that providers are reimbursed on time and in accord with their contracts; the data warehouse or operational data store receives complete and accurate data in a timely manner; and the data is in the correct format to be stored in the warehouse.

Most process owners are focused on the success of their own process (the second bullet). Some may not account for the first and third points at all.

In complex organizations, data is produced and used by a wide array of people and processes. Data is not "owned" in the way sometimes envisioned by data management professionals. However, these processes are interconnected by data, sometimes in ways that producers and consumers do not always understand or even need to understand. These interconnections mean that "ownership of data" is complicated. Because data continually moves through organizations, is incorporated into many processes, and can be copied and transformed without being lost or diminished, no single person or process has complete control over the data. Data's organic characteristics make it a wild thing that is difficult to pin down and "own."

Add to this that people are people. People will not be able to be accountable unless accountabilities are defined, and it is unfair to make them "accountable" for things that are out of their control and beyond their sphere of influence. In advocating for data ownership, we should be advocating that process owners be accountable for the data their teams create. Processes generally are "owned," often at the executive level. I advocate for giving up the pursuit of "data owners" and replacing it with a commonsense understanding that there must be accountability for data along the internal data supply chain; that is, as data is created and moves through the organization, accountability for it at any given point rests with owners of the business process that is creating or moving it. In short, processes owners would be accountable for the quality of the data they produce as they already are accountable for other process outputs.[13] If this approach were in place, then the executive responsible for data, ideally a CDO, could work with process owners to manage the overall data supply system.

Poor-Quality Data Is Costly, Dangerous, and Tolerated

Although data has sped up and grown bigger, and some organizations strive to transform themselves, the approach many organizations take to managing their data has not improved much since 2001. There is still "widespread failure of management boards to give data issues the attention they deserve" (PwC, 2001, p. 6) and "widespread failure by companies to both appreciate the strategic importance of data management and to institute structures reflecting that importance" (PwC, 2001, p. 9). It is true that most large organizations have a data governance function, and many even have CDOs. Privacy and security risks around data are better managed than they were previously. Yet these risks are also much greater now, and many organizations would be out of business had there been no improvement (Information is Beautiful, 2021).

The bottom line is that organizations continue to lose money, increase risk, and miss out on opportunity because they have not taken action to improve the quality of their data. To quote the Leader's Data Manifesto: "Data offers enormous untapped potential to create competitive advantage, new wealth, and jobs; ... and otherwise improve the human condition. [But] organizations are far from being data-driven" (Data Leaders, 2017). The big difference is that fewer people seem to be talking about the quality of data in relation to the potential benefits of the data. As noted previously, some even naïvely assert that with the emergence of Big Data, the quality of data does not matter.

The focus on data governance and security has brought the focus away from data quality. Yet refocusing on quality may very well improve both governance and security. Deficiencies in quality reduce the potential value of data by increasing both the costs of data management and the risks associated with data use. Despite the recognized importance of data, few organizations actually define what they mean by high-quality data. Fewer still manage their data to improve and sustain its quality. Instead, most organizations make do with the data they produce through their business operations. At the same time, they budget millions for and ardently seek a holy technological grail that will unlock their data's power.

In this pursuit, they miss the obvious: poor-quality data is costly and dangerous. It does not take much imagination to understand why. It does take a bit of common sense and a willingness to

---

[13]McGilvray (2021) takes a similar approach, placing accountability for data in the hands of people who are already accountable for the processes that create or use data.

acknowledge the levels of waste and risk associated with many organizational processes that do not account for the quality of the data they produce and consume. Estimates about these levels of risk and waste are generally very high. Most organizations do not want to admit that they have been so slack with valuable resources.

Costly

Every year, experts produce statistics about the direct and indirect costs of poor-quality data. Reports differ, but most estimate that between 10% and 30% of productivity is lost as a result of poor-quality data; estimates for lost revenue are between 15% and 25%. Even these estimates seem low. One report indicated that data scientists spend 60% of their time cleansing data; another report set this figure at 80%. In 2016, IBM estimated that data quality problems cost the United States $3.1 trillion (Redman, 2016).

These costs can be categorized in different ways. The most obvious direct costs of poor-quality data include scrap and rework (including detection, analysis, and remediation of issues; work-arounds; and hidden correction processes[14]) and fines associated with compliance failures. The indirect costs are more insidious and more difficult to associate with hard numbers because they are hidden by their nature. Yet a quick look at the list should leave very little doubt that they have a large impact. Costs of poor-quality data include the following:

- **Scrap and rework:** Direct costs of issue detection and remediation; indirect (often hidden) costs or workarounds and corrections
- **Inefficiencies:** Process failures and delays, impact to project timelines, reduced productivity resulting from activities such as time spent looking for and cleansing data
- **Customer impact:** Customer dissatisfaction, increased customer service costs, customer attrition
- **Organizational impact:** Mistrust, interpersonal conflict, employee dissatisfaction
- **Impediments to improvement:** Failure in reengineering or reorganization efforts; inability to innovate
- **Inability to execute a business strategy:** Bad decision making, missed opportunities, limits on execution, failure to gain competitive advantage
- **Reputational costs:** Direct costs of noncompliance (e.g., fines) and public relations/damage control; indirect costs of a poor reputation

In the 1980s, quality guru Philip Crosby pointed out that, "Quality is free." He meant that when people assume that it costs more to produce a high-quality product than a low-quality product, they point to the costs of improving processes and input, and they ignore all the costs associated with making up for the repercussions of poor quality; that is, they ignore the costs of inefficient processes, failed products, and dissatisfied stakeholders that they are already incurring. If they focus on quality from the beginning and throughout the production process, quality pays for itself. Crosby estimated that the price of nonconformance was 30% of revenue: "One in every three

---

[14]Tom Redman refers to these kinds of practices as "The Hidden Data Factory." See also Alter (2014) for a full-length discussion on the implications of workarounds. Workarounds are likely to result in poorer-quality data, but they are also often a sign of other problems, such as poorly designed processes, lack of training, or lack of awareness.

dollars is flat out wasted" (Crosby, n.d.). This is very close to the estimates of losses resulting from poor-quality data. W. Edwards Deming made the same argument: "Low quality means high costs .... Defects are not free. Somebody makes them and gets paid for making them." Further, somebody gets paid to correct or repair them (Deming, 1986, p. 11).

Both Crosby and Deming put the blame for low-quality products squarely on management. If leaders compromise on quality, they encourage their organizations to accept low-quality outcomes. If they adopt a quality management philosophy, they "deliberately create an environment where all transactions are completed correctly each time, and where relationships with employees, suppliers, and customers are successful" (Crosby, n.d.). Unfortunately, although many leaders today see the potential value in data, few seem to understand their role in getting their organizations to manage data and other information assets in a way that taps into this value (Evans & Price, 2020).

The key to reducing the costs of poor quality is the prevention of defects. It is much more costly to fix a defect or respond to a defect than it is to prevent a defect in the first place. The significant impact of early detection is summarized in the "Rule of Ten" or the "1-10-100 Rule." In product manufacturing, the cost of preventing a problem is about one-tenth of the cost of correcting an existing problem. The cost of failure is about ten times greater than the cost of correction (Canic, 2019) (Fig. 7).

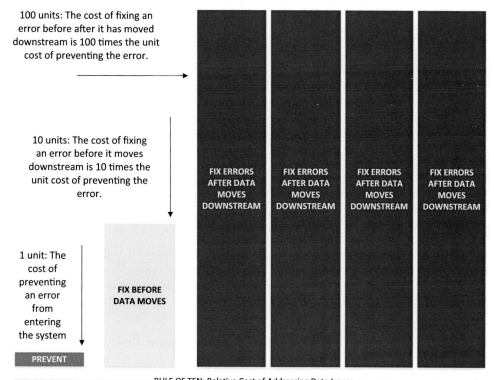

FIGURE 7

The rule of 10 (units drawn to scale).

The progression, which can be applied to any process, is as follows:

- **Costs of prevention:** Prevention includes designing processes to produce output of required quality and training employees to execute these processes correctly so output meets expectations (in short, doing things right the first time). Prevention represents 1 unit of work.
- **Costs of correction:** *Correction* is another name for *scrap and rework*, that is, fixing things after a problem is detected. The costs associated with correction represent ten times the costs associated with prevention. Correction represents 10 units of work.
- **Costs of failure:** Failure includes any costs incurred when addressing the downstream impacts if a problem is not fixed. Fixing downstream impacts cost ten times more than correcting the errors: 100 units of work. In fact, it may cost more because the cost of failure is the largest source of customer dissatisfaction and poor reputation, which can have long-term repercussions.

In software development, the terms are slightly different, but the idea and the ratios are the same. If addressing a defect found in unit testing costs $100, addressing the same defect in system testing will cost $1,000. Addressing it in user acceptance testing will cost $10,000. In a production system, it will cost $100,000 to fix the problem and clean up its effects (Standish, 2014).

Given this perspective, it also does not take much imagination to identify the benefits of high-quality data, not only to those who use data for analytics, but also to those who use data directly to execute operational processes:

- Higher productivity
- Improved customer experience
- Reduced risk that data will be misused
- Higher capacity to act on opportunities
- Increased revenue
- Competitive advantage gained from insights about customers, products, and processes

These benefits are all things we expect to happen anyway because we expect processes to work and produce the desired outcomes, even though most of us have directly experienced the results of poor-quality products, services, and data.

Dangerous

Almost anything of value or potential value is also connected with risk. If nothing else, there is the risk that value may be lost or never realized. People who extol the value of data but do not account for the costs of poor-quality data ignore the risks associated with data, including the following:

- Inconsistencies in how data is created and structured
- The work required to integrate different data sets
- The role that interpretation plays in both data creation and data use
- The potential for unethical or criminal use of data

The glowing talk about data as an asset assumes that data can be used in the ways that people envision, and that, through these uses, data will generate value. Usability depends, in part, on accessibility. People must be able to access the data, and the data must exist in a form that is suitable for how they want to analyze and manipulate it. More importantly, usability depends on the quality of the data, access to knowledge about the data (metadata), and skills and experience to use it properly (data literacy). The absence of these things increases the risk that the data will be misused. When data is misused, it becomes the opposite of an asset. It is a liability.

But with today's data, risk goes far beyond the potential failure to derive value from an asset. Many organizations collect highly personal data. Through it, one can trace the actions and behaviors of individual people and learn things about them that in previous generations would have been considered very private, such as whom they call, how long they talk, where they spend their time, what books and articles they read, what they eat, what medications they take and why they take them, how much money they have, and what they buy with their money. Data collection about the daily activities of individual people is almost constant. The surveillance society is securely in place.

Enabling surveillance of individuals and groups is a political problem and a threat to individual freedom and to Western political institutions that depend on well-informed, literate citizens. I will not address these problems in this book because they are not my areas of expertise. But I will recommend that data management professionals educate themselves in these risks and recognize both the ethical implications of the misuse of data and the potential political implications of the availability of the kind of data we routinely collect, store, and use (Schneier, 2015; Stephens-Davidowitz, 2017; Zuboff, 2019).

This book focuses on data quality in the context of professional data management. Collecting all of this data presents multiple challenges from both a general data management and a specific data quality management perspective. As discussed earlier, one of these challenges is data protection. Personal and private data represents risk to the individuals it references. If this data is accessed and misused, individuals will suffer financial damage and personal distress. This data also represents risk to the organizations that want to get value from it. Organizations must protect personal data. If they do not and they are breached, they will lose customers and suffer reputational damage. They may even be sued for reparations. Organizations must also ensure that they do not themselves misuse this data. If personal and private data is also inaccurate, it presents additional risks, for example, the possibility that a person will be associated with a disease or health condition they do not actually have or will not be associated with a health condition they do have.

If organizational data is incomplete, inaccurate, or incorrectly integrated, it also presents risks. Even if personal data is not breached, an organization's business data can be breached with the potential loss of competitive advantage. For example, poor-quality data presents the risk that the organization will misunderstand its customer base, financial standing, or level of compliance with regulatory requirements. Because data represents the organization and its customers, it must be protected, but it also must be of high quality.

Given the importance of data protection, imagine someone asking the following questions:

- How much data protection is enough? It doesn't have to be "perfect," does it?
- What is our threshold for allowing bad actors to take advantage of the information we have about our customers, suppliers, and employees? Should we let them have 1% of this data?
- Names, birth dates, and Social Security numbers are all personal identifiable information (PII). Should the minimum viable product for data protection be to just start with the Social Security number and put the others on the backlog?
- How many Social Security numbers and how much credit card information will we allow hackers to get before we do something about it? Should we do this as a percentage of customers or a raw number?

Of course not. Anyone who talks openly about tolerating an "acceptable" level of hacking or criminal activity would be seen as completely irresponsible. Yet people do ask analogous questions about the quality of data. In doing so, they miss the point. Organizations operate based on their data. They should know what condition their data is in and what risks it poses to the organization, and they should manage these risks accordingly.

The point of these comparisons between data quality management and data security is not to diminish the importance of data protection, but to point out the obvious: organizations should not have to choose between data protection and data quality. In fact, organizations that understand risk management have the cultural attitude to have both high-quality and well-protected data. This may be related to the root causes of poor-quality data: if an organization has poor-quality data, it is often because its management does not know their business as well as they could or should. This is risky in and of itself.

Tolerated

The research for this chapter covers published perspectives on data and information quality beginning in the mid-1990s. The story could go back even further to the beginning of data warehousing or even to the development of "data banks" (Ackoff, 1967; Ivanov, 1972; Kent, 1978). Ever since we reached a point where we tried to integrate organizational data into data banks, warehouses, and marts, smart, well-informed people have raised concerns about the costs and risks associated with poor-quality data. They have said, essentially, "Yes, data is very valuable. But not if it is poorly managed, ungoverned, and of poor quality." Further, they present a vision of how an organization can move from a state where their data is a liability to a state where it is truly an asset and a competitive differentiator (Fig. 8). But few organizations have acted on this knowledge. Most organizations imagine that they work in the top half of the graph, where data is truly an asset, and high-quality data provides a competitive advantage. They may not even imagine that there is a bottom half, but this is where they actually live. They do not know the condition of their data, and therefore data is as much a liability as an asset.

There is almost a willful ignorance involved in this level of toleration, as evidenced from Gartner's 2018 Data Quality Tools Magic Quadrant Survey referenced earlier in this chapter (57% of the respondents do not measure the financial impact of poor-data quality).

Olson (2002) summarized reasons why organizations fail to address data quality problems. His list sheds light on the reasons organizations tolerate poor-quality data:

- There is a low awareness of the cost of data quality problems.
- There is a low awareness of the potential value of improvements.
- There is a high tolerance for errors in primary systems.
- Issues are treated as isolated problems instead of symptoms of wider process problems.
- People learn to cope with issues and accept poor-quality data; they develop workarounds and give up hope of resolving problems.
- The business case for improving quality is not presented as a compelling alternative to overcoming organizational inertia and living with issues.
- People become skeptical about the ability to improve things and to get return on investing in improvement.

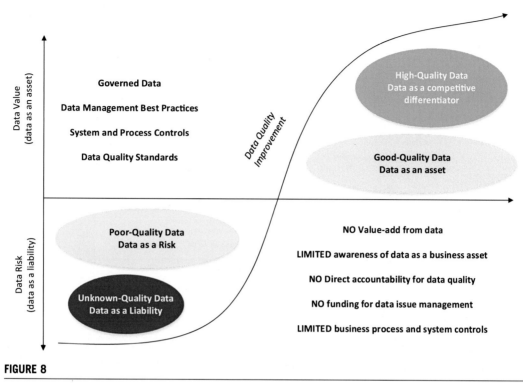

FIGURE 8

Data as a liability versus data as an asset.

In a nutshell, most organizations accept the status quo rather than identifying and acting on opportunities for improvement. Olson also provides insight on the conditions needed to improve data quality. The approach must be as follows:

- **Proactive not reactive:** Improvement comes from getting ahead of the problems.
- **Holistic:** It is not enough to address symptoms of poor quality, such as individual data issues. The underlying causes must be addressed.
- **Long-term:** Short-term fixes are often necessary, but improvement takes longer and requires sustained commitment.
- **Enterprise-wide:** Data reflects and connects the enterprise. The approach must ultimately be organization-wide and involve changes in behavior. If it is limited to a few people, it will not have the desired effects and probably will not be sustained.
- **Based on higher expectations:** High-quality data must be a requirement of projects. The organization should cease to tolerate low-quality data.

McGilvray, Price, and Redman (2016) shed further light on the tendencies of organizations to tolerate low-quality data (Fig. 9). Based on research by Evans and Price (2012), they identify five categories of root causes and 23 contributing factors to the general problem of information assets not being properly managed. Their analysis, which includes concerns in addition to quality, shows

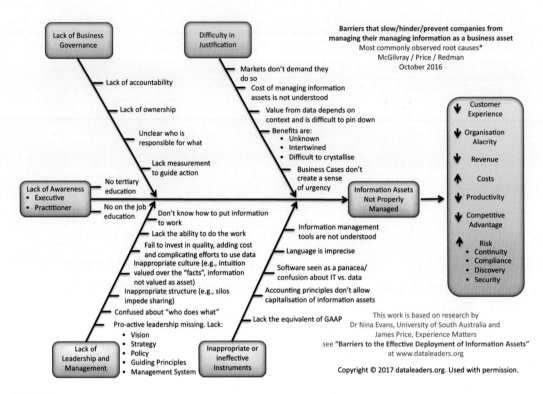

FIGURE 9

Barriers to managing information as a business asset — detailed fishbone diagram.

Copyright © 2017, dataleaders.org. Used with permission.

the connection between these other challenges (business governance, awareness of data value, difficulty in measurement, leadership commitment) and the quality of data. The root causes of why information assets are not managed properly include the following:

- **Lack of awareness:** Among both executives and staff, including data management practitioners, there is limited education about the importance of managing information assets and limited on-the-job training for how to manage information and data effectively.
- **Lack of business governance:** The business governance category recognizes problems with accountability, ownership, and responsibility for ensuring that assets are well-managed. Lack of business governance (not just data governance) includes a lack of measurement and the feedback it provides to guide action.
- **Lack of leadership and management:** Lack of leadership is connected to the absence of vision, strategy, policy, and principles. People do not know how to get value from their information, or they simply do not have the skills to do the work. Organizations add costs because they do not invest in quality at the start, but these hidden costs are not acknowledged. The lack of leadership promotes organizational culture that does not see the value of data or that has structures in place that impede sharing.

- **Difficulty in justification:** When there is no vision for how the organization will get value from data and information, it is difficult to justify the effort to improve data quality or change practices that result in poor-quality data in the first place. This is connected to a lack of knowledge about the actual costs and benefits of managing information assets. It also makes it difficult to develop the sense of urgency required to change practices within an organization.
- **Inappropriate or ineffective instruments:** Finally, organizations lack the means to improve their practices. They may not understand information management tools. They may argue about the vocabulary of data management. Some will seek technical tools to solve the problems, not recognizing that a misplaced faith in technology often contributes to data problems. Also, they do not have the equivalent of a set of general acceptable accounting principles to guide information management activities.

This set of root causes leads to improperly managed information and the associated costs of poor quality, including diminished customer experience; reduced organizational clarity, revenue, competitive advantage, and productivity; and increased costs and risks. These root causes are also directly connected to five challenges: (1) understanding the nature of data and managing its production and use, (2) the role of process design in ensuring quality, (3) the impact of technology on data quality, (4) the need for knowledge and data literacy skills among people who use data; and, most importantly, (5) the role of leadership in establishing a culture focused on quality, where accountability for data is made clear.

The costs are also clear: organizations lose money and opportunity because they manage their data poorly and their data is, consequently, of poor quality and unreliable.

Meeting the Challenges

When organizations strategize about becoming data driven or going through a digital transformation, they are working on the assumption that they have the data to do so and that their data is reliable and complete, even if history indicates that few of them should have this confidence. They envision getting value from their data, which is admittedly a lot sexier than managing data liabilities. Maybe they are not aware of the work required to produce high-quality data, or maybe they do not like to talk about this part of the process.

The tolerance for low-quality data paints a bleak picture, but there is a reason for optimism in this bleakness. Because so few organizations have the wherewithal to address the challenges of managing data quality, those that do are likely to see great benefits, just as organizations that focus on product quality will gain a significant competitive advantage.

The best way to approach the work of data quality management is to identify the obstacles to success and remove them or to reduce and manage their impact. Many obstacles are directly related to the five challenges (data, process, technology, people, culture/organization). To do so, it is important to understand these challenges both in general terms (what they are and how they affect most organizations) and in specific terms (how they manifest and what their effects are in a particular organization). It is not possible to address all of these challenges at once. Instead, it is necessary to do the following:

- Understand them within your organization.
- Determine their impact on organizational success.
- Prioritize them based on costs and benefits.
- Address the high-priority items within the context of your organization.

The rest of this book will present information and techniques to help focus on those goals. Chapter 2 provides a high-level overview of each of these challenges and an approach to meeting them. Chapter 3 discusses the relationship between data quality and business strategy. Chapters 4 to 8 discuss each challenge in depth (data, process, technology, people, culture/organization). Chapters 9 to 11 describe the core data quality management functions that support an organization's ability to improve and sustain data quality.

Organizational Data and the Five Challenges of Managing Data Quality

2

"I have not failed. I've just found 10,000 ways that won't work."

Thomas Edison

Introduction

This book focuses on managing the quality of organizational data, that is, the data that any organization creates in the process of executing its operations, transacting business with its customers, and evaluating its own performance. This chapter starts by exploring the concept of the organization as a system and the multiple roles that data plays in this system. Together, the organization and its data provide the context for the work of data quality management.

In Chapter 1, we reviewed the evolving state of data in today's world and identified a range of conditions that prevent organizations from getting value from their data. These conditions provide the backdrop for the rest of the book. Chapter 1 also described five challenges that can get in the way of data quality management. In this chapter, we will unpack these five challenges and recognize how each has an impact on the quality of data. These include the data challenge, the process challenge, the technical challenge, the people challenge, and the culture challenge.

The Five Challenges of Managing Data Quality

The five challenges of managing data quality interact with and reinforce each other (Fig. 10). The data challenge is directly connected to the people challenge, as both require knowledge about data. The process challenge is directly connected to the technical challenge, as most organizational processes are dependent on the technical tools used to carry them out. All of these pieces (the data, process, technology, and people) are part of the overall culture of the organization. If accountability and responsibility for data are not made clear, the cultural challenge will not be met, and it will be very difficult to meet the other challenges.

The Data Challenge

The data challenge includes knowing how different forms of data are structured and what conventions are used in data's representation of facts; understanding how data sets are created and their limitations; defining what is meant by high-quality data; and recognizing low-quality data.

Meeting the Challenges of Data Quality Management. DOI: https://doi.org/10.1016/B978-0-12-821737-5.00002-X

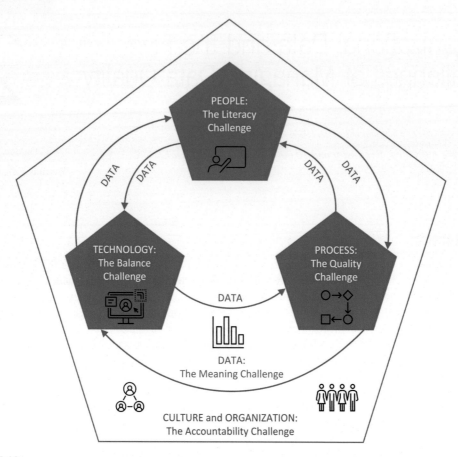

FIGURE 10

The five challenges of managing data quality.

Managing the quality of data requires knowledge of how data works as part of a representational system, the choices made in creating it, the ways it can be used and misused, and its connection to other data. Addressing this challenge requires data management skills and knowledge, including specialized skills related to data quality management and metadata management.

The Process Challenge

The process challenge includes defining and managing organizational processes so they result in higher-quality, more reliable data and ensuring that data producers understand how their choices affect the usability of data by data consumers. Producing higher-quality data requires understanding how its condition may be influenced by the processes through which it is created and the ways the data is likely to be used. Addressing this challenge requires managing the processes that produce, move, and use data by recognizing that there are customers for these processes, they have expectations related to the quality of data, and these expectations can be met.

The Technical Challenge

The technical challenge involves understanding how choices related to technology affect the creation, accessibility, use, and quality of data. Producing higher-quality data and using data both require understanding how data is connected to and separable from technology and how technical choices leave an imprint on the data created through them. Addressing this challenge requires focusing on the data before focusing on the technology and meeting the requirements for data as well as technology.

The People Challenge

The people challenge includes ensuring that data producers and data consumers have the knowledge, information, and skills they need to access, understand, and interpret data. Using and interpreting data requires that data consumers build their knowledge of how data works in general and how their organization's data works in particular and that they hone their skills in interpreting and communicating about data. Addressing this challenge requires building data literacy skills and managing explicit knowledge (metadata) within the organization.

The Culture Challenge

The culture challenge includes ensuring that there is oversight of data within the organization and accountability for data along the data supply chain to enable the organization to generate expected value from its data. Improving and sustaining the quality of data requires aligning the organization's people, processes, and technology behind the goal of creating high-quality data assets and using the insights gained from these assets to create value for the enterprise and its constituent parts. Addressing this challenge requires defining accountability goals and establishing a program of oversight that is appropriate to the organization. Such a program must be supported by managed culture change.

The Sixth Challenge: Vocabulary

Another factor that gets in the way of data quality management is the way we talk about it. For example, even the words *data quality* can cause confusion. Sometimes people use the term *data quality* to refer to the condition of data (its level of quality). Other times they use it to refer to the processes required to fix data, to the team charged with doing so, or to an abstract or undefined thing. (We need data quality!) In presenting the challenge to data quality management, this chapter will define the key terms needed to understand processes. Definitions are also compiled in the glossary for reference.

Organizational Data

Organizational data is data that any organization creates in the process of executing its operations, transacting business with its customers, and evaluating its own performance. This is sometimes referred to as *administrative data* (Keller et al., 2017), but this term can be misleading.

Organizational data can be understood to include multiple subtypes of data, such as master data, reference data, operational data, transactional data, metadata, and even external data (data created outside of the organization that may be brought in to augment organizational data). These data sets are created, used, and combined in different ways to meet the goals of the organization.

Improving the quality of data requires a perspective on the organization as a complex system with interconnected elements working together to achieve goals. Data and information are important elements within the system. They are also critical to connecting the different parts of the organization. Playing multiple roles, data and information are critical to the evolution of the organization.

Although many organizations have the same categories of data (e.g., lists of customers, vendors, employees, and products; transaction records; quarterly sales figures), the data of a given organization is unique to that organization. Company A and Company B will both have a list of customers, but their lists will differ from each other. Even if Company A and Company B have many of the same customers, these customers will have purchased different products from each organization at different times for different reasons. Each organization's data will tell a different story about these customers. An organization's data not only reflects the activities of the organization, but it also would be impossible for any organization to recreate its data if it were lost (Redman, 1997).

In a certain sense, organizational data has existed since recordkeeping began. But with the rise of computing, the capacity to capture, store, and share organizational data has changed significantly. The emergence of data warehousing technology enabled organizations to integrate and analyze their data in ways that were previously impossible. This enabled new insights – a "business intelligence" – about customers, products, and processes. Technological advances now allow organizations to capture and process larger and more complex data sets. Organizational data can be used in new forms of analysis (e.g., predictive analytics, machine learning, artificial intelligence).

People use data and information not only for analytics, but also to carry out operational processes and to meet organizational goals. When processes are messy and inconsistent, so is the data produced through them, and so is the organization. Data is often created in organizational verticals (departments, siloed teams), but it moves horizontally within organizations, across verticals. When people create data to meet the immediate needs of their own process and are not aware of the ways in which their data may be used by others in the organization, they cannot account for the requirements of other data consumers. They may create usable data, but it is more likely that the data they create will have gaps or require cleansing or manipulation to be usable. Raising awareness of the uses of data within an organization, even in simple ways (e.g., understanding that many functions require information about the organization's customers and therefore keeping current and accurate customer records), can help improve the quality of data within the organization.

Organizational data is the focus of professional data management efforts that nowadays must account for the fact that many organizations are very large and complex and that most data is managed via technology that itself requires a high degree of management. Yet many of our assumptions about data and data quality are based on a view of data that stems from how data is created and used in science and statistics. Data as we know it in most business enterprises is not created with the same care that scientific or statistical data is created. It is created through the activities of the organization, largely as a by-product of these activities. Unfortunately, because activities such as sales, marketing, enrollment, and underwriting are executed separately, the data produced through different processes does not always fit together.

The chronic problem of disparate or heterogenous data (the variation challenge that has plagued both data warehousing and efforts to get value from data lakes) is usually blamed on the data having been "created in silos." However, because data represents the activities of an organization's data, even unplanned and underdesigned data can provide a means through which the organization can learn about its operations, customers, products, partners, and processes. That said, this data can be managed purposefully, as a product of these activities intended to provide input into reports and analyses. If it is managed with intention, the organization will learn more and be more confident in what it learns. It will also improve the efficiency of its learning, because the mechanisms that are used to manage data (i.e., reliable, high-quality metadata; data literacy skills; and robust system controls) are also valuable in using data.

Organizations are complex entities with many moving parts. Because organizations are complex, managing organizational data with purpose requires recognizing and managing this complexity. If people within the organization can understand the organization as a whole, which includes how the parts are intended to fit together as well as how they may have been forced to fit together through workarounds and inconsistencies, it increases the chances of producing data that is comprehensible, usable, and represents the characteristics that are important to the organization. Knowledge about data is a specialized form of knowledge about an organization. As we will discuss in Chapter 7, an organization can get more value from its data if this knowledge itself is managed and cultivated.

While data greatly benefits from planning and design, organizations also evolve over time. They must be flexible enough to respond to new opportunities. Data also must be able to evolve. In fact, data's ability to change in a somewhat organic way can be a catalyst that enables an organization to take advantage of new opportunities and to respond to the evolving needs of its customers. There are many benefits to designing data with a view to its potential for change while also balancing this change with a degree of control that enables the data to remain meaningful.

For example, for many years, the attribute of gender was used as an example for how to standardize codes. System A has gender codes of M = Male, F = Female, and U = Unknown. System B has 01 = Male, 02 = Female, and 00 = Unknown. To standardize these, one must determine what the standard representation is and map other codes to it. This could mean transforming M, F, and U to 01, 02, and 00; transforming 01, 02, and 00 to M, F, and U; or transforming both to another set of values. Gender provided a simple example of data transformation when the concept of gender was assumed to be simple and stable. But in recent years, as a society we have recognized the concept of gender itself as multifaceted and fluid. To provide appropriate health care, for example, it may be necessary to know both the physical sex of an individual and their gender identity. Therefore the range of concepts represented by a set of gender code values must evolve to account for biological males identifying as female, biological females identifying as male, individuals who are transitioning from one sex to the other, and individuals who do not identify as either male or female. Indeed, many people recognize two different attributes: physical sexual identity at birth and gender identity.

These general conditions within organizations represent a challenge to data quality management. No one in data quality management starts with a clean slate or a green field. There is always organizational history to contend with, not only in the form of existing data, but also in the form of people, processes, and technologies. Past projects, unfulfilled architectural visions, and an ongoing battlefield of competing priorities and varied interpretations of strategy can get in the way of addressing the root causes of existing data quality problems and of preventing future problems.

Organizations must actively work on ensuring that data is of the highest possible quality. This work includes defining criteria for quality and applying these criteria in business and technical processes. Individual data quality practitioners and teams dedicated to improving the quality of data must understand their organization's goals, articulate the value of high-quality data, and advocate for the behavioral, process, and technical changes required to improve data quality.

Organizational Data and Systems Thinking

To understand the importance of data to organizational self-knowledge, one can apply concepts from systems theory. Systems theorist Donella Meadows defines a *system* as an interconnected set of elements that is coherently organized to achieve a purpose (Meadows, 2008, p. 11). This definition is very similar to that of quality pioneer W. Edwards Deming, who defined a system as "a network of interdependent components that work together to try to accomplish the aim of the system. A system must have an aim. Without an aim, there is no system. The aim of the system must be clear to everyone in the system" (Deming, 1994). Deming's formulation emphasizes that systems must be purposeful. However many components a system has, the point of their existence is to be part of the complex whole.

Meadows emphasizes how the components of any system (i.e., elements, organization/structure, interconnections, and purpose) over time create the behaviors characteristic of the system. Though systems are defined as *coherent* because of their focus on purpose, they also include tensions. Systems are composed of subsystems that may have conflicting or misaligned goals. Indeed, we can recognize most organizations as what John H. Holland calls *complex adaptive systems*, which "involve great numbers of parts undergoing a kaleidoscopic array of simultaneous interactions" and which "exhibit and aggregate behavior that is not simply derived from the actions of the parts" (Holland, 1992).

Although systems are complex, they work well because they are resilient, self-organizing, and structured. System behavior is determined largely by system structure, and system structure is not easy to change. Systems depend on feedback loops to modulate their behavior. Systems are also prone to what Meadows describes as *system traps*, which are connected to limitations in feedback loops. These system traps are as follows:

- Resisting change (policy resistance)
- Difficulty ensuring that people act responsibly toward shared resources (the tragedy of the commons)
- Relying on past performance to influence future expectations (drift toward low performance)
- Internal competition spiraling out of control (escalation)
- Systemic rewards to previous successes (success to the successful)
- Disguising system limitations by shifting burdens within the system (workarounds)
- Encouraging people to game the system by beating the rules
- Producing incorrect or undesirable results by defining goals poorly

Even though systems, like businesses and other organizations, are not technically alive, they nevertheless take on characteristics of living things. They evolve, anticipate, and exhibit behaviors characteristic to themselves. Even organizations that do the same work, such as two manufacturing firms or two health care companies, "behave" differently from each other because they are distinct systems and have evolved their own characteristic approaches to getting work done — their own "behaviors." When we recognize that different organizations have different "cultures," we are acknowledging that their approach to problems and the ways people work together within them differ from each other in noticeable ways.

Systems thinking can inform many aspects of data quality management (Evernden & Evernden, 2003; Hillard, 2010; Ivanov, 1972; Orr, 1996). Systems thinking informs the five challenges in the following ways:

- **The Data Challenge:** Data and information play multiple roles within an organization. They are elements of the system; they are the means by which interactions are executed and documented; and in many cases they are part of the purpose of the system. This means the quality of information exchanged within the organization directly affects the relationship among other elements within the system as well as the system's ability to achieve its goals.
- **The Process Challenge:** Thinking of an organization as a system connected by data also sheds light on the process challenge in quality management. Because processes are often developed independently of each other, people developing them may make incorrect assumptions about input or pay limited attention to uses of the output beyond their immediate needs. But if they see their process as a component part of a greater whole, they are more likely to make these connections. Seeing these connections allows them to present their requirements for quality to suppliers and to listen to the quality requirements of downstream consumers of the output from the process.
- **The Technical Challenge:** Data and information are part of the overall system (the organization), and they are managed within information technology (IT) systems. IT systems have additional characteristics that are directly connected to quality. They contain information that is assumed to correspond to real-world objects, events, and concepts. To achieve this correspondence, design of both the system (a system model) and the data (a data model) is required. Using any IT system requires some knowledge of how the system itself represents the real world. If an IT system is not well-designed or if people do not understand how it works, then people using it will often resort to workarounds to get information into the system. If they cannot change the IT system, they will "force reality to fit the [system] model" (Ivanov, 1972). Workarounds cause the information in the system to be further out of alignment with the objects, events, and concepts it is supposed to represent. Much of the information in IT systems is about the organization itself. People designing IT systems will do a better job of it if they understand the organization holistically. This is one reason why enterprise architecture is such a critical function.
- **The People Challenge:** People are also "elements" in the system that is the organization. Those creating and using data need knowledge and skills to get value from it. The better they understand the organization as a system connected by data, the better able they will be to use and interpret organizational data.
- **The Culture Challenge:** Seeing the organization as a system with its own behaviors provides a clearer perspective on the challenges of culture change, especially with respect to governance. The overall goal of data governance is to establish and sustain appropriate behaviors toward data in the organization by defining decision rights and accountabilities toward data. If an organization is a system and a system generates its own behavior, then one route to a successful data governance program is to understand this behavior and evolve it in an intentional way. This requires both engagement with the purpose of the organization and a thoughtful approach to potential system traps.

The Data Challenge: The Mechanics of Meaning

There is so much data in today's world and so much focus on data being everywhere, that many people take it for granted and may not think about what data actually is or where it comes from. Our commonsense understanding of data is that it represents facts about the world. Indeed, the following standard dictionary definitions back this up:

- The Latin root of *data* is *dare*, the past participle of "to give." *Data* means "something given." In math and engineering, the terms *data* and *given* are used interchangeably.
- The *New Oxford American Dictionary* defines *data* as "facts and statistics collected together for reference or analysis."
- The American Society for Quality (ASQ) defines *data* as "a set of collected facts" and identifies two kinds of numerical data: "measured or variable data ... and counted or attribute data."
- The International Organization for Standardization (ISO) defines data as a "re-interpretable representation of information in a formalized manner suitable for communication, interpretation, or processing" (ISO, 2016). ISO defines information as "knowledge concerning objects, such as facts, events, things, processes, or ideas, including concepts, that within a certain context has a particular meaning."

Because facts are facts, many people do not think about the work that goes into creating data. However, facts require structure (e.g., times, dates, measurement scales, records, and attributes), and establishing structure requires a set of choices about what to leave in and what to leave out of that structure. Data is an abstraction of information about the world. Creating data implies a model of the world as it involves decisions about how to encode, represent, and communicate information about people, objects, concepts, and events. Do you use the metric system or the imperial system? Do you use the Fahrenheit or Celsius scale? People have different ways of representing the same concepts. Data representing the same concepts can take on heterogeneous shapes. Data is like a language; it includes vocabulary and grammar. To speak it, you follow rules, but these rules have a certain amount of flexibility. And, of course, while although all languages have rules, they differ with respect to the specifics of these rules.

Because choices around data imply a model of the world, creating data requires knowledge and planning about which characteristics comprise effective representation, how to organize them in relation to each other, how to capture them in a usable form, how to share them, and how to understand them. This last point is particularly important. Data is not only an interpretation of the world. Data is also an object to be interpreted (Sebastian-Coleman, 2013). Using data requires information about what characteristics are being encoded and how these are encoded. (This information about data is usually referred to as *metadata*.) Interpreting data provides a means to understand the world. In this sense, data is a form of knowledge. Our ability to use data is constrained by our own knowledge, skills, and experience as well as by the knowledge, skills, and experience of the people who create data.

So, even though data is so integral to today's world that many people can and do take it for granted, data is not natural. It does not make itself. It does not speak for itself. People create data and the mechanisms and devices that collect, store, and maintain data. Data has all the flaws and limitations of anything made by people. It also has an incredible amount of inherent power. Because data formally encodes characteristics about the world, the existence of data influences our understanding of the world and the choices we make in creating more data. On one hand, when data is designed based on a scientific paradigm and used to explore questions and test hypotheses, it can create new knowledge about the world and can, indeed, change the world for the better. On the other hand, when designed and used to "prove" politically or economically motivated assumptions, it can also be used to change the world for the worse.

Despite being created by people, data also has organic characteristics. It not only grows in volume; data also changes form as it is accumulated, aggregated, and combined. Uses of data beget more data. It evolves as collection methods and uses change. As people use data, they learn from it and want to refine it.[1] Organizational data has organic characteristics because organizations are complex systems that evolve their own behaviors over time. Data is both an element in the organizational system and a means of enabling relationships among other elements (Meadows, 2008).

Organizations require data to execute operational processes. They need accurate names and addresses to ship products and bill customers. They need accurate product information to maintain inventories and meet customer needs. For the same reason, they need accurate metadata. Many organizations also get value from their data through the insights they can mine from it. Data enables them to learn about their customers, products, processes, and partners. The data we will focus on in this book, commerce-based organizational data, has particular challenges because, in most cases, it is not planned for or designed in the way that scientific and statistical data are. Much of it originates accidentally as a by-product rather than the product of processes that themselves are evolving. Also, organizational data evolves quickly as organizations attempt to meet their goals and respond to new opportunities. Data brings value only when it is used. To be successful with data, that is, to get value from data and the work required to manage data, organizations must account for and manage their knowledge about data (metadata) and cultivate data-related skills (data literacy).

The description of data so far implies that all data is structured data (data that is organized in columns and rows). The definition of *data* has expanded since the introduction of the computer in the mid-20th century. The term *data* is now used to refer to any information captured in an IT system (*New Oxford American Dictionary*). In Chapter 4, we will discuss the implications of this newer definition of *data*. For now, it is important to note that the expansion of electronic media means that many things we would not have called *data* a few decades ago (e.g., photographs once would more likely be called *artifacts* than *data*) are now considered data, albeit "unstructured" data.

Unstructured data presents the same challenge as structured data: to get value from it, you must be able to use and interpret it. As with structured data, this process requires knowledge of what the data represents and how it was created. Indeed, the first step in using "unstructured" data is usually to impose some level of structure on it so it can be understood. Or as data quality thought leader Tom Redman puts it, "There are two kinds of data: structured data and data that has not yet been structured."

Vocabulary

Throughout this book, we will use the following definitions of critical terms related to data:

- **Data**: Data is the representation of selected characteristics (attributes) of objects, events, and concepts (entities) that is expressed and understood through explicitly defined conventions related to their meaning, collection, and storage. Since the introduction of the computer in the mid-20th century, the word *data* has also been used to refer to any information captured in or processed by a computer or other IT system.

---

[1] A quick example of evolving uses of data: mail order companies used to collect address data because it was needed to deliver products to customers. Now they use address data as a means of understanding customer demographics. This is an example of refinement. The International Classification of Diseases (ICD) is updated as medical professionals refine their knowledge about the nature of diseases.

- **Data Quality**: Data quality is a measure of the degree to which data fits the purposes of data consumers. Synonyms include: *quality of data* and *condition of data*.
- **Data Quality Management**: Data quality management is the process of controlling of a set of activities intended to ensure that data fits the purposes of data consumers. Core data quality management activities include the following:
  - Defining data quality requirements and the characteristics of high-quality data
  - Assessing the quality of data based on these definitions and requirements
  - Measuring, monitoring, and reporting on data quality levels to data consumers and providing feedback to data producers
  - Detecting and facilitating the resolution of data quality issues
  - Recommending and implementing improvements to the processes that produce data so data is made fitter for evolving purposes
  - Institutionalizing practices, standards, and policies for producing high-quality data
- **Metadata**: Metadata is explicit (i.e., documented) knowledge about data that enables data to be created, understood, and used.[2] Metadata is required for the use of data. The absence of metadata is a data quality issue because lack of information about data is an obstacle to the use of data. A wide range of information is included under the umbrella of metadata. For example:
  - Definitions of what the data represents and how it relates to other data (e.g., table and column descriptions, data dictionaries, business glossaries, data models and their detail about data types, data format, table joins)
  - Descriptions of how, where, and by which processes data was created (e.g., data provenance, business process descriptions and rules, system design diagrams, tool-generated data lineage diagrams)
  - Ways to classify the data (e.g., data domains, business functions, security levels)
  - Details about how data is technically instantiated (e.g., system descriptions; specifications; copy books; extract, transform, and load [ETL] code)
  - Descriptions of how data moves through processes and systems (e.g., data flows, architectural diagrams)
  - Descriptions of what happens to data as it moves through processes and systems (e.g., data lineage, data supply chain, information life cycle)
  - Records of specific instances of data movement (e.g., system logs, control reports)

The Process Challenge: Managing for Quality

People often think of quality in general and data quality in particular as amorphous and subjective. They get distracted by the idea that "fitness for purpose" implies an infinite range of purposes, each with its own standard for quality. Or they buy a data profiling engine, set up a few rules, and say they "have data quality" without saying what it means for data to be of high quality. But the history of product and service quality management shows that the quality of any product or service

---

[2]*Metadata* is often defined as "data about data," a formulation that I find singularly unhelpful. Kenett and Redman (2019) define *metadata* as "data that assists in the interpretation of other data." I find this definition quite useful because it focuses on how metadata is used, rather than on trying to draw a line between data and metadata.

can be defined, managed, and improved. This history also demonstrates that high-quality products are not created by accident but by intention, whereas low-quality products result from a lack of attention, especially lack of attention to the requirements of customers.

This is why the best way to manage the quality of data is by design, by understanding how and why data is produced and how it is used across the data life cycle and throughout the data supply chain. This process requires that an organization explicitly define what it means by high-quality data. Quality requirements come in many forms, such as definitions, standards, policies, and process flows, all of which can be grouped under the umbrella of *metadata* — explicit knowledge about data.

When data does not meet the expectations of data consumers, then it is by definition of low quality. Low-quality data may be associated with a range of conditions: records may be out-of-date or missing, values may be absent or incorrect, desired information may not have been collected at all, or data consumers may simply not understand the data. Any of these conditions can be an obstacle to using the data and therefore an obstacle to getting value from it. They are all data quality issues.

Because data brings value only when it is used, quality matters and can be understood only in the context of data use, keeping in mind that many processes that produce data do so in order to use it. Organizations must plan for high-quality data based on how the data is likely to be used and the requirements of the people and processes that will use it. Doing so requires a kind of organizational self-knowledge. Leadership must see the connections between their business strategy and their data and focus on ensuring that the data that the organization depends on for its critical functions is highly reliable. Because in any organization, the largest proportion of critical data is created by the organization itself, this means ensuring that the organization manages its internal data supply chain and understands its data value chain.

Vocabulary

Based on the preceding discussion about the process challenge, we will use the following definitions throughout the rest of the book.

- **Data Producer:** A data producer is any person, process, or system that creates, generates, or makes data available. Synonyms include *data creator* and *source system*.
- **Data Consumer:** A data consumer is any person, process, or system that uses data. Synonyms include *data customer*,[3] *end user*, and *target system*. Note: Through their uses of data, many data consumers also produce data.
- **Data Environment:** The data environment is a broad term for the collection of factors that influence the creation and use of data: the business processes through which data is produced, the technical systems through which it is produced and stored, the data itself, metadata (including data standards, definitions, specifications), technical architecture (including data

---

[3]Information quality pioneer Larry English argued against the use of the word *user* with regard to data: "The only people who call their customers 'users' are IT and drug dealers." I do not use the term *user* because it connotes the use of an application, rather than the use of data. Tom Redman argues for the term *data customer*, rather than *data consumer*, correctly pointing out that data is not consumed when used. Use of the word *customer* also emphasizes that people depend on other people's data, and it draws on the history of quality management, which focuses on customers as the arbiters of quality. Despite this strong argument, I have chosen to use the term data *consumer* because it is used more widely and because it also accounts for systems as "consumers" of data.

access tools), and data uses. All of these have implications for understanding data quality. The data environment includes the people, processes, and technology involved in creating and using data (English, 1999; McGilvray, 2021).

- **Data Supply Chain:** The set of processes through which data is created and distributed within an organization or among organizations.
- **Data Value Chain:** The set of processes and activities through which the creation and use of data contributes value to an organization's products and services.
- **Data Life Cycle:** A series of phases or stages through which data progresses from its initial definition and creation, enablement, and design through its maintenance, use, enhancement, and disposal. As part of its life cycle, data can be used multiple times. Often the life cycle includes feedback and improvement data, which starts the cycle again.
- **Data Quality Issue:** Any obstacle to a data consumer's use of the data, regardless of its root causes or why it is an obstacle.
- **Data Quality Issue Management:** The process of removing or reducing the impact of obstacles to the use of data by data consumers. Issue management includes the identification, definition, root cause analysis, quantification, prioritization, and remediation of issues, supported by tracking and reporting on issues.
- **Designed Data:** Data that has been created through processes that account for its potential uses. Designed data includes characteristics that help enable its use; for example, it is supported by high-quality metadata.

The Technical Challenge: Data-Technology Balance

Much of the data we produce and use today depends directly on the technology used to create it (we cannot collect sensor data without a sensor and a means of storing the data stream), so it is easy to confuse data and technology and to think that technology properly accounts for the quality of its own output — data. Historically, it has also been easier to focus "data" management on technology solutions for collecting or storing data than on the data itself.

Such technologies are often sold on the interesting potential that they represent, rather than on what organizations will actually accomplish with them. Most technologists are deeply interested in new technologies. Some will even admit to chasing after shiny objects. This is not wrong in and of itself. Lots of new technology is pretty cool and comes with the promise of enabling new business opportunities. The challenge comes when technologists ignore the data, assume that the data will always be okay (despite many reasons not to assume this), or see its condition as someone else's responsibility (e.g., the data "belongs to the business" or "IT has no control over the data"). Of all people, technologists should recognize the interdependence between data and the technology used to create it. Often, they overlook the dependence of any technology initiative on reliable data. For example, artificial intelligence can quickly become artificial stupidity if training data is of poor quality.

Added to this is the problem of hype. Organizations facing data quality problems can easily be duped into thinking that a new data quality tool will make everything right with their data. This causes them to purchase tools before defining the problems they are trying to solve and without a plan to get value from them. More importantly, if they have not identified the root causes of poor-quality data in their organizations, which research shows are largely cultural and process-based, then tools may simply make a bad situation worse.

Most importantly, technology can have a direct effect on the data itself. Anyone who has used *Excel* will recognize that things like data format and precision can throw off results if one is not aware of how they work and does not account for them. In larger systems as well as in business intelligence tools and other applications used to prepare or visualize data, the same data set may produce different results in different technologies (Saey, 2015a, 2015b). Even research science, which is built on a foundation of reproducing similar results under similar conditions, is experiencing a replication crisis because of the challenges associated with the use of different tools and technology to prepare and visualize data. The following was reported in *Science News* in 2015:

> Just keeping track of Big Data is a monumental undertaking. Sharing the data with other researchers, a critical piece of transparency and efficiency in science, has its own set of problems. And the tools used to analyze complex datasets are just as important as the data themselves. Each time a scientist chooses one computer program over another or decides to investigate one variable rather than a different one, the decision can lead to very different conclusions (Saey, 2015a).

Smart organizations will take a strategic approach to both data and technology and ensure that they achieve the best balance for the organization. By putting business goals first and identifying the data they need to meet those goals, they will support data creation and use through technology decisions that create value, by improving efficiency and the capacity to act on evolving opportunities.

The People Challenge: Knowledge and Data Literacy

Data is complex, and there is more of it than ever. Creating high-quality data requires planning and intention, including planning for the impact of technical choices on the quality of data. Using data requires knowledge of how data is produced and the conventions it uses to represent the world, skill in organizing and manipulating data to answer questions, and experience interpreting the results. Organizational data is as diverse and complicated as the organization that produces it. A single individual cannot know all of the data in an organization. But, collectively, the organization must be smart about its data by building explicit knowledge (metadata), including knowledge of what is meant by high-quality data, and by ensuring that employees understand how data works and how to use and interpret it.

All of this means that organizations must invest in *data literacy*, that is, in ensuring that data consumers have the knowledge, experience, information, and skills they need to access, understand, and learn from data in different contexts and to communicate with other people about data. Data literacy includes both the thinking skills needed to understand and use data, domain knowledge, and experience with the organization needed to interpret what organizational data implies about customers, products, and organizational activities. The working definition of data literacy used throughout this book is: *Data literacy* is the ability to read, understand, interpret, and learn from data in different contexts. It also includes the ability to communicate about data to other people.

The Culture Challenge: Organizational Responsibility for Data

Awareness of data uses will not solve all data quality problems, however. Data is a source of knowledge about the organization, its customers, products, and partners as well as its management, employees, and processes. Knowledge is power, and control over knowledge and the exchange of information is political. This political aspect of data prevents many organizations from developing the capability to make consistent, enterprise-level decisions about data. People do not want to give up their own control of data. Particularly, no one wants to feel exposed because their data and information are not "good."

Although many organizations have implemented data governance programs to address these challenges, data governance, as a set of practices, has not delivered on its promise. Misconceptions about the goals and role of data governance have even contributed to the problems some organizations have in managing data quality. In some organizations, the data governance team is viewed as imposing intrusive policies and needless bureaucracy that complicate projects and processes or as a policing function, enforcing petty rules that prevent people from getting work done. In other organizations, the data governance team is perceived as the only team responsible for data, charged with making all decisions and solving every problem, stewarding every data element, thus letting everyone else off the hook. Neither of these models reflects the intention of the people who originally conceptualized data governance, and neither will solve the political problems related to data. Similar challenges exist with the role of the chief data officer (CDO). Although originally conceived as a means through which data would be accounted for in the C-suite, the CDO role has fragmented to include many aspects of data use. Successful organizations hire a CDO and implement data governance based on clear goals related to their overall business strategy.

Vocabulary

Throughout this book, we will use the following definitions for concepts related to organizational responsibility for data.

- **Chief Data Officer:** The CDO is a senior executive responsible for the use and governance of data across the organization. The CDO may have responsibility for data strategy, data management, data quality, and life cycle management. The CDO is generally considered a business role, rather than a technical role.
- **Data Governance:** *Data governance* is organizational oversight of data and data related processes. The Data Governance Institute describes it as "a system of decision rights and accountabilities for information-related processes, executed according to agreed-upon models which describe who can take what actions with what information, and when, under what circumstances, using what methods."
- **Data Stewardship:** Stewarding data is a way of interacting with data, specifically, acting with accountability for data for the good of the organization. Data can be *stewarded* at different levels using informal and formal approaches. Stewardship is required of every individual who creates or uses organizational data.
- **Data Steward:** Informally, a subject matter expert in a data domain, data set, process, or data element who acts accountably toward data and upon whom others rely for information and

expertise. Formally, as a job title, a person who has specifically defined responsibilities related to helping the organization create, manage, govern, use, and derive value from its data.

- **Accountability:** To be accountable means to be answerable, literally "liable to be called to account" (*Online Etymological Dictionary*). Accountability means that a person is expected to act in a defined manner and must be able to explain their actions. To have accountability for data means having overall responsibility for a data set and defining clear responsibilities for those that produce the data; people accountable for data also ensure that data is in its expected condition and are able to explain the condition of the data under their control.

- **Organizational Culture:** *Organizational culture* refers to "the pattern of beliefs, values and learned ways of coping with experience that have developed during the course of an organization's history, and which tend to be manifested in its material arrangements and in the behaviors of its members" (Brown, 1998). More simply put, culture describes the way people work within an organization, with some reflection on why they work the way they do. The culture of an organization may be described through characteristics such as the attitude toward work itself, leadership style, and so on.

Meeting the Challenges

While the specifics will differ across organizations, these interconnected challenges are present in every organization that produces and uses data. It is not possible to address them all at once; however, by taking a strategic approach, it is possible to make improvements that reduce their impact, limit risk, and enable improvement over time. The ability to meet these challenges requires a vision of the desired future state, an honest self-assessment of the current state, leadership, and the ability to define and execute an improvement plan. Moving from the current state to a future state requires culture change management, the ability to prioritize and formalize activities to meet immediate- and long-term goals, and an investment in people who are ready, willing, and able to build and apply their skills. In short, fitting these pieces together requires a data strategy.

Data Quality and Strategy

3

"Strategy without tactics is the slowest route to victory. Tactics without strategy is the noise before defeat."

Sun Tzu

Introduction

Data, processes, technology, people, and culture all influence the ability of an organization to achieve its goals. For an organization to get value from its data, these elements must be aligned. They must interact in ways that produce data that meets the needs of data consumers. Data consumers must also have the knowledge, skills, and experience needed to interpret data and apply what they learn from it to meet organizational goals. Just as high-quality data does not happen by accident, neither does alignment. Alignment requires planning and practice. It is best achieved in the context of the organization's overall mission and vision—its strategy.

A strategy is "a plan of action or policy designed to achieve a major or overall aim" *(New Oxford American Dictionary)*. The concept has a military origin. *Strategy* derives from the Greek word *strategia*, meaning "generalship." Its second definition is "the art of planning and directing overall military operations and movements in a war or battle." Its third definition is "a plan for such operations." Thus, strategy implies both the work of planning and the plan itself.

The goal of a military strategy is to win a war. The goal of a business strategy is to enable an organization to compete effectively in the marketplace. Many organizations approach strategy by defining the organization's desired state (its vision) and the route to achieving its goals (its mission). Strategy, then, is the plan for success. It describes how an organization will move from its current state to its desired future state. Strategy includes a set of choices that are based on the goals it is trying to reach:

- **Goals:** What it hopes to gain from the actions (e.g., competitive advantage, market share, customer loyalty) versus what it does not expect to gain. An organization that is competing on price is not expecting to gain customer loyalty.
- **Scope:** Areas the organization will focus on and areas it will not focus on. An organization that decides to focus on quality may not be able to focus on market share.
- **Actions:** Activities executed to achieve the goals and activities the organization chooses not to execute because they do not contribute to the strategy. An organization that focuses on market share will have different marketing activities than one that focuses on customer loyalty.

Meeting the Challenges of Data Quality Management. DOI: https://doi.org/10.1016/B978-0-12-821737-5.00003-1

If this were done in a vacuum, the path would be clear, and the organization would move itself forward unencumbered. However, organizations do not exist in vacuums. They compete with other organizations for customers, market share, and so on; they develop new products, take advantage of new technologies, and manage their processes to gain efficiencies so they can meet their goals and serve their stakeholders. Strategy must also account for the following:

- **Feasibility:** Does the organization have the resources required to achieve the strategy? If not, can it get the required resources (people, technology, products, suppliers)? What are its options for moving forward in the absence of the required resources?
- **Obstacles:** What can get in the way of the strategy? What are the options for overcoming impediments?

So even though running an organization is not the same as waging a war, the ability to achieve goals has similar requirements: the ability to use knowledge, planning, decision-making skills, and imagination to gain a competitive advantage or achieve other defined goals. Imagination—the ability to envision new opportunities, anticipate how conditions may change, and develop contingency plans to respond to this evolution—is a critical component of strategic thinking.

Strategy sets direction, but it must be flexible. A military strategy will fail if its initial assumptions are incorrect and the people executing it do not realize this and fail to make adjustments; if those executing the strategy fail to account for information gained through interactions with the enemy; or if tacticians fail to respond to changing conditions on the ground. Executing a strategy depends on the ability to make choices among options that contribute to the overall goal in different ways. It also depends on willingness to take advantage of new opportunities as they arise (e.g., by adopting emergent technologies or applying new uses of data). Organizations make tradeoffs to achieve their goals, building on strengths and minimizing weaknesses. The better they understand their own strengths and weaknesses, the better they will be able to respond to opportunities and threats.

US President Dwight D. Eisenhower, recollecting his military career, once stated, "Plans are worthless, but planning is everything." By this, he meant that the process of thinking through possibilities and options for responding to them—in short, preparing oneself to respond across a wide range of possible events—enables a person to understand the context of any decision he or she may make. Doing so puts a person in a better position to make smart, informed decisions, even when events take unpredicted turns.

In Chapter 1, we discussed a range of social, technological, and political forces that influence the ability of any organization to use its data, including the speed with which data is created and shared, the range of forms it may take, the need to protect it, and the risks of not doing so. These forces influence the ways organizations respond to opportunities and threats.

This chapter will explore how concepts about strategy apply to planning and decisions that organizations make about their data. Specifically, we will discuss how data strategy is connected to overall business strategy and how to account for the challenges particular to managing, improving the quality of, and getting value from data. The details of any one organization's strategy will differ from those of other organizations (i.e., what data they focus on first, what processes they improve, and what technology they adopt), but the categories of problems they face and questions they address will be similar. These categories are connected to the five challenges of managing data quality: the data itself (data challenge), the processes (process challenge), the technology used to create and manage data (technical challenge), the people who use and apply data (people challenge), and the culture of the organization that establishes or fails to establish accountability for data (culture challenge).

Thinking Strategically

A data strategy is not an end in itself. It is a plan for getting value from data. Value is measured by the ways in which the use of data contributes to business goals—the overall business strategy. This means that the better the organization defines its overall business strategy, the better able it will be to understand opportunities presented by its data. An organization that builds a full business strategy does the following:

- **Articulates its vision, mission, and goals**. These concepts help the organization define success, envision the organization's desired future state, and recognize the steps required to get there.
- **Accounts for industry-specific factors and competitors** to determine how to compete. What opportunities can it create or take advantage of? What may get in the way of success?
- **Accounts for forces beyond its control** that may affect its industry, for example, the impact of regulation, the possibility of economic downturns, and the risk of natural disasters or global pandemics.
- **Realistically assesses its current state**, its own strengths and weaknesses, to understand what may get in the way of success and what actions are required to move it toward its desired future state.
- **Uses what it has learned to plan** the specific activities required to move it toward its future state, commit resources (people, technology) to those activities, and begin working the plan. The plan should:
  - Prioritize its actions and define its scope
  - Define what the organization expects to gain from the actions and how it will measure success

These components of an overall business strategy speak to the need for an organization to have additional characteristics, specifically, an openness to innovation and a willingness to change its culture (how people work together) to reach its goals. Strategy is not about business as usual.

An organization that knows what it is trying to accomplish, how it differentiates itself, and what is likely to get in its way is in a position to answer the most important questions relevant to a data strategy:

- What data does it need to support its goals?
- What data does it already have, and what opportunities may be addressed with this data?
- What does it want to do with its data?
  - Sell it directly?
  - Embed it in products and services?
  - Reduce risk?
  - Improve efficiency?
- How will the organization obtain, manage, and use data to support its goals?
- How will the organization manage data to meet legal and regulatory requirements?
- What skills will the organization need to get value from data?

- How will the organization prepare its employees to get value from data?
- What behaviors will the organization expect of employees with respect to data?
- What technology will be needed to support the work and reduce data-related risks?
- How can the organization evolve its data knowledge and skills to support the effort?
- How will the organization measure the success of these efforts?

Very few organizations know themselves this well. But the questions provide a starting point to build this knowledge specific to data and to act on the insight it provides.

Data plays a role in thinking strategically. One can readily see how reliable data about customers, suppliers, sales, markets, emerging products, and competitors can provide valuable insight about these market forces (Porter, 2008). Informed by data, an organization can anticipate and plan for how to respond to opportunities and threats. This insight about the role of data in supporting strategic decisions should prompt an organization to begin thinking strategically about data. To compete effectively and serve its customers, an organization can ask the following questions:

- What data does the organization need about itself, its customers, its products, its vendors, its supply chain, the market, potential substitute products, and its competitors?
- What questions will it ask of this data? What does it want to learn?
- How will the organization respond if the data shows it something different from what it anticipated?
- What risks are represented by the data?
- How will the organization manage and protect the data?
- How will the organization ensure that the data is trustworthy and reliable?

Data Strategy

Different organizations define strategy to different degrees and with different focal points. Some may focus just on their own industry. Others may take a long view and account for a wide range of external forces. All of them require data and information to build their business strategy. To maintain a strategic edge, they should also define a strategy for data.

MIT Center for Information Systems Research makes data strategy sound very sexy: "A data strategy is a central, integrated concept that articulates how data will enable and inspire business strategy." Gartner also comes on pretty strong: "A data strategy is a highly dynamic process employed to support the acquisition, organization, analysis, and delivery of data in support of business objectives" (Gartner Glossary, n.d.). Marr (2017) describes data strategy as a means of understanding how data can help an organization achieve its goals. Data contributes through improved decision making; improved operations; and monetization (by selling data or data products).

The Enterprise Data Management (EDM) Council's Data Management Capability Assessment Model (DCAM) provides a lot of practical advice on what to include in a data strategy. Its definition of data management strategy describes a set of components that anyone thinking about data strategically should account for. As a blueprint or master plan, the data management strategy:

- Determines how data management is defined, organized, funded, governed, and embedded into the operations of the organization.
- Defines the long-term vision including a description of critical stakeholder or stakeholder functions that must be aligned.
- Demonstrates the business value that the program will seek to achieve.
- Describes how the organization will evaluate, define, plan, measure, and execute a successful and mature data management program.[1]

DalleMule and Davenport (2017) present data strategy as a coherent means of "organizing, governing, analyzing, and deploying an organization's information assets [that] enables superior data management and analytics—essential capabilities that support managerial decision making and ultimately enhance financial performance." All of these definitions recognize that a data strategy is not about the data alone, but about how data will be used and how it will need to be managed so it supports these new uses. For DalleMule and Davenport, the ability to manage data strategically entails tradeoffs between "defensive" activities that manage risk and "offensive" uses of data that allow the organization to act more quickly on opportunities. This balance involves a set of choices about the degree and type of control an organization asserts over its data:

- For which data sets and under which conditions does an organization require a "single source of truth" that provides exactly the same data throughout the organization?
  - For these data sets, the organization will need to establish data standards, data management processes, and controls that enforce the use of data from the source/system of truth and prevent the creation of other versions of this data.
- For which data sets does the organization allow multiple "versions of the truth," customized to meet specific business needs?
  - For these data sets, the organization can allow flexibility with how people change this data but will also need to ensure that data consumers are aware of differences among versions of "the same" data sets.
- Perhaps as importantly, how does the organization manage the balance between these two options?

For a truly strategic organization, achieving the right balance will be part of an ongoing process. In whatever way it balances between offensive and defensive components, a data strategy is a plan for getting value from data. As such, it must account for how the organization wants to use data, the data it requires, and the processes related to managing the life cycle of that data:

- **Data Opportunities:** Defining how the organization wants to use the data to gain a competitive edge or to generate or add value. These organizational opportunities drive the data strategy.
- **Data Requirements:** Identifying what data the organization needs to generate to respond to opportunities and manage threats. Data requirements include quality expectations and defining what condition this data must be in to achieve organizational goals.

---

[1]Enterprise Data Management Council (2014). I highly recommend this document for anyone looking for a clear set of steps to apply the concepts discussed in this chapter. It is available on the website of the Data Governance Professionals Organization (DGPO).

- **Existing Data:** Determining what data the organization already has, what its condition is, and what formal knowledge is documented about the data and the processes that create it. This knowledge should include assessment of data quality that is based on data requirements.
- **Managing the Data Life Cycle:** Determining how the organization will obtain or create the data it needs, make it available for use, and manage it over time. As with understanding data requirements, managing the data life cycle for specific data requires knowledge of that data and the organization. It also requires data management skills and reliable data management processes.
- **Technical Requirements:** Ensuring that the organization has the technology it requires to support the people and processes that create, manage, and use data and that the technical architecture and governance of information technology (IT) align with and support the data strategy. This is especially challenging as organizations try to take advantage of technologies like the cloud, while still being dependent on legacy technology (e.g., mainframe).
- **Data Skills, Knowledge, and Experience (Data Literacy):** Understanding what skills data analysts and other data consumers will need to apply to interpret data and determining how to build these skills within the organization.
- **Governing Data:** Defining expected behaviors and accountabilities around data as well as how the organization will make decisions about data over time to enable use and reduce risk. How an organization chooses to govern its data reflects organizational culture overall. Focusing a data governance program on behaviors required to support the strategy can be a key to success.

In other words, a data strategy must account not only for the data, but also for people, processes, technology, and the interaction among these—that is, the organizational culture.

Such a strategy might also be called a *data management strategy, data governance strategy*, or *data quality management strategy* because it must account for how data will be managed, what condition the data must be in to meet organizational needs, how the organization will make decisions about data, and the ways data will be used. It could be called a *process improvement strategy* because to produce higher-quality data, an organization must design its processes with this goal in mind. Because technology is required to create, use, and manage data, a data strategy must both account for existing architecture and influence choices about technology. In addition, people within the organization must be able to use and understand data as well as adopt appropriate behaviors toward it. Adopting a strategy to get more value from an organization's data requires training, cultivation of data knowledge, and managed culture change. In some organizations, a data quality management strategy will be embedded in a data strategy or a data governance strategy. In others, it will be executed separately.

Strategic Alignment: People, Process, and Technology

Any strategy must account for people, process, and technology and the relationship among them (culture and organization). If people, process, and technology are not aligned in a purposeful way, the organization will not be successful (Fig. 11). These relationships are particularly important in relation to data because the ability to get value from data is directly dependent on the processes

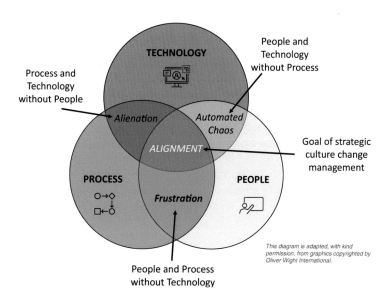

FIGURE 11

Results of failure to align people, process, and technology to achieve strategic goals.

Modified with permission from graphics copyrighted by Oliver Wight International.

through which data is produced and the technologies through which it is stored, maintained, and accessed.

- Implementing a new technology without clearly defining its relation to new and existing processes requires people to figure things out on their own. They will figure things out, but at the cost of creating multiple inconsistent approaches that will reduce the value that the technology is intended to bring. Automating processes without understanding them first is a recipe for disaster.
- Implementing a process and technology to support it without aligning people to execute the process causes resistance and alienation. People will see both the process and the technology as impositions that prevent them from doing their work. If people do not adopt process and technology improvements, then the organization will not get value from these efforts and will get less value from its people.
- Even if people are on board with process changes, implementing a new process without appropriate technology is bound to frustrate them, especially if the process is intended to improve efficiency.

On the positive side, if people, process, and technology are aligned, then the organization has improved its potential for success. This is especially true with data. When people know what they are trying to accomplish and have a clear process for accomplishing it, and that process is well-supported by appropriate technology, then they can do their work efficiently and consistently. If they do their work efficiently and consistently, they will produce better output—better products and services for customers. When much of this output is data, the people using that data are more likely to understand and trust it. They will spend less time and fewer resources cleansing it and more time analyzing and getting insights from it.

Assessing Strategic Readiness for Data Quality Management

Whatever name it goes by, a strategy to get more value from data has a starting point: the business strategy and the current practices around creating, managing, and governing data. It also has a process: assessing the current state and defining the actions required to move from that current state toward the desired future state.

The next two subsections, "Understanding the Business Strategy" and "Assessing the Current State," present sets of questions aimed at understanding the value of high-quality data to an organization as well as the current state of the data, processes, people, and technology that enable the data. These questions provide the basis for developing a data strategy with data quality management components by aligning quality requirements with business strategy and identifying existing conditions that support or may prove to be impediments to data quality improvement.

Understanding the Business Strategy

The starting point for an organization's approach to data quality is its business strategy and the data strategy that supports the business. Therefore the first step in formulating a data quality strategy is to understand the business strategy, the role data plays in that strategy, and the requirements for high-quality data implied by the business strategy. This requires asking some fundamental questions:

- What is the organization's vision, mission, and goals? (i.e., Why does it exist? What are its goals?)
- What are the organization's strategic drivers?
  - How does it differentiate itself from competitors?
  - What opportunities does it want to take advantage of?
  - What obstacles does it face?
  - What are its strengths and weaknesses?
  - What is its appetite for risk?
- What role do data and information play in the organization's ability to achieve its goals?
  - How does it want to use data operationally to provide products and services to existing customers? How can it get more value from these processes?
  - How does it want to use data tactically to meet shorter-term goals and to build a foundation of strategic knowledge?
  - How does it envision using data strategically to gain insight about its markets, manage suppliers, build its brand, and differentiate its products and services?
    - What analytics does the organization require to understand its performance?
    - Does organizational strategy include data monetization; that is, directly selling data or incorporating data into products and services?
- What data is most critical to supporting these goals?
- Have quality requirements for this data been defined?
- Is the quality of this data known?

If the organization has a data strategy, these questions may already have been answered. If the organization does not yet have a data strategy, answers to these questions provide the initial context for formulating one. It is not necessary that these questions be answered in detail. It is necessary to have enough information and understanding to make connections between data and opportunities the organization wants to take advantage of.

Assessing the Current State

Strategy is forward thinking, but its starting point is the organization's current state. (You cannot plan a war if you do not know how many guns and soldiers you have.) The organization's current state is a picture of the effects of past choices the organization has made. It also reflects how choices have been made, whether explicitly through formal process or implicitly through habits that staff and management have adopted less consciously. For example, if people in the organization do a lot of data work in an ad hoc way, "off the sides of their desks," it may be because the organization has not defined clear accountability for data or because they have not seen the value in formal data management. If it has not invested IT money in building applications to support business processes, then it may be because IT projects have not delivered the results that businesspeople expected. Thus a current state assessment not only defines the baseline for improvement but also provides insight on how an organization works. Among the benefits of assessing how work is getting done is to determine how to do the work in better ways and to make decisions about how to do it as effectively as possible to meet goals.

From a data perspective, understanding the current state requires collecting information about the what, who, where, why, and how of the organization's data and how it is managed:

- What data does the organization have?
- Where does the data come from?
- Who is responsible for creating data?
- Who uses the data?
- What business capabilities does the data support?
- What condition is the data in? Does it meet the needs of data consumers? If not, in what ways does it fall short?
- How is data managed, both technically and from the perspective of business processes?
- How are decisions made about data? Are they made formally or informally? Are they made in an enterprise context or a departmental context?
- What behaviors may become obstacles to getting value from data?
- What behaviors, skills, and knowledge should be cultivated to increase the value the organization can get from its data?

The questions in the following section provide prompts for making observations about the current state in relation to the five challenges of data quality management.

The Data Challenge: Organizational Data and Knowledge About Organizational Data

Assessing the current state of data in the organization starts with general questions. The goal of these questions is to understand the context of data creation and use in the organization. These questions can be answered through a combination of interviews, group workshops, and review of existing documentation. They do not need to be answered in great detail, but the general condition must be understood.

- What data does the organization produce?
- What processes produce the data?

- What data does the organization purchase?
- What data does the organization receive from vendors, customers, and other suppliers?
- In what ways is data inventoried? For example, does the organization know how much and which type of data it has about its customers, products, and vendors?
- What is known about the quality of data from internal sources? External sources?
- How much and what kind of documented knowledge (e.g., metadata, training materials, process flows, specifications) does the organization have about its data?
- How is this knowledge managed?
- How do people access information about data?
- What are the known risks associated with organizational data?
- What are the known obstacles to data use?

In addition to understanding what data and metadata content exists, it is also important to understand the current state of data management practices for the organization's most critical data (the data it relies on to serve customers; meet strategic goals; ensure compliance with laws, regulations, and contractual obligations; and measure its own success). Again, these questions do not need to be answered in great detail. They should provide enough information to understand potential obstacles to executing the strategy:

- Which data is managed centrally with an enterprise perspective?
- Which data is managed by individual departments?
- Is master data (e.g., data about products, customers, vendors) managed as such?
- How is reference data managed? How effective is this approach?
- To what degree do data management practices account for the concepts of a data life cycle and a data supply chain?
- What data quality management practices are in place in the organization? What are they focused on? How effective are they?
- How is data made accessible to data consumers?
- Are the tools available to data consumers robust enough to meet current needs? Will they meet strategic needs?

Most organizations have more data than they can effectively manage, and taking a strategic approach means that you do not want to manage every piece of data. Once you understand the general condition of data, the next level of questions should quickly focus on the data that supports the strategy.

- Which data is most critical to meeting strategic goals?
- Who are the most critical consumers of this data?
- Do they trust the data? What are their data pain points?
- Is the quality of this data managed? If so, what is known about the condition of this data (i.e., its quality, reliability, and trustworthiness)?
- Is the data reliable enough to meet strategic goals?
- What gaps are there in the data? How are these gaps currently being filled?

Data required to support an organization's strategy is, by definition, among the most critical data. It may be owned by a single department, but it must be managed for use in support of strategic goals. Data management includes the technical reliability of processes and applications that make data available for use as well as those that ensure its quality. If data is not reliable enough to meet strategic goals, then the strategy must include improving its quality. Organizations that want to leverage their data strategically must develop processes to manage their data and knowledge around their data, including criteria for quality and knowledge about the data life cycle itself.

Organizations that want to leverage their data in support of strategy must understand how to manage different data sets to that end. For example, if the strategy includes improving customer service, then management of customer data must focus on meeting the quality criteria of customer service people. It must be accurate, current, complete, and integrated across the organization to provide the customer service organization with a complete view of the customer.

The Process Challenge

Managing the data life cycle is a process challenge. The processes that create data must ensure that its quality is high enough to support organizational goals. One component of assessing strategic readiness for data quality management is understanding the processes that create critical data and the ways in which critical data moves within the organization:

- To what degree is the internal data supply chain for critical data documented and understood?
  - Do data consumers know who creates the data they depend on?
  - Do data producers know who uses the data they create and what these customers' requirements are?
- To what degree are processes that create the most critical data managed to ensure that data consumers' quality expectations are met? (i.e., How mature are these processes?)
- What business and technical controls are in place during data creation to prevent errors?
- What technical controls are in place to manage data movement?
- What risk management protocols are in place to respond to problems and issues?

The Technology Challenge

The processes that create data and enable data use must be supported by technology. The design of this technology should account for the quality of data produced. In addition, data moves through the organization for use in business processes via the data supply chain, which is dependent on technical systems and processes. People responsible for moving data through the organization should understand the overall data supply chain so they can ensure that the data retains its integrity as it moves.

Because an organization's ability to create and use data is dependent on technology, so is its ability to execute a data quality strategy. The ability to leverage technology depends on the following:

- The technology itself: how reliable it is and how well the applications work together
- The alignment of that technology with the business processes it supports: Can the business processes be executed efficiently and produce reliable output?
- The understanding and motivation of the people who develop and support the technology: Is IT aligned with and incented to achieve business goals, or is IT an island unto itself?

Assessing the current state in this way includes asking questions about the technology itself, the relationship between IT and business functions, and the people who build and support the technology.

- The technology
  - Does the organization have the technology it needs to support the business processes critical to data strategy?
  - Has the organization developed a future state architecture to support the strategy?
  - To what degree does existing technology support the creation of high-quality data?
  - How does IT define the quality of data in its systems? If IT does not have a definition of high-quality data, why don't they?
  - What standard controls does IT have in place to assure the integrity of data as it moves among systems?
  - Is there a data architecture function within the enterprise architecture team? If so, how much and what kind of influence does it have over other IT functions?
- The relationship between IT and business functions
  - How is IT funded?
  - In what ways does the IT funding model support the business strategy?
  - In what ways might it be an obstacle to executing the strategy?
  - What level of partnership or collaboration exists between the IT department and the people who use the applications that IT creates and supports?
  - How are conflicts between IT goals and business goals mediated?
- The people who build and support the technology
  - How do technologists see themselves? Is it primarily as part of the organization they work for or primarily through their technical roles (e.g., as programmers, developers, database administrators, architects)?
  - How are people who work in IT incentivized? Is it based on budget? On time delivery? Quality? A combination?
  - How do existing incentives support the business strategy? How might these incentives be obstacles to the strategy?
  - What kinds of incentives would support the strategy?

Organizations that want to get strategic value from their data must work to ensure that IT goals are aligned with business goals. This alignment is likely to pay off in multiple ways. Technologists have specialized knowledge of how parts of the organization interact through their data. If they also understand business goals and how data supports these goals, they can and should provide insight on the opportunities offered by new technologies.

The People Challenge: Data Knowledge, Skills, and Experience

Ultimately, people are the key to getting value from data. They use it to understand the organization's products, customers, risks, and opportunities. Using data requires skills and experience. An organization that wants to get value from its data should assess how well prepared its people are to do the work, that is, how "data literate" they are.

- How much experience do individuals have with data as part of their core work? Do employees use data regularly and directly (e.g., as underwriters and actuaries in insurance do), or is core work separated from data (e.g., most people in service industries are not working directly with data)?

- What is the organization's perspective on data? What kind of data does leadership use to describe and measure business performance?
- Are employees interested and excited about the possibilities presented to learn from data, or are they intimidated by the complexities of data? Is data seen as "technical," or is the use of data integrated into multiple aspects of managing the organization?
- Does the current workforce have the skills and experience required to meet the goals of the strategy? If not, what are the options for closing the gap?

Data literacy includes data quality components. Data consumers are the ultimate arbiters of quality; they are customers of the people and processes that create data.

- How do data consumers characterize the challenges they face using data? Do they talk directly or indirectly about quality?
- How does the organization define requirements and expectations for data quality? How effective is the process in meeting the needs of data consumers?
- How well do data consumers understand data quality measurement and assessment results? What value do they get from these? Are they actively involved with defining measurements that will help them understand the condition of the data they use?
- What kinds of feedback do data consumers provide to the people and processes that create data?

Nowadays, almost every organization wants to take advantage of its data. Strategist Bernard Marr (2017) echoes many others when he asserts that "every business is now a data business." However, not every organization can easily make this leap. In some industries (e.g., financial services, insurance, health care), the use of data is integrated into core processes. In other industries, it is not. Working with data takes a combination of knowledge, skills, and experience. A data strategy should account for the organization's starting point and define actions (e.g., training, hiring) that will help individuals build and hone the skills required to get value from data.

A data quality strategy should include building out a meaningful vocabulary around quality—one that enables data consumers to articulate their requirements and contribute to the overall improvement of data quality.

The Culture Challenge: Data Governance Practices

To be strategic about data, an organization should assess how it currently defines accountability for data and makes decisions about its data. As with any aspect of the current state, an organization's existing governance practices are a snapshot of the effects of past decisions. If formal data governance is in place, then the program should be assessed for alignment with the strategy. Indeed, in some organizations, the data governance program may facilitate the data strategy or the data quality components of the strategy. If formal data governance is not in place, then informal practices for making decisions and providing oversight should be assessed.

- If the organization has a formal data governance program, where does it reside within the organization, and what is its focus?
- How does it define success? How effective is it? What limits or enables its effectiveness?

- If the organization does not have a data governance program, how are decisions made about data within the organization? To what degree are decision-making processes formalized? To what degree are formal processes actually followed?
- How are expected behaviors around data defined? Are they defined by formal policies, ad hoc expectations, or something in between?
- In what ways do the behaviors as defined in data governance policies support the business strategy? In what ways might they be an obstacle to the strategy? What behaviors are required to support the strategy?
- How is accountability toward data defined? Are *data ownership*, *process ownership*, and *system ownership* formally defined? If not, how are they understood?
- In what ways does the approach to data accountability support the strategy? In what ways might it be an obstacle?
- What definition of *data accountability* would support the strategy?
- In what ways are data governance practices expected to contribute to the organization's ability to extract additional value from its data?
- In what ways are data governance practices designed to manage risks around data?
- Is there a concept of data stewardship? If so, how is *data stewardship* defined? In what ways does this definition support the strategy? In what ways might it be an obstacle to executing the strategy?
- What definition of *data stewardship* would support the strategy?
- How well is data use supported?
- To what degree is metadata managed to ensure that data consumers have the information they need to use data? Are there any gaps in metadata that will be obstacles to meeting strategic goals?
- Is data quality management part of the Data Governance Program, or is it a separate function? If it is separate, then the data quality and data governance functions will need to align on strategy.

Strategy sets direction, but it also requires flexibility. Organizations must be able to adjust to new conditions and unexpected situations while still moving forward. One key to staying on course while accounting for evolving conditions is to define clear accountabilities and oversight of decision-making processes to ensure that they are followed. This is especially true for data because most organizations find it difficult to define and enforce accountability and consistent decision making around data. Meeting this need is why data governance is critical to data strategy.

Data governance was originally envisioned as providing oversight of processes related to data from an enterprise perspective. It was not necessarily seen as a strategic function. However, because few organizations have an enterprise perspective on their data and this perspective changes how an organization sees its data, a well-executed data governance program has the potential to provide important insight on data strategy. Unfortunately, as discussed in Chapter 8, many data governance programs either never establish focus, lose it, or become so weighed down with bureaucracy that they do not contribute to forward motion.

However, this is not their only fate. Because data governance is focused on defining required behaviors and accountabilities toward data, a data governance program can make an important contribution to the execution of an overall data strategy as well as a data quality management strategy. Much of the battle in getting more value from data is clarifying responsibilities for data, ensuring that people have the tools and training they need to carry out these responsibilities, and reinforcing desired behaviors by rewarding people when they do act with accountability. People want to do the right things, but they may not know how to do the right things. Governance can help define the best ways to act around data. Organizations that want to leverage their data strategically should align and focus their governance programs to support this effort.

The Culture Challenge: Organizational Culture Change

Ultimately, the effectiveness of a business strategy and any data components to support it depends on the organization's ability to execute. Execution is work. It depends on people being able to work together. This is where culture comes in. One definition of *culture* is how people work together. Culture can be characterized across different axes (e.g., in terms of their level of cooperation, hierarchy, supportiveness). It is greatly influenced by the tone set by leadership. People will try to do what leadership asks them to do and behave in ways that leadership asks them to behave.

When assessing the current state, the goal is to understand how people within the organization work together; in systems thinking language, it is to understand the aggregate behavior of the organization.

- How do people working in the organization characterize the culture of the organization? What is working well? What areas need improvement?
- What is the organization's leadership style? Is it command and control? Laissez-faire? Something in between?
- Are teams hierarchical or flat?
- What findings came from the process assessment? What opportunities do these present? To what degree are people willing to change their processes in support of the strategy? What effects are expected on the quality of the data the organization produces?
- What findings came from assessment of technology and the IT space? Is IT prepared to support the data strategy?
- What findings came from assessment of the organization's current approach to data governance? What behaviors does the organization want to cultivate to support the data strategy?
- What findings came from assessment of the organization's current level of data literacy? How data-literate is the organization? What skills and knowledge does the organization need to build to be successful in its data strategy?
- How well prepared is the organization to execute a data strategy? Is it able to make decisions about data in ways that account for enterprise objectives?
- Is leadership committed not only to the idea of getting value from data, but also to the cultural changes required to be successful?
  - Are the vision and mission clear?
  - Do employees understand the relationship of data to the business goals?
  - Do they have the skills they need to use and get value from data?
  - Are there obstacles to adopting new behaviors around data?
  - Does leadership understand data-related opportunities?
  - Does leadership understand data-related risks?

Any new strategy requires changes in what people do and how they do it. (If they are already doing things the way they need to, then a new strategy would not be necessary.) Many people tend to resist change (some consciously and others subconsciously). Even people who are committed to changing require help along the way.

Organizations that want to get strategic value from their data, especially those that want to improve the quality of their data, will need to support this effort with training and communications that build commitment to the changes and make them sustainable by enabling employees to meet the new goals. This should include training about data as data, training that increases knowledge of the organizational data chain, and training about responsible behaviors toward data.

Defining the Future State

An assessment of the current state will surface a range of knowledge about the organization's data, processes, technology, and people. If done honestly and with the intention of improvement, the assessment will identify gaps and potential obstacles to meeting strategic goals. It should be closed out with a formal deliverable (white paper, presentation, or a combination of both) that draws focused conclusions about strengths and weakness, opportunities, and threats to executing the strategy and provides recommendations in each of the categories that require action:

- Organizational knowledge about data
- Data management practices
- Technology to support data creation and use
- Employees' data skills, knowledge, and experience
- Data governance practices
- Organizational culture

Fig. 12 provides an example of a simple analysis of strength, weaknesses, opportunities, and threats (SWOT). Documenting strengths, weaknesses, opportunities, and threats in this way enables people to see them in relation to each other. Strengths and weaknesses often mirror each other, as do

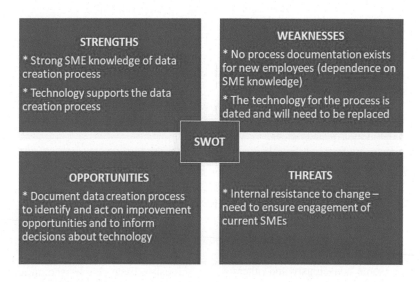

FIGURE 12

Example of a SWOT analysis.

opportunities and threats. Once the organization has a picture of its current state, strategists can use it to define changes required to move toward the desired future state.

Defining the future state provides a way of addressing gaps, obstacles, weaknesses, and threats through simple statements about what the future should look like. This is essentially a way of creating mini vision statements to address individual conditions that may present obstacles to the strategy.

For example, on the topic of organizational data and knowledge of organizational data, goals may include the following:

- To meet the goals of the data strategy, we will...
  - Create an enterprise domain model that describes the relationships among critical data sets
  - Create data flow diagrams that describe the movement of data among business functions within the organization
  - Ensure that when data is ingested into the data lake, it is automatically inventoried, so that data consumers can find it
  - Require that critical systems maintain data dictionaries in a central metadata repository
  - Enable a knowledge-sharing site in which contributors receive credit when their posts are referenced positively by other users

For data management practices, goals may include the following:

- To improve the overall management of critical data, within the next two quarters, we will...
  - Identify and implement processes to prevent errors in the two most critical data collection systems
  - Define "sources of truth" for data about products and vendors
  - Propose an approach for managing enterprise reference data in a central repository
- Within the following year, we will...
  - Implement a master data management (MDM) program to support customer relationship management
  - Enforce standards for collecting customer data in systems outside of the MDM system
  - Require that critical data in enterprise systems be profiled and assessed for quality on a scheduled basis

With respect to technology, goals may include the following:

- This year, we will implement a training program that ensures that...
  - Technologists understand how the systems they develop support business processes that are critical to the business strategy
  - IT systems are recognized for the quality of the data they produce
  - Data consumers can access data with confidence using reliable tools
  - When issues are found with data, teams from different systems collaborate to address the root causes
  - Standard system controls exist for processes that feed the data warehouse

With respect to data literacy, goals may include the following:

- Employees who create data have access to data flow diagrams to understand which people and processes consume the data they create
- Employees in targeted departments have been trained in basic statistics
- The organization has published standards and guidelines for how to develop effective data visualizations

For data governance practices, actions may include the following:

- Define accountability for data as part of the organizational data chain
- Define standard requirements for obtaining data from outside vendors
- Implement a policy that no new data may be added to the data lake unless metadata is provided to support it
- Establish standards for the quality of critical data and relationships within the customer domain
- Provide training on what employees should do when they find issues with data
- Formalize data quality management practices based on Total Quality Management (TQM) methodology

With respect to culture, actions may include the following:

- Six months after management has implemented a culture change management program to build commitment to quality and responsibility for data, all employees who create or use data will be able to:
  - Understand and speak about the role data plays in their own work and the relationship of that work to the overall business strategy
  - Understand and be able to act on their responsibility for the quality of the data they create
  - Receive training on the tools they need to access the organization's data
  - Find information about data when they have a question
  - Report data issues
  - Understand the value of data to the organization, and take steps to protect data and prevent misuse of data
  - Use data with confidence

Making a Plan

Future state assertions can be collected as part of brainstorming about the findings from the current state assessment. They help identify requirements related to understanding data and how to manage it, improving processes to produce higher-quality data, managing technology in ways that put data first, cultivating data literacy, and establishing a culture in which people take accountability for the data they create and use. They are aspirational and intended to provide perspective.

To move from a list to a plan requires further alignment and prioritization. Decisions about what actions are required and their relative importance will be specific to the relationship between the current state of the organization and the strategy. The level of detail in the plan will also be influenced by organizational culture. That said, some basic questions can get the process moving:

- What are the three most important things to *do* to support the strategy?
- What are the three most important things to *stop doing* to support the strategy?

Thoughts can also be organized around the five challenges:

- What do we need to know about our data to be successful?
- How can we improve metadata management so we retain knowledge about our data?

- How do we improve our processes so we create better data?
- How do we better manage our data supply chain to ensure that data meets the needs of data consumers?
- How do we focus technology funding in support of the data strategy?
- What training and incentives do we put in place to cultivate data literacy?
- How do we define accountability for data?

The answers to these questions will differ depending on the organization, its current state, the direction it wants to move, and why it wants to move in that direction. Executing a strategy requires the ability to make choices among alternatives. You cannot do everything, and you should not try to. Accounting for component pieces of a strategy sometimes means deciding not to take certain actions. This is much better than not taking action because you were not even aware of the option to take it.

The Five Challenges in Depth

Section 2 explores the five challenges. Each chapter discusses one challenge, connects it to the other challenges, and proposes ways to address the challenge under discussion.

Chapter 4: The Data Challenge: The Mechanics of Meaning presents an extended definition of the concept of data through the lens of history. All forms of data encode information about the real world. Using data always involves interpretation, so it is important to understand how data works, to understand "data as data." But what we mean by data and how we create and use data in science, statistics, and commerce have changed over time. Many assumptions about data quality are rooted in this evolution. A better understanding of the evolution of data helps us define and manage specific expectations related to data quality.

Chapter 5: The Process Challenge: Managing for Quality presents foundational principles of quality management and applies these principles to data. Organizations do not produce high-quality products by accident. High-quality results depend on planning and commitment. Data is both a product of organizational processes and a resource required to execute those processes. While data differs from other products and assets, especially with respect to its life cycle and the *ways in which organizations can derive value from it, the product model of data nevertheless provides the foundational components on data quality management. It also allows us to see the connections between the process challenge and the other challenges at different points in the life cycle.*

Chapter 6: The Technical Challenge: Data/Technology Balance discusses the deep connection between the data we produce and the technology through which we create, collect, manage, access, and use it. Data brings value only when it is used. Without reliable technical management of data, people cannot access and use data. Unfortunately, incorrect assumptions about the relationship between technology and data often result in poorer-quality data. Organizations must manage their technology to support their data strategy while avoiding the risk of being sucked into technology hype. Both data and technology must serve organizational goals.

Chapter 7: The People Challenge: Building Data Literacy addresses the skills, knowledge, and experience people require to create, use, and interpret data. Data literacy is the ability to read, understand, interpret, and learn from data in different contexts and to communicate about data with other people. The people challenge is both a skills challenge and a knowledge challenge. No single individual can know everything about an organization's data. But together, people can solve more problems in better ways if they understand data as a construct, recognize the risks associated with data production and use, cultivate a level of skepticism about data, and develop skill in visualizing and interpreting data. They will solve even more problems if the organization supports these efforts through disciplined metadata management and data quality management.

Chapter 8: The Culture Challenge: Organizational Accountability for Data addresses the need to change organizational culture and establish clear accountability for data. Improving data quality is, unfortunately and unavoidably, political. People must behave differently to do the work associated with making better data and making data better. Efforts in this direction (e.g., implementing data governance and stewardship programs, hiring a chief data officer) have met with limited success, due to lack of vision, conflicting demands, unclear priorities, and bad faith. Better data quality management demands a reexamination and refocusing of data governance and stewardship as well as leadership commitment to the work required to unlock data's potential for value.

The Data Challenge: The Mechanics of Meaning

4

"Science, as you know, my little one,
is the study of the nature and behaviour of the universe.
It's based on observation, on experiment, and measurement,
and the formulation of laws to describe the facts revealed."

Neil Gaiman, "The Mushroom Hunters"

Introduction

This chapter will explore the evolution of the ideas about data to demonstrate how our assumptions about data influence our assumptions about data quality. The chapter addresses the data challenge—understanding the mechanics of how data contains and conveys meaning—by providing historical context about data that data-literate people should be aware of. This context also informs the process challenge—understanding how data structure depends on the processes and instruments through which it is created or collected.

To this end, we will focus on data's semiotic function, that is, how data historically has resulted from an effort to represent facts about the world. We will discuss why seeing data from the perspective of its capacity to convey meaning provides a basis for measuring its quality. We will also show that in the mid-20th century—with the introduction of the computer and the association of data with "transmittable and storable information by which computer operations are performed" *(Online Etymological Dictionary)*—a shift in the meaning of the word *data* has influenced the technical perspective on what data is and how it is managed. Rooted in the separation of data (transmitted signals) from meaning (the information conveyed by the signal), this shift has had detrimental effects on the quality of data.

Data: A Short History

The definition of *data* has changed over time as different disciplines (mathematics, physical sciences, history, theology, statistics, computer science) have adapted the term for different purposes (Tables 1 and 2).

Once upon a time, the word *data* was understood to mean "givens," based on its Latin root, *dare*, "to give." The *Oxford English Dictionary* defines *datum*, the rarely used singular of the Latin plural *data*, as "a thing that is given or granted; something known or assumed as fact and made the

Meeting the Challenges of Data Quality Management. DOI: https://doi.org/10.1016/B978-0-12-821737-5.00004-3

Table 1 Definitions of data and assumptions about data quality, part 1.

Context of use	Mathematics, logic	Physical sciences	History	Government statistics
Origination period	Pre-Renaissance	16th century	17th century	Late 18th, early 19th century
Definition	Data as "givens": input into logical arguments or proofs	Data as observations, measurements, outputs from experiments	Data as "givens": undisputed facts and assumptions about historical events	Data as aggregated records about life cycle events
Where data comes from	Asserted as part of a logical argument (e.g., $x > y$, "All men are mortal")	Data is collected through designed experiments that enable consistent measurement/ observations. Accuracy depends on well-designed, consistently calibrated instruments	Historical records and artifacts, written histories (i.e., narratives of historical events accepted as true representations of those events)	Public records: census counts, births, deaths, marriages, suicides, deaths in battle, and so on
What data represents	Logical structures	Evidence of physical "laws" that can be expressed mathematically	Accurate information about the chronology of events and the people who participated in these events	Numerical patterns that reflect laws about human life cycle and social behavior
Intended use	As a foundation for argument or analysis, to build knowledge, to demonstrate expertise	As the basis for discovering patterns or relationships related to the objects and processes being observed, to understand how the world works	As the basis for constructing and interpreting a narrative of historic events	As the basis for describing patterns and laws that govern human behavior, to plan for predictable events
Basis for data's authority	Acceptance of logical conditions	Credibility of the scientific method, reproducibility of the observations	Credibility of the authors and texts cited as the source of facts	Assumption that there are "laws" of behavior that can be discovered through statistical analysis. Confidence that the records are accurate
Basis for judging data quality	Logical assumptions cannot contradict each other and cannot be disproven	Reproducibility under consistent conditions	Completeness and accuracy of the set of agreed-to facts about history	Trust in completeness and accuracy of records. Explanatory power of statistical models. Believable explanations for patterns

Table 2 Definitions of data and assumptions about data quality, part 2.

Context of use	Commerce	Information theory	Machine-generated data	Social media data
Origination period	Late 19th century	Mid-20th century	Late 20th/early 21st century	Early 21st century
Definition	Data as by-products of transactions	Data as signals sent through a channel	Data as any information captured electronically	Data as any information captured electronically
Where data comes from	Business transactions, related to the manufacture and sale of goods and procurement of services, collected manually or through business machines (e.g., cash registers)	Data is anything that needs to be transmitted (e.g., Morse code, radio signals, telephone communications)	Data generated via sensors, Internet of Things (IoT), and through the use of electronic/digital systems	Data is content created or shared; transactions executed through the use of electronic/digital systems
What data represents	An accurate record of exchanges of goods and services	Instances of messages to be transmitted	Activities executed by machines and logged by computers; exchanges among devices	Activities executed using electronic devices
Intended use	As a means of ensuring that business is transacted fairly, as a way to plan for future ventures	Use depends on the message (Shannon's effectiveness problem)	Analysis of the activities executed via electronic devices to gain insight into machine operations and sometimes also human behavior	Analysis of the activities executed via electronic devices to gain insight into human behavior and to predict or influence future behavior
Basis for data's authority	Accurate and consistent recordkeeping	Authority depends on the sender and the message	Design of the devices that collect the data	Belief that the activities recorded reflect meaningful patterns and that these patterns are correctly interpreted by people or machines analyzing the data
Basis for judging data quality	Balanced books, reliable basis for decision making	Signal-to-noise ratio	Calibration of devices. Ability to interpret the data (e.g., predict events or behavior based on the data). Ability to use insights from patterns to influence behavior	Ability to use insights to predict and influence behavior

basis of reasoning or calculation; an assumption or premise from which inferences are drawn" (*Oxford English Dictionary*, 1989). The concept of the datum was also associated with the idea of a standard or reference point. For example, in the late 19th century, sea level was referred to as a "datum-line," a stable point from which to take other measurements. There is a lot to unpack in these definitions. It is worth exploring them a bit more.

Data as "givens" in mathematics and logic are associated with "facts." As the foundations of arguments and calculations, they are assumed to be true. They are input into logical arguments and calculations, such as a given like "$x > y$" in algebra or a premise like "All men are mortal" in logic. Today, most of us probably first think of data in relation to science. Data comprise sets of observations or measurements. But the idea of data as a set of assumptions or givens, rather than observations, did not go away. In 17th-century philosophy, natural philosophy, theology, history, and mathematics, the term *data* referred to "that category of facts and principles that were, by agreement, beyond argument" (Rosenberg, 2013).

In the 18th and 19th centuries, the term *data* began to be used to refer to the output from, as well as input to, calculations and analyses. Data included not only what is given but also what one seeks to discover and what one analyzed to make discoveries. For example, data included facts established through observation and further experimentation. The development and use of statistics to understand patterns in marriage, birth, suicide, and other social phenomena combined these two meanings, as believers in statistics discovered through aggregated observations what they saw to be unchangeable laws—the givens—of social behavior (Porter, 1986).

Ideas about data did not evolve in a vacuum. While the meaning of the word *data* was evolving, so were the meanings of the closely associated words *fact* and *information* (Burke, 2000). The *Oxford English Dictionary* defines *fact* as "Something that has really occurred or is actually the case; something certainly known to be of this character; hence a particular truth known by actual observation or authentic testimony, as opposed to what is merely inferred, or to a conjecture or fiction; a *datum* of experience, as distinguished from the conclusions that may be based on upon it" (emphasis added).

While in the 18th century, the word *information* referred to things that were known about a particular thing, in the 19th century, people began to use the word to refer to the idea of abstract general substance that exists in the world (Nunberg, 1996, p. 9). The change in meaning was directly connected to the rise of newspapers and other media through which "objective" information has been shared over the past several centuries (Daston & Galison, 2010). This usage led to an understanding of information as a neutral set of unconstructed "facts" that existed independently of human interpretation and were reported on by disinterested observers. Of course, all facts, even if they are generally accepted as true, are nevertheless constructed, as is all information and all data.[1] As the use of the word *data* has evolved, so have ideas about where data comes from and what it represents. These ideas influence people's assumptions about and perceptions of the quality of data. A summary of different perspectives on data—mathematical, historical, scientific, statistical, commerce-based, and Big Data—will make this clearer (see Tables 1 and 2).

---

[1]Shapiro (2003) describes how the word *fact* begins as a legal term, referring to a human action or event that requires proof. The meaning of *fact* (and later its plural, *facts*) evolves into a reference to agreed-to truths through its use in history, theology, natural philosophy (science), and newspapers and through its contrast with fiction, poetry, and lies. See also Nunberg (1996) and Poovey (1998).

Scientific Data

Scientific data refers to data created through the scientific method, for example, quantitative and qualitative observations collected using a disciplined methodology to test hypotheses and answer scientifically formulated questions (Fig. 13). As it started to be used in the 17th century, the concept of scientific data included sets of observations that, depending on how and to what purpose they were collected, could be used to make general assertions about how the world works. In many cases, these observations resulted in "laws" that could be expressed mathematically. Galileo and Newton are the heroes in this view of data.

Ideas around scientific data have evolved as scientific practices have evolved during the past 400 years. But remarkably, the ideas about what makes scientific data of high quality have remained stable as they are based on principles related to the scientific method itself, that is,

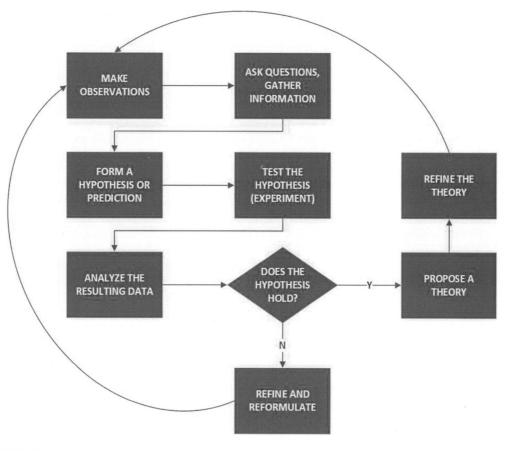

FIGURE 13

The scientific method.

the process of observing a phenomenon, positing questions about how it works or why it takes place (causes/effects), formulating a hypothesis, testing the hypothesis via a designed experiment (which produces data about the phenomenon), and revising the hypothesis based on the results of the experiment.

The quality of scientific data is associated with several factors:

- **The design of the experiments** by which a hypothesis is tested or the observational method by which data is collected.
- **The reliability of instruments** used to collect data (Daston & Galison, 2010). Much scientific data comprises direct measurement of objects or other phenomena, through measurement instruments invented specifically to understand the phenomena that they measure. Examples include the clock, thermometer, and barometer. The reliability of the data scientific instruments collect depends on the following:
  - Their design: Do they measure the characteristics they purport to measure?
  - Their calibration: Do different individual instruments produce the same measurement values under the same conditions?
- **The explanatory strength of theories, categories, models, or laws proposed** through the observations. In other words, the degree to which the interpretation of the data makes sense is itself a means of assessing the quality of the data. Strong theories successfully account for observations about the phenomena they describe, and such theories enable a level of prediction about some phenomena. This strength includes, for example, the ability of Newton's laws of gravitation to predict the results of a new instance of force and mass interacting and the ability of Darwin's theory of evolution to identify potential gaps in the evolution of a particular species of animal or plant. Weak theories do not possess these characteristics.
- **The use of clearly defined, consistently applied standards**. We can think of the standardization of scientific data in several ways:
  - In the organization of data collection (Johannes Kepler's tables of measurements come to mind)
  - Consistent representation of measurement results and other observations
  - The appropriate and transparent use of calculations
- **An attitude of scientific skepticism**. The idea of continually questioning the world has been inherent in scientific thinking since its emergence. Scientific knowledge is progressive knowledge. Progress depends on the capacity of scientists to question their own data and conclusions. Data is subject to scrutiny. For analysis to be taken seriously, scientists must clearly describe what data they produced and how they produced it. The results themselves must be reproducible.[2]

---

[2]An approach akin to scientific skepticism is reflected in SR 11-7 Guidance on Model Risk Management published by the US Federal Reserve regarding the conceptual soundness of financial models used in banking (US Federal Reserve, 2011). The guidance identifies two fundamental risks related to models: "(1) a model may have fundamental errors and produce inaccurate outputs when viewed against its design objective and intended business uses; (2) a model may be used incorrectly or inappropriately or there may be a misunderstanding about its limitations and assumptions." In other words, risks are related to the model's creation and its use. The guidance on risk management centers on "effective challenge" of models, which is, ultimately, adopting a skeptical position toward any model before using it: "critical analysis by objective, informed parties that can identify model limitations and produce appropriate changes. Effective challenge depends on a combination of incentives, competence, and influence."

- **The effort to reduce bias**. Like other human activities, science is susceptible to bias. But the scientific method combined with practiced skepticism are aimed at reducing the biases of individuals and groups. Scientific data that is clearly biased is perceived as of low quality.
- **Falsifiability**. Science requires not only that the results of experiments must be reproducible, but also that the questions science is trying to answer are themselves falsifiable. This concept requires a bit of explanation, in part because the word *falsifiable* in close proximity to the word *data* causes a bit of cognitive interference. The principle of falsifiability was formulated by philosopher Karl Popper. He asserted that, for statements to be ranked as scientific, they must be "capable of conflicting with possible, or conceivable, observations" (Popper, 1963). A synonym for *falsifiable* is *refutable*. The idea is best explained through an example.[3] In early 2021, there has been renewed controversy of a purported case of demonic possession that was documented in the early 1980s in the book *The Devil in Connecticut*. The family of the person involved has disputed the assertion that he was possessed by a demon. The book's author, Gerald Brittle, said his research convinced him that demonic possession is real (Hartford Courant, June 6, 2021). This means he has looked at a lot of cases of presumed demonic possession, and they show similar characteristics. The problem is that once a person concludes that they are looking at a case of demonic possession, there is no way to prove that it is not a case of demonic possession. Following the logic of a tricky double negative, there are no conceivable observations that can be made to show that a demon is not involved. And every possible observation can be attributed to a demon. Conspiracy theories have similar characteristics (Witze, 2021).
- **The role of interpretation**. Falsifiability is critical to scientific data quality because it goes to the heart of how experiments are designed, how observations are collected, and how evidence is synthesized to create a model of the world. Falsifiability informs the very questions science asks. Popper's argument has implications not only for the quality of scientific data but also for the role of interpretation in creation and use of any data:
  - In creating data, we make choices about what questions we are trying to answer and what characteristics of the world we choose to abstract to answer them.
  - To advance scientific knowledge, scientists must ensure that they are measuring things that actually matter to the questions they are trying to answer. If their predisposition to a particular answer governs their selection of characteristics, then they will merely be collecting data to prove what they already believe to be true.
  - If their theories do not allow for the possibility of refutation, then they are not scientific and should not be treated as such.
  - This idea can be extended to other forms of data as well, as any data selection implies a kind of model of the activities the data represents. If we "believe" in a model that cannot be tested, then we risk creating a skewed, if self-fulfilling, view of those activities.[4]

---

[3]Popper explained falsifiability in reference to Sigmund Freud's psychological theories. Acknowledging the internal consistency of Freud's theories, he nevertheless saw them as "unscientific" because there was no question that could be asked that could possibly show them to be incorrect. Each example to counter the theory becomes another piece of evidence to support the theory.

[4]See O'Neil (2016), Schryvers (2020), and Derman (2011) for the effects of nontested analytic models on how we perceive the world. See also Perez (2019) for the implications of a mental model of the world that does not account for women.

Statistical Data

The term *statistical data* is almost redundant. *Statistics* as an area of knowledge is defined as: "The mathematics of the collection, organization, and interpretation of numerical data, especially the analysis of population characteristics by inference from sampling." The word *statistics* is also a synonym for *numerical data*, and a statistic is defined as "a datum that can be represented numerically" (Farlex, n.d.). As with scientific data, to understand statistical data requires understanding not only the data itself, but also the methodology through which the data is collected and the techniques used to analyze and interpret it.

Because we live in a world full of statistics and understand the world through many everyday uses of statistical data, it is easy to forget that looking at the world through a statistical lens is a relatively recent phenomenon. An early use of what we now think of as statistics, the first life tables or mortality tables that established the probability of a person dying before his or her next birthday were created in the late 17th century. By the 1750s, these tables had developed into a foundational piece of the life insurance business. More widespread use of statistics as a set of practices began in the late 18th century with the numerical study of social phenomena, both natural (birth, death) and voluntary (marriage, suicide). These studies were connected to the effort to understand the connection between levels of population and the wealth of nations. They were driven by the desire of governments of emerging nation states to understand characteristics of their citizens. Early "statists" were pleased to find, within social complexity, instances of "statistical laws" that implied stability and aggregate uniformity, despite individual variety (Porter, 1986).

The numerical science of society, statistics, developed quickly and greatly influenced other sciences as statistical methods were applied to them. Largely a result of work performed in the 1930s, we now emphasize the fundamental importance of uncertainty and error within statistical analysis. However, in some circles in the late 19th century, there was a high level of confidence that, "any phenomenon composed of numerous independent events could be expected to exhibit impressive regularity in mass" (Porter, 1986).

Much early statistical data was "found" data. Those studying social phenomena looked at parish birth and death records and government records related to taxation, military service, and the like. Once an understanding developed around the knowledge that might be gained through it (e.g., through its use by governments and life insurance companies), the collection of statistical data became intentional and planned for. Indeed, this is one reason why the requirement to take a census of the population was included in the Constitution of the United States. Government statistics quickly took on characteristics similar to scientific data. The quality of statistical data depends on similar factors, most importantly the following:

- The definition of population about which data will be collected (i.e., what object or entity is being observed?)
- The definition of the characteristics, attributes, or variables about which to collect data (i.e., knowing what questions the data will answer enables collection of required data)
- The means by which data is collected (i.e., the limitations of the instruments for collecting data)
- The type of analysis to be conducted (i.e., the statistical techniques applied to interpret the data)

The quality of such data can thus be understood through the design and consistency of data collection, the comparison between expected results and actual results, and, for many questions, the consistency of data over time. For example, to test the hypothesis that the marriage rate is stable over time but can be influenced by events such as wars, bad harvests, or global pandemics, one must start with a measure of the baseline rate and obtain measurements over time (e.g., an annual rate or a decade-based rate). These measurements will show how stable or unstable (i.e., how predictable) the rate is over time. If the rate is stable, then the hypothesis will appear strong and can be used in other ways. The baseline can serve as the basis for detecting changes or anomalies. Correlated with other measurements (e.g., the timing, type, and duration of economic events, wars, diseases), a measurement for a given year or decade can be used to infer causes and effects. These uses explain why statistical techniques appeal to scientists and historians as well as governments.

One of the strengths of statistical analysis is that statistical techniques themselves can be employed to test the consistency and quality of data collected (e.g., measures of internal consistency, confidence levels). Statistical techniques can be applied to all kinds of aggregated data to discover patterns and, through these, to predict the continuation or disruption of such patterns. Data science is basically the application of statistical techniques to large data sets. With the advance of software developed to support data science, there are emerging opportunities to use the techniques of data science to perform data quality analysis. These techniques are an extension of applying concepts related to statistical process control to data quality analysis and management (Loshin, 2001; Redman, 1997; Sebastian-Coleman, 2013) (see Chapter 5).

Commerce-Based Organizational Data

A significant amount of work done by data scientists is focused not on data that is collected systematically with an eye toward ensuring its quality, but on data created through the operational processes of businesses or other multifunctional enterprises (see Chapter 2). This data is "commerce-based" because it is created and captured as part of the process of exchanging goods and services. Examples include records of transactions or information about customers, employees, vendors, and products sold. Of course, not all organizations that want to manage their data are commercial. Governments, educational institutions, and nonprofit organizations all share this need. However, the focus is on data that reflects the operational practices of these organizations as well as the people and other organizations with which a given organization interacts.

Data about the exchange of goods and services has existed since recordkeeping began, but it began to grow in importance in Europe at the end of the 16th century, with global economic competition arising from the discovery of the Americas, the rise of mercantilism, and the introduction of new ways of thinking about wealth, new approaches to banking, and new methods of financing and insuring commercial activities. By the late 18th century, when the mercantilist approach was largely superseded by the emerging concept of free trade, double-entry bookkeeping and other forms of recordkeeping had matured significantly. This meant that a lot of data was being captured in the process of executing commercial activities. This data was not an end in itself. It was produced as a by-product of harvesting and selling crops, manufacturing, importing, exporting, and paying for goods and services. Even so, because it was captured to track these activities, it also allowed these activities to be seen in a different way than they would be if they had not left these traces. As such, this data provides significant insight into a range of human activities and informs our historical knowledge in ways that few other sources can.[5]

Today, most people who talk about getting value from data or managing the quality of data are talking about operational data in the organizations that they work for. As it was before computers, most operational data today is created as a by-product of buying, selling, shipping, financing, enrolling, paying claims, and so on. People who manage organizations know that knowledge about the market, customers, and competitors is necessary to make good decisions about strategy and execution. This recognition has driven a lot of discussion about the value of data and other forms of organizational knowledge. With the rise of computing systems that can integrate data from different parts of an organization, it has also led to the concept of business intelligence and, with Big Data, predictive analytics. These uses of data drive the idea that data itself is an organizational asset.

The profession of data management has arisen in response to the need to transform this by-product into a usable asset because even though most people would agree with the idea that data has value, few organizations actually treat data as an asset (Evans & Price, 2012). As defined by the Data Management Association (DAMA), data management includes a set of eleven functional areas that, together, enable organizations to deliver, control, protect, and enhance the value of data and information throughout their life cycles (DAMA, 2017).

Much of the work of one of these functional areas, data governance, focuses on ensuring that organizational data is documented in metadata and depicted in data models and other architectural artifacts so it can be integrated and used effectively. The technical processes of integrating data are the focus of many information technology (IT) departments. Integrated data enables an organization to get a picture of itself via its data. But integrating data is hard. Because commerce-based data includes data from multiple organizational processes that are logically connected (e.g., if an organization sells products to customers, transactions of customer buying products should align with both customer data and product data), we expect it to fit together "naturally," or logically. However, it does not always actually fit together because often these processes are executed in different systems, and there is always some level of variation among the ways that systems create, store, and make data available for use.

Organizational data lends itself to information architecture, a practice that depicts the way data flows or should flow into and through an organization, and to data modeling, a practice that can depict actual or desired relationships between data sets produced via different organizational processes. Because they describe expectations related to data relationships, information flow diagrams and data models can provide information that is critical to data quality management.

---

[5]And this data, of course, now represents a form of historical data. For example, Historian David Eltis describes how a database of voyage-by-voyage shipping records from the Atlantic slave trade from the 16th to 19th century has enabled historians to revise estimates of the total number of individuals taken out of Africa and enslaved in the Americas. This data enables a better understanding of the ethnic mix of Africans enslaved in different areas in the Americas as well as the degree to which different European powers engaged in the slave trade. It is difficult to imagine how this knowledge could be gained other than through such a set of records. Eltis's 2001 article that summarizes findings to that point is a fascinating study in data quality as he assesses not only the content of the data but also its limitations. For example, he discusses the difficulty, in some cases, of determining the country of origin of some slave ships because slavers often carried multiple sets of shipping papers to hide their national affiliation or to represent different national affiliations, depending on what naval vessels they were likely to encounter. Much additional analysis has been done with this data since 2001. See https://www.slavevoyages.org/

The goals of data quality management, as a functional area within data management, are to reduce the risks associated with poor-quality data and enable the benefits of high-quality data so organizations can get value from their data assets. As we will discuss in Section 3, data quality management accomplishes the goals first by making data quality known to the organization and then by working with process and system owners to improve the way the organization creates or obtains, stores, maintains, and uses its data.

From a data management perspective, it is helpful to recognize different categories of organizational data because they are associated with different criteria for quality (DAMA, 2017; pp. 30, 126, 350):

- **Transactional or Operational Data:** Data that records the activities of an organization (e.g., purchases, sales, claims, grades, enrollments).
  - The quality goals in relation to transactional data are straightforward: transaction records must be associated with the correct goods and services; the correct customers, clients, vendors, students, or patients; and the correct prices. They also must include correct information about the time, place, and nature of the transactions themselves.
- **Master Data:** Data that describes the entities that define the parts of the organization (e.g., products, services, store locations, schedules, employees) or with which an organization interacts (e.g., clients, prospects, customers, vendors, members, students).
  - The quality goal in relation to master data is to have a complete and current set of records for the entities the organization interacts with and a means to identify any individual entity across multiple interactions with the organization. Customer master data is the easiest example to illustrate this abstract idea. An organization can provide better customer service if it has current and accurate information about each of its customers (a master record, with a master identifier for each customer) and if it can correctly associate this information with each customer at every transaction.
- **Reference Data:** Data that is used to characterize other data in the organization (e.g., product types, customer types) or to relate data to information beyond the boundaries of the organization (e.g., geolocation codes, industry classification codes) (Chisholm, 2001).
  - For reference data to be of high quality, it must be complete (contain all required values and all definitions of those values), current (if the meaning of values changes over time, then the data must reflect the time frames for individual meanings, and when data is used, all definitions must be up-to-date), and well-defined (the definitions of the values must be clear and comprehensible).
- **Metadata:** Metadata represents information about other data. For example, definitions of data elements collected by the organization, or stored tables and columns, logs of system activity, depictions of data flows. A general principle is that metadata is data and subject to the quality principles of other types of data. The range of metadata is wide, and these principles are applied differently depending on what the metadata represents and how it is created.
  - At one end of the scale is technical metadata, such as logs of system activity, the quality of which depends on the technical means by which the data is captured: Is all the necessary data captured? Is it captured at the necessary level of precision? Is it captured at the appropriate frequency? And the ability of people or machines to understand the implications of this data—a problem that is solved by having metadata about the metadata.
  - At the other end of the scale, *business metadata* includes definitions, requirements, training documentation, and the like. For business metadata, quality depends on the clarity, accuracy, level of detail, and comprehensiveness of definitions and other written information about the data. Standards for the quality of written metadata are, essentially, standards for good writing.

- **Organizational Metric Data:** Data that is aggregated from transactional and master data to describe the performance of the organization. Such data may be used to manage processes (e.g., ordering products from a supplier, shipping products to customers, receiving payment for services rendered) or to report to stakeholders (e.g., profit and loss at the business line level in the annual report).
  - The quality of organizational metrics depends on the quality of the inputs (master, transactional, reference, and metadata), the soundness of the models on which the metrics are based (Are they measuring the characteristics they purport to measure?), and the calculations used to generate the metrics (Are the measurements being taken in a way that reflects the reality of the organization's performance?).
  - In addition, organizational metric data is often created through the use of business intelligence (BI) tools. Different tools can have different effects on the perceived quality of data, based on the quality of their presentation layer and the techniques for visualizing data. And, of course, the knowledge, skill, and choices of the people preparing the visualizations have direct effects on the perceived quality of the data.

Organizational data is not the only data that can be understood in terms of subcategories. Scientific and statistical data also include metadata, master data, and reference data. And both scientific and statistical data include aggregate detailed measurements or observations into larger categories that serve a purpose similar to that served by organizational metrics in business. However, the modern profession of data management is focused on helping organizations manage commerce-based data. This data is rarely planned for or designed to the degree that scientific or statistical data is. Most often it is a by-product of organizational processes, few of which produce data based on clearly defined, consistently applied standards. Recognizing the historical condition of organizational data as a by-product, one goal of data management is to apply this knowledge by intentionally designing data and the processes that produce it to produce higher-quality data that accounts for the needs of these other uses (i.e., to recognize that there are customers for organizational data).

The goal in describing these different types of data—scientific, statistical, and data associated with commerce—is not to imply that they are mutually exclusive. Instead, it is to show that our understanding of data is multifaceted. The different ways that data can be created, especially the degree to which data is consciously created for a purpose (i.e., the degree to which it is designed), inform our understanding of what actually constitutes data as well as what we can do with data. Scientific data is designed with intention and rigorously tested before being interpreted. Modern statistical data is also designed with intention. When statistical techniques are applied to data that is not intentionally designed (e.g., organizational data, social media data), these techniques can be used to characterize the consistency and reliability of the data—how much confidence we should have in it.

The core of commerce-based data has remained stable for several centuries. This data comprises the information generated through the exchange of goods and services: ledgers, purchase orders, sales receipts, inventories, shipping orders. The rise of the Internet and technical developments that have enabled us to capture and store many more types of data have expanded our ideas about what data is and how organizations may use it to serve their customers and gain a competitive advantage. Now organizations not only want to know what you buy, but also what you looked at and did not buy. They want to mine social media feeds to better understand what their customers may be saying or thinking about their products. They want to predict and perhaps even control buying behavior, not merely record it.

Data Since the Introduction of the Computer

We have looked at many different facets of data that inform our current use of the term. In this section, we will discuss the effects that the emergence of computer technology has had on our understanding of data and how we understand the quality of data.

The first definition of data in the *New Oxford American Dictionary* is "facts and statistics collected together for reference or analysis." This commonly understood meaning is based largely on the way the concept of data is used in science, as discussed previously. The second definition reads "*Computing:* the quantities, characters, or symbols on which operations are performed by a computer, being stored and transmitted in the form of electrical signals and recorded on magnetic, optical or mechanical recording media" (*New Oxford American Dictionary*, 2005). This meaning of the word *data* is quite different from its previous meanings. The idea of data as "transmittable and storable information by which computer operations are performed" was introduced in the late 1940s (Online Etymological Dictionary). It has had a significant impact on our modern understanding of the concepts of both data and information. Indeed, it adds a qualitatively different meaning to both because it separates data and information from their function of representing reality and from their relationship to something like "truth" or "fact." It defines them solely in terms of the medium in which they are stored—the computer. The computer is also, especially in the 21st century, the medium through which most data is created and used.

This definition would not necessarily present a problem (the same word can mean different things, depending on context), except when people fail to see the difference and apply a meaning (data = facts) in a context in which it does not apply (any information captured in a computer or "digitally"). In today's world, even in contexts in which the word *data* refers simply to "information stored in a computer," it nevertheless carries with it the strong implication of the idea of data as facts. Namely, simply because the information is in the computer, it must be meaningful and true. These implications influence expectations for and perceptions of the quality of data and, more dangerously, our perceptions of what is truthful or factual.

The measurement of information by the bit has morphed into the idea that any information stored electronically is "data," regardless of the relationship of the bits to "given" assumptions or what we understand as "facts." Because much of the information we used to capture on paper is now captured digitally (along with a whole lot of information that was not previously "captured" at all), data now includes all kinds of stuff we did not even imagine in the 1940s, from sophisticated sensors capturing terabytes per minute to streaming video and social media postings—all of which have a different relationship to truth than do measurements, facts, and statistics. The measurement of amounts of data has also led to much of the hype around our current information "ecosystem," the "digital world," and the "information universe," as described in Chapter 1.

Consider, for example, estimates of how much "information" (i.e., number of bits) exists on the Internet. If you Google "How much data is in the world?," you will find numerous charts showing the exponential increase in the world's information accompanied by assertions about how much information is or will be created each day or each year. For example, you will find that the digital "universe" is doubling every year (Marr, 2018; Schultz, 2019). These claims promote the idea that the volume of information we produce is good and important in and of itself—because the commonsense understanding is that information is meaningful, and meaningful things are good and important. These statistics also imply a dubious equality among all forms of information. Just because Newton's *Principia Mathematica* occupies the same number of bits as a John Grisham novel, do they contain the same "amount" of information? Does a similar "amount" of bytes imply a similar value to society?

Our technological ability to store information electronically has many repercussions, the most important one being that, for better and worse, we can now learn a lot more about people's activities and interactions than we could before we had the capacity to collect, store, and analyze their electronic trails. The considerable amount of electronically stored information about our daily lives creates new risks in our society, the implications of which we are only starting to explore (Zuboff, 2019).

If we set aside the risks—and there are many personal, ethical, and political risks—the collection of massive amounts of data has made data management a very significant challenge. To manage a thing means to be in charge or control of it and to use it to meet aims or goals. Data management includes "the supervision of plans, policies, programs, and practices that deliver, control, protect, and enhance the value of data and information assets throughout their life cycles" (DAMA, 2017). How does one manage "transmittable and storable information" when almost all information is "transmittable and storable"? There is so much data with potential value that it is difficult to know where to start managing it in ways that help unlock this value, especially given that in many cases we do not know why it was created or how its meaning is encoded. When we do not know what to expect from "data," it is difficult to judge whether it represents what it purports to represent or what purposes it might be fit for.

Big Data and Data Quality

The variety of "unstructured" data extends the concept of data itself. At one end of the scale are things like information generated through sensors and other measurement devices designed to meet particular purposes. We know what a sensor is measuring, so we have a foundation on which to interpret its data. In this sense, some machine-generated data resembles scientific data. It is dependent on the calibration of instruments that collect it. At the other end of the scale are things like social media posts, which are essentially just things people say. These may be tagged with times, dates, and number of likes, and they can be mined through sentiment analysis, for example, but understanding what they mean often takes a lot of context. What position is the person speaking from? What motivates them to share this piece of information? Is the person deliberately lying or just misinformed? Am I misinformed? Interpretations can be wildly contradictory.

Although there are ways to measure the quality of machine-generated data, based on how it is produced and what it represents, the standards by which we would measure the quality of social media data are essentially nonexistent because it may be created for a wide range of purposes, and it has no obligation to fact, method, or discipline. Social media "data" is mined by algorithms for indicators used to present advertisements and political messages to users. Such algorithms do not always do this basic job very well. (What is more annoying than getting flooded with ads for something you have already purchased?) To actually understand what social media data represents, to interpret it beyond the surface, would take the skills of historians, anthropologists, and psychologists. There is little foundation to assess the quality of social media data.

Tables 3—5 contrast the characteristics of "traditional" and "Big" data using some simple examples. Many aspects of data quality assessment depend on understanding the structure of data. All data, even "unstructured" data, has a degree of structure (see Table 3). Types differ based on what drives this structure. Relational data is characterized by a high degree of design focused on the data itself. Social media posts are structured based on user interface, which does things like limit the number of characters per post. The application provides a bucket for content. Users can put anything they want in the bucket.

Big Data is characterized by the three Vs: variety (see Table 3), volume, and velocity. Some people will add a fourth V: veracity (see Table 4). Even traditional data can come in large quantities at great speed. But traditional organizational data is also more predictable, largely because it reflects organizational processes. It has a firmer obligation to veracity—accurately representing the real world—than does social media data. The veracity of data at the other end of the unstructured scale, machine-generated data, is dependent on the design and calibration of the devices that collect this data.

A data quality dimension is a general, measurable category for a distinctive characteristic (quality) possessed by data. Dimensions of quality are to data what length, width, and height are to physical objects. Data quality dimensions help define expectations for data and provide a basis for the measurement and quantification of data quality levels. Through them, we can understand

Table 3 Types of data contrasted by inherent structure.

Variety	Type of data	Example	Inherent structure	Structure driven by
Traditional	Mainframe output	Extended Binary Coded Decimal Interchange Code (EBCDIC) files	High, but messy	Design of the originating system
Traditional	Relational database	Warehouse tables	High	Data model
Big/unstructured	Machine-generated	Streaming sensor data	Very high	Design of the collection device
Big/unstructured	Social media posts	Twitter	Low	Application interface, language of user

Table 4 Types of data contrasted by volume, velocity, and veracity.

Type of data	Volume	Velocity	Veracity
Mainframe	Large but predictable	Potentially fast but predictable	Measurable (compare with real-world or other data)
Relational database	Large but predictable	Potentially fast but predictable	Measurable (compare with real-world or other data)
Machine-generated	Potentially huge	Super-fast, variable	Dependent on design and calibration of instrument/collection device
Social media posts	Potentially huge	Variable	No obligation to truth; no basis for comparison

Table 5 Dimensions of quality applied to different types of data.

Type of data	Completeness	Format consistency	Validity	Integrity	Consistency
Mainframe	Number of records generated/time period. Comparison to a known real-world population	Constrained by system rules	Constrained by rules defining valid values and relationships	Can be systematically constrained	Expectation based on the process the data represents
Relational database	Number of records generated/time period. Comparison to a known real-world population	Constrained by model, can be systematically constrained	Constrained by rules defining valid values and relationships	Can be systematically constrained	Expectation based on the process the data represents and on the data model
Machine-generated	Rate at which data is collected	Constrained by collection device	Based on calibration of collection device	Depends on consistent collection devices	Expectation based on the process the data represents
Social media	No general definition of "completeness"	Constrained through application interface	Not applicable; no criteria for validity	Not applicable; no criteria for integrity	Not applicable; no criteria for consistency

quality in relation to a scale and in relation to other data measured against the same scale or different scales whose relation is defined (Sebastian-Coleman, 2013). We will discuss dimensions of quality in depth in Chapter 10. I introduce them here to show how they can be applied to both structured and unstructured data. An answer to the question of what makes data "complete" depends on both what the data is intended to represent (why it was created) and what it will be used for. Correct format is focused on whether the data is in a shape that enables its use. Validity answers the question of whether data follows defined rules. Integrity reflects how well different pieces of data fit together. Consistency focuses on whether data follows expected patterns, including those discernable in other data and in the populations represented by the data. All of these characteristics depend to a large degree on the assumption that data itself represents some form of truth against which its quality can be understood.

Dimensions are critical to determining which data characteristics to measure and how to interpret measurement results. At the heart of data quality measurement is the effort to understand how well data represents what it is intended to represent. Traditional organizational data largely represents business processes (transactions) between stakeholders associated with the organization. Machine-generated sensor data reflects the measurements taken by a device. Social media data reflects whatever words and images people decide to share for whatever reasons they care to share them (see Table 5).

What History Teaches Us About Data Quality
More Information Is Now "Data"

Having reviewed a wide range of definitions about data and their implications, it is worth revisiting and expanding on the definition of data from Chapter 2.

> *Data* is the representation of selected characteristics (attributes) of objects, events, and concepts (entities) that is expressed and understood through explicitly defined conventions related to their meaning, collection, and storage. Since the introduction of the computer in the mid-20th century, the word *data* has also been used to refer to any information captured in or processed by a computer or other IT system.

We can elaborate on this definition to capture the breadth of meaning now associated with the concept of data.

- Scientific, statistical data, and commerce-based data are abstract representations of selected characteristics of real-world objects, events, and concepts, expressed and understood through explicitly definable conventions related to their meaning, collection, and storage. These types of data, which are intended to represent facts about the world, are created through systematically recorded observation of these characteristics. The meaning and accuracy of these types of data must be understood and interpreted within the context of their creation. These contexts are purposeful. Scientific and statistical data are specifically created to build human knowledge. Commerce-based data is collected as part of the process of organizations creating or exchanging goods and services. It can also be used to build knowledge.
- In the digital age, data is also understood to be any information created or captured in electronic form and sharable through computers and other technological systems, regardless of why this information was created or of the relationship of this information to fact or truth. The meaning, accuracy, and intention of this type of data must also be understood and interpreted within the context of its creation. There are often severe limitations in gaining accurate knowledge of the contexts and the motivations for creating some forms of electronic data.

The two component pieces of this definition are unlikely to play well together. This is intentional. To manage the quality of data, we must acknowledge what we are looking at. Data quality management requires the ability to measure meaningful data characteristics in meaningful ways. There are limits to what can be measured about "data" that is simply electronic "stuff" captured by a computer. To make meaningful use of this "stuff" requires that it be structured—turned into purposeful data. This structuring is itself an act of interpretation.

Much About Data Remains the Same

Our understanding of what data is and where it comes from has changed over time—from the idea that data are "givens" or inputs to the idea that data results from observations and calculations to the idea that any digitally captured information is data. With these changes, ideas about the relationship of data to truth, fact, and knowledge have also evolved, but some core ideas have nevertheless remained stable and central to the concept of data. If we confine ourselves to the first part of the definition, among these ideas are the following:

- **Data's function is semiotic:** In representing and conveying meaning, the primary function of data is to serve as a sign of things other than itself (Chisholm, 2010). How well it carries out this function is a characteristic of its quality. Data's semiotic function directly influences what we use it for. Using data means interpreting data's meaning. In aggregating facts and looking across sets of observations (sometimes with the help of statistical calculations and other times with visual representations that summarize and compare data), people can see patterns and connections that imply relationships and correlations. But data does not speak for itself. People interpret data. Not all interpretations are of equal value. It takes skill and knowledge to understand what data can tell us.
- **People make data:** Data does not just exist, even in its function as "givens," until it is created by people (or machines made by people). The choices people make when creating and using it imply a set of assumptions about the reality that they are representing. Data is, in this sense, a model of or interpretation of reality. One must understand these choices to assess the quality of data.
- **Data influences the shape of reality:** Because data represents the world and is a means by which we interpret the world, it also helps construct the world. This means that reliable, well-planned, well-understood data can change the world. Deftly manipulated untrustworthy "data" can also change the world, which is another reason why metadata describing data's origins and the processes through which it is created is so important to assessing data quality.
- **Knowledge of data quality equals knowledge of data:** Because data encodes meaning, using and understanding data requires knowledge of the context in which it was created and the ability to interpret the conventions by which data encodes information. Knowledge of data includes knowledge of how and why it was created, what it represents, and how well it functions as a sign of the things it represents. Knowledge of data includes knowledge of what we expect data to represent and how data enacts this representation. This means that understanding data requires understanding the expected qualities and characteristics of the data.

Each of these assertions has implications for how we understand data and therefore how we understand data quality.

Data's Function Is Semiotic

The goal of creating data is to represent facts and truth about the objects and events that the data describes. This makes sense, given its close connection to science, the goal of which is to understand the material world. To create data, one must account for both attribute-level observations and larger patterns of meaning. Data at the attribute level is atomic, focused on small singular characteristics. Data about these characteristics is also often aggregated to create or discern meaning, largely through the ability of data interpreters to see patterns. Though data can be used to tell a story, it functions differently from other representations, especially from narrative. Data represents the pieces. The interpretation of data is required to understand correlations, causes, effects, and "stories" implied by the data (Knaflic, 2015; Taylor, 2020).

One difference between data that is structured through a data model and data that is unstructured is that we may not immediately see the relationship among entities, attributes, and values. Even more than traditional data, unstructured data gives the impression that it pre-exists its own creation and only needs to be collected. That said, part of the work of interpreting unstructured data is imposing some degree of structure on it.

Data represents objects, events, and concepts in the world. Data functions as a sign. It represents things other than itself for the purpose of conveying meaning about the objects and events it represents (Chisholm, 2010). This idea is often missed because we think of data as pre-existing our efforts to "gather" or "collect" it and because we sometimes talk about data as if it is something more than a representation—as if it had an existence outside of this representational function. For example, data quality pioneer Larry English defines data as "an *equivalent reproduction* of something real. If all facts that an organization needs to know about an entity are *accurate*, that data has inherent quality—it is an electronic reproduction of reality" (English, 1999; emphasis in the original, p. 22). Data is not the equivalent of reality or a reproduction of reality any more than a musical score, by itself, is a reproduction of musical sound or a scoreboard is a reproduction of a sporting event. Data is a means of representing selected characteristics of reality. We choose to represent these characteristics because abstracting them out will help us understand the objects, events, or concepts we want to learn about. Literacy of any kind involves the ability to hold abstract thoughts in our head (Wolf, 2016). Creating and using data requires general literacy skills and knowledge of characteristics particular to data.

Signs work by encoding information. This means that creating data involves encoding information, and using data involves decoding it. Every use of data requires interpreting it by decoding what it represents. Sometimes this process is simple. A product number represents a single product, and a customer number represents an individual customer; by bringing them together, you can understand which customers purchased which products as well as how many people buy the same product multiple times, and so on. Sometimes it is more complicated. A population of people who died of Covid-19 also shared socioeconomic and ethnic characteristics (Centers for Disease Control and Prevention, 2020a). In what ways are these characteristics related to the death rate? Answering a question like this requires knowledge of statistics, the ability to create and test models of causes and effects, and the ability to refrain from jumping to conclusions.

Decoding data is required not only because data is encoded, but also because some of data's characteristics are not directly about its meaning but instead are about how that meaning is encoded. Data is often encoded using established conventions of representation associated with measurement (e.g., the use of a specific scale to express temperature). Encoding happens at many levels when data is created or produced. When a physician "takes" a patient's temperature, he or she uses a thermometer (a measurement instrument designed to collect a specific kind of data) to obtain a "reading" (a number of degrees that represents the patient's temperature) based on a specific scale (Fahrenheit or Celsius). There is a reality to be measured. By definition, a patient's body will be of a specific temperature when that temperature is measured, and if the patient is sick, he or she is sick, whether or not the doctor takes the patient's temperature. But to understand the patient's condition and to measure one of its effects on the body (an increase in heat), we encode it within a system of signs designed to quantify degrees of heat. Because we have a scale and the anchor point of a normal body temperature (98.6°F), the temperature reading provides the physician with an interpretable signifier. A temperature of 103°F will generate more concern than a temperature of 99°F.

Because signs encode information, all signs require interpretation to be understood or decoded. In the case of body temperature in which the conventions of representation are now common knowledge, interpretation is straightforward. A patient with a temperature above 98.6°F may have a fever; a patient with a temperature of 98.6°F, by definition, does not have one. Before the invention of the thermometer and its application in medicine, people only knew that certain sicknesses could cause a person's body to heat up.

In the case of less familiar data, people must learn these conventions to understand what they are looking at and to attribute meaning to it. This means that much data cannot be understood and interpreted without sufficient context. To determine whether or not data is reliable, you not only must understand what data is intended to represent, but you also must know how it is encoded. Some encoding conventions are so familiar that we do not think about them (e.g., weather reports, stock market results, our bank balance, in addition to temperature). Nevertheless, when we judge data quality, we are judging data's representational effectiveness as well as its content. When we are looking at unfamiliar data, our lack of knowledge about the means by which data is encoded can make the data incomprehensible. Understanding and using data require knowledge about data, so managing data quality involves managing knowledge about data, that is, managing metadata.

Consultant Malcolm Chisholm has written eloquently on the semiotic aspects of data. In opposition to the standard definition of data quality as "fitness for purpose," he advocates a definition of data quality that focuses on data's representational function: data quality is "the extent to which the data actually represents what it purports to represent" (Chisholm, 2012, 2015, 2017). His definition makes a lot of sense. Data represents something, and it must be understood by something—a person or a machine (what semiotics pioneer Charles Sanders Peirce calls an *interpretant*). An interpretant can misunderstand the data. This does not make the data itself wrong. Likewise, a person can use data for something that it is not supposed to be used for. This does not make the data itself wrong. Falsifying data may make data "fit for purpose," but it also means the data is fake. It does not represent what it purports to represent. We will revisit Chisholm's paradigm when discuss the product model of data in Chapter 5. I agree with what he is saying and have used the term *representational effectiveness* to refer to this aspect of data quality (Sebastian-Coleman, 2013). The only difference is that I do not think we need to choose between high-quality data being "fit for use" and high-quality data "actually representing what it purports to represent." I think we need both.

People Make Data

Perhaps because of its original meaning as "givens" or because it is the basis for discovering relationships that can be expressed mathematically (force = mass × acceleration), or because it conveys information about the world that we know exists whether or not we measure it (a fever is a fever), we often take data for granted. We do not often think about how data is created though human design. We think of it as something we "collect" or "gather," and we forget that humans had to develop the models and design the instruments required to turn observations about phenomena into data.

When we think about the massive amounts of data that can be collected by sensors and scientific instruments, we may think these are very far from people creating data through data entry or even manual measurements. But these sensors were designed by people to function in a particular way and to gather data to serve specific purposes.

For anything to function as a sign requires an element of design and an acceptance of the conventions of design, such as mathematical formulas or other means of encoding. As importantly, data conveys meaning by representing only selected characteristics of reality, which means we leave out a lot of characteristics. Models are always simplifications. In this sense, choices about what to collect data about and how to construct data create a kind of model of the world. They are based on a set of choices about what constitutes reality in the first place. This means data is thus both an interpretation of the objects it represents and an object that itself must be interpreted (Sebastian-Coleman, 2013).

Because people create data in different ways, interpreting and using data requires information about these choices. Data is a kind of language. Translating it requires context and definition. In data management, *metadata* is the term used to describe the knowledge required to use data. We often talk about metadata and data as if they are separable, but they are not. Metadata, documented knowledge of what data represents and what conventions of representation are used to encode it, is necessary for data to be interpretable.

Data Influences the Shape of Reality

Just as written language does, data enables human communication across time and space. In this sense, data enables us to see patterns and characteristics that we would not otherwise be able to see. For example, it also enables us to comprehend patterns in large sets of observations or measurements. Knowing that India has 1.38 billion people, the United States has 331 million, and Monaco has 38,000 enables us to understand the size of the three populations in relation to each other (Worldometer). But relative size is a simple example. Data also enables us to see more complicated patterns and even to discern reliable laws about how the physical world works and how people behave. Because data allows us to see the world differently, it also enables new forms of knowledge. The invention of statistics as a science of society is itself an example of this, as are Newtonian physics and the theory of evolution.

Data not only represents reality; the use of data has direct effects on reality (Kent, 2000). In helping to construct reality, data influences how we perceive reality. We see in day-to-day life how the availability of data influences our actions and our world view. We are barraged with data about the weather, traffic, the stock market, and our health. In *Weapons of Math Destruction*, Cathy O'Neil describes how even poorly constructed or untested models of value have far reaching effects (O'Neil, 2016). For example, the criteria used for the *U.S. News and World Report* annual rankings of colleges not only influence which colleges high school students think they should apply to, but they also significantly influence the behavior of the people running the colleges, who apply resources to criteria that increase their rankings. As O'Neil describes it, these original criteria were not tested against student needs or any other foundational standard. They were set up based on which schools were known to be "good" when the report was initially conceived. Now they are produced through an "algorithm," so people believe them, despite the lack of a firm and tested analytic foundation and despite flimsy original ranking criteria.

Sometimes data can change reality in profound ways. We can see these effects in relation to scientific discoveries. Newton's laws ushered in a new understanding of the world as a machine that worked according to discernible laws of nature. Of course, insights gained through scientific data and the theories it supports and enables are not always greeted with open arms. Galileo was forced to deny the truth of what he saw because the implications undermined the world view of his contemporaries. Darwin's insights into evolution are still controversial because some people find it difficult to reconcile them with religious scripture. And sometimes a scientific veneer can cover data that represents a skewed or malicious view of reality, as with 19th and early 20th century theories on race (Gould, 1996). Other times, as in the case of climate change, despite resting on firm scientific foundations, data is not taken seriously because the implications of what it represents are too difficult to imagine (Ghosh, 2017). The wide range of reactions to the Covid-19 pandemic illustrate both the ways in which data evolves as we use it to try and understand the world and the ways it can be used and misused; interpreted well and completely misunderstood; or praised as a source of knowledge leading us to a solution and condemned as a misleading hoax, sometimes all by the same person.

Knowledge of Data Quality Equals Knowledge of Data

We associate data with the ideas of accuracy, precision, and truth. We want to trust that data accurately represents what it purports to represent. When we find out that data is inaccurate or that people have misrepresented it, we feel betrayed. The reason that statistics are found in company with "lies and damned lies" is that people do purposefully misuse them.[6] This misuse is a kind of betrayal of our assumptions about the idea that truth and knowledge can be represented through data.

We have inherited a set of assumptions about what data is that should cause us to think carefully about how we define the quality of data. The different ways that the concept of data has been used to understand mathematics, history, science, society, and commercial enterprises has shown that we create and collect data for particular purposes. We want to understand how the world works. We ask questions about the world and collect data to answer them. Sometimes trying to answer these questions shows us things we did not expect to see, such as apparent underlying patterns in social behavior. But the way we ask questions about the world and the way we create data to answer these questions is directly connected to the expectation that we can see something in the results. Even when we do not like what we see, we can still understand it if we have designed our data collection with integrity and purpose and analyzed the results with proven methods for detecting patterns and relationships.

For data as well as for physical products and services, quality is judged based on the expectations people have about the object being assessed and the alignment between expectations and the reality of what they see. People cannot know what to expect from data unless they understand what data represents and how it enacts this representation. When they do know these things, then they also have expectations related to the quality of data: what makes the data complete, valid, cohesive, and trustworthy. Understanding data is central to understanding data quality, and understanding data quality is central to understanding data. In many ways, they are two sides of the same coin.

Meeting the Challenge of Understanding Data

The history of the concept of data clearly shows the strong relationship between data and knowledge. The primary means of meeting the challenge of understanding data is to manage knowledge about data and help the organization and the individuals improve their data literacy. The questions then become: What forms of knowledge must be managed? And how does the organization build its skill in using data?

---

[6]It's not clear whether Samuel Clemmons (Mark Twain) or Benjamin Disraeli said it first, but somewhere in the late 19th century, one of them apparently observed: "There are three kinds of lies: lies, damned lies, and statistics."

Teach the Organization About Its Own Data

Knowing an organization's data is a means of knowing the organization itself. Data should not be viewed as the purview of IT or of "experts." Data and information are part of all organizational interactions. Establish and document the expected relationship between business process and data; recognize data as input to and a product of business processes; and raise awareness of the uses of data within the organization.

Manage Metadata

Documentation has a bad name these days, but, given the proliferation of data in most organizations and the desire to get value from data, documentation is more necessary than ever. Organizations must set and meet a reasonable standard for the minimum documentation of business processes, data definitions, technical processes, and the relation between these things. They also must build into project work the initial collection of business metadata.

Manage the Processes That Create Data

Because people make data, we have a great deal of control over how we make data. As we will discuss in depth in Chapter 5, designing the processes that create data to produce a higher-quality product can reduce the costs and risks associated with poor-quality data.

Cultivate Data Literacy

We will discuss data literacy in depth in Chapter 7, but I will make a few comments here because knowledge about how data works is critical to data literacy. For decades, people have used the term *knowledge worker* to refer to how we work together in the Information Age (Peter Drucker coined the term in the mid-20th century). If we are knowledge workers, then what are we expected to know and what skills do we apply in our work? *Data literacy* has become the term of the day to refer to the ability to work with data. *Literacy* refers to a set of skills and knowledge required to read, understand, and use written texts. Data literacy is similar. It includes the knowledge, skills, and experience to read, understand, interpret, and learn from data in different contexts, along with the ability to communicate about data to other people. Data literacy must be cultivated at both an individual and organizational level.

Formalize Data Quality Management Practices

Formalizing data quality management practices, including data standards and appropriate controls, so people understand their purpose and value and they can be executed consistently, helps the organization produce more consistent, usable data. These practices also create a valuable form of knowledge about the organization and its goals. Data quality management practices can become a means of building data literacy by teaching the organization about data in general and about its data in particular.

Develop Appropriate Data Governance Practices

Organizational data is created in many different places to serve many different needs in an organization. Everyone involved wants their own needs met, but few people have the perspective to account for the organization as a whole. Without this perspective, organizational data will get more complicated and disparate over time. Solving this problem requires oversight and governance of decisions involving data. Notice that I did not say, it requires that you "implement data governance." As we will discuss in Chapter 8, current definitions of data governance have not delivered on the promises they made. Yet the problems data governance was intended to solve have not gone away. We must rethink how we govern data, and organizational leadership must commit in good faith to implementing change if organizations are to solve these problems.

The Process Challenge: Managing for Quality

"Be not deceived; . . . for whatsoever a man sows that shall he also reap."

Galatians 6, 7−8

"Quality begins with intent."

W. Edwards Deming, *Out of the Crisis*

Introduction

This chapter presents basic principles and concepts of quality management in the manufacture of physical products and services and discusses what can be gained by applying these principles to data. It starts with definitions of quality to ground the discussion and then explores in-depth the concept of "quality by design" as formulated by quality pioneer Joseph Juran. It presents a set of principles for quality management derived from a range of quality thought leaders. The goal of discussing these principles is to show the ways they support the management of data quality. Data is a product of organizational processes and an organizational asset, but it differs from other products and assets in important ways, especially with respect to its life cycle. These differences affect our understanding of data quality and our approach to data quality management. The final section of the chapter will discuss the insights from and limitations of applying the product model to data quality in light of the particular challenges data presents as an object of quality management.

Quality Is Not an Accident

One of the most obvious reasons that managing the quality of data is challenging is that managing the quality of any product is challenging. Few products or processes, goods or services work exactly right the first time. Success requires commitment, thought, planning, and, most importantly, practice. Quality is achieved when organizations produce the intended outcome of a defined process. All thought leaders in quality emphasize that the point of producing quality products is to satisfy customers. Because customers' needs evolve over time, an organization focused on producing quality products must learn continuously how to improve its products to meet these evolving needs. All of this means that high-quality products are not created by accident, but poor-quality products many times are.

Meeting the Challenges of Data Quality Management. DOI: https://doi.org/10.1016/B978-0-12-821737-5.00005-5

Another obvious reason that managing the quality of data is challenging is that data differs in important ways from other products. Data is not a physical product with height, weight, length, and width. It is abstract. To even understand it requires an understanding of the context and purposes for which it was created and the ways in which it may be used. And data can be used in ways that are completely unimagined at the time it was created. There may be a lot of time and space between the data "product" and the data consumer or "customer." Still, the ways we produce and use data, particularly within the contexts of science, statistics and commerce, are meaningfully informed by the concept of data as a product and the application of quality management principles to data management. This is because data consumers (the people and processes who use data) have expectations related to the characteristics that make data meaningful and usable.

Definitions of Quality

Quality is defined as "the standard of something as measured against other things of a similar kind ... general excellence of standard or level ... a distinctive attribute or characteristics possessed by someone or something" (*New Oxford American Dictionary*, 2005). Data quality is most often defined as "fitness for purpose." This concept comes directly from quality management in the manufacture of physical products. It has been expressed in different ways by quality thought leaders. W. Edwards Deming associates quality with meeting standards expected by customers: "Good quality means a predictable degree of uniformity and dependability with a quality standard suited to the customer" (Deming, 1994). Joseph Juran defines the quality of any product as its "fitness for use" (Juran, 1992). He adds that organizations succeed best when their products not only meet their customers' requirements but also please customers in some way. Such organizations must also ensure that they do not displease their customers by having products fail in service at unacceptable rates. Philip Crosby defines quality simply as "conformance to specifications." In each case, quality is understood in comparison with a set of expectations: a standard expected by customers, a use/purpose, or documented specifications (Crosby, n.d.).

The definition of *data quality* as "fitness for purpose" also aligns closely with the processes through which scientific data is produced. In science, data is designed in the sense that it is collected to answer a particular question and thus meet a specific purpose. In some cases, measurement instruments are developed specifically to collect data. And scientific data is tested for validity, consistency, and reproducibility to ensure its quality.

Quality Data

ISO 8000, the international standard for data quality, defines quality data as "portable data that meets stated requirements" (International Organization for Standardization, 2016). This definition focuses on two things:

- **Portability:** The idea that data is technology-agnostic and should be able to convey the meaning of the information it represents, regardless of what technology is used to store and access it
- **Requirements:** The idea that standards exist that describe the characteristics required to make data usable and trustworthy

The definition implies that high-quality data, like any other high-quality product, is the result of intention and planning, that customers have expectations related to the quality of data, and that characteristics of quality can be clearly defined and understood.

As the history of quality management makes clear, the surest way to produce a high-quality product is to design quality in. Quality management is exactly that: a set of practices to ensure that quality is designed into a product or service. Quality management requires helping an organization create a cultural commitment to quality and to managing processes in a way that ensures quality outcomes. Many organizations fail to ground data quality management in principles of overall quality management. They do not recognize that the people and processes using data are customers of the people and processes that create the data. They treat data as a by-product of their processes, rather than a product of those processes. They do not plan for high-quality data, so they do not produce high-quality data.

Data quality has its own challenges because people have different and often incorrect assumptions about what data is, how it is produced, how it may be used, and how it should be managed across an organization and over time. Without a clear understanding of these things, it is difficult to define what an organization even means by high-quality data, never mind put in place the people, processes, and technology required to manage data quality.

This problem is made more difficult by a misguided assumption that data quality is somehow "subjective." This comes in the form of oddly phrased questions like, "How much data quality is good enough?" I say "oddly" because the question itself seems to imply that some number associated with data quality is an end in itself, rather than that data quality management processes are a means to the end of satisfying data consumers' expectations by better understanding and meeting their needs.[1] In doing so, the question ignores the fundamental purpose of data: to represent characteristics of people, events, and concepts in ways that enable a common understanding of these things among and between people. It also ignores the assumption that, with effective analysis and skilled interpretation, data can reveal characteristics about these things that would otherwise not be visible or comprehensible. With regard to organizational data, analysis includes developing insight about the organization's processes, products, and customers as well as learning from these how to make better products or services. The question should not be, "How much quality is good enough?" but "Why is the data unusable (incorrect, missing, wrong, or "bad") in the first place?"

The question, "How much quality is good enough?" ignores some basic assumptions about what makes data of high quality. At its simplest, quality is about the difference between the characteristics a data consumer expects the data to have and the characteristics the data actually has. Ideally, these expectations are based on knowledge of the data, what it represents, and the process through which it is created.[2] The better defined a data consumer's expectations, the better able the customer will be to judge the quality of the data.

Expectations about data come from several sources, starting with common sense and reasonability derived from knowledge about what the data is intended to represent (usually a business process). Other sources of expectations about data include documented knowledge about the data (metadata), such as

---

[1] The desire to put a cap on quality seems to be a perennial problem in quality management. Deming mentions it in the introduction to *Out of the Crisis*. In data management circles, it often comes in the form of questions about thresholds. People are eager to set thresholds, sometimes even before they define the characteristics they are measuring.

[2] I put it this way because someone is sure to say, "What if you *expect* low-quality data?" The simple answer is: If you expect low-quality and you get low-quality, then you are still able to judge quality using your expectations.

business rules, data models, definitions, and process flows. First, one must be able to understand the data. Then one must have confidence that:

- The data represents the things one is asking questions about
- The data looks as expected
    - From a technical perspective, this includes formatting, and so on
    - From a content perspective, this includes recognizable congruity between the data and the things the data represents

Most people who use data want to know that their data is complete, whether completeness is defined in terms of the number of records included, the population of customers included, the time-frame under analysis, the characteristics represented, or some other criterion. They also want the values for each characteristic to accurately reflect the objects being represented. They want data to be comprehensible and organized and formatted in a way that enables its use. Importantly, and the place where many organizations get into trouble because so much data is produced in silos, data consumers want to be able to combine data from different parts of the organization to answer questions about performance, products, and customers. They expect data to fit together because the processes that produce the data reflect the organization as a whole.

Defining what is meant by high-quality data is a necessary first step to producing high-quality data. This definition can come in the positive form of standards, definitions, rules, requirements, specifications, or other documented expectations from data consumers, or in the negative form of customer complaints. (For most organizations, it includes both forms.) Measuring data against the definition of quality is the second step and is the beginning of data quality management. Taking action to improve data is the third step and the route to reducing costs, mitigating operational risks, and increasing the value the organization realizes from data.

Data as a Product

Before associating the concept of data with the concept of a product, it is worth understanding what is meant by a product. Juran has a very simple definition: a product is the output from any process (Juran, 1992, p. 5). This definition comprises physical things (goods), work performed for someone else (services), and information (reports, plans, instructions, advice, commands). Although Juran does not specifically call out data, it is easy to see why the early thought leaders in data quality saw the analogy between products as output from a process and data as output from a process, especially given Juran's acknowledgment that information is part of process output (Fig. 14).

Given the obvious similarity between data as a product and the manufacture of physical products, we can gain some perspective on data quality problems by asking what physical products would look like if we created them in the same way that we create data. For example:

- If we engaged a small team of people to create a physical product but gave them no standards or requirements?
- If we had multiple teams working separately creating different parts of the product, but did not tell them that their output would be integrated with the output of another team at the end of their process?

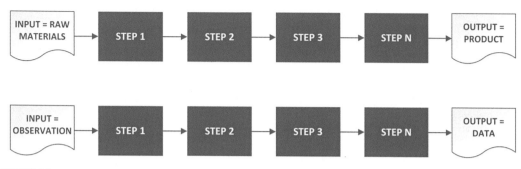

A product is the output from a process, data is the output from a process.

- If we allowed each team to choose a different measurement system and a different set of materials to develop their product?
- If we said, "Don't worry about documenting how you make the product or how to use it. We can do that later."

The short answer is that the pieces would not fit together. Each team would make their own choices. There is very little chance that these choices would align. Fitting the product together would require adjustments on all sides.

A *process* is a series of steps that turns inputs into outputs.[3] In a data process, the inputs and the outputs are both data. Data quality problems are usually identified in the output—the data product. When outputs look as we expect them to look, we see good-quality data. When they look different from what we expect, we see poor-quality data. However, the problems detected in the output may be rooted at any point in the production or consumption process. For example:

- **Inputs** may be poorly defined, missing, or incorrect, or assumptions about inputs may be incorrect.
- **Process steps** may be poorly defined, missing, redundant, or poorly executed.
- **Controls** on process steps may be:
  - Insufficient: They may not control to the degree that they should control
  - Poorly designed: They may not control what they are supposed to control
  - Not properly placed: They do not control when they should control
  - Neglected: No one is paying attention to the feedback provided by the control
- **Outputs** may be perceived as low quality because:
  - The data is actually wrong
  - Data consumers have incorrect assumptions about the data
  - The data is poorly designed and hard to use (e.g., the data is highly complex)
  - The data does not actually meet the data consumer's needs

---

[3] I first heard *process* described in this very useful way from a colleague of mine who did Business Process Engineering at Cigna. Unfortunately, I cannot remember her name, so I can only acknowledge that the formulation is not my own.

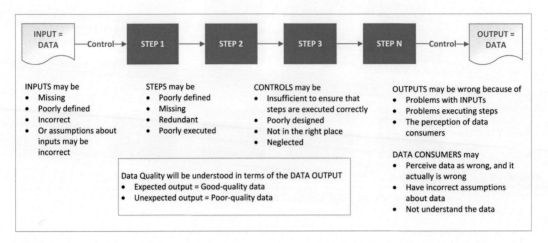

FIGURE 15

What can go wrong in a generic data production process.

These risks related to data and the processes that create it increase as data moves along the data chain from process to process, system to system (especially as it is reformatted or otherwise transformed to meet the requirements of different systems) and from use to use. Because data can be a product at one point in the data chain and an input to another product at another point in the data chain, it is easy to understand why clear expectations for quality are important to the data chain as a whole. It is also easy to imagine the negative effects of errors reverberating throughout the chain (Fig. 15).

The product metaphor for data is central to the work of several leading thinkers in data quality management.[4] For example, in the influential article "Beyond Accuracy: What Data Quality Means to Data Consumers," Richard Wang and Diane Strong define data quality as "data that are fit for use by data consumers" (Wang & Strong, 1996). Their definition draws directly on Juran's definition of quality as "fitness for purpose." They emphasize understanding how quality is perceived by people who use data, rather than how data quality is perceived by people charged with building and maintaining databases and other technologies or even by people executing business processes. They argue that most organizations produce data as a by-product of business and technical processes. When data is treated as a by-product, little attention is given to its quality from the perspective of people who may want to use it in downstream operations or analytics. Even things that should be simple at the moment of creation, like defining what the data represent to the creation process, become complicated when other people try to understand and use the product. If data were treated instead as a product—the result of a well-defined information production process—the quality could be designed into the production process, and data would better meet the needs of data consumers.

---

[4]English (1999, 2009), Loshin (2001), McGilvray (2008, 2021), Redman (1997). Each of these thinkers has also developed a set of data quality dimensions. See Sebastian-Coleman (2013), Appendix B.

From this understanding, Wang and Strong propose a set of four categories through which data quality can be understood. Within each category, they propose dimensions of data quality:

- **Intrinsic data quality** denotes that data has quality in its own right; it is understood largely as the extent to which data values are in conformance with the actual or true values. Intrinsically good data is accurate, correct, and objective, and it comes from a reputable source. Dimensions include accuracy, objectivity, believability, and reputation.
- **Contextual data quality** points to the requirement that data quality must be considered within the context of the task at hand and is understood largely as the extent to which data is applicable (pertinent) to the task of the data user. The focus of contextual data quality is the data consumer's task, not the context of representation itself. For example, contextually appropriate data must be relevant to the consumer in terms of timeliness and completeness. Dimensions include value-added, relevancy, timeliness, completeness, and appropriate amount of data.
- **Representational data quality** indicates that the system must present data in such a way that it is easy to understand (represented concisely and consistently) so the consumer is able to interpret the data; the concept is understood as the extent to which data is presented in an intelligible and clear manner. Dimensions include interpretability, ease of understanding, representational consistency, and concise representation.
- **Accessibility data quality** emphasizes the importance of the role of systems; the concept is understood as the extent to which data is available to or obtainable by the data consumer. The system must also be secure. Dimensions include accessibility and access security.

Wang and Strong recognize that there are customers for data products and that these customers judge the quality of data they are using in ways that are more complex and multifaceted than the assumptions that IT professionals make about data quality. Each of their categories implies the need for metadata—documented knowledge that enables people to understand and use data—in support of quality data.

As noted in Chapter 4, another way of looking at data quality is by determining how well data represents what it purports to represent (Chisholm, 2012). As I hope was clear from the earlier discussion, the need for data to represent what it purports to represent is inherent in any use of data. Wang and Strong account for it in their concepts of intrinsic and representational data quality. Their use of the product metaphor emphasizes that there are customers at the end of the data chain. These customers will choose data based on what it represents and judge the quality of data based on how they want to use the data. The choice, then, is not between data that "represents what it purports to represent" and data that is "fit for purpose" (to be of high quality, data must do both). It is between data that is created accidentally as a by-product (an insignificant and disposable output from a process) and data that is created through a well-defined process, as a product, with the knowledge and awareness that it will be used after its creation because of what it represents.

The Juran Trilogy: Quality Management Processes

Knowing these general characteristics, let's look closely at the work of Joseph Juran to understand how the drivers of quality management work together. Juran describes the process of managing quality as analogous to financial management. Strategic financial planning starts with setting financial goals, determining the actions and resources needed to meet them, establishing performance measures, comparing actual performance to results, and rewarding people based on results (Juran, 1992, p. 301). Well-executed financial management works in organizations in which performance against financial goals is given "substantial weight in the system of merit rating," there is universal participation, a common language centered on a unit of measurement (money), and training that enables even nonfinancial managers to understand financial concepts, processes, and methods (Juran, 1992, p. 302). A strategic approach to finance enables an organization to make financial decisions in the context of the overall goals of the organization.

Juran's quality trilogy presents a similar vision of quality management. It has three basic components: planning, control, and improvement (Fig. 16). Within each of these processes is a set of "universal sequences" necessary to bring about the desired outcomes. These sequences have been "discovered again and again by practicing managers" (Juran, 1992, p. 15). They include the following:

- **Quality planning:** The activity of developing the products and processes to meet customers' needs
  - Establish quality goals
  - Identify the customers
  - Determine the customers' needs
  - Develop product features to meet these needs
  - Develop processes to produces these features
  - Establish process controls, and transfer to operating forces
- **Quality control:** The activity of monitoring performance in relation to quality goals
  - Evaluate actual quality performance
  - Compare actual performance to goals
  - Act on the difference
- **Quality improvement:** Activities focused on raising quality performance beyond original quality goals
  - Establish the infrastructure needed to secure annual quality improvement
  - Identify the specific needs for improvement, and set up improvement projects
  - Establish project teams with clear responsibilities
  - Provide resources, motivation, and training for teams to
    - Diagnose causes of poor quality
    - Stimulate establishment of remedies
    - Establish controls to hold the gains

Juran describes the quality planning phase in great detail through the concept of quality by design. The intention of quality by design is to reduce the gap between customer expectations and customer perceptions of quality. This gap may be established at the beginning of the product design process if an organization does not understand its customers' needs. With each stage of the process, the gap can grow. The overall perception gap results from the combination of the understanding gap, the design gap, the process gap, and the operations gap (DeFeo & Juran, 2014, p. 93).

Juran points out that "product features and failure rates are largely determined during planning for quality" (Juran, 1992, p. 2), that is, during the effort to understand what the quality

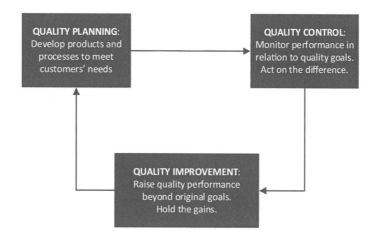

FIGURE 16

Juran's quality trilogy.

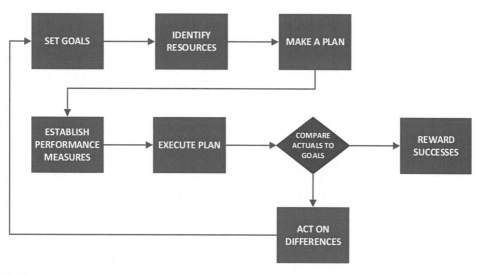

FIGURE 17

Juran's process steps.

goals are. The planning process includes setting goals for quality, based on customer expectations, and establishing processes to meet these goals (Fig. 17). When organizations fail to plan for high-quality outcomes, they do not get high-quality outcomes. As he succinctly puts it, "Our quality problems have been planned that way" (Juran, 1992, p. 3), meaning that a lack of attention to quality during the planning phase results in low-quality outcomes. Deming made a similar observation about the connection between design and results: "Every system is perfectly designed to get the results it gets."[5]

Juran's trilogy provides a quick and easy way to describe what is needed to manage quality: planning, control, and improvement. Juran argues that the trilogy is more than just a way to explain quality to upper management. It provides a unifying concept for the organization to understand the connection between planning, control, improvement, and high-quality outcomes (Juran, 1992, p. 15). The quality by design approach stresses the "dual responsibility of those who plan to provide the features to meet customer needs and to provide the process to meet operational needs" (Defeo & Juran, 2014, p. 90).

One final note. Juran points out that information about the product (e.g., assembly instructions, operating manuals, and maintenance requirements) is part of a high-quality product because it is necessary to the customer's success in using the product. Within data management, the same can be said about metadata. Metadata is part of the data product. Data consumers require it to use data. Its absence reduces the quality of data because the lack of knowledge about the data is an obstacle to using the data.

Dimensions of Product Quality

In "Competing on the Eight Dimensions of Quality," David Garvin provides an update on Juran that helpfully informs discussions on data quality (Garvin, 1987). Most organizations today are not talking simply about having higher-quality data; they want to leverage data as a strategic asset to gain a competitive advantage. This means they must think differently about how they produce and use data. Most importantly, they must determine what aspects of their data require improvement work.

Garvin's analysis is about how to gain advantage through improved product quality. He points out that most American manufacturers in the post-World War II era did not take quality seriously as a strategic opportunity. They saw it only as something that could hurt an organization if it were completely ignored. Although they were smart enough to try to prevent defects, they missed the idea that they could also please their customers with a higher-quality product. Garvin refers to this approach as "defensive quality" and adds, "One thing is certain: high quality means pleasing consumers, not just protecting them from annoyances" (Garvin, 1987).

Garvin introduces the idea of dimensions of quality to discuss a more strategic approach to meeting customer expectations. Importantly, he points out that to get to a customer perspective and take a strategic approach to quality, managers must develop a vocabulary that allows them to talk about quality in a strategic way. Garvin's eight dimensions include both objective and subjective facets. They enable a quality strategy because an organization may have to choose among them to determine how it can gain advantage over its competitors:

- **Performance:** The product operates as expected.
- **Features:** The product has additional characteristics that please the customer.

---

[5]The attribution of this quote is in question. It may have originated with Paul Batalden or Arthur Jones, rather than Deming; https://deming.org/quotes/10141/

- **Reliability:** The product works well; the customer can use it.
- **Conformance:** The product meets standards.
- **Durability:** The product lasts for the expected amount of time.
- **Serviceability:** If the product breaks or stops functioning, it can be fixed.
- **Aesthetics:** The product is attractive and pleasing.
- **Perceived quality:** The customer feels good about the product.

Wang and Strong's perspective on data quality is similar in many ways to Garvin's perspective on product quality. It is based on the customer's (data consumer's) perspective, not just the manufacturer's (IT's or, more properly, upstream business process') perspective. In taking this view, Garvin recognizes that customers want to use products. How they perceive quality is directly connected to use. This means that meeting specifications and minimizing defects or failures are necessary but not sufficient conditions for quality. Garvin's multidimensional approach also points to the idea that customers are concerned with more than just price. They also care about long-term reliability and serviceability of products. Just as product quality goes beyond the obvious (price), data quality, in Wang and Strong's parlance, goes "beyond accuracy."

We will discuss data quality dimensions in depth in Chapter 10. In the meantime, it may be helpful to do a quick synopsis of the basics to see how some basic dimensions of data quality align with concepts of product quality a la Garvin, from the perspective of the customer ("You"):

- **Accessibility:** You can access the data you need.
- **Completeness:** You have all the data you need to meet your purpose (and you do not have extra data that you do not need).
- **Currency:** The data reflects the current state of what it represents; it is not old or out of date.
- **Format correctness:** All pieces of data are in the shape you expect them to be in (ideally, following enterprise standards).
- **Validity:** The values in the data belong to the set of possible (expected) values.
- **Integrity:** The pieces of data fit together in the ways you expect them to fit together.
- **Consistency:** The data follows patterns that you expect it to follow (including reasonable alignment with known facts about the real world).

There is a logical progression to these concepts. If you cannot access the data, you cannot do anything with it, including determining if it meets your needs. If you do not have all of the data that you need or the data is out of date, then it does not really matter whether it is correctly formatted. If it is not correctly formatted, then in many cases, values also technically cannot be valid. Unless data is formatted as expected and contains valid values, it is unlikely to fit together with other pieces of data. And it if does not fit together, then you will not be able to determine whether it follows expected patterns. If you can determine that it does not follow expected patterns, you then must figure out why: Changes in patterns or errors in the data?

Of course, these also presupposed that data you need exists in the first place. It will also be great if the data is supported, that is, people and information are available to help you use the data if you have trouble understanding what you are looking at.

Quality Management Principles

Organizations committed to quality must invest time and talent to ensure that their products and services meet the quality levels their customers expect. Quality management in all fields—manufacturing, health care, financial services, and other service industries—follows several critical principles, which are outlined in the following sections. We will define these principles here and then revisit them after discussing the ways in which data differs from other products.[6]

Establish Organizational Commitment to Quality

Quality does not just happen. Quality is the result of a set of choices about how to prioritize and deploy resources. Quality starts with leadership commitment. This commitment requires a vision of how different functions will work together toward a common goal. Leadership must engender a culture committed to quality processes and outcomes. Individuals and teams must be empowered to act in ways that support the overall goal of creating quality products and services. Kaoru Ishikawa's quality circles provide a means of changing an organization's culture through collaboration and empowerment, as does Crosby's "common purpose."

Deming's 14 points, which call for management to create "constancy of purpose" toward the improvement of products and services are the clearest expression of the relationship between leadership commitment and the ability to produce quality products (Deming, 1986). Point 5, "Improve constantly and forever every process for planning, production and service," point 13 "Institute a vigorous program of education and self-improvement for everyone," and point 14 "Put everybody in the company to work accomplishing the transformation" emphasize the need for a comprehensive approach, engaging people throughout the enterprise. Point 7, "Adopt and institute leadership," point 8, "Drive out fear," and point 9, "Break down barriers between staff areas," describe the role of leadership in enabling transformation of the organization.[7]

Focus on the Customer

The customer is the arbiter of quality. Through their decisions to purchase or not purchase a product, customers decide what is "fit for purpose." They have expectations that are either met or not met by a product. Some customers know exactly what they expect, but many are not consciously aware of their own expectations. They may never have put them into words or stated them out loud. Nevertheless, they judge quality based on their expectations. An organization that wants to satisfy its customers over time must be in conversation with those customers to understand their needs and expectations as these evolve. Juran's quality by design process starts and ends with understanding customer requirements.

---

[6]These are derived from multiple works by Deming, Juran, Ishikawa, and Crosby. Kaoru Ishikawa (1915–1989) is credited with developing a specifically Japanese approach to quality strategy, which includes broad involvement in quality across the organization (not only top to bottom within the organization) and start to finish in the product life cycle (ASQ.org).
[7]Early thought leaders in data quality, Redman (1997), English (1999), Loshin (2001), and McGilvray (2008), all discuss the importance of Deming's 14 points to the improvement of data quality. More recently, O'Keefe and O Brien (2018) apply them to data ethics.

Manage the Production Process

There is a direct connection between product and process. It takes a sound, predictable process to produce a consistently high-quality product. Predictability depends on having consistent inputs from suppliers and on consistently executing process steps. Obviously, the steps themselves must be executed in the right way to produce the desired outcome. (You can have a predictable process that consistently fails to produce a high-quality product.) Shewhart's[8] statistical process control methods are used to understand and improve the production process. Ishikawa's analysis techniques (e.g., the fishbone diagram) enable organizations to identify root causes of production errors and act on process improvements.

Manage the Supply Chain

Products are made of multiple parts or ingredients. The quality of a product (the output from a process) depends on the quality of the inputs. Inputs are themselves products of a preceding process. Each part must meet the specifications (i.e., expectations) of the production process, or the product will not meet required levels of quality. This means that quality depends on partnership with suppliers whom an organization counts on to produce reliable parts and deliver them within expected timeframes. To deliver to specification, suppliers must know the requirements and act accountably toward the quality of their own products. Juran's quality by design approach recognizes supply chain management as a key element in producing quality products, as does Feigenbaum's Total Quality Control.[9]

Measure and Monitor the Process Against Quality Goals

The only way to know if a process is operating as predicted or a supplier is producing high-quality parts or a product has met quality expectations is to measure these things. The degree to which processes create consistent output can be measured using the statistical process control methods introduced by Walter Shewhart, suppliers' quality can be measured against specifications, and product quality can be measured against customer expectations (usually documented in a specification).

Build Quality into the Product Life Cycle

The overall process by which products are managed, the product life cycle, has several phases. It starts with conceptualizing and planning for the product, developing or acquiring it, using or applying it, and supporting its use by the customers. Expectations related to quality must influence all

---

[8]Walter Shewhart (1891–1967), a pioneer in quality management, was among the first to apply scientific and mathematical methods to reducing the costs of poor quality in manufacturing. The control chart, which he developed, is a critical tool in quality management.

[9]Armand Feigenbaum (1920–2014), an engineer and economist, formulated the concept of Total Quality Control (TQC), which advocates for integrating quality development, quality maintenance, and quality improvement efforts across the organization to reduce costs, improve efficiency, and better serve customers. He also introduced the concept of the "hidden factory" to describe the extra work required in most organizations to correct mistakes.

FIGURE 18

The Shewhart improvement cycle.

phases of the life cycle. That is, the product life cycle provides the context for making decisions about products that result in their ability to meet customer expectations. As discussed earlier in this chapter, Juran's trilogy describes how to manage the overall life cycle of a product (we will discuss the data life cycle in-depth in Chapter 11).

Continuously Improve

This combination of principles is aimed at two things. The first is ensuring that an organization creates products that are consistently of high quality. The second is that the organization identifies and acts on opportunities to improve quality. The idea of continuous improvement is best summarized in the Shewhart Cycle: Plan, Do, Check, Act (PDCA; Fig. 18). This problem-solving methodology, based on the scientific method and similar to the Juran trilogy, captures the intention of an organization that seeks to learn from its customers and the feedback they provide. Improvement comes through a defined set of steps. Planning involves defining the requirements; doing is implementing the requirements; checking is comparing the results against the plan and actively determining how to address gaps or problems; and acting is implementing improvements.

Data Is Different from Other Resources

This chapter began with the observation that the first and most obvious reason that managing the quality of data is challenging is that managing the quality of any product is challenging. I hope the discussion of quality management principles and processes has made the first point clear, while at the same time pointing to a set of methodologies and a body of knowledge that describe how to meet the challenge of defining and measuring quality.

The next and perhaps less obvious reason why managing the quality of data is challenging is that data differs from physical products and from services in ways that complicate how we think about quality.[10] Cars and jewelry have clearly defined physical characteristics associated with quality that are based on the materials they are made from and the features they include. Services are similar. You know you are getting good service at a restaurant if you are seated promptly and comfortably, your order is taken when you are ready to give it, the food arrives in a timely manner, the food smells wonderful, and it tastes even better. But we do not tend to think about data in these terms because it is not physically present.

In addition, data is also talked about in data management circles as an organizational *asset*. This term itself is not well-understood by non-accountants, and the ways that data is understood to bring value to organizations have not yet achieved the status of "generally accepted accounting principles." But whether we think of data as a product or as an asset, it differs in important ways from both physical products and other organizational assets.[11] In the following discussion, I will refer to *data* as both an asset—a useful or valuable thing, a kind of property available to meet debts and other commitments—and as a product—using Juran's definition, "a product is the output from any process" (Juran, 1992).

Because data is not a physical object, it is not constrained by the limitations of physical objects.[12] It does not wear out when used, for example. Unlike money or other financial assets, it can be used multiple times without being "spent." Especially in electronic form, data is also easily copied, transformed, and manipulated without the original data being changed or degraded. It can even be stolen and not be "missing." It can be used by more than one person or process at a time. Data is not subject to the law of the conservation of mass. It can be used to create new data, without "using up" the original data. The idea that data is often used to create new data gives data an organic quality that other assets do not have.

Organizations that manufacture physical products control the production, storage, inventory, and distribution of these products. They know how many widgets they make, to whom they sell them, and how the widgets are likely to be used. Data is different with respect to these processes:

- **Production:** Data is created in many places inside and outside of the organization, but no one is counting/cataloging how much is produced (again, the by-product problem). Controls are likely to be inconsistent across the range of places where data is created. Once created, data can easily be copied.
- **Inventory:** There are no standards for counting how much data an organization has. Efforts to do so usually focus on technical aspects of data—how many databases are managed and how many bytes these databases contain. Keeping an inventory of data is complicated by the ease with which data can be copied as well as how it can be transformed through use (e.g., aggregated, standardized). In short, many organizations do not know what data they have, never mind what condition the data is in. (This is one reason why data catalog technology is currently all the rage for Big Data environments.) But inventory is not about knowing how full your warehouse is. Inventory

---

[10]Much of the information in this section derives from Redman (2008), Chapter 1: The Wonderous and Perilous Properties of Data and Information in Organizations.

[11]As I hope is clear from the discussion, product and asset are not opposites. Data is both a product (it is created) and an asset (something from which value can be derived). It can also be thought of simply as a resource (a thing that can be used).

[12]Undoubtedly, even a junior DBA is likely to point out that there are physical constraints on data storage and manipulation. I get that. You still cannot touch data.

is about knowing what products are available for sale. For data, this means having metadata that describes data contents, at least at the level of the object. Knowing product inventory is also necessary to account for the value of the products on the balance sheet. With data, there are no standards for defining this value.

- **Storage:** Data can be easily stored. And, as with physical products, the manner in which it is stored has a direct impact on its quality. For example, how data is stored influences how it is maintained. In addition, different kinds of data need different levels of protection, and storage methods must account for these requirements. As noted in the comments about inventory, the organization may be able to measure how much data is stored, based on the size of data sets and other technical considerations. To know the content of stored data, and therefore any special requirements for storage, requires metadata.
- **Distribution:** Most organizations tightly control who can access data from their systems and what data they can access. The functionality of applications that enable access is critical to customer perception of quality ("I have access to the data, but I cannot sort it or filter it."). Once data is out of an organization's systems, the ability of an organization to control it is very limited, even among their own employees. Many organizations have limited, if any, documented information about who uses data and to what ends.
- **Usage:** Although there is often a direct connection between data production and data uses, new uses of data evolve over time. This means quality requirements evolve. Because most organizational data is produced in the context of a specific business process, there is not always a direct connection between data producers and data consumers. In addition, the challenges with creating an inventory of data also reverberate on data use: data can be used multiple times without being used up. And it lasts for a long time, so data created for one purpose can often be used in unanticipated ways for other purposes.

As we have seen, historically, especially within the business realm of transactions, a lot of data is created not intentionally, as the product of a well-defined process, but accidentally, as a by-product of organizational operations. Per Juran, data quality management must begin with making this "by-product" an intentional product. This idea has implications for how data quality can be managed, but it also tells us something about data: commerce-based organizational data is very difficult, if not impossible, to reproduce or replace. As Tom Redman succinctly put it, data is non-fungible (Redman, 1997).

A *fungible* asset is interchangeable with any other of its kind. Any individual dollar bill, euro, or yen is the same as any other dollar bill, euro, or yen. But can the records of two transactions replace each other? No. An organization may be able to replace its customer list, but it is unlikely to be able to replace the history of transactions of any given customer if this data were to be lost. While all records representing the same type of thing, say the sale of a product, may have the same structure, the details of the individual events they represent will differ from each other. If two people buy the same product, they remain two different customers. Even if they purchase the same product at the same location, they cannot do so with the same clerk at the same time. If a single person buys the same product twice, they will have purchased it at different times or locations. As anyone who has had to document their medical history (multiple times, on paper, at a doctor's office) will realize, it is hard to reconstruct the events and dates for even one person. Imagine if a large health care insurance company needed to reconstruct the claim records of all of its members. Even for a single day's worth of data, the task would be impossible.

An organization's data—its customer list, product information, and sales history—is unique to that organization. It is like a fingerprint. This is why data represents so much potential value. It records organizational activities and events in ways that will enable the organization to learn from itself.

These characteristics that make data different from other assets also make it difficult to associate data with concepts that are used to manage other assets, such as ownership, inventory, risk management, auditability, and consistent valuation (Ladley, 2019).

Limitations of the Product Model for Data Quality

Producing a quality product requires intention; quality is not an accident. Although data is recognized as a valuable organizational resource and in rare cases is even treated as an asset, data is also different from other organizational resources. Because we think about data differently from how we think about assets and physical objects, there are recognizable limitations to the product model for managing data quality. The first limitation is that data plays multiple roles within an organization, which also makes it difficult to characterize it as an asset or a product. This is why I prefer the term *resource*, which brings more focus to how a thing is used rather than the more financially focused concept of an "asset." Data is:

- **An operational necessity:** Data is required to transact business and is produced through the transaction of business. It is a critical resource required to use other resources.[13]
- **A type of organizational knowledge:** In capturing information about the organization and its activities, data is the means through which the organization knows itself and its customers.
- **A meta-asset:** Data describes other assets, such as financial instruments, inventories, and people.
- **An asset:** A thing from which value can be derived. Data provides value when the benefit gained from applying the insights gleaned from it surpasses the costs of collecting, organizing, storing, accessing, and analyzing it.
- **A risk:** Much has been written about data as an asset, but unmanaged data is also a liability. If data is misused or breached, the organization can be called to account for the consequences (see Fig. 7).

The second limitation is a level of confusion about the product model's definition of quality as "fitness for purpose," especially if the word *intended* is added to the mix. Many people balk intuitively when they read that data quality is "fitness for *intended* purposes" because they recognize that a lot of organizational data is not created specifically for the purposes that data consumers put it to. For example, sales data is not created specifically to enable analytics about sales. It is created as part of the process of selling products. Data about adjudicated health care claims is not created to enable health care analytics. It is created to make accurate payments for services.

---

[13]Michael Brackett's *Data Resource Design: Reality Beyond Illusion* uses the term *resource* rather than *asset*. From both a personal and a professional point of view, I wish that the idea of data as a resource had caught on more strongly than data as an asset. Data is an asset (see the fourth bullet in this set), but too often, the "asset" comparison brings focus to the problem of putting a direct monetary value on data and obscures the range of roles that data plays within an organization.

Related to this argument is the recognition that much of the data used for business intelligence, analytics, and other efforts to gain insights about customers and products is produced internally by the organization and is not available through any other means. While internally produced data may be augmented with external data, most data consumers do not have a lot of choice in which "data products" they use. If you want to do an analysis of sales figures, you must use the data collected by the organization about sales figures. If you want to analyze trends about payments to health care providers, you must use adjudicated claim data. You cannot go shopping for a different data set. That said, once people in the organization recognize what they want to do with data, they can set requirements for how data is collected and organized, for example, what attributes sales figures should require.

In addition, data consumers are constantly coming up with new ways to use data. Recognition of this fact leads people to take "fitness for purpose" to mean that to manage data quality, you must know or be able to envision every purpose to which data can be put—an impossible task. Discussion on this aspect of quality seems to be based on the assumption that data uses differ so significantly from each other or that each person who uses data has unique quality requirements that must be met on an individual basis. Fortunately, this is an unlikely situation. It is also why it is helpful to recognize that data quality is not only about "fitness for purpose" but also about representational effectiveness: "the extent to which the data actually represents what it purports to represent" (Chisholm, 2012).

People who get caught up in the possible complexity of "fitness for purpose" forget that most uses of data are directly related to the reasons the data was created in the first place. If you are looking at sales data, it is probably because you want to understand how well your products are selling, who is buying them, or who does a good job of selling them. If you are analyzing sales data for a retail company, your expectations for quality are probably similar to those of other users: you want the data set to contain all transactions for the time periods you are concerned with; you want the transactions that represent details of the sales, for example, what was sold in each location, along with the sale price; and you may want other details, such as the name of the salesperson or transactions related to returned items or what coupons or discounts were used in the transactions. You would expect this data to correctly reflect the details of the process (e.g., item numbers, prices). All of the other people analyzing sales data want essentially the same things as a starting point for their analyses.

People who get caught up in the possible complexity of "fitness for purpose" also forget that the most important directive related to the product model for data quality is about the process of creating data: data should be created as the product of a well-defined process, as opposed to being created as a by-product (potentially, of a poorly defined process). Producing higher-quality data in the first place, data that is designed to represent the world in clearly defined ways, is one of the keys to managing data quality within the organization and over the data life cycle. A second key is ensuring that this data is supported by explicit knowledge (metadata) that enables data consumers to understand the choices made when the data was created.

Meeting the Process Challenge: Apply Quality Management Principles to Data

Now that we have looked at the general principles of quality management and at quality management from a process perspective, as described by Juran, we will discuss how these ideas apply to data quality management. These general principles have been at the center of data quality management since its inception, especially among those who advocated for the idea that data is a product.[14] However, the ideas are complicated by the ways that data differs from other resources. For example, it is difficult to focus on the data consumer when the data may have multiple types of customers with different needs, and their needs evolve over time. Although it should be possible to control the initial conditions of data production, data is still often seen as a by-product of core business processes, rather than a product of those processes. At this point, with the rise of analytics and the desire to get value from data, there is really no excuse to tolerate treating data as a by-product, when clearly there are customers for data as a product. But there are obstacles to doing so. Ensuring that data is of high quality takes a level of planning and ongoing commitment similar to that required for physical products. And similarly, failure to plan for high-quality outcomes constitutes planning for lower-quality outcomes (Juran, 1992, p. 3).

Establish Organizational Commitment to High-Quality Data

Quality for any product starts through a commitment to quality, a shared purpose for the organization, to ensure that their products and services meet the needs of their customers. Any organization that wants to improve its products has recognized that it must change what it is doing. This means it must change how people work together—change its culture. Cultural change does not come easily or naturally to most organizations. It requires leadership and commitment, intention, planning, and practice. In the first of his 14 points, Deming refers to this as establishing "constancy of purpose." It must be executed in good faith.

Because many problems with data originate from the lack of an enterprise perspective and the tendency of functional teams to work in silos, any approach to improving data quality must articulate the enterprise perspective—even if improvements must be implemented incrementally. A big part of culture change involves raising awareness of the internal data supply chain. People who produce data must recognize that they have customers who use that data. Other parts include defining what is meant by quality and setting standards that can be applied consistently. Data consumers need a way not only to make their quality requirements known but also to have those requirements met. This also requires leadership. Without direction and incentives from leadership to account for the enterprise stake in data, individual departments will operate to meet only their own goals (i.e., they will work in silos because the incentive system encourages them to work in silos). The only way they will change their behavior is if leadership shows them why it is important to do so.

Quality is not an end in itself. It is a means to several other ends, among them better customer service, improved process efficiency, increased employee satisfaction, and cost reduction. These are indirect benefits of improving the processes that produce data. Improved data production will ultimately enable more effective use of data. And because data quality is not an end in itself, the conversation to engage leadership must not be focused solely on data or on "data quality for the sake of data quality." It must be focused on the expected benefits of higher-quality data, such as improved efficiency, higher productivity, and improved ability to meet the needs of the organization's customers.

---

[14]See Redman (1997, 2008), English (1999, 2009), Wang and Strong (1996), Loshin (2001, 2011, 2019), and McGilvray (2016, 2021). These founding texts of data quality management are rooted in "the product model" of data. For a case study on product life-cycle management and data quality management, see Davidson, Lee, and Wang (2004). See Pierce (2007) for an overview of articles and books related to the product concept of data.

- **Bottom line:** Frame organizational commitment to data quality in the context of the organization's overall strategy and purpose, especially its relationship with its customers.

Focus Data Quality Improvement on the Data Consumer

Focusing on the customer is about knowing who the customers are and helping them define their requirements for quality so the organization can meet these requirements. In product quality, there is an obvious customer: the person or organization that buys and uses the product. In data quality, the "data customer" or "data consumer" may be a new concept for some organizations. To improve data quality, it is necessary to build awareness of data uses. Data producers may not know or think of themselves as data producers. If they recognize that the data they create has a life after they create it and view the people who are using data within the organization as their internal customers, they will produce better data. Simple awareness can bring about significant improvements, even without detailed knowledge of the specific expectations of the organization's data consumers.

If the first challenge is to raise awareness, the second is to define the requirements of these customers. The third challenge is putting in place the well-defined processes needed to meet these requirements, that is, the processes that will enable data producers to create the data their customers need in the condition their customers need it to be. Ultimately, the value an organization gets from data is generated when that data is used, so one goal of data production should be to remove obstacles to data use that arise from the conditions of production.

Raising awareness may be complicated because any data production process is likely to have multiple data consumers. People do become confused about data quality requirements when they assume that customers will have widely different expectations for data. Conversations can get sidetracked through questions related to the "correct" tolerances for errors or other details of data quality management. Underlying the hesitation in setting data quality requirements is sometimes a concern about getting quality expectations wrong. In these cases, it is important to remember that data quality is based not only on fitness for specific purposes, but on representational effectiveness. Does the data represent what it purports to represent? This recognition can help focus the conversations on the common requirements that are connected to data content, rather than the nuances of measurement. Data quality management is about making the data better. Every step that helps build knowledge and understanding of data and the processes that produce it contributes to that goal.

Although a lot of good can be accomplished by raising awareness and enabling data consumers to articulate their expectations for quality, it is not possible to improve all data production processes and even less possible to change them instantly. Many obstacles to data use may be based in the technical environment, where change is expensive and time-consuming and has little chance of being funded. Other obstacles may be embedded in business process limitations, which are also challenging to change—and another reason why leadership commitment is required to improve data quality.

- **Bottom line:** All improvements start with awareness. Before they can improve their data products, data producers must understand that they have data consumers and that these customers have quality requirements and expectations. This requires knowledge of how the organization should fit together from a data perspective. It also requires the ability to talk about organizational data in a way that allows people to see the connections and the benefit of acting on them.

Manage the Data Production Process

The quality of a product depends on the process through which it is created. The process must be well defined so it achieves its goals. It also must be consistently executed so the quality of the output is predictably high. The most important facet of managing any process that produces data is to recognize that data is one of the products, not merely a by-product, of the process. For example, making a sale means that a customer obtains a product, and an organization obtains payment. The other result is that the organization obtains data about the transaction—data that can be used to better understand the customer, the product, and the transaction process. The internal customer for this data may be the sales department, the product development department, the customer service department, marketing, finance, or analytics. It is likely that all of these departments use sales data. If the data consumer's data quality requirements are known, then the data production process can be managed to meet them. This may be as simple as putting edits in place that make it mandatory for an upstream process to collect information required for downstream users. Or it can be more complex, such as putting in place a master data management process around customer data and enforcing its use across the enterprise so there truly is a single view of the customer.

This is how quality outcomes are achieved. Once you know who your customers are and what they mean by quality, design the processes required to meet the needs of the customer.

Like quality management itself, process improvement is sometimes seen as an add-on or a "nice to have," rather than as a necessity. Process improvement as a discipline requires applying analysis and people skills to bring about changes in behavior. It requires sponsorship and leadership support. Process improvement starts with knowledge of the current state: How is the process actually executed? Where are the risk points for data? How can it be simplified or better controlled? This knowledge can be gained by recognizing the connections between data producers and data consumers and engaging them in the effort to improve. Doing so will have the added benefit of raising awareness and improving the conversations around data.

Because existing data production processes may be greatly influenced by the technology through which they are executed, there are likely opportunities to improve process execution through edits and other technical controls. However, this should be done based on how the process is intended to operate, not merely as a means of patching the problems. Implementing technical controls can be expensive, and there is sometimes a limited appetite for implementing them. The controls themselves can be perceived as obstacles to the business process through which data is produced, and they will be if they are poorly designed.

- **Bottom line:** Process knowledge is the key to process design and improvement. The process improvement approach provides opportunities to better understand the impact of the process on the quality of the data. When it comes time to make recommendations, frame the suggestions for changes in terms of benefits to the organization. Invest in technical changes only after understanding the primary business process.

Manage the Data Supply Chain

The quality of a product depends not only on a well-designed process, but also on the quality of the inputs. In manufacturing, the idea of a supply chain recognizes that products are made of parts, and each of the parts must be of high quality for the end product to be of high quality. Data moves horizontally (e.g., across verticals) within an organization. This means, even within a single organization, a "data supply chain" will deliver data to the people and processes that require it. This data chain has both process and technical aspects. Data is created by business processes, using specific technology. It is delivered to be used in other business processes that may rely on different technology.

The concept of a data supply chain complicates the idea of focusing on customers. First, it raises the problem of "fitness for purpose." If there are multiple purposes, who gets to decide what makes data "fit"? Keep in mind that "fitness for purpose" is only one side of the coin in understanding data quality. There is a direct connection between what data represents, how it is produced, how well data consumers understand data structure and other conventions of representation, and how data consumers are likely to define its quality. Although there may be some differences in tolerances for error among different uses of data, there is not an infinite variety. Data consumers usually have a common set of expectations that can provide the foundation for evaluating quality. The second problem comes back to clarifying and clearly communicating about requirements and expectations. Managing a supply chain requires each "link" in the chain to declare its quality requirements to its supplier and each "link" to meet the quality requirements of its data consumers. Ideally, quality requirements can be articulated to meet needs across the supply chain.

Much of the potential for getting value from data comes through its use in business intelligence and analytics. These uses of data require that data from multiple sources be integrated in a data warehouse, data mart, or data lake. Many of these sources will be internal to the organization, so a simple data supply chain may be composed of just internal data. An obvious starting point to understand the data supply chain is through depictions of the organization's data architecture. Unfortunately, many organizations produce data in silos, through disconnected business processes and each with its own technical system. While the processes are connected to each other logically (e.g., in health care, membership information in the eligibility system is ultimately intended to ensure that members get the services they need and that claims are paid correctly), in many cases, the systems and business processes are not set up to supply data to each other. They may have been put in place at different times without a vision of how their data may be used together. Data from different processes may be perfectly useable for those processes and still be hard to integrate because of differences in levels of granularity, values used to represent the same concepts, or formatting. All of these conditions are obstacles to data integration and use.

- **Bottom line:** Before you can manage a supply chain, you must understand what it looks like. You can begin by understanding the organization's data architecture and the internal data supply chain. This will allow you to identify risks and opportunities for improving the data supply chain. It is not possible to redesign all systems within an organization so data fits together as logic says it should, so it is necessary to view the data within an organization with an eye toward both risk management and quality. You should expect and identify differences among data from different systems, rather than being surprised by these differences. You should also recognize that the supply chain will evolve as new applications are developed and use these changes as opportunities to define quality requirements up front.

Monitor the Data Production Process

Manufacturing requires a well-defined, well-executed process and reliable inputs. Without these, outputs will be inconsistent. Manufacturing also requires controls to ensure that both the inputs and outputs continue to meet standards and that the process is consistently executed as designed. In addition, the execution of a process may surface flaws in design. Monitoring provides feedback that can be used to improve even a well-designed process.

Data quality can be improved (and to a certain level enforced) through systematically enforced controls. However, data also has organic characteristics. It changes over time in ways that may not be predictable, and there are benefits to allowing its evolution—evolution represents the potential for innovation. But you also must be aware that this evolution is taking place. Measuring data quality allows an organization to detect and respond to emerging changes. As noted earlier, data requirements also change over time. So, for multiple reasons, monitoring data content is critical to keeping knowledge about data current, to helping data consumers use data, and to ongoing improvement of the processes that create data.

The most obvious way to monitor data is to measure it against defined standards. In product management, standards are provided by specifications that clearly describe the expected size and shape of parts. In data quality management, standards are formal rules or other expectations for data, including data quality rules, business rules, or baseline data sets. The idea of measuring against standards depends on the ability to measure, the existence of standards against which to measure, and the ability to interpret the results of measurements in ways that help people better understand the data.

The most obvious way to improve the data supplied to a process is to set clear expectations for the data. Standards used to manage the data supply chain describe requirements for data use. The same standards can be used to measure data quality. Assessment of the data supply chain provides a starting point for characteristics that require standardization for technical reasons. Data that is shared among processes should be created at the same level of grain, using the same values to represent the same characteristics. It should be formatted so that it can be loaded into downstream systems with the least amount of manual intervention.

Standards for measurement should be focused on characteristics of data that are meaningful to data users. Standards should also embody and clarify expectations related to what the data represents. People make data; therefore people can set standards for what they expect from data. For example, address data for customers based in the United States requires accurate Zip codes. Zip codes and the geographic areas associated with them are defined by the US Postal Service. This standard can be used not only to measure the validity of Zip codes, but also to prevent incorrect Zip code/address association. As we will discuss in Chapter 10, the dimensions of quality provide another means to define data standards and meaningful measurements.

Many organizations do not think about data meeting standards. They may have never been asked to think about data this way, or they may simply view data as a "natural" output from a system or process. It's either right or wrong, even though they have not clarified what it means to be right or wrong. Getting people to think about data standards is part of the cultural change required to get them to think differently about data quality as a whole.

- **Bottom line:** Processes will not work as designed by their own accord. They require monitoring that provides feedback on what is working to expectation and what is not. This is why appropriate controls are so important. It also takes time for people to learn processes, recognize their inherent risks, and identify appropriate controls and other opportunities for improvement. Organizations should recognize this and build in time to mature processes. Data standards provide a way to get feedback about the quality of data. It is not necessary to set standards for every piece of data, but it is necessary to establish standards for the most critical data. By taking all three together—the need for standards, the usefulness of controls, and the benefits of actively using feedback to improve processes—organizations can become more efficient as they prevent errors and produce higher-quality data.

Manage the Data Life Cycle

Product quality management advocates that organizations take a comprehensive view of their products by managing for quality through the different phases of the product life cycle (in Juran's terms, this means planning for quality, controlling for quality, and improving quality). This approach accounts for the impact of each phase on the quality of the end product. It requires that, from the start, the organization understands its customers and strives to meet their expectations.

When data is viewed as a by-product, it is an accidental output from a process and does not have its own life cycle. But when it is seen as a product, we can understand it through a life-cycle model and associate quality management processes with the different phases of this life cycle. Data must be created or obtained. If it is designed to any degree, it is designed to meet the requirements of the process through which it is created. (What data is needed to complete a sale? What data is needed to pay a claim? What data is needed to ship a product?) But if it is also viewed as having a purpose beyond this initial stage, it can be created in ways that serve those additional purposes. (What data is needed to assess the potential future sales of a product? What data is needed to help members better manage a chronic health condition? What data is needed to improve on-time delivery?) This idea is extremely important. It goes to the heart of what is meant by "getting value from" or "unlocking the potential of" organizational data. Data represents knowledge about the organization. But this knowledge and its value can only be unlocked if data is used—that is, if it is interpreted and people act on what they learn from it. Put in terms of the data life cycle, data creates value only when it is used. All other phases of the life cycle represent costs. The reason for incurring these costs is to enable an organization to get the value that comes from data use.[15]

The challenges with managing the data life cycle are similar to those of building awareness of data consumers and of managing the data supply chain. Teams work in silos, in part, to get their work done. Not everyone will have time to consider data from an enterprise perspective. They need to only insofar as doing so allows them to do their part. However, some people will need to think

---

[15]Tom Redman has asserted in numerous publications that the two most important moments in the data life cycle are data creation and data use. Danette McGilvray is the person who specifically pointed out to me the observation that data brings value only when it is used (in her POSMAD formulation, "applied"). See Chapter 11.

about the overall enterprise, for example, enterprise architects who have a similar stake in understanding the data life cycle and data governance professionals who want to enable the organization to make better decisions about data. This is especially important because the data life cycle can be complex. It is not as straightforward as the life cycle of physical products. Data can be copied, shared, and transformed as it is used, just as links can be added to the data supply chain each time an application is developed.

- **Bottom line:** To manage the product life cycle of data requires applying all of the principles described here: an enterprise view of data, a commitment to quality, knowledge of data consumers' requirements, the ability to manage production and the data supply chain, the ability to set and measure against standards, and the ability to effectively monitor the processes through which data is produced. As this review shows, the product metaphor for data is not perfect, but it allows us to identify a range of opportunities for improving data quality within an organization. To apply quality principles to data, you must understand not only the quality principles but also the ways data itself works and the role of data within the organization.

Continuously Improve

Continuous improvement includes addressing the root causes (not just the symptoms) of data issues and anomalies. We all know issues arise, but few organizations know this well enough to plan for remediation, even though they could. As importantly, like other products, data evolves. Especially in today's environment, where technology is developing rapidly and organizations are seeking opportunity through data, continuous improvement must be built into the plan.

Coda: Build Quality In

As Juran argues, quality is not an accident. It takes the commitment of the organization, including leadership commitment. Focusing on quality involves a reorientation and requires significant organizational and cultural change. To establish organizational commitment, you will need to engage leadership to change the approach. You must understand the organization, including what it does, how people interact with each other, the role that data plays, the attitude of leadership toward quality in general, and the attitude toward data quality in particular.

The first step is raising awareness and articulating how high-quality data contributes to business strategy and how poor-quality data is an obstacle to the ability of data consumers to do their jobs. It is especially important to raise awareness of the relationships between data producers and data consumers in the organization. Data consumers are customers of data producers. If the two are not aware of this relationship, then data producers do not have the opportunity to meet the requirements and expectations of data consumers. Simple mapping of these relationships will help bring awareness. This can be the starting point to designing data quality requirements into organizational processes.

The Technical Challenge: Data/Technology Balance

6

"The system designer was surprised and said that by sheer 'luck' I had found one of the few errors made by the system.... [Management] would not have allowed a hand-operated system to get so far out of their control."

Russell Ackoff, "Management Misinformation Systems" (1967)

Introduction

This chapter discusses the challenges associated with the interdependence of data and technology, given the rapid evolution of both in today's world. To manage the quality of data, organizations must account for various and evolving forms of data and the technology through which data is created, stored, and used. Technology choices influence the structure of data, the accessibility of data, and the ability to move data into, within, and out of the organization. They influence what data can be collected and how it can be used, even if the data, to a certain degree, can also be made independent of the systems in which it is created. In addition, technical tools are critical to assessing, monitoring, and improving data quality.

The more pressing challenges are organizational. Organizations spend a lot of time and money focused on technology decisions and management of the evolution of technology. This is often to the detriment of the data, which some technologists feel they have no control over (the old "garbage in/garbage out" mentality). If organizations spent as much time focused on data as they do focused on technology, they would have better data and a better basis on which to make decisions about technology. Common misconceptions about the relationship between data and technology contribute to poor-quality data. And technology hype can become a monkey wrench in the works.

Technology and Data

Historically, data has been closely linked to the technologies that enable it to be captured, stored, and analyzed. Although data can be separated from the technical applications through which it is created, our ability to use data in new and potentially advantageous ways is directly connected to advances in technology that enable us to create and store new and different forms of data and to analyze data in ways that offer new perspectives. New technologies are continuously changing the data landscape. But a technology-based understanding of data often ignores the question of data quality because technology is usually indifferent to the core of data quality: data content and meaning. To produce high-quality data, we must understand the impact of technology on data production and use.

Meeting the Challenges of Data Quality Management. DOI: https://doi.org/10.1016/B978-0-12-821737-5.00006-7

New technologies offer significant opportunity to create or enhance the value of data. Value can be understood as increased knowledge and insight from data, increased opportunity to buy and sell data, or a combination of these. Organizations wanting to take advantage of these opportunities can get caught up in the hype around technology and lose sight of the fact that technology, by itself, does not solve problems or capitalize on opportunity. As Evans and Price (2020) have argued: "Business decisions are not based on the availability of technology; they are made on the information delivered by the technology." They further point out that, in the absence of a strategy for managing information assets, "information systems are unlikely to be usable or fit for purpose" (Evans & Price, 2020). High-quality data is required to deliver on the promise of technology. Delivering on this promise also requires people with the knowledge and skills needed to get value from data (see Chapter 7).

Data Is Everywhere

If data were just another process input or output, managing it would take no more thought than managing other inputs and outputs. But data is not just another input or output. Because so many of our transactions and interaction are executed electronically, data is integral to almost every process we execute in business and even in daily life. If we are selling a product, we start with data about that product (e.g., type, size, color, quantity). We collect data about the transaction (e.g., where and when it happened, who sold, who bought, what credit card was used, price, tax). At the end of the month and end of the quarter, we aggregate this data, compare it with past performance, and determine how well the organization is performing. In health care, when a doctor sees a patient, their interactions are captured via electronic data that describes symptoms, diagnoses, procedures, and the like. Similar data collection and storage activities take place if we are applying for a job, making a donation, or even sending an email or text to a friend. In our device-based economy, data production and collection are pervasive. We are living in the middle of a data explosion or a data tsunami—pick your metaphor.

Information Technology Is Evolving Rapidly

The primary reason that data is everywhere is that the technology for capturing, storing, analyzing, and sharing data is everywhere. In far less than a century, we moved from a world in which computers were the stuff of science fiction to one in which almost every device we use is computerized—from our actual computers, to our phones, watches, household appliances, and cars. Even our pets have chips. We are "connected" to each other via electronic devices, and many of our devices themselves are connected to each other via the Internet of Things (IoT). Not only is there more data, but data is also produced much more quickly and in many more different forms than it ever has been before. This change is summarized in data management practices through reference to the three V's of Big Data: volume, velocity, and variety.

Technology is usually seen as a great enabler, and it certainly does enable a wide range of uses of information. The fact that we can collect and aggregate significant amounts of data about what products customers buy under what conditions, how they use these products, and so on, means that businesses can make better informed decisions as they attempt to meet customer needs. They can also more effectively measure the impact of these decisions. In addition to enabling business success, collecting, aggregating, and analyzing data also have the potential to make the world a better place. Better data can help us better understand people's health and safety, our capacity to produce and distribute food, ways to manage the environment, and other processes that affect our quality of life.

But the new technologies and the data they enable also present risks. The amount and type of data that we now routinely collect as part of daily life can just as easily be used for criminal or unethical purposes as for good. And it has been. Data breaches are common, as are examples of data being misused or used in ways that are clearly detrimental to the greater good as well as to individuals (O'Keefe & O Brien, 2018).

Information has always represented both risk and opportunity, and modern technological innovation has increased the potential for both. Poor-quality data generally represents greater risk than high-quality data because poor quality is often the result of processes and applications that are badly designed or badly executed in the first place (O'Neill, 2016).[1] From a data quality management perspective, the rapid evolution of technology is a fact of life and not likely to slow down. Although organizations cannot anticipate every change, they can better account for the condition of constant change. To do so, it is critical to understand how new technologies define, collect, and manipulate data (i.e., how they influence the production of data products) and to work with data consumers to define their expectations and criteria for the quality of data produced in innovative ways.

As noted in the chapter introduction, many challenges with technology management are not technical but organizational. Technology is expensive. It takes technical expertise to implement new technologies so they operate efficiently and reliably. Large projects organized to implement new applications or new tools often go more slowly than planned. People get frustrated. Once an organization has sunk money into a project, it is difficult to pull back and cut losses. Information technology (IT) departments get a bad rap. Businesspeople create workarounds. Tensions flare. None of this helps the work get done or improves the quality of data. Instead, these situations make it more difficult to clarify and meet data consumers' requirements.

The Dangers of Technology Hype

The rapid evolution of technology creates opportunity to create value through data in the form of increased knowledge and insight. It also creates a lot of hype. The word *hype* refers to intensive publicity or promotion. Hype about new technologies is almost always misleading because it focuses on the most interesting or provocative possibilities offered by new technologies, without accounting for costs or limitations (Funk, 2019). The hype around technology is such a big challenge that the consulting firm Gartner developed a way to analyze it to help organizations

---

[1] In *Weapons of Math Destruction*, a study of the use and impact of Big Data on daily life, Cathy O'Neill describes numerous instances of poorly designed analyses that have direct negative effects on individuals. For some of the easiest examples to understand, she draws on her experience in the financial industry before the 2008 depression. Much less obvious examples include ways that algorithms are used in granting mortgages, hiring, rating colleges, and other processes that significantly affect the lives of individuals. Added to the problem of poor design producing unreliable data that people nevertheless believe in because it comes from an "algorithm," the resulting bad information can now be spread much more rapidly and affect many more people. For additional examples, see Schryvers (2020).

understand what to believe about new technologies—the Gartner Hype Cycle (Fenn & Blosch, 2018). One of the first things people hyping new technologies seem to forget is that the value to be gained through these technologies depends on the quality of the data.

The hype around data lakes provides a good example. Just the title of the 2014 book, *Big Data: A Revolution That Will Transform How We Live, Work, and Think* by Viktor Mayer-Schönberger and Kenneth Cukier, provides a sense of it (Mayer-Schönberger & Cukier, 2014). In case you did not get the message from the title itself, the book's description continues, "Big Data is a revolution occurring around us, in the process of forever changing economics, science, culture, and the very way we think.… What we have already seen is just the tip of the iceberg.… *Big Data* is the first major book about this earthshaking subject." Obviously, part of the hype here is simply an effort to market the book. That said, Mayer-Schönberger and Cukier make this "revolution" seem easy by downplaying the importance of data quality in Big Data environments and, with it, the work required to manage data: "Often, Big Data is messy, varies in quality …. What we lose in accuracy at the micro level we gain in insight at the macro level."

As discussed in Chapter 1, people who first hyped the possibilities of data lakes presented them as alternatives to data warehouses. In a data lake, data scientists will be able to bring in all of the data they need and mash it together to magically produce "insights," without having to go through all of the work required to set up a data warehouse—all of the data modeling, metadata management, documentation of transformation rules, and coding of extract, transform, and load (ETL) processes required for traditional data warehouses and marts. These people forget that data warehouses were also hyped as somewhat magical solutions to the problem of data integration. And we now have statistics that show data scientists spend 60% of their time cleansing or preparing data for use and only 40% of their time doing productive data analysis (Press, 2016).

In the early 2020s, there is a lot of hype around machine learning (ML) and artificial intelligence (AI). Even *Forbes* magazine cannot restrain itself when it talks about "mind-blowing things AI can already do today." Similarly, a 2019 article in *Built-in*, "The Future of Artificial Intelligence: 7 ways AI can change the world for better…or worse," can hardly contain its enthusiasm. After describing the use (or potential use) of AI in transportation, manufacturing, health care, education, the media, and customer service, the author declares, "But those advances … are only the beginning; there's much more to come—more than anyone, even the most prescient prognosticators, can fathom" (Thomas, 2019). But the biggest risks involved with ML and AI are directly related to the quality of the data used as input. As data quality thought leader Tom Redman puts it:

> Poor data quality is enemy number one to the widespread, profitable use of machine learning. While the caustic observation, "garbage-in, garbage-out" has plagued analytics and decision-making for generations, it carries a special warning for machine learning. The quality demands of machine learning are steep, and bad data can rear its ugly head twice—first in the historical data used to train the predictive model and second in the new data used by that model to make future decisions (Redman, 2018).

As noted earlier, organizations wanting to take advantage of the opportunities presented by advances in technology can lose sight of the fact that technology, by itself, does not solve problems. People must make decisions about how to use technology to support the organization's mission. And data is required to deliver on the promise of technology. By itself, technology cannot overcome the limitations of low-quality data.

Leadership should also recognize that not every technology must be adopted by every organization. In this respect, managing the hype is necessary to managing strategy. In planning for the technology required to support the business, the organization must focus on its own goals, not on the goals proposed by vendors. When these do intersect, there is opportunity. Reliable technology that improves efficiency and quality can provide a competitive edge. When they do not intersect, however, there is waste and shelfware.

With regard to data quality management, technology hype has additional repercussions. Data quality is often talked about in terms of technology. Organizations purchase "data quality tools" that are touted as the solution to undefined or vaguely defined data quality problems or to every possible problem an organization might have with data (except, of course, poorly define business processes). These tools will cleanse data, profile data, and even evaluate "data quality and structure within and across heterogeneous systems."[2] They don't say: These tools will only do these things if you can tell them what your expectations for the data are. Data cannot be cleansed without cleansing rules or validated without validation criteria. It cannot be standardized without standards. In other words, if you do not know what you mean by high-quality data, the tools cannot help you improve your data because you will not know what you want to accomplish with the tools. Technology alone will not solve data quality problems, and in the absence of clearly defined standards and reliable processes, technology can make these problems worse by providing the organization with a false sense of confidence that they are doing something to improve the quality of their data, when what they are really doing is turning data assets into liabilities.

Even Gartner sends mixed messages. On one hand, their proposed Data Quality Operating Model recognizes the need to address perennial problems: addressing issues reactively, not measuring data quality, implementing initiatives and solutions in silos, and failing to build strong partnerships across the enterprise, not to mention business leaders' continued belief "that data quality is a technical concern, rather than a business concern" (Chien et al., 2020). On the other hand, Gartner's definition of *data quality* ("The term *data quality* relates to the processes and technologies for identifying, understanding and correcting flaws in data that support effective data and analytics governance across operational business processes and decision making") completely leaves out the process of data creation and the opportunity to prevent errors in the first place (Chien & Ankush, 2021). This definition equates data quality with data correction.

The Tension Between Data and Information Technology

The rapid evolution of IT brings attention to the relationship between any technology and data created through it. Creating data has long entailed creating data-collection instruments. Some of these instruments have become integral to our understanding of the world and to everyday life. Think of the clock, the telescope, the microscope, the barometer, and the thermometer. The thermometer is

[2]IBM's marketing for Infosphere. https://www.ibm.com/us-en/marketplace/infosphere-information-analyzer. See also https://www.gartner.com/reviews/market/data-quality-tools.

not only a measurement device. It is through the invention of the thermometer that we develop the very concept of temperature. It is through the clock that we developed our concept of time.

Most people associate IT with data, not only because of the modern definition of *data* as "transmittable and storable information by which computer operations are performed," but also because before we started calling IT *information technology*, it was called things like *data processing, data management*, and *database administration*. Large computers that stored data were called *data banks*. The idea was that we can put a lot of data into these machines.

Still, almost since the introduction of computers and IT, there has been an ambivalent relationship between the information/data and the technology—or better put, between the people who create or use the data and the people who manage and develop the technology. Data does not always behave in ways technology and technologists would like it to. This has become even more the case as the ability of computers to collect different kinds of information has expanded.

At the heart of this ambivalence is a gap. Technologists recognize that they do not have control over a lot of data. If the data is not as expected, then the technology will not produce reliable results. They express this recognition through the oft quipped refrain: "Garbage in/garbage out." This ambivalence has existed for a long time. The founding document of information theory, Claude Shannon's *A Mathematical Theory of Communication* (1948), starts with the separation of meaning from information. Shannon asserts that, "These semantic aspects [i.e., the meaning or content of the data] of communications are irrelevant to the engineering problem. The significant aspect is that the actual message is one selected from a set of possible messages" (Shannon, 1948). At its worst, this means that from an engineering perspective, the message can be "garbage" as long as the "solution," to paraphrase Shannon, "enables the receiver to select the intended garbage from the set of possible garbages." Warren Weaver makes clear that Shannon used the word *information* in a very technical sense (Shannon & Weaver, 1949).

One effect of the ambivalent relationship between technologists and data is that there is a strong separation between people responsible for the technology that is used to manage data and the data itself. Even though they work in "data management," technologists generally do not see themselves as responsible for data. They are responsible for the hardware, the software, and the execution of technical processes, not for the data content. Sometimes, they disown even the responsibility to have a basic understanding of what the data represents.

This position is symptomatic of a general problem in complex organizations: no one is seen as directly responsible for data. But it is also a problem because, ultimately, the data represents the processes through which it is created; and everyone who works for an organization should have a basic understanding of what the organization does and how it does it. For example, I work in health care. Though I have never processed a claim, I know what a claim is and what information it contains. I also understand what it means to process one. It would be irresponsible of me not to know fundamental things about how a health care company operates. Technologists can bring a type of knowledge that others do not possess; specifically, knowledge of the details of how data is brought into and integrated into complex systems, how it is structured, and the best ways to access it. Without this knowledge, it can be difficult for the people who execute data production processes to understand and use the data. But if the two pieces are not connected—if the business process and the technical process are not perceived as two sides of the same coin—then they may not correspond in expected ways, including what the output (data) looks like.

Codd, the Relational Model, and Data Independence

In the early 1970s, another IT thought leader, E.F. Codd, introduced the relational data model, which offered a different way of looking at the relationship between data and the technology used to store and access it (Codd, 1970). Codd was trying to solve several problems connected with data management practices at the time, including reducing maintenance costs and improving the ability of end users to understand and access data. At the time, the two most common practices for structuring data for retrieval were trees and networks. Both practices required detailed knowledge of how data was physically situated in a specific system. You could not get the data out of the system if you did not know how it went into the system. The relational model greatly simplified how data could be stored and retrieved. It also helped people better understand concepts around data structure.

Among the goals of Codd's work was what he called the "data independence objective" by which he meant separating the logical purpose of the system (its data) from the physical setup of the application (the representation of the data within a database system). In addition to simplifying data structure, Codd's relational model accounts for the idea that data will evolve. The data independence objective acknowledges that data evolves through "growth in data types and changes in data representation—and certain kinds of data inconsistency which are expected to become troublesome, even in nondeductive systems" (Codd, 1970). Codd also recognizes that different systems create data in different ways and that the relational model also enables "communication of bulk data between systems which use widely different representations of the data" (Codd, 1970).

Codd's work ushered the concept of the data model and practices around modeling data. In creating a relational data model, an organization prepares itself to integrate data from different systems. Data modeling depends on defining the meaning of entities and attributes and the ways entities relate to each other. It provides an opportunity to define data separate from systems and to precisely define specific data requirements (Hoberman, 2009).

The International Organization for Standardization (ISO) acknowledges the connection to technology in its definition of *data* as "re-interpretable representation of information in a formalized manner suitable for communication, interpretation, or processing" (ISO 11179).[3] ISO's standard for data quality (ISO 8000), which defines quality data as "portable data that meets stated requirements," recognizes a debt to Codd's insight that data should be separable from the system in which it is created. Data that is completely dependent on the system in which it is created is not high-quality data, by definition, because it can be used in only one place. To ensure portability, ISO 8000 "specifies requirements for the declaration of syntax and semantic encoding." This means, for data to be used outside of the system in which it is created (and often, for it to be used within such a system), the meaning of the data and the technical and nontechnical means by which that meaning is encoded (the conventions through which information is represented) must be known to the people and processes that use the data. In other words, metadata is required for people and processes to understand and use data.

---

[3]An alternate ISO definition of *data*: A representation of facts, concepts, or instructions in a formalized manner, suitable for communication, interpretation, or processing by humans or by automatic means (ISO 2382-4).

Accounting for the Imprint of Technology

Codd's work is important for many reasons. One of them is that he does not think of data simply as "transmittable and storable information by which computer operations are performed," as Shannon put it. Instead, he recognizes that data conveys meaning and that the people who use data are using it because it conveys meaning. That said, there are some purists who take Codd's principle of data independence to an extreme and imply that data should always be seen as completely separate from technology, and that, because of this, technology does not directly affect data. This ignores the fact that technical choices have direct effects on the quality of data.

For purposes of access and retrieval (the problems Codd was focused on), the data independence approach is vitally important. However, when we consider the other end of the supply chain—data production or creation—we cannot ignore the imprint of technology on data. The technical applications through which data is created influence many aspects of data, including the attributes that can be collected, the relationship among attributes, the values that may be used to represent specific attributes, data granularity, the precision of data within a column, the level of validation, the data format, and details of the conventions of representation. While it is possible to separate data from the system in which it is created, that system will nevertheless leave an imprint on the data. Not only does technology have direct effects on the structure, format, and content of data, it also has indirect effects. People may not be able to use technology as designed. Or they may not want to because the technology may not actually work the way they need it to. In such cases, people may develop workarounds, which result in lower-quality data (Alter, 2014). This is another argument for designing the data before designing the technology through which it will be produced.

Although the relational model brings us closer to data independence, data almost always bears the marks of the systems in which it is created, whether those systems are notebooks, spreadsheets, mainframes, or Python programs. Some technological solutions produce data that does not play nicely with other data. This can be the result of technical choices (e.g., the platform on which the data is created, the format in which the data is generated) or for nontechnical reasons (one system records measurements using the metric system, another one uses the imperial system). Differences in units of measure and in the values of codified data are obvious. They should be easy to discern and address—if data requirements are assessed and understood before systems are developed. Structural differences should also be detectable, but people do not always look for them. Two examples can show this. The first focuses on differences in data format; the second focuses on differences in the assumptions built into tools used to query data.

Example: Format Differences in Tax Identification Numbers

A tax identification number (TIN) is a nine-digit identifier issued by the US Internal Revenue Service (IRS) to aid in the administration of tax laws. TINs function similarly to Social Security numbers (SSNs). Within health care data, a provider's TIN is often used as a de facto identifier for doctors, hospitals, and other provider entities. TINs can be used to aggregate all claims. They are also critical to understanding which entities are being paid for which services. Unfortunately, the rules around TINs can be somewhat confusing. For example, a simple Google search will reveal that a TIN must contain nine digits and cannot begin with a leading zero, but individual providers can use their SSN as a TIN, and SSNs can have a leading zero.

Table 6 Counts and percentages of provider TIN formats from four claim systems (~1 month of medical claims).

TIN length	System A (count)	System A (%)	System B (count)	System B (%)	System C (count)	System C (%)	System D (count)	System D (%)
9	65,787,627	95.8024	49,220,583	94.8576	9,971,828	97.8970	6,595,216	100
8	2,747,086	4.0004	2,533,048	4.8817	214,038	2.1013	0	0
7	5,097	0.0074	4,939	0.0095	158	0.0016	0	0
6	3	0.0000	1	0.0000	2	0.0000	0	0
5	2	0.0000	2	0.0000	0	0.0000	0	0
4	130,324	0.1898	130,322	0.2512	11	0.0001	0	0
0	6	0.0000	0	0.0000	6	0.0001	0	0
Total	68,670,145		51,888,895		10,186,043		6,595,216	

The problem comes with how TINs (and in some cases SSNs) are stored. If they are stored as numeric data (data type = number), the leading zeros will be dropped. If they are stored as characters or text, the leading zeros will be retained. The benefit of storing these identifiers as numbers is that it makes data processing simpler. It is easier to sort and organize numeric data. Also, if they are stored with the knowledge that they require leading zeros, then they can be presented to data consumers in the correct format (with leading zeros). However, if they are stored as numbers and the people developing the system do not know that the leading zero is important, then the data will not meet the needs of data consumers. If TINs are stored with different data types in different systems, then additional challenges will arise with data use.

Table 6 shows the counts and percentages of different formats for TINs across four claim systems. The table aggregates 1 month's worth of claim data. In systems A and B, over 4% of the data does not meet the simple format requirement that the TIN be nine digits long. In system C, a little more than 2% of the data does not meet this expectation. In all three systems, most of the problem is associated with records that have TINs that are eight digits long. Analysis showed that the problem was caused by storing the TIN as a numeric data type, rather than storing it as text or as character data type.

The data reveals other problems as well. In systems A and B, approximately 0.2% of records have only four digits. This issue was connected to another tax identifier, the PIN, which the IRS issues to some taxpayers. Here, the TIN owners submitted the wrong identifier on some claims (the PIN instead of the TIN). Table 6 also shows that, in both system A and system B, a set of records have seven digits. In both cases, these records comprise less than a thousandth of a percentage of the total, but there are still several thousand of them in each system. It is not clear why these records are populated in this way. There are also a few records with lengths of six and five as well as some that are missing altogether. In contrast, in system D, which has a rule in place to format the TIN, all records have the same format—the correct length of nine digits for all TINs.

Example: Differences in Querying Tools

Just as different systems may use different data types and lengths to store the same logical data attribute, so too will query tools embed different assumptions about the precision of data that they present. Here is an example. An analyst wanted to compare a set of records for a month of data to results in the general ledger, using a column that captured year-to-date actuals data. The analyst used "the same" query twice; running it first using Apache Hive, Hadoop's native querying capability, and then using SAS.

The analyst knew there was a problem because the two queries returned different record counts. SAS returned over 8,000 records, while the Hive query returned only 7,200. The analyst observed that all of the records in SAS and missing from Hive had year-to-date actual amounts of less than 50 cents absolute value. After inspecting the records, the analyst concluded that Apache Hive excluded records with values that rounded to zero. Twenty-two percent of these records contained values of either one cent or negative one cent (0.01 or −0.01). The difference in the total amount represented by the two record sets was less than $20. But the cost of this issue was high. Identifying the problem, defining it, doing the analysis, determining the root cause of the difference, and reviewing this with stakeholders amounted to more than 20 hours of work.

What these examples imply for data quality management is straightforward to describe, even if it is difficult to implement: the people designing the systems through which data is produced must recognize and account for the impact of technology on the creation, storage, and use of data. The primary criterion for whether a technical solution will meet business requirements should be whether it supports the production and use of high-quality data. Again, drawing on the product model of data, the idea of data design is critical to high-quality data. Planned data is higher-quality data than accidental data. Data that is standardized across an organization via the production process can be integrated more easily than data that is not standardized. Its quality can be more easily managed because expectations for quality can be defined in the standards. Most importantly, it will be easier for data consumers to use, because they will understand what it means and how it fits together.

Yet planning and design for the data itself is sometimes ignored during the process of application design. Planning requires information architects to understand data meaning (what the data is intended to represent) and to develop and apply data standards. But it is also critical that they understand how data is created and what impact the technical means of its production may have on the output. Even data consumers need at least a basic understanding of how data production technologies work, what problems they are intended to solve, and how they interact with other systems. If an organization does not plan for usable data, then it will most likely create data that is difficult to integrate and, ultimately, difficult to use.

IT Funding Models Contribute to the Tension

The conceptual data/technology divide is mirrored by the organizational business/IT divide. Joe McKendrick (2018) from *Forbes* describes the scramble for funding: "Every effort tends to be departmentalized and gets funded by separate business units, who don't necessarily want to share with the rest of the enterprise. Even if corporate announces some kind of centralized funding initiative, a scramble takes place among departments for supporting their individual efforts."

Although McKendrick is writing in the context of digital transformation, his characterization of the process is accurate more generally as well. IT funding is not usually about executing a comprehensive strategy. It is about competing for resources within the enterprise, almost always without regard for the greater good. This is not good for the organization, not good for the people, and not good for the data. It increases the risk that IT will succumb to technology hype because hyped products make big, sexy promises that make everything sound simple and can be quickly converted to business cases that look good on *PowerPoint* slides. When promised benefits fail to materialize or take significantly longer than planned to materialize, the tensions between IT and businesspeople reemerge or intensify.

Meeting the Challenges

Meeting the challenge of putting data and technology in the right relationship is a matter of perspective and balance. This is not an easy task, especially because there is a long history of separating the two. In addition, in many organizations, funding structures and organizational politics work to re-enforce the perspective that the two should be kept separate. The people who work in technology rarely use the data they manage. The people who use data often do not understand the intricacies of technology. There are many visible and direct costs to managing technology. There are many hidden and indirect costs to managing the quality of data. It is easier to see the costs and benefits of technology and harder to see those related to data. Technology is a defined thing. There are systems and applications to be built, operated, and maintained. These are owned and managed by named people. Data is everywhere in the organization, and it moves around. Ownership is not clearly defined, so no one is advocating for the data itself when the scramble for funding launches. Yet data and technology are also obviously and directly connected. The creation and use of data depend on technology. Technology applications are put in place to enable the organization to execute processes that create or use data, or both.

No one would disagree with the idea that gaining perspective and achieving the right balance requires looking at the organization holistically, understanding it as a system, and aligning technology and data goals with business goals. Most organizations try, at some level, to do this. However, very few put data before technology, and very few actively cultivate the idea that as the customers of IT teams, businesspeople see data, not technology, as the product that IT delivers. And these two things are what must change.

Put Data First

The need to understand requirements for data before requirements for technology has long been recognized by people within the data quality management space (English, 1999; Redman, 1997) as well as in the information architecture space (Evernden & Evernden, 2003).

Success depends a lot on the kind of organizational self-knowledge that can be gained by clarifying the desired relationship among business process, data, and technology. An enterprise architecture team can play a critical role in defining this relationship because by definition, it is charged with developing an enterprise perspective on data and technology. It is not only enterprise architects, but IT overall, who can change their relationship to data. IT sees data in ways that businesspeople often do not. This can be incredibly valuable. The challenge is acknowledging this perspective and enabling more productive knowledge sharing between technical and nontechnical people.

Design Quality In

Putting data first necessarily means ensuring that data is of high quality. Here technology can truly be part of the solution. Systems can be designed to build quality in, through controls that prevent errors and guide the success of business processes. Building them to do so requires a combination of knowledge: knowledge of the goals of the process the system supports, the data it requires or produces, and an understanding of the ways that technology can improve efficiency or reduce the complexity of the process. A single individual will not be able to do this on his or her own. Getting there requires a combination of the following:

- **Process improvements:** For example, ensuring that project processes include the definition of data quality requirements and the assessment of data against quality expectations and standards.
- **Improved collaboration and communication** between IT and their customers—the business process owners who want to gain efficiency through automation and the analysts who want to gain insight from data.

Remember That Businesspeople Are IT Customers

For better or worse, IT funding models, project processes, and organizational politics can mess up the relationship between IT and their customers, often to the point where people forget that they work for the same organization. To their credit, many in IT try to improve the situation though the adoption of Agile and other development methodologies, which are structured to promote better interactions between project teams and their customers. Improvement begins by acknowledging the customer relationship. This does not mean adopting a "Just following orders" mentality. It means helping customers understand their needs and figuring out how to meet these needs.

Improving an organization's ability to get value from data requires having technology that supports these efforts and people who understand that technology. It also requires having people who understand and can use data—people who are data literate. This will be the subject of Chapter 7.

Bringing about sustainable change to long-ingrained habits and ways of interacting, however, requires defining desired behaviors around data and working with people to adopt these behaviors. It also means making these behaviors part of organizational culture through agreed-to accountability models for data. This data governance work, supported by managed culture change driven by organizational leadership, is the subject of Chapter 8.

The People Challenge: Building Data Literacy

7

"This is indeed a mystery," I remarked. *"What do you imagine that it means?"*
"I have no data yet. It is a capital mistake to theorize before one has data. Insensibly one begins to twist facts to suit theories, instead of theories to suit facts. But the note itself. What do you deduce from it?"

Dr. Watson and Sherlock Holmes, "A Scandal in Bohemia"

"Waste of knowledge, in the sense of failure of a company to use knowledge that is there and available for development is ... deplorable."

W. Edwards Deming, *Out of the Crisis*

Introduction

The same challenges that get in the way of managing the quality of data can also be obstacles to creating and using data: the nature of data itself; its function in representing human observations about the world; the heterogeneity of data within organizations; the technical, process, and cultural challenges that can make data seem opaque and indecipherable; and the lack of clarity about who should be accountable for data and in what ways accountability should be defined. Some of these can be addressed through better data design, better metadata, and the production of higher-quality data in the first place. But data still does not speak for itself. The people using data within an organization must have the knowledge, skills, and experience to understand and interpret it. They must be, to some degree, "data literate."

Data literacy is the ability to read, understand, interpret, and learn from data in different contexts. It also includes the individual's ability to apply what is learned to different contexts, including communicating about data to other people.[1] This chapter will explore the concept of data literacy in order to propose ways to improve and cultivate the skills needed to be data literate. We will start with assertions and models of general literacy and then propose several different models of data literacy. With these models in mind, we will do a short experiment that involves looking at data about data literacy. This experiment will demonstrate basic skills required to understand data. We will describe the components of data literacy—the

---

[1]Gartner defines *data literacy* as "the ability to read, write and communicate data in context, including an understanding of data sources and constructs, analytical methods and techniques applied—and the ability to describe the use case, application and resulting value" (Gartner Glossary). This definition, which is referenced in multiple articles on data literacy, is useful and appears to be emerging as a standard, but I wish it were a little less jargony. In contrast, EWSolutions defines *data literacy* simply as "the ability to derive meaningful information from the proper understanding and use of data."

Meeting the Challenges of Data Quality Management. DOI: https://doi.org/10.1016/B978-0-12-821737-5.00007-9

knowledge, skills, and experience that people and organizations must build and cultivate if they are to understand and learn from their data. We will end by discussing the implications of not building data literacy.

The focus here is on data literacy within the organization. Higher literacy levels help the organization meet the people challenge by ensuring that those who create and use data have the knowledge and skills to access, use, and interpret data. Data literacy, which rests on a foundation of general literacy, requires both general knowledge about data and specific knowledge about data in their organization. Along the way, I will call out some observations that are particularly important for people working in data quality management.

A Few Assumptions

Data Literacy and General Literacy

Data literacy skills are directly dependent on general literacy—the ability to read, understand, and learn from written texts—as well as knowledge of mathematics and science. Understanding data is a specialized form of reading. *Numeracy*, the ability to understand and interpret numbers, from basic mathematical functions (addition, subtraction, multiplication, division) through complex statistics, describes a skill set necessary to data literacy. Knowledge of the scientific method, which describes how to define data and collect data required to answer questions and test hypotheses, is also part of data literacy.

Literacy as a Continuum

General literacy skills are understood as part of a continuum, or a set of stages, in which a person develops the skills and knowledge that provide the foundation for the next stage. Reading starts with learning the alphabet, developing comprehension skills, comprehending the role of grammatical structures, all the while gaining knowledge and experience needed to understand and engage with texts of increasing complexity. All stages require knowledge of words and grammar, but as a person reads more, he or she will also develop skills in interpreting and evaluating texts.

As with general literacy, people can have different levels of data literacy. Just as you do not need to be a literature professor to be literate, you do not need to be a scientist or statistician to be data literate. However, you do need to understand something about "data as data." Throughout this chapter, as I discuss general data literacy skills, keep in mind that these are part of a continuum. Just as there are different levels of general literacy, there are different levels of data literacy.

Let's look at some examples of how people understand general literacy. Tables 8–11 present phases, or progressions of skills that describe the literacy continuum. Each implies a different story about what it means to be literate. Table 7 describes the stages a child goes through when learning to read. This information comes from the Edvocate, a website that advocates for "education reform, equity, and innovation." The story it tells is that of the emergent reader. The child, exposed to print materials early on, at first struggles to comprehend them, but begins to develop the necessary skills,

Table 7 The five stages of reading development.[2]

Reading stage	Reading stage description
Stage 1: The emergent reader (6 months to 6 years)	During the initial phase of the reading development process, children sample and learn from a full range of multiple sounds, words, concepts, images, stories, exposure to print, literacy materials, and just plain talk during the first five years of life.
Stage 2: The novice reader (6−7 years)	During the second phase of the reading development process, children are learning the relationships between letters and sounds and among printed and spoken words. The child begins to read stories with high-frequency words and phonically regular words and uses emerging skills and insights to "sound out" new one-syllable words.
Stage 3: The decoding reader (7−9 years)	During the third phase of the reading development process, children are beginning to read familiar stories and text with increasing fluency. This is accomplished by consolidating the foundational decoding elements, sight vocabulary, and meaning in the reading of stories and selections that the child is already familiar with.
Stage 4: The fluent, comprehending reader (9−15 years)	During the fourth phase of the reading development process, reading is used to acquire new ideas to gain new knowledge, to experience new feelings, to acquire new attitudes, and to explore issues from multiple perspectives. Reading includes the study of textbooks, reference works, trade books, newspapers, and magazines that contain new ideas and values, new vocabulary, and syntax.
Stage 5: The expert reader (from 16 years)	During the fifth phase of the reading development process, the learner is reading from a wide range of advanced materials, both expository and narrative, with multiple viewpoints. Learners are reading broadly across the disciplines, including the physical, biological, and social sciences as well as the humanities, politics, and current affairs.

[2]*From Lynch, M. (2019). What are the Five Stages of Reading Development? The Edvocate (website). March 13, 2019. https://www.theedadvocate.org/what-are-the-five-stages-of-reading-development/.*

Table 8 Progression of skills associated with analyzing texts.[3]

Level and year	Sub-element: Interpret and analyse learning area texts
Level 1—End of Foundation Year	Students interpret simple texts using comprehension strategies.
Level 2—End of Year 2	Students interpret and use texts to explore topics, gather information, and make some obvious inferences using comprehension strategies.
Level 3—End of Year 4	Students interpret literal information and make inferences to expand topic knowledge using comprehension strategies.
Level 4—End of Year 6	Students interpret and analyse information and ideas, comparing texts on similar topics or themes using comprehension strategies.
Level 5—End of Year 8	Students interpret and evaluate information, identify main ideas and supporting evidence, and analyse different perspectives using comprehension strategies.
Level 6—End of Year 10	Students interpret and evaluate information within and between texts, comparing and contrasting information using comprehension strategies.

[3]*From Australian Curriculum, Assessment and Reporting Authority (ACARA) (n.d.). F-10 Curriculum, General Capabilities, Literacy (website). https://www.australiancurriculum.edu.au/media/3596/general-capabilities-literacy-learning-continuum.pdf.*

and at last is able to master the complexity of the written word. This process enables the learner to gain knowledge, experience new feelings, and recognize multiple viewpoints.

Table 8, based on information from the Australian Curriculum, Assessment and Reporting Authority (ACARA), focuses on a specific skill set—interpreting and analyzing texts. This list is part of a larger matrix that describes the overall set of skills students are expected to learn as part of public education in Australia. The student starts the journey of interpretation simply by trying to comprehend basic texts. Over time, the student develops skill in making inferences, evaluating evidence, and recognizing different perspectives. This set of skills allows the student to evaluate information by comparing and contrasting different sources. At the end of year 10, the student is able to apply these skills to comprehend a wider a range of texts.

Table 9 is published by the Literacy Cooperative, an Ohio-based group that seeks to "bring broad attention to issues of access, quality, and learner progression and transitions" and to influence public policy. This list focuses not on the development of skills in students, but on the activities that adults are able to engage in at different levels of literacy. The list itself is based on US federal government standards for literacy. Its story contains an underlying message: some people have not mastered skills in reading. Their opportunities are limited. Let's educate people to ensure that they have the skills they need to succeed in today's world.

Finally, from an international study of adult literacy levels, Table 10 describes criteria for tasks that a person might accomplish at different levels of literacy, based on both the complexity of the texts themselves and the ability of the reader to process and use written information (Goodman et al., 2013). These criteria are defined to be tested against so literacy levels can be measured. At "below level 1," a person has some ability to read, but very limited ability to learn from written information. As we move to the higher levels, the skills required to understand written information develop and are honed as the complexity of that information increases. A person at level 5 not only possesses a foundation of background knowledge of the text's context, he or she is also able to recognize and understand the nuances in texts and the implications of subtleties in presentation. At this level, a person is able to evaluate the reliability of different sets of written information based on a wide range of factors.

Table 9 Adult literacy skills as defined by the US federal government.[4]	
Literacy level	**Example skills/abilities**
People at Level 1 can	Locate one piece of information in a sports article Locate the expiration date on a driver's license Total a bank deposit entry
People at Level 2 can	Interpret appliance warranty instructions Locate an intersection on a street map Calculate postage and fees when using certified mail
People at Level 3 can	Write a brief letter to explain a credit card billing error Use a bus schedule to choose the correct bus to take to get to work on time Determine the discount on a car insurance bill if paid in full within 15 days
People at Level 4 can	Explain the difference between two types of benefits at work Calculate the correct change when given prices on a menu
People at Level 5 can	Compare and summarize different approaches lawyers use during a trial Use information in a table to compare two credit cards and explain the differences Compute the cost to carpet a room in a house

[4]*From The Literacy Cooperative. (n.d.). Literacy Levels. https://www.literacycooperative.org/literacy-facts/literacy-levels/.*

Table 10 Adult literacy levels as defined in the study: Literacy, numeracy, and problem solving in technology-rich environments among U.S. adults: Results from the Program for the International Assessment of Adult Competencies 2012.[5]

Proficiency level	Literacy task description
Below level 1	The tasks at this level require the respondent to read brief texts on familiar topics to locate a single piece of specific information. Only basic vocabulary knowledge is required, and the reader is not required to understand the structure of sentences or paragraphs or make use of other text features. There is seldom any competing information in the text and the requested information is identical in form to information in the question or directive. While the texts can be continuous, the information can be located as if the text were non-continuous. As well, tasks below level 1 do not make use of any features specific to digital texts.
Level 1	Most of the tasks at this level require the respondent to read relatively short digital or print continuous, non-continuous, or mixed texts to locate a single piece of information which is identical to or synonymous with the information given in the question or directive. Some tasks may require the respondent to enter personal information onto a document, in the case of some non-continuous texts. Little, if any, competing information is present. Some tasks may require simple cycling through more than one piece of information. Knowledge and skill in recognizing basic vocabulary, evaluating the meaning of sentences, and reading of paragraph text is expected.
Level 2	At this level, the complexity of text increases. The medium of texts may be digital or printed, and texts may be comprised of continuous, non-continuous, or mixed types. Tasks in this level require respondents to make matches between the text and information and may require paraphrase or low-level inferences. Some competing pieces of information may be present. Some tasks require the respondent to cycle through or integrate two or more pieces of information based on criteria, compare and contrast or reason about information requested in the question, or navigate within digital texts to access-and-identify information from various parts of a document.
Level 3	Texts at this level are often dense or lengthy, including continuous, non-continuous, mixed, or multiple pages. Understanding text and rhetorical structures become more central to successfully completing tasks, especially in navigation of complex digital texts. Tasks require the respondent to identify, interpret, or evaluate one or more pieces of information, and often require varying levels of inferencing. Many tasks require the respondent construct meaning across larger chunks of text or perform multi-step operations in order to identify and formulate responses. Often tasks also demand that the respondent disregard irrelevant or inappropriate text content to answer accurately. Competing information is often present, but it is not more prominent than the correct information.
Level 4	Tasks at this level often require respondents to perform multiple-step operations to integrate, interpret, or synthesize information from complex or lengthy continuous, non-continuous, mixed, or multiple type texts. Complex inferences and application of background knowledge may be needed to perform successfully. Many tasks require identifying and understanding one or more specific, non-central ideas in the text in order to interpret or evaluate subtle evidence-claim or persuasive discourse relationships. Conditional information is frequently present in tasks at this level and must be taken into consideration by the respondent. Competing information is present and sometimes seemingly as prominent as correct information.
Level 5	At this level, tasks may require the respondent to search for and integrate information across multiple, dense texts; construct syntheses of similar and contrasting ideas or points of view; or evaluate evidenced based arguments. Application and evaluation of logical and conceptual models of ideas may be required to accomplish tasks. Evaluating reliability of evidentiary sources and selecting key information is frequently a key requirement. Tasks often require respondents to be aware of subtle, rhetorical cues and to make high-level inferences or use specialized background knowledge.

[5]From Goodman, M., Finnegan, R., Mohadjer, L., Krenzke, T., Hogan, J. (2013). Literacy, numeracy, and problem solving in technology-rich environments among U.S. adults: Results from the Program for the International Assessment of Adult Competencies 2012: First Look (NCES 2014-008). U.S. Department of Education. Washington, DC: National Center for Education Statistics. https://nces.ed.gov/pubs2014/2014008.pdf.

Models of Data Literacy

Each of the literacy tables represents a model of what general literacy means by describing how literacy may evolve through a progression of stages. In doing so, each table provides insight on what such a progression may look like for data literacy. We can think of a series of continuums that describe the movement from:

- Being a novice data analyst to being an expert data analyst
- Comprehending basic data characteristics to possessing a wide range of strategies to understand and interpret data
- Using data to answer simple questions to using data to answer complex questions
- Using simple and familiar data to being able to explore, evaluate, and describe the reliability of data as part of the process of interpreting it and sharing insights with others

There is still a lot of work, hopefully research-based,[6] required to create sound models of data literacy that provide ways of understanding the skills people need to use data within organizations. As starting point, it helps to propose working models. Tables 11−13 present three sketches of possible models of data literacy, each with a different purpose and a different level of detail. Again, these are intended as starting points for discussion.

- Table 11 identifies basic knowledge people should possess about data, skills they should develop around data, and experiences they should have to help them apply their knowledge and develop their skills.
- Table 12 takes one component of this general list—data visualization—and presents additional detail.
- Table 13 associates knowledge required to perform activities in different roles within an organization.

Table 11 describes the types of knowledge, skills, and experience a data-literate person is likely to possess. This includes knowledge of data structure, processes that create and use data, ways to interpret and communicate with data, and skill and experience in accessing, preparing, and sharing insights from data.

The general model of literacy presented in Table 11 provides a starting point to build out more detail related to knowledge, skills, and experience associated with particular data-related activities, as is done for data visualization in Table 12.

Table 13 presents a model for data literacy within an organization. It outlines the activities performed by people in different roles and the knowledge required to perform these activities. This model recognizes that anyone creating or using data requires some knowledge of how data works—how data input becomes data output. As roles require more direct use of data, the ability to access, organize, manipulate, and present data become important skills. Roles that involve interpreting data for the advancement of the organization will also need to have a deep knowledge of statistics. As do models of general literacy, any model of data literacy must account for the increasing complexity of data as well as of the work involved with using data.

---

[6]There is a lot of data literacy research focused on the educational environment. Interestingly, much of this research focuses on ensuring that teachers are data literate (see Gummer & Mandinach, 2015). Two books that I became aware of after I drafted this chapter (Jones, 2020; Morrow, 2021) focus on data and analytics within organizations. They look very promising. I wish I had had more time to read them in depth.

Table 11 General data literacy knowledge, skills, and experience.

Literacy component	Data literacy component	Detail
Knowledge	Knowledge of "data as data"—structure and life cycle	Understanding of how data can be collected, structured, and organized for use, how data may change over time and have different uses in different circumstances (e.g., knowledge of the data life cycle).
Knowledge	Knowledge of the things that can go wrong with data	Understanding of how a process relies on data input and creates data output; ability to see data as the product of a process and to recognize factors that contribute to or diminish the reliability of data.
Knowledge	Knowledge of ways of looking at data	Knowledge of data visualization and understanding of how data may be combined, aggregated, and calculated before visualization techniques are applied. This knowledge contributes to the ability to "tell a story" (interpret) data.
Knowledge	Knowledge of statistical methods	Basic understanding of statistics and how statistical techniques are applied to data. Knowledge of the risks associated with applying inappropriate techniques.
Knowledge	Knowledge of data domains	Knowledge of data domains, whether understood through industry (health care data, financial data, educational data) or by master data concepts (customer, product, geography).
Knowledge	Knowledge of peculiarities of data within a given organization	Understanding of data as the DNA of an organization, the source of knowledge about the ways the organization works.
Knowledge	Knowledge of the impact of technology on data	Understanding of how different tools work, how they enable one to manipulate and use data, and what the best tool is for the job in any given instance.
Knowledge	Knowledge of the quality expectations for data	Knowledge of what it means for a data set to be complete, valid, and current. This includes understanding concepts related to data quality management in general, and knowledge of the particular data quality requirements of the organization or industry.
Skills	Technical skills that enable access to data	Ability to query data effectively.
Skills	Skill at identifying and evaluating the appropriateness of a data set to the task at hand	Understanding of the level of detail, criteria for completeness, and ability to inform the question at hand.
Skills	Skill at organizing data for analysis	Getting data at the right level of detail, de-normalizing it, combining it, and aggregating it.
Skills	Skill at applying appropriate analysis techniques	Determining the best ways to test hypotheses.

(Continued)

Table 11 General data literacy knowledge, skills, and experience. *Continued*

Literacy component	Data literacy component	Detail
Skills	Skill at robustly testing hypotheses while interpreting data	Avoiding cognitive traps.
Skills	Skill at organizing data for presentation	Ability to make a business case, influence decisions, or solve problems; ability to use data visualization to support both interpretation of data and communications around data.
Experience	Experience querying data	Finding the appropriate data through querying for specific analyses.
Experience	Experience evaluating the quality of data	From basic inspection and comparison to rules to assessment of the reliability of the source.
Experience	Experience preparing data for presentation or analysis	From the basics of choosing the appropriate data to present, getting rid of the noise, combining and visualizing data, and so on. This starts with running reports and actually thinking about the results and continues through being able to create sophisticated models. It may include anything from a cost-benefit analysis to an annual report. Preparing data for presentation or analysis is really a way of learning to *think* about data.
Experience	Experience tracing the root causes of data issues	Although root cause analysis is usually associated with data quality work, many analysts who find data issues do a lot of digging to try to uncover the sources of their frustration; doing so increases their knowledge of organizational data, the data chain, and the risks associated with not managing data purposefully.
Experience	Experience interpreting data	Evaluating quality is a necessary step to interpreting data (actually drawing conclusions from what you see, or at least formulating hypotheses that can be tested). Interpreting data is more than just saying what you think it means. For complex data, it also includes learning how to apply different analysis techniques and choosing techniques that are most appropriate to the task at hand.
Experience	Experience using data tools	From basic query tools and spreadsheets to more sophisticated data visualization tools, all the way through to tools that allow you to combine disparate data sets for complex analyses. This is not so much about "reliance on technology" as it is about understanding how empowering some technologies can be and choosing the right one for the job.

Table 12 Knowledge, skills, and experience required for data visualization.

Literacy component	Data literacy category	Item
Knowledge	Data visualization	Understanding how basic graphs (time sequence, bar, pie, Pareto) work and how they differ from each other
Knowledge	Data visualization	Understanding the role of scale in the creation of data visualization
Skills	Data visualization	The ability to read and interpret a graph or chart
Skills	Data visualization	Determining an appropriate visual option based on the data to be presented
Experience	Data visualization	Preparing a set of graphs as part of delivering a presentation

Table 13 Data literacy levels, based on activities, knowledge, and roles.

Level	Activities	Knowledge	Roles
1	• Create business requirements for data. • Maintain knowledge of the relationship between their business processes and the data created and managed through these processes. • Appropriately access and use the data and metadata they need to execute their work. • Control the quality of the data they collect and manage through business knowledge, procedures, and best practices.	Knowledge of data input and output of business processes for which they have direct responsibility.	Basic Data Creation and Consumer roles
2	• Organize and manipulate data for presentation or use (e.g., create basic data visualizations in Excel or similar software). • Analyze data for patterns, and offer interpretations based on trends, patterns, or apparent correlations. • Inform the ways the organization is tied together through different data sets.	Knowledge of data-as-data, how to organize and prepare data for presentation or use.	Beginner/Junior Business Intelligence (BI) and Reporting roles, Business Analysts, Developers

(Continued)

Table 13 Data literacy levels, based on activities, knowledge, and roles. *Continued*

Level	Activities	Knowledge	Roles
3	• Query and manipulate data to understand it better and share their knowledge with others. • Report on or steward data within a domain(s) of expertise. • Provide subject-matter expertise about the quality of data and risks related to the data sets they know well. • Leverage their understanding of the organizational data chain to mitigate risks associated with other uses of the data. • Track and trace data; formulate hypotheses about root causes of data issues.	Knowledge of how to query and manipulate complex data and prepare it for presentation or use; can use data to influence decisions or to formulate options for solving problems.	Senior BI and Reporting Analyst roles, Data Analysts, Business Analysts, Data Quality Analysts, Data Stewards, Developers, Data Engineers, IT and Business Architects
4	• Leverage existing programs to prepare and use data in comprehensive analyses based on knowledge of the relationship among multiple data sets. • Apply statistical techniques and advanced visualization to interpret data. • Maintain a full understanding of the organizational data chain and the risks and limitations associated with different data sets.	Knowledge of how to combine data and how to apply statistical methodologies to existing data to understand and interpret data.	Advanced Business Intelligence and Analytics roles, Actuaries
5	• Apply advanced knowledge of statistics to create and train predictive models. • Define problems, test hypotheses, and recognize the risks and limitations of proposed models. • Produce analyses based on multiple complex data sets, including unstructured data. • Apply knowledge about the organization and its behavior through data to identify opportunities for additional insight.	Advanced knowledge of statistics, knowledge of how to create predictive models through data selection, hypothesis formation, testing, and training.	Data Scientists Data Strategists

Data Literacy and Organizational Data

Because data is always created or used within a specific context, creating or using it requires knowledge of this context. The focus of this book is on organizational data—the context is the organization itself. You cannot get value out of organizational data without knowledge of the organization itself as a complex system composed of interconnected elements driven by goals and purpose. But to realize value from data, it also helps to understand data itself at an abstract level: "data as data"—how it is created, captured, and organized, how it changes through its life cycle, and how it can be brought together or taken apart to reveal observations below the surface of the rows and columns.

Data Literacy and Thinking Skills

Just as understanding literature, mathematics, and science requires the ability to conceptualize in different ways, understanding and interpreting data requires that people develop their thinking skills as well as their knowledge. Math requires the ability to think in logical steps. Science requires the ability to define problems, test hypotheses, and recognize the limits of one's own knowledge. Data literacy requires both critical thinking (the ability to analyze, synthesize, reflect, and reason based on observation and experience) and systems thinking (the ability to see and understand the relationship between the structure and behavior of the component elements in a system) as well as the ability to understand data-as-data.

Data as a way of representing the world requires a specialized way of thinking. One must be able to see entities (the things that data represents), attributes (the characteristics that entities possess), and values (the specific meaning of an attribute for a particular entity at a point in time). For example, dogs (an entity type) are animals that can be classified by breed, color, weight, and characteristic behaviors (attributes). My dog (an entity instance) is a shepherd-hound mix, is brown/black, weighs 65 pounds, and loves to chase chipmunks (specific values). Understanding data as data requires being able to see these relationships and to move between them at different levels of abstraction. This means being able to formulate and use categories. I can compare my dog to dogs in general or to animals in general. One must also be able to recognize the limits of data as a means of representing the world. Any model of a dog is not an actual dog. (To quote George E.P. Box's famous observation, "All models are wrong, but some are useful.")

Building these skills takes time because honing the skills depends on building both knowledge and experience while thinking through actual problems. A person with some level of this knowledge, these skills, and actual experience is a data-literate person. They can improve their level of data literacy by practicing these skills and building their knowledge through experience.

Data About Data Literacy: An Experiment in Observation

Before we jump in and start solving the problem of data literacy, I am going to perform a little experiment using data about the concept of data literacy. This process will be similar to the one a literature teacher might use in parsing a poem. I will draw attention to features of the data so you can consciously observe the data. Then I will describe how I see these features coming together in ways that shed light on both the quality of the data and the meaning of the data.

The data set we will look at comes from the Google Books Ngram Viewer. The Ngram Viewer is a specialized search engine that charts word frequencies from the large corpus of

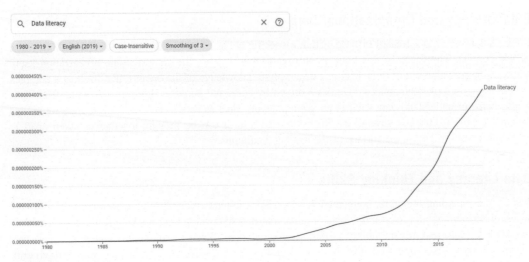

FIGURE 19

Google Ngram Viewer, Data Literacy 1980–2019, Smoothing = 3 (https://books.google.com/ngrams/graph?content=Data+literacy&year_start=1980&year_end=2019&corpus=26&smoothing=3).

books available through Google Books. It can be used to trace the history of concepts based on the frequency of words and phrases published in these books. As Google touts it, the Ngram Viewer "allows for the examination of cultural change as it is reflected in books." The tool is easy to use. (To follow along at home, go to https://books.google.com/ngrams). Enter a word or words, choose a timeframe and language or a subset of books (e.g., English, American English, English Fiction, American Fiction), click, and ta da! A graph appears. The viewer also presents links to the books referred to in the graph. Once you have made your selection, scroll down below the graph and select timeframes to access information about the books represented in the graph. To document my experiment, I did it three times (in January, February, and April 2021), with slightly different results each time.

The question we want to answer through this experiment is: To what degree does the use of the term *data literacy* reflect something we could call *cultural change?* Based on the Google Books Ngram Viewer, the term *data literacy* first appeared in English language texts in the early 1960s (1962 was the earliest instance I could find; 1974 was the next). It was not used much, however, until the turn of the 21st century (2001–2002). Its use spiked upward starting in 2011 and has been increasing since then (Fig. 19). This makes sense, given the development of computers and the emergence of the "information age."

The Ngram Viewer includes a feature called *smoothing* that simplifies the visualization of the data. Smoothing averages the counts of references over a period of years and reduces the detail present in the graphs displaying trends. As one commentator stated, this process makes the data "more legible and thus easier to analyse."[7] The Ngram Help page points out, "Often trends become

---

[7]Part of a case study on text mining, published on the website of the School of Advanced Study, University of London. https://port.sas.ac.uk/mod/book/view.php?id=554&chapterid=328.

more apparent when data is viewed as a moving average." When looking at the Ngram with a smoothing of three (its default), we see a steady increase in the use of the term *data literacy* between 2000 and 2011 and an exponential increase in the use of the term starting in 2012. If we reduce the smoothing to zero (thus seeing the "raw data," not the averages), we see fluctuation within this increase. Between 2005 and 2011, *data literacy* appeared to have become a commonly used term. Then its use tripled between 2011 and 2012, declined a bit during the following years, and then tripled again between 2015 and 2016 (Fig. 20). So, although it may be "more legible and thus easier to analyse," smoothing reduces the precision in the data and affects how one sees change over time.

The Ngram Viewer allows a user to enter and compare the frequency of multiple words. For example, the term *numeracy* has a longer history than the term *data literacy*. It was introduced before 1820. It had a resurgence of use in the mid-1940s, experienced its first exponential climb in the 1960s and 1970s, and saw a second surge starting in the mid-1980s and lasting until 2004 (Fig. 21). Like *data literacy*, its use declined a bit for the next 5 years, but then picked up again in 2010 and increased steadily until 2015. Both terms are being used at a much higher frequency than they were in the early 1960s, but not at as high a frequency as they were in 2015.

Searching both words in the Ngram Viewer (Fig. 22) allows us to contrast their relative frequency, something that would be a little difficult to do any other way given the small percentage of each term within the overall data set. Helpfully, the Ngram Viewer allows the user to limit the timeframe for comparison. Thus we can look at the data starting in 1980, when both terms are in active use. If you are following along at home and want to see additional contrasts, add the term *data fluency* to the mix. Although the term is used much less frequently than either *numeracy* or *data literacy*, its use follows a similar pattern, with use starting to increase in 2002−2003 and sharply increasing in 2011. Add plain, vanilla *literacy* to the search, and all three other terms, *data literacy, data fluency*, and *numeracy*, will flatline.

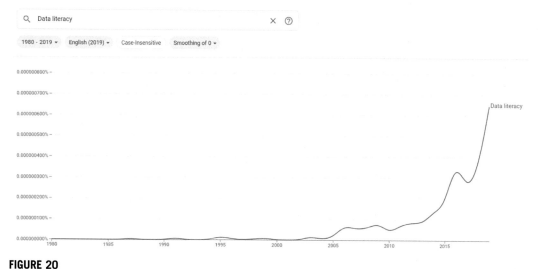

FIGURE 20

Google Ngram Viewer, Data Literacy 1980−2019, Smoothing=0 (https://books.google.com/ngrams/graph?content=Data+literacy&year_start=1980&year_end=2019&corpus=26&smoothing=0).

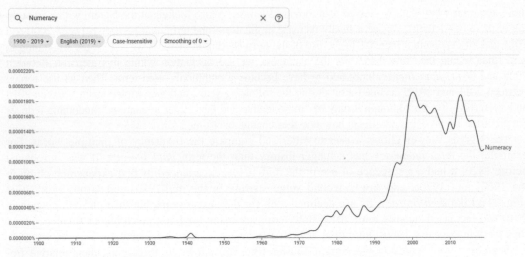

FIGURE 21

Google Ngram Viewer, Numeracy 1990–2019, Smoothing = 0 (https://books.google.com/ngrams/graph?content=Numeracy&year_start=1900&year_end=2019&corpus=26&smoothing=0).

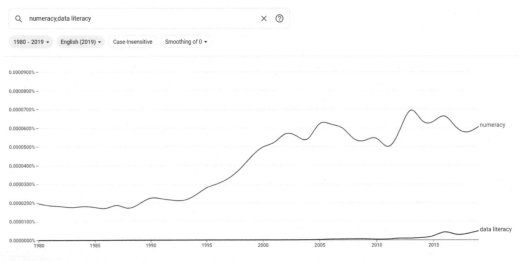

FIGURE 22

Google Ngram Viewer, Numeracy and Data Literacy 1980–2019, Smoothing = 0 (https://books.google.com/ngrams/graph?content=numeracy%2Cdata+literacy&year_start=1980&year_end=2019&corpus=26&smoothing=0).

The challenge with the Ngram Viewer is, of course, that it is hard to know exactly what constitutes the population being measured for any given trend; that is, what is the denominator for the measurements? For example, when I first looked at this data at the beginning of January 2021, I found the early references to both *data literacy* (1960s) and *numeracy* (1820s). But when I pulled the graphs at the end of February 2021, they were no longer there. Between the two visits, books from 2019 had been added to the population. Perhaps the earlier references are now too small to be picked up. But when I looked again in April 2021, I was able to see them—maybe I was not focused enough in February. The data set includes over 5 million books. But there is no claim that these are "representative," and there has been criticism of the data set as biased toward scientific texts (Google: How reliable is the Ngram Viewer?).

When beginning to look at the detailed data, the books related to data literacy, one can see that most, not surprisingly, are directed at educators. A few are directed at programmers or data management professionals. But, one can also see that some references probably should not be there at all. For example, the following two sentences from *The Encyclopedia of Law and Society* by David S. Clark (2007) generate a reference to data literacy that is picked up by the Ngram Viewer: "What accounts for the statistical relationship in Robinson's state-level **data? Literacy** rates among the native-born varied substantially from one state to another."

Should the bolded words be counted as a reference to data literacy? I don't think so. Although the terms *data* and *literacy* are next to each other on the page, they do not represent the concept of data literacy. They are in two different sentences. That Ngram has a little trouble sorting out these details brings the data into question. From the data I can see in the graphs, I am confident that the use of the term *data literacy* is increasing, but from a cursory inspection of the detail, I have little confidence that the details of the chart are "correct" or "accurate" in an absolute sense. For my uses, however, it does not matter. I am looking for a general trend, not a precise analysis. I can formulate an initial conclusion to my question (To what degree does the use of the term *data literacy* reflect something we could call "cultural change"?) by saying that it looks like there is a kind of "cultural change" reflected in the term *data literacy*, but to understand the nature of this change would require a much deeper dive into the "raw data"—the books that provide the counts used in the graphs.

At the time of this writing (January to February 2021), Ngram did not have data for 2020, but a Google search of the term *data literacy* on January 16, 2021, returned 180,000,000 results (in 0.59 seconds!). In contrast, a search on the term *numeracy* returned only 14,300,000 results (in 0.58 seconds). When the data for 2020 becomes available, it is likely to show another increase and substantiate my impression that data literacy has become something of a hot topic in the past several years. Or maybe not, because much of what is written about data literacy is published not in books, but in articles, which are not included in the Ngram database. In any case, I will need to hold off on testing my hypothesis because I have no means to test it until the necessary data becomes available.

What did this experiment tell us about data literacy? It illustrates some points about process and thinking:

- **Iterative inspection:** Understanding data involves an iterative process of inspection. One must look at the data itself in different ways and ask questions about what population the data represents, what the representation includes, and what it excludes. In this case, iterative inspection includes expanding and reducing the timeframe for inspection and comparing results for *data literacy* with results for similar terms.

- **Comparison:** One must make a set of comparisons to understand the context of the data and the specific data. How the data is aggregated and, in this case "smoothed," will influence the perception of the trend as will obvious choices such as the timeframe for the data. Comparison to related words, such as *numeracy* and *data fluency*, will allow one to see the wider context of the use of the term *data literacy*.
- **Parts and whole:** In the process of iterative inspection, one of the most important comparisons will be between the wider context (the big picture) and the detailed parts. Sometimes, to see and understand the whole, one must dig into the details. And vice versa.
- **Visualization:** A lot of data comparison depends on the ability to visualize data, the types of visualization chosen, and the details of the visualization. Displaying data in a graph or chart allows one to see patterns that are not visible in tabular data—you will not be able to look through 5 million books by yourself. But there is a need for caution. In the examples shown, the scales of the graphs differ along both the vertical axis (y-axis, in this case the percentage of texts in which the term appears) and the horizontal axis (x-axis, in this case the amount of time displayed on the graph). These differences create differences in the perception of the data itself.
- **Source, structure, and quality:** One must account for conditions that influence the quality of the data: where the data came from, what population it represents, how it is displayed, what may be wrong with it, as well as what one does not know about it. In other words, just like the data itself, errors or anomalies must be understood in context.
- **Verbalize/describe/think:** Many times, one must put ideas into words to check the level of understanding. For example, recognizing when an upward trend increases exponentially provides a moment of insight. This kind of change is unusual and should be called out for further iterative inspection. The ability to describe in words what one sees in the data brings us back to the insight that data literacy skills are directly connected to general literacy skills, and that part of being data literate is being able to communicate to other people about data.
- **Building "intuition" through knowledge and experience:** Data does not speak for itself, and understanding and interpreting data takes knowledge, skills, and experience. It does not become "intuitive" until you have done a lot of it over a period of time. Even then, interpreting data requires patience and the capacity to hold oneself back from the temptation to jump to conclusions.

Data Literacy: The Extended Definition

Data literacy is directly connected to what we traditionally think of as literacy. Literacy is fundamentally about people cultivating their ability to take in abstract information and to think about this information in a range of ways: to imagine and visualize Tintern Abbey as a ruin and in its glory as we imagine Wordsworth doing the same, to empathize with Madame Bovary even as she destroys her marriage, to envision Juliet envisioning Romeo, to put together a bookcase from Ikea. Written information allows us to communicate across time and space as well as to move across time and space within our own brains. Data plays a similar role in human culture. It is a specialized form of written information.

The United Nations Educational, Scientific and Cultural Organization (UNESCO) defines *literacy* as "the ability to identify, understand, interpret, create, communicate and compute, using printed and written materials associated with varying contexts. Literacy involves a continuum of learning in enabling individuals to achieve their goals, to develop their knowledge and potential, and to participate fully in their community and wider society" (UNESCO, 2004, 2017, cited in Montoya, 2018; Goodman et al., 2013). UNESCO's perspective is broad reaching. It is not limited to simple "reading and writing"; instead, it recognizes the role that the ability to learn from written materials plays in improving the quality of life for individuals, communities, and, indeed, human society as a whole.

Literacy is not just the ability to read words on a page or screen. It is the ability to understand, evaluate, and use any information conveyed through text. Through reading, individuals build knowledge, not only about the subject matter they read, but also about the process of reading. All human cultures have language, but not all of them have reading and writing. Though we live in a time in which we are flooded with written information, reading is not natural. It must be learned. Studies have shown that reading physically changes the human brain. In *Tales of Literacy for the 21st Century: The Literacy Agenda*, Professor Maryanne Wolf describes the process: "When we learn to read, our brain has to create a totally new circuitry that reflects many important influences, beginning with the type of writing system to be learned" (Wolf, 2016, p. 4; see also pp. 28–35, 59, 68, and 73).

Just as it takes time and commitment to get your body in shape, it takes time and practice to become literate. The more you read, the better you become at reading, seeing how stories and other information fit together, and seeing how details support or contradict each other. Just as playing music is not simply about hitting the correct note at the correct time, reading is not merely sounding out the words. It is about learning to think differently because of what you can see and think about in written text. Written language, like data, is a group of symbols that must be interpreted in the context of their origin. The same word can have a different meaning in different languages. In French, the word *demand* simply means "ask." In English, the word *demand* implies something beyond a simple request—it means asking with a sense of urgency or authority.

Because reading requires people to think outside themselves, it enables them to imagine and empathize with others and to see situations from multiple perspectives. Literacy includes a set of intellectual skills, not the least of which is imagination. In applying these skills, individuals not only learn about the materials they are reading; they also become more capable of learning new things. It is not surprising that the term *data literacy* has emerged strongly in the past few years. Many of the same skills required to interpret literature and to understand scientific or other texts are required to interpret data: the ability to understand overall structure and perceive patterns, to see details in relation to the whole, and to detect and ask questions about apparent contradictions and anomalies.

The need for data literacy is directly connected to the value proposition of literacy in general (to achieve goals, develop knowledge, participate fully) and of data in general: data is valuable because we can learn things from it that we cannot learn any other way. There are patterns in the behavior of people or populations that are not visible except through data analysis. This is one of the reasons why people were so excited about statistics in the 18th and 19th centuries (Porter, 1986). Because patterns in large populations are not self-evident, it requires knowledge and skill to see them, just as it requires knowledge and skill to comprehend written texts.

Unlocking value from data depends on literacy skills—the ability to understand what data represents, to see patterns in it, and to interpret and draw conclusions from it. People count on data performing its basic function: to represent people, events, and concepts in the real world. But skepticism is also part of the picture. Just as when we read a novel, we know that we cannot believe everything a character says (as most American high school students learn, Nick Caraway, who narrates *The Great Gatsby*, is an "unreliable" narrator), when we look at data, we must understand the context in which it was created and its limitations. Data can be biased, incomplete, poorly designed, and out of date. People can manipulate it and misinterpret it. They can even simply lie about it. Part of being a data-literate person is knowing these risks and being able to respond to and account for them. For example:

- Being able to ask questions about the origin and reliability of data to make good decisions about whether and how to use data
- Evaluating the quality of data
- Recognizing the potential for bias in data
- Acting responsibly by informing stakeholders about known limitations of data, including gaps and other quality issues

There are now vendors that offer certification in data literacy or provide frameworks through which data literacy can be "adopted." Training is certainly necessary to cultivate data literacy skills (no one should have to teach themselves statistics). However, taking a few training courses does not make a person data literate. And literacy cannot be "adopted." It is not something you buy or pick up. People must develop data literacy skills. Data literacy takes time. It requires not only the acquisition but also the cultivation of skills, including the ability to make connections among disparate experiences and to apply knowledge in different contexts. It is about people learning to be smarter about data. There is no app for it.

Data Literacy Skills, Knowledge, Experience

Any kind of literacy can be understood as derived from a combination of knowledge, skills, and experience. Literacy begins when a person learns the alphabet and begins to recognize how words are represented in written form. It develops through an explicit knowledge of the structure of written language—sentences, paragraphs, chapters. More importantly, as a reader reads more, he or she begins to understand nuances in texts. Experience reading literature hones skills in seeing connections, understanding structure, and recognizing how an author's choices in revealing information enrich the experience of the story. Experience reading nonfiction, science, history, and even technical information has similar effects as all of these require a person to abstract information and understand it from different perspectives. Reading data requires similar knowledge and skills. Knowledge is gained and skills are honed through the experience of using and thereby interpreting data.

Skills

In *The Data Loom: Weaving Understanding by Thinking Critically and Scientifically with Data*, Stephen Few describes some of the core skills associated with what he calls *data sensemaking* (Few, 2015a). Data sensemaking starts with domain knowledge. For most of us, this means understanding the data you are working with in the context of your organization. If you work in health care, you must understand the health care system (how patients, providers, and insurers interact). Depending on what you do in health care, you may need highly specialized domain knowledge. Medical coders develop deep knowledge of the structure of diagnostic and procedure code sets, the criteria for coding accurately, and the implications of different choices in coding. Not all individuals in health care have this level of specialization, but anyone who works in health care should know the importance of these codes to the system as a whole.

Few does not use the term *data literacy*, but his discussion, focused on the set of thinking skills that are at the heart of understanding and using data, provides one of the best descriptions of core data literacy skills that I have seen. Using Few's list as a starting point and adding a few pieces from other writers, these skills include the following:

- **Critical thinking:** The ability to clarify ideas, to recognize how you think (metacognition), to avoid logical fallacies and other cognitive traps, to be open to the possibility that you may be wrong in your assumptions or conclusions, and to be willing to adopt new ideas and perspectives for the purposes of increasing your understanding of a subject.
- **Scientific thinking:** Knowledge of the scientific method and scientific principles (such as falsifiability), the ability to apply a scientific approach to ask better questions, formulate and test hypotheses about possible causes and effects, and maintain perspective on your own conclusions.
- **Statistical thinking/quantitative reasoning:** Knowledge of how statistics work (including some of the pitfalls and misconceptions about statistics), an understanding of numbers, and the ability to apply quantitative reasoning to problems (including making good decisions about what and how to measure and avoiding making poor decisions about the same) (see Paulos, 2001).
- **Systems thinking:** The ability to comprehend the organization as a system of interconnected elements organized to meet goals, to see the relationship among the parts and the whole, and to recognize how interactions among parts influence each other (see also Meadows, 2008).
- **Visual Thinking:** The ability to understand and interpret information conveyed visually through graphs, charts, and other means; the ability to determine the most effective ways to visualize different kinds of information; and the ability to recognize questionable features of such representations (see Cairo, 2016; Knaflic, 2015).
- **Curiosity:** A level of engagement with data, a desire to understand it and learn from it, and the ability to ask meaningful questions about how it works and what one may learn from it. It is important to recognize that critical thinking, scientific thinking, skepticism, and ethical thinking all involve a degree of curiosity and a willingness to ask questions.
- **Skepticism:** Willingness to question the data, to go beneath the surface, and to understand the context in which data is created (data sources) as well as the standards for relevance, accuracy, representativeness, and completeness used to create it. The ability to know the limitations of the data and use it appropriately, to recognize when and in what ways data may be biased, and to account for potential limitations of data when interpreting it (see O'Neil, 2016; Schryvers, 2020).
- **Ethical thinking:** Understanding the potential for good or harm of any actions or conclusions from data and recognizing the need to actively prevent harm (see O'Keefe & O Brien, 2018).

- **Communications skills:** The ability to share insights with others and to help them see what you are able to see in the data.

Few also provides simple, practical advice about how to develop these thinking habits, not only as an individual (prevent distraction, take notes, give yourself time to think), but also as an organization (teach each other, raise questions, encourage feedback, allow people to admit their mistakes, give people time and space to think, help them cultivate their thinking skills).

Ultimately, these skills support a person's ability to use data because they contribute to a person's ability to interpret data: to understand its meaning and be able to explain that meaning to other people. Although these skills are called out separately and you can focus your study to develop them separately, they work together. Think of it this way: when you work out at the gym, your routine may focus on your core, your upper body, or your lower body, depending on your specific goals. But your overall goal and the overall result of working out is to be more fit. And although you may focus on one thing at a time, your body as a whole benefits from the exercise. The same goes for intellectual fitness.

Knowledge

Domain knowledge and knowledge about the organization and the industry in which one is working are required to understand and learn from data created by and used by an enterprise. Thinking skills are at the core of data literacy. But to use data, it is helpful to understand data-as-data. As we will discuss in more depth in Chapter 9 when we look at data quality in the context of data management, a data-literate person should have general knowledge of how data is created, organized, managed, transformed, and used as well as specific knowledge of these processes within his or her organization:

- **Data creation/collection:** How data is created in science, statistics, social science, commerce, and other settings. This includes understanding the influence that data collection devices (forms, surveys, sensors, measurement approaches) have on the data that can be created and on the quality and reliability of that data. This goes for Big Data as well as traditional data.
  - Within an organization, this requires knowledge of the processes that create, collect, or obtain data. For example, within health care in the United States, knowledge of how accounts are underwritten, how claims are submitted and adjudicated, how providers are contracted, and so on.
  - Knowledge of data creation/collection within an organization also requires understanding what can impact the quality of data. For example, when data is collected manually, how are the people who collect it incentivized? If they are evaluated based on speed rather than accuracy, they may take shortcuts that affect the quality of data they collect (e.g., entering 99999 for a Zip code). For automated data collection processes, what controls are in place to prevent errors and ensure integrity?
  - An obvious risk point for data creation is the level of awareness among people who create data of the uses to which this data is put. If the people creating data are not aware that others depend on them to create complete and accurate data and if they are incentivized for speed, then data will be of lower quality. Simply raising awareness can measurably improve quality.
- **Data uses:** Common-sense uses of different kinds of data, such as knowing that customer information is used by marketing, sales, product management, and accounts receivable; that

multiple processes feed the general ledger; and that administrative data is used to measure organizational goals.

- Within an organization, it is important that data producers are aware of how people and processes use the data they create. For example, within health care, knowing that adjudicated claims will be used to provide patients with quality ratings for medical providers should result in submission of more accurate claims by providers, who have a direct stake in these ratings.

- **Data structure/organization:** Knowledge of how data is organized (whether into tables, columns, and rows or into charts, graphs, and so on) contributes to the ability of people to understand the data. This is not to say that everyone must be a data modeler. Instead, it is to recognize the ways data structure contributes to data meaning.
  - Within an organization, this means knowledge of the enterprise data model (if one exists), which describes the connections among data produced in different parts of the organization. For example, in health care in the United States, members obtain coverage from their employers, who are the clients of the health care company. These same members are patients who visit providers who contract with the health care company.
  - Again, knowledge of data structure provides insight into factors that can affect data quality. If the organization does not have an enterprise data model or an architectural vision that captures an enterprise perspective on data and if it does not have data standards, then departments, which necessarily operate in silos, will develop their own habits around collecting and creating this data. Siloed data tends to be heterogeneous data. Although it is likely to meet the needs of the people who create it, it may not meet the requirements of other data consumers.
  - Knowledge of data structure is important to meeting these requirements. Differences in the structure of data sets (e.g., granularity, level of detail) are more difficult to account for than differences in representing particular values. It takes time and costs money to transform and standardize data for downstream uses. Also, the process of transforming data from different sources complicates and introduces risks in the data supply chain.

- **Data management:** Knowing the different types of data (transactional data, master data, reference data) that exist in the organization, who is responsible for them, how they are maintained, how they relate to each other, and how they influence each other's reliability and quality.
  - Within an organization, this requires knowledge of critical reference and master data sets and the ability to use them. For example, critical health care codes sets, such as the Current Procedural Terminology (CPT), Healthcare Common Procedure Coding System (HCPCS), and International Classification of Diseases (ICD) Diagnostic and Procedure Codes, are updated annually. New codes that come into effect each January are made available in October of the preceding year. These codes affect how claims are paid and how clinical analyses are conducted. They should be maintained so new codes are available for use each January. A person using these codes should know whether or not the code set is current and complete.
  - It also requires understanding who is accountable for the quality of data and how decisions are made about data, especially about shared data.

- **Technology for data collection and storage:** How the technology for data collection may influence characteristics of data, such as accuracy, completeness, and currency.

- Within an organization, this includes knowledge of how the systems that process data work. For example, most data used in analytics and reporting is moved from transactional systems to marts or other applications for access and use. Data completeness and currency depend on the timing and type of updates.
- It also means recognizing the risks related to data orchestration, storage, and access. Having multiple systems with versions of "the same" data creates risks related to data redundancy as well as data disparity.
- **Data movement/data supply chain:** How within an organization, such as a government or corporation, data moves between processes so it can be used to serve different purposes. Data created in one technical system for a particular purpose may be used in another part of the organization for a different purpose.
  - Within an organization, knowledge of the supply chain includes understanding how different data sets are connected and dependent on each other. For example, within health care in the United States, master data about providers will be required to adjudicate claims. It will also be required in the systems that manage provider contracting and produce provider contracts. To ensure that these interactions work as desired, it helps for data consumers to provide input to data producers about their quality requirements.
  - Data movement involves risk. Each time data is "touched," there is a risk of data loss or unexpected transformation. Having explicit requirements for quality can help manage these risks because these requirements draw attention to and make technicians aware of characteristics of data that are important to the people and processes that use data.
- **Data transformation and aggregation:** How different data inputs may be calculated or aggregated to create summarized data points and how changed or manipulated data relates to the atomic data from which it is created.
  - Within an organization, knowledge of transformation and aggregation includes understanding how data sets are brought together for purposes of measurement or analysis. For example, within health care, aggregating claim data related to particular health conditions and associating it with data on patients and providers to understand which treatments are most effective in managing a chronic disease.
  - Changing data introduces the potential for misunderstanding. When data is aggregated by different methods and different standards, the "same" data becomes disparate. People must know how data has been changed to make appropriate comparisons between different versions of the "same" data.
- **Technology for data analysis:** How the technology for data analysis may have effects on data aggregation and visualization.
  - Within an organization, this includes being clear about which tools are used to present analytics and how these may affect the interpretation of the data.
  - Because different tools have different effects, data-literate people must develop the ability to know how analytics tools work and to learn new tools. They must also understand the most appropriate ways to analyze data (rather than having the tools themselves determine and limit what analysis can be done).
- **Data protection and security:** The ability to distinguish between appropriate and inappropriate uses of data; the risks associated with some data uses; and how data can be misused.

- Within an organization, knowledge of data uses is critical to data security as well as to ensuring data quality. All people who handle data should be aware of ways that data can be misused, intentionally or unintentionally. They must have basic knowledge of legal, compliance, and regulatory requirements, including knowledge of protection levels for specific data such as protected health information (PHI) and personally identifiable information (PII) in health care. They also should understand the potential for unethical uses of data and actively work to prevent such misuse.

If these topics seem technical and focused largely on data management concerns rather than data literacy, it may be because data creation, organization, and use are going on all around us, and we take them for granted. For example, we routinely understand information about sports, the economy, and the weather without necessarily thinking about how the data that contributes to this information is created, transformed, and prepared before we see the results. And yet, this data goes through a life cycle. It is created through defined processes. It is organized for use, enabled, but also limited and manipulated through specific technologies, maintained for quality, moved, transformed, and aggregated, before being ultimately published and shared. Basic knowledge of these processes can help analysts better understand the limitations and risks associated with using particular data sets. Data quality practitioners will need to have more in-depth knowledge if they are to help prevent data errors and recommend data controls.

Metadata: Managing the Organization's Explicit Knowledge

This brings us to the most important form of organizational support for data literacy: metadata management. Even a very data-literate person cannot know everything about organizational data. For an organization to be data literate and for data-literate people to get value from data, data use must be supported by metadata, and metadata itself must be managed. Metadata management amounts to stewarding explicit knowledge about data. If the organization does not manage its metadata, data is harder to find and harder to use. If an organization does not manage its metadata well, analysts will have an inconsistent understanding of data. Metadata management also goes directly to the problem of waste within organizations. An International Data Corporation (IDC) survey of more than 400 data professionals in Europe and the United States found that they spend a disproportionate amount of time (40%−60%) either searching for data or building information assets that already exist elsewhere in the organization (Jewell, 2018).

Metadata requires governance as well as management. Processes and policies should be in place to ensure that fundamental semantic metadata (entity and attribute definitions) is documented and maintained. People should be trained on how to access and use metadata as well as where to go when they have questions related to the metadata they use. Use of metadata builds knowledge of data structure. It also can create a feedback loop between data producers and data consumers.

Metadata is an essential ingredient for data quality management, and data quality management processes should be a major contributor to metadata because they look at data through the lens of customer expectations for the data.

Data Knowledge: An Example

We can think through these processes using an example with which many people will be familiar, the collection of census data by governments. The US Constitution requires that a census be conducted every 10 years. This data influences the composition of the US House of Representatives and is used to allocate funds for infrastructure and services. For the decennial census, data is collected via forms that are mailed to all households and via census workers who visit a sample of households. The US Census Bureau augments data from the decennial census with data from state and local governments and agencies that administer programs.

The US Census Bureau shares this data on its website (https://www.census.gov/en.html). It not only provides tables, but also data visualizations to help people see what is in the data. Not surprisingly, many of these visualizations include maps that portray observations about the population across the geography of the United States. It provides information about data sources, tools for analyzing data, and analyses that the US Census Bureau has collected.

In putting together and using the data from the census, the US Census Bureau employs a lot of statisticians. But you do not need to be a statistician to understand much of the data presented on the website. You do need to understand what the data represents, how it is organized, and how to use contextual information provided by the US Census Bureau to understand its limitations, including that the categories and questions change with each execution of the census. In short, you need a measure of data literacy. Looking at this data, using the tools, trying to understand what you see will also contribute to your ability to look at other data sets.

Experience

Data literacy includes domain knowledge and thinking skills. The best way to build these skills is through hands-on experience creating, using, or resolving issues with data. For example:

- **Creating data to answer a question** shows a person what can go wrong with the data collection process and what is necessary to make it successful. For example:
  - Data collection questions: Creating a form, survey, spreadsheet, or other data collection device to meet a specific goal, including formulating appropriate questions. Then conducting the survey and analyzing the results. This type of activity will teach a person how to think about the design of data and will show how the questions one asks frame the possibilities of what one can see in data. One goal is to reduce the ambiguity of any results while at the same time not predetermining the results.
  - Collecting measurement data: Developing a hypothesis about a problem or opportunity and creating a data collection process to obtain measurement data that tests the hypothesis. This requires determining what characteristics to measure and how to collect accurate, usable measurement data that is relevant to the hypothesis. In other words, thinking about the goal (understanding the validity of the hypothesis) and designing questions that will meet that goal.
- **Preparing and using data** in a report or presentation can uncover unexpected characteristics of existing data sets. These activities require a person to understand existing data structures and compare their assumptions with the actual data. Preparing information to share with other people (e.g., preparing charts as part of a presentation) also builds the following skills:
  - Applying appropriate forms of statistical analysis to uncover patterns in the data
  - Choosing the best options for visualizing data
- **Root cause analysis of data issues** helps analysts build the following skills:
  - Seeing patterns in the data itself using techniques such as distribution analysis and Pareto analysis to isolate the issue
  - Tracking and tracing the movement of data within and between systems as they analyze the data chain

- Asking "Why?" at least five times to develop understanding of a chain of causes and effects that can affect the quality of data
- Process analysis, including by developing flowcharts and other visualizations of activities that show where data may be created or transformed incorrectly
- Defining appropriate controls as they look at ways to prevent problems

Even in an organization that aspires to be data driven, not everyone must be a data scientist, an information architect, or a data quality analyst working on the root causes of data problems. But many people will be involved, directly or indirectly, in creating, using, and understanding the implications of data. Even a small amount of hands-on work collecting data, preparing analysis, or creating a visualization can help raise awareness of the ways in which the organization is connected through its data and the ways in which individuals can do more to ensure that data quality is maintained in their part of the data chain.

The Data-Literate Organization

Literacy of any kind is about skills and knowledge and the ability of people to apply skills to knowledge to better understand the world. Author and data management consultant Daragh O Brien describes *data literacy* as "the ability of an individual to understand the meaning and purpose of data in context; not only to perform immediate job functions but also to extrapolate, correlate, and apply knowledge about data to new contexts and unforeseen or novel situations" (O Brien, 2020b).

Although literacy in general is fundamentally about individual skills and knowledge, written texts are also a way of connecting groups of people (e.g., nations, religions, communities). Groups of people, including organizations that produce and use data, can raise their overall literacy by making a commitment to the education of their members. In a literate community, individuals develop their skills because they are expected to use these skills and because the skills themselves are valued for the contribution having them makes to overall quality of life. Within a commerce-driven organization of the type we have been discussing here, this will not happen naturally. There will always be some people who work hard and build their own expertise, but these folks are few and far between. Most people are simply trying to do their jobs the best they can. They do not carve out time for development unless the organization encourages them to do so. Leadership within the organization must promote data literacy by setting the expectation that employees should always strive to get smarter at what they do. Leadership also has to support this effort through training and other opportunities for professional development. Leadership should reward people who contribute because they have taken advantage of these opportunities. Advocacy of improved data literacy should be the natural outgrowth of leadership's recognition of the value of data and the value of work that enables higher-quality data.

In *Executing Data Quality Projects: Ten Steps to Quality Data and Trusted Information*, data quality consultant Danette McGilvray makes several important observations about the connection between organizational and individual data literacy and the data life cycle:

> Given the importance of data in our lives, many organizations are taking up the cause of data literacy. That is a good thing. However, definitions of data literacy vary and may depend on which organization is doing the defining or what product a vendor wants to sell. Most definitions

include the ideas of working with data, analyzing data, representing data in context, communicating, and even arguing with data. These definitions emphasize being able to comprehend and interpret data. What is lacking in the definitions of data literacy is an acknowledgement of the need to understand the sources of the data and a means to determine if sources can be trusted. A person is not data literate if they use data from a source that is lying about the data or whose facts are inconsistent with more reputable sources or if they are not aware that they should even be checking these in the first place. The definitions also fail to recognize that the ability to adequately prepare the data for use is part of data literacy (McGilvray, 2021, p. 13).

In a data-literate organization, employees can be expected to apply their skills and knowledge to new situations connected with the use or interpretation of data. As individuals build their own skills, they also influence the organization. By demonstrating these skills, they help others develop them. If the organization supports, encourages, and invests in this kind of interaction, over time they build overall organizational capability.

In addition to the thinking skills described earlier in the "Skills" section, what is required to build this kind organization?

- **Knowledge of the organization itself:** People in the organization should know the industry and the organization itself. This will help them know what data is critical to organizational success.
- **Knowledge of the organization's data supply chain:** How, why, and by whom critical data is created, how it is used, and how it influences and contributes to the organization's ability to meet its goals.
- **Knowledge of data-as-data:** Understanding data structure, the creation of data through calculations and aggregations, the risks associated with data use and misuse, what can go wrong with data, and how data problems can be prevented.
- **Knowledge of data management:** How data is managed in the organization, how decisions are made about data, and what makes data of high or low quality.
- **Knowledge of technologies for storing data and tools for accessing data:** Understanding how data is stored and shared and being able to use tools to query data and organize it for analysis.
- **Skill in designing data:** The ability to create or obtain the data the organization needs and to ensure that it fits together in the ways the organization needs it to.
- **Skill in using data:** The ability to prepare, aggregate, analyze, and visualize data in ways that help the organization understand itself, its products, and its customers; to apply relevant data to organizational problems and questions; and to interpret basic statistical functions.
- **Skill in presenting data:** The ability to communicate findings and insights in ways that help other people understand what the data implies.

As stated previously, building a literate organization requires leadership commitment. Leadership commitment comes from recognizing value. This includes understanding the following:

- The value of data
- The costs of poor-quality data
- The benefit to the organization of managing data

Data literacy implies a commitment to quality data. People within a data-literate organization will have high standards for data and little tolerance for low-quality data. They will understand how data is created and how it can be affected by poor process design or unwise choices about technology. They will also value the role that data plays in enabling the organization to meet its goals and want to leverage data to these ends. Data literacy is critical to any organization that wants to get value from its data assets as it addresses both sides of the value equation by improving the quality of data being created and reducing the risks associated with data use. This does not mean that everyone must be a data expert. (Literacy is best understood as a continuum of skills and knowledge.) It means that everyone must have a reasonable level of knowledge about the critical role that data plays within the organization and a reasonable amount of skill in understanding and interpreting data.

A quick comparison illustrates this point. Every US health care company requires every employee who might create or use data to be trained in data protection, especially with respect to PHI and PII. The goals of such training are to ensure that each and every employee understands the following:

- PHI, PII, and other sensitive data exists within the organization's systems.
- The exposure of PHI, PII, and other sensitive data is a risk to the company and its customers.
- This data must be protected.
- Any employee or contractor who fails to take common-sense actions to protect this data is at risk of losing their job.

This training does not turn ordinary employees into experts in data protection and security. But it does raise overall awareness, and it makes employees accountable for their actions toward sensitive data. Building data literacy within an organization will expand at least this level of awareness to other aspects of the data life cycle. Employees do not have to be experts in data management, but they should know that data requires management and that their actions, as data producers or data consumers, have an impact on the organization's ability to get value from its data.

The Alternative: Data Illiteracy

If my assertions about data literacy seem idealistic, consider the alternative: data illiteracy. Using O Brien's definition, data illiteracy would amount to the *inability* of an individual to understand the meaning and purpose of data in context; the *inability* to perform immediate job functions; and the *inability* to extrapolate, correlate, and apply knowledge about data to new contexts and unforeseen or novel situations.

This idea of a deep gap in organizational capability is pretty frightening. It becomes more frightening in light of research that shows that people who do not cultivate scientific literacy are more susceptible to both misinformation and actual, physical brain disease than those who do. In other words, just as literacy changes the brain by building circuitry, a lack of literacy leaves the brain less able to think about abstract problems and even makes it more susceptible to disease. Writing in *Scientific American* about support of dangerous anti-science beliefs and behaviors, such as belief in conspiracy theories related to the Covid-19 pandemic, Serggio Lanata and Bruce L. Miller assert:

> Low educational attainment is a risk factor for Alzheimer's disease and other forms of dementia, suggesting that high educational attainment is associated with fostering neuroanatomical

conditions that protect our brain from the pathophysiologic changes of Alzheimer's disease. This remarkable scientific finding supports the idea that high quality education and science literacy physiologically and functionally strengthen the brain, protecting us from the threat of false beliefs during times of uncertainty and crisis (Lanata & Miller, 2021).

The level of science literacy Lanata and Miller advocate for is closely aligned to what I have described in relation to data literacy. They point out that careful interpretation of data requires training and practice, but that "The ability to evaluate data scientifically . . . is not just for the few with professional training in science or medicine but can be learned and practiced by anyone as part of standard primary, secondary or more advanced education. Indeed, people who do not practice science can understand scientific principles and tools and apply them to their personal and professional lives."

It is tempting to think of data illiteracy resulting largely from a lack of education, but there is also another source: data enthusiasm—naïve belief in the power of data in and of itself—can blind people to the work required to create high-quality, usable data as well as to understand and interpret data.

In *Big Data Revolution: What Farmers, Doctors and Insurance Agents Teach Us About Discovering Big Data Patterns*, Rob Thomas and Patrick McSharry share stories of innovation brought about by the use of Big Data in a range of industries (Thomas & McSharry, 2015). Many of their examples shed light on how better data can lead to better products and more efficient use of resources. (This is not a new insight, but an important reminder about the benefits of high-quality data.) However, their depiction of what they call "the data era" depends on some naïve assumptions about where data comes from and how it works. For example, their repeated assertions that the term *data* will replace the term *opinion* or *perception*—as if there had been a pre-data era in which decisions were made without data, information, or knowledge and as if data and opinion were opposite to each other instead of intimately connected to each other.

They use health care as one of their examples, pointing out that "a medical industry that starts with the collection of data and ends with science-based analytics of data is very different from how the industry began many centuries ago." It is hard to disagree with their observation, except to question whether there was a medical "industry" many centuries ago. (There was not.) They continue: "Any time a person walks into a new physician's office, he is a stranger. He becomes a known quantity through what he tells the physician, but he is rarely sharing facts; he is sharing perception. Contrast this situation with a world where his medical history, his data, is provided the minute he walks into the office. His chances of receiving the proper care increase exponentially" (p. 42).

The critical thinker in me asks, "Really?" Let's look at just the logic here. Most people go to the doctor because they want to solve a health problem. So, shouldn't we assume that most patients are at least *trying* to share "facts" with their doctors? More importantly, aren't their own perceptions of their condition valid input to any diagnosis? (If not, then why do doctors insist on asking: "How are you feeling today?") If a patient is sharing only "perception" in a conversation with a new doctor, then hasn't he shared only "perception" with all his previous doctors? That means all of his medical history (his data) is just a collection of his perceptions. Is the medical history better just because someone entered it into an electronic medical record and made it "data"? Does the mere existence of the electronic medical history guarantee better medical care?

If this history is "provided the minute he walks into the office," then chances are that the doctor has not even had a chance to read it. (If a medical record exists in a database but no one uses it, does it help a doctor diagnose a patient?) What if the doctor has never seen a person with the symptoms this patient exhibits? Even if the doctor has the person's medical history, he may not know how to interpret the symptoms, or he may interpret them incorrectly. What if the doctor has an implicit bias because of his specialty, the community he works in, an interesting paper he just read, or a discussion he had with a colleague yesterday afternoon?

Thomas and McSharry's example is not helped by misuse of statistical thinking. It is undoubtedly true that some doctors, through their knowledge, skill, and experience working with patients, as well as their access to better data, are better diagnosticians than others. But does it follow that having a complete medical history "exponentially" increases the chances of receiving the proper care? An exponential increase of a quantity over time is proportional to the quantity itself. The more you have, the more what you have increases, for example, when you multiply a value by 2 (2, 4, 16, 32, 128, 256, and so on). An exponential increase can be understood in contrast to a linear increase, for example, when you increase by a set amount, such as adding 2 to a value (2, 4, 6, 8, 10) (Fig. 23).

Given that any doctor in the United States will have attended 4 years of college, 3 years of medical school, and 2 years of residency and will be licensed through a set of standard examinations

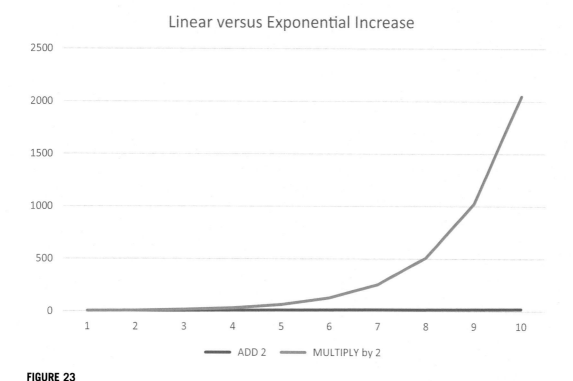

FIGURE 23

The difference between a linear and an exponential increase.

required of all physicians, any time you walk into a doctor's office, you should already have a pretty good chance of receiving proper medical care. Is there even the potential for an *exponential increase* in the chances of receiving proper care? There may be. However, given the structure and behavior of the medical system, "an exponential increase" seems unlikely.

I don't want to be completely snarky. There is a lot of benefit to having an electronic medical record that provides accurate information about the timing of illnesses and injuries, medications, surgeries, and so on. It can and should be more reliable than a person's memory. But its existence does not guarantee "proper medical care" any more than the existence of your gym membership guarantees that you will be physically fit. Data does not work by magic. It must be used by the doctor. The doctor must interpret it. Interpretation includes knowing that data in the records was created by other human beings who have recorded their own interpretations. And medical history does not tell a doctor how a patient is feeling today. There is still a need for doctor-patient communication and an interpretation of that history.

My point is this: Untempered enthusiasm for data is a form of data illiteracy. Data does not speak for itself or solve problems on its own. Asserting that it does amounts to hype and is a form of magical thinking. Data can help us better understand the world and can provide insight into how to solve problems—if

LOW POTENTIAL DATA VALUE	HIGH POTENTIAL DATA VALUE
HIGH DATA LITERACY	
Potential Data Value: Low • The data itself is unreliable, but the people using it recognize it as such. • Reduced risk of data being misused, resulting from less overall use of data. • Less overall use of data implies fewer opportunities to derive value from data.	**Potential Data Value: High** • The data itself is reliable, and the people using it understand it. • Low risk of data being misused. • High data use, and therefore more opportunity to derive value from data.
LOW DATA LITERACY	
Potential Data Value: Very Low • The data itself is unreliable, and the people using it do not recognize this condition. • High risk of data being misused. • High cost to figure out and fix.	**Potential Data Value: Low** • The data itself is reliable, but people do not know how to use it. • High risk of data being misused. • Capacity to derive value depends on the ability to develop data skills.

FIGURE 24

Data literacy four square.

we know how to use it and if we actually use it. Data and facts are not the opposite of opinions. Reliable data should be valuable input into how we form opinions, that is, how we develop perspective and gain insight into the problems we are trying to solve and the opportunities we are trying to take advantage of.

Data illiteracy is a risk to organizations. Lack of knowledge and understanding about data can lead to lower-quality data (and its associated costs) and to misuse or inappropriate use of data. It is more likely to lead to lost opportunity. Organizations want to get value from their data assets. They cannot do so without a data-literate workforce. In 2019, Gartner reported that data literacy was ranked as the second-biggest internal roadblock to the success of the office of the CDO (Panetta, 2019). (They actually meant to say that *data illiteracy* was the roadblock, but we can let that go.)

Data literacy has direct effects on data quality. People who are more data literate (more aware of how data is created in and used in their organization) are more likely to create high-quality data and to take action if data is of low quality. If organizational structures are in place to report, prioritize, and remediate data issues, then knowledge about the data and feedback about it can lead to data quality improvement. If these structures are not in place, then, unfortunately, discovery of data issues can lead to workarounds and other hidden costs.

The quality of the data itself combined with the organization's ability to use it contribute to the value equation for data. Fig. 24 summarizes the risks low data literacy presents in connection with underutilization and misuse of data and sets, both in relation to data quality. The combination of high data literacy and high-quality data offers the highest potential to get value from data. Data only brings value when it is used. If data is used by people who do not understand it, it creates risks for the organization. If people understand data well enough to recognize when it is of low quality, then they may refrain from using it or at least recognize its limitations when they do use it, thus reducing the risk of misuse.

Data Literacy and a Growth Mindset

I have worked in banking, education, manufacturing/distribution, commercial insurance, and health care. All of these have required knowledge about how data and information influence organizational success. But it was not until I worked in a data warehouse that I learned there was a perceived distinction between "data people" and other people. I had worked there only a few weeks when a colleague, a trainer for the warehouse, told me that I was a "data person." I did not want to say I wasn't (after all, my job title contained the words *data quality*), but in the next sentence she showed her hand. "I am not a data person," she said. "But you're training people on the query tool!" I thought, "How can you not be a 'data person'? And what does it even mean to say that?"

Many people who work with data do divide the world into "data people" and "not data people." I do not like to make this distinction, but I understand where it comes from. Some people have more interest in data-as-data than other people have. And people with an analytic bent may "get it" faster than those without that bent. This can be scary to people who feel like they do not "get it." People who understand data can be intimidating to those who find data somewhat impenetrable.

The differences between data people and non-data people seem to come down to three characteristics: a general attitude toward data, the ability to recognize patterns and structure in data, and a comfort level with data analysis. Data people find data interesting. They are curious about it. They understand data structure and enjoy the process of finding patterns in data. Because they can see patterns in data, they are comfortable with manipulating data—taking it apart and putting it back together again. In contrast, non-data people either find data intimidating or they simply cannot find what is interesting about it. To them, all data looks the same. It is opaque. They do not feel comfortable moving data around or taking it apart to put it back together again.

Because some people think there is a kind of permanent difference between data people and non-data people, cultivating data literacy requires a growth mindset. Much has been written about the impact of mindset on learning, but it boils down to this: If you think that intelligence is static (either you are a data person or you are not a data person forever and ever—a fixed mindset), you learn less and have less chance of mastering new skills. But if you have confidence that you can learn new things (growth mindset) and you are willing to persist in the face of setbacks, then you will learn and master new skills. Organizations and individuals who want to get more value from their data should start by adopting a growth mindset about data literacy.

Even people who do not have a strong interest in data-as-data can learn about data in ways that enable them to help an organization get more value from its data. Sometimes just a really good example of what one can see in data is enough to pique the interest of a non-data person. When I first started working in data quality management and learned to use control charts, I was amazed by what they revealed about the data. It was eye opening, especially when I was able to directly correlate spikes in data quality measurements with increases in help desk tickets reporting defects in the data.

Having once been an educator, I believe in a growth mindset. Anyone can learn a subject if they put their mind to it. The differences between data people and non-data people have to do with knowledge, skills, and experience, rather than with personality or disposition. If a person has not had the opportunity to work with data, if they have not experienced the "Aha!" moments that come with recognizing a pattern in data, then it makes sense that they have limited interest or feel they lack the actual ability to work with data. But if they are given the opportunity to see how data can work, then they can develop the interest; if they develop the interest, they can develop the required skills. The goal, after all, is not to turn everyone into a data scientist, but to raise awareness and understanding.

Meeting the People/Knowledge Challenge: Build Data Literacy

Building a data-literate organization takes time and commitment. Even more than the other challenges we have discussed, meeting the people challenge requires leadership and culture change. It takes some courage on the part of individuals and leadership to move in this direction because it requires being open-minded about oneself and the organization, giving and receiving feedback, and being willing to fail. Organizations must commit to training their employees and providing the tools that allow them to use their training and cultivate their skills.

But at the heart of such an effort is a recognition of data's potential to show us things we cannot see in any other way. As the Leader's Data Manifesto asserts: "Data offers enormous untapped potential to create competitive advantage, new wealth and jobs; improve health care; keep us all safer; and otherwise improve the human condition" (Dataleaders.org). Tapping this potential requires people with skills, knowledge, and experience using and interpreting data. Moreover, for most organizations, the best opportunities for organic growth lie in data. When people in an organization are excited about data, ready to learn, willing to experiment, and not afraid to make a few mistakes along the way, that organization will be more successful than one in which people are not engaged.

Coda: Books for the Journey

As I have said several times, data literacy depends on basic literacy. Just as a literate person will want to read the classics, a data-literate person should also do some core reading. In the bibliography and in the text of this chapter, I have referenced a range of books that can help people improve their data literacy. Below is a short list of essential reads.

Stephen Few, *The Data Loom: Weaving Understanding by Thinking Critically and Scientifically with Data* (Few, 2015a). This short book is focused entirely on the skills people need to use data. I was delighted when I read it. His *Signal: Understanding What Matters in a World of Noise* (Few, 2015b) is also a delight. With stunning clarity and purpose, Few explains and makes comprehensible a range of concepts related to data structure, statistics, and visualization. Few has also written on data visualization and dashboard design, again, making the material accessible and usable.

Darrell Huff, *How to Lie with Statistics*. Originally published in 1954, this book still holds up as a field guide to ways people try to dupe each other with data (Huff, 1954). It is an essential read for the data skeptic.

Daniel Kahneman, *Thinking, Fast and Slow* (Kahneman, 2013). An economist and psychologist, Kahneman specializes in the psychology of judgment and decision making. This book helps you think about thinking and shows specific ways in which you may not think the way you thought you were thinking.

Douglas Laney, *Infonomics: How to Monetize, Manage, and Measure Information as an Asset for Competitive Advantage* (Laney, 2017). Laney's book helps you think about the value of data in organizations. He brings in-depth thinking about data, finance, and economics, supported by numerous examples and case studies.

Danette McGilvray, *Executing Data Quality Projects: Ten Steps to Quality Data and Trusted Information*, 2nd edition (McGilvray, 2021). McGilvray describes the relation between data quality improvement and process improvement in general. Her methodology will help people in the organization become more data literate as they solve data problems. The second edition is supported by numerous case studies.

Katherine O'Keefe and Daragh O Brien, *Ethical Data and Information Management: Concepts, Tools and Methods* (O'Keefe & O Brien, 2018). This book focuses on how data is used and how it can be misused. It makes direct connections between the need for quality and the ethical handling of data. More importantly, from a data literacy perspective, it helps you understand data-as-data, with no technology hype. At all.

Cathy O'Neil, *Weapons of Math Destruction: How Big Data Increases Inequality and Threatens Democracy* (O'Neil, 2016). As with *Ethical Data and Information Management*, Cathy O'Neil's book allows you to see how data can be used and misused. Her examples draw attention to the sometimes cavalier, sometimes intentionally destructive ways in which influential data is created.

Thomas Redman, *Data Driven: Profiting from Your Most Important Business Asset* (Redman, 2008). Among Redman's many contributions to the field of data quality management, the concept of the Management System for Data and Information, described in the third section of *Data Driven*, is among the most important. This book will help you build your systems-thinking perspective while you learn more about data within organizations.

Kenett and Redman's *The Real Work of Data Science: Turning Data into Information, Better Decisions, and Stronger Organizations* (Kenett & Redman, 2019). Kenett and Redman offer numerous insights about data literacy. Not to give away the ending, but the "real work" involves teaching others in the organization about data. Though I did not find the term *data literacy* in the book, this book is about how to think about and communicate with data.

Edward Tufte, *The Visual Display of Quantitative Information* (Tufte, 1983). Tufte is a recognized pioneer in the field of data visualization. He not only helps you see data differently, but he also helps you understand why seeing data clearly matters to your ability to think about and use data.

The Culture Challenge: Organizational Accountability for Data

"The fundamental concept in social sciences is Power, in the same sense in which Energy is the fundamental concept in physics."

Bertrand Russell

"The principle of acting in good faith is at the heart of all decent work."

Richard Eyre, Film Director

Introduction

We have looked at the challenges of understanding data and managing product quality. We have seen that the rapidly evolving technical environment continually presents new data management challenges. And we have explored the ways in which people and organizations can improve their data knowledge and skills in using data. Cultivating data literacy is one component of improving behaviors toward data. But the hard work of individuals, in and of itself, will not change the organization as a whole. Changing organizational culture (i.e., changing how people work together) requires leadership. In this case, it requires that organizational leaders take accountability for data as an asset by ensuring that there is oversight of the processes that create and use data. It also means they provide funding and resources to improve and maintain data quality and get the organization to adopt a data-driven culture. This takes commitment supported by the desire for change and belief in the ability of the organization to change.

Ultimately, data quality improvement depends on changes in behavior. People must behave differently if they are to accomplish the work of ensuring that data is of high quality and of using this data to generate value. Organizations have hired chief data officers (CDOs) in an effort to establish executive oversight of data. They have implemented data governance and data stewardship programs in an effort to change behavior. To build accountability, they have named people data owners. These efforts have had limited success, but the problems the CDO, data governance, and data stewardship were intended to solve have not gone away. This chapter will look at why this is so and suggest ways to rethink how we implement these concepts.

Meeting the Challenges of Data Quality Management. DOI: https://doi.org/10.1016/B978-0-12-821737-5.00008-0

Accountability, Responsibility, and Good Faith

Let's start with a frank admission of two related problems that provide the context for the discussion in this chapter[1]:

- First, many people assert that organizations must establish accountability for data, but few people actually want to be accountable for data.
- Many data governance initiatives have hit brick walls because the organizations that implemented them did not do so in good faith.

Failed data governance initiatives are often blamed on things like people not understanding data governance or what it means to be accountable for data. This is a lame excuse. People who work in organizations that are talking about getting value from data certainly understand governance and accountability for other aspects of their business. It does not take a gigantic cognitive leap to see how these apply to data. But often data governance initiatives, like data quality initiatives, fail because executives do not recognize the value of their information assets, the cost of managing these assets, and the benefit of managing them well (Evans & Price, 2012, 2020), despite workable models for assessing this value (Laney, 2017).

The dictionary definitions for *accountability* and *responsibility* are essentially the same: they both mean "answerable, liable to be called to account, ... accountable for one's actions" (Online Etymological Dictionary). But in modern business parlance, we recognize different levels of answerability; accountability is the highest, and responsibility is next.

Accountability stipulates who makes what decisions. Accountability is imposed by senior executive leaders (i.e., the board and the chief executive officer [CEO]) who are themselves accountable for the overall success of the organization. For example, because the board and CEO make the chief financial officer (CFO) accountable for the effective management of an organization's financial assets, the CFO will lose his or her job for mismanaging the organization's money. Accountable people delegate authority to people responsible for day-to-day management and use of assets. For example, the CFO delegates authority for spending money to managers. Managers are expected to report back to the CFO (account for) how they use that money. Non-managers who incur expenses are expected to follow company policy and obtain approval from management in doing so.

For critical asset categories, there can only be one accountable person. This person must have the authority to enforce standards and behaviors across the organization. There can be many people responsible for using assets and reporting on their use. Responsible people are expected to follow standards and behave according to organizational policy.

In the case of data and information assets, the data management profession has proposed the CDO as the accountable person (Aiken & Gorman, 2013; DAMA, 2017), and many organizations have established a C-level position for data and information. Given this model of accountability and responsibility and given how data and information are created and used in organizations, every single person who creates or uses data must be responsible for their behaviors around data.

---

[1] I am indebted to James Price for the ideas at the core of this section.

One thing the CDO should be accountable for is defining these expected behaviors. In many organizations, these behaviors have not been defined, or, to the extent that they have been defined (e.g., through data governance policies), they have been very hard to enforce. This is a big problem. As discussed in Chapter 1, among the barriers to managing information as an asset are a lack of business governance and a lack of leadership and management (see Fig. 8). This means many CDOs have been hired and many data governance programs have been implemented essentially in bad faith. Organizations have not committed to the cultural, behavioral, process, and technical changes required to unlock the power of their own data.

Data Requires Oversight

The data environment is complex, and the technical environment is constantly evolving. Technological innovation enables an organization to produce, purchase, store, access, combine, and manipulate more and different forms of data. This means that data moves more rapidly within and between organizational units. Data can quickly be copied, moved, manipulated, and reused. Data from different departments and different systems may be structured or formatted differently, so integrating it involves cleansing and transforming it. Through a range of processes, data sets that were originally supposed to represent the same real-world entities (e.g., all of the organization's customers or vendors, sales for the third quarter) can quickly become disparate.

No one doubts that data and information are valuable and, if used well, they offer a key to competitive advantage. But few organizations succeed in fully unlocking this value (Evans & Price, 2012). Although good planning and reliable architecture help mitigate the risks, technical challenges are not generally the root cause of this problem; organizational choices and culture are. Success in getting value from data depends on an organization's ability to implement appropriate processes and skilled people around data management, including data quality management. To combat all of this potential for disparity, an organization must establish oversight for data.

The need for oversight has long been recognized. Organizations that want to get a clear picture of themselves must understand the connections among their parts. This need was first recognized as such with the advent of data warehousing, when it quickly became clear how heterogenous organizational data was and therefore how difficult data integration could be. People must perform a lot of work to get value and insight from data. They must organize and prepare data for analysis and reporting. If data has not been designed to account for the connections among different parts of the enterprise, then it will not serve the purposes people want it for. In such circumstances, data and data quality become objects of contention and politics within an organization. That is, the very thing that is supposed to enable success and insight becomes an obstacle to success.

Because data moves horizontally as well as vertically within organizations, it is not usually controlled by a single organizational entity with a single executive. And because it can be copied, restructured, combined, and reused, it cannot be controlled in the same way as other organizational resources. To get value from data, people must use it, so organizations want to balance control of data with their ability to leverage data. Data requires a form of oversight that accounts for the need for collaboration and cooperation about how data is produced, protected, and managed for value throughout its life cycle.

The Politics of Data Within Organizations

Data offers great potential for innovation, especially because it can provide insight about customers and products. However, because the quality of an organization's data reflects the quality of organization's processes, it also can expose vulnerabilities within an organization. This is one reason why discussions about the quality of data can easily become politicized. They can be perceived simply as an indictment of existing processes, teams, and technologies, rather than as a means to improve processes and enable teams to be more successful. As noted, managing data requires managing knowledge about data as a reflection of the organization. Knowledge is power, so managing data knowledge includes managing political perspectives that often include different views about the importance and even feasibility of quality as well as different assumptions about accountability and decision making around data.

Although data and technology are separable, they are also directly connected. Many people within a given organization have a direct stake in how the organization makes decisions about its data and its technology. These interests can conflict with each other. Technology decisions have a large impact on the quality of data, but this impact is often obscured by organizational processes for managing technology. For better or worse, it is easier to focus on technology than to address people's behavior and change processes. Technological change can be described, planned for, and measured, whereas the cultural and behavioral changes needed to focus on quality are hard to implement and measure. Moreover, because of the financial implications of decisions about technology, when these decisions are formalized through the budgeting and planning process, the focus is solely on the technology itself, not on the data that the technology manages.

Organizations not only must define what they mean by high-quality data; they also must develop the skills and processes required to ensure that they consistently create high-quality data, which is the foundation for many products and services. Some of these skills are technical, but many of them are interpersonal and, ultimately, cultural. They are about how people work together to ensure that the organization produces any high-quality outcome.

Data plays a role in an organization's daily operations. Consequently, much of it must be managed locally. But there is also an expectation that organizational data will fit together. Oversight of data must therefore be driven by an enterprise perspective. This does not mean that all decisions about data must be made centrally. It means decisions related to different parts of the organization must account for the context of the enterprise and their connections to other parts of the enterprise.

Because of its organic nature, data will change over time. Unless there are clear standards and controls to manage change and to ensure that data is produced to work consistently across the organization, data, like anything else, will tend toward entropy and become more disparate, chaotic, and random over time. All of this means that if an organization wants to get value from its data, it must establish enterprise-level oversight of data. Oversight includes the following:

- **Policy:** Describing expected behaviors around data
- **Accountability:** Defining what accountability for data means within the organization; identifying who is accountable for specific processes that create and use specific data sets
- **Knowledge management:** Ensuring that knowledge about data is documented and shared, including knowledge about quality expectations
- **Standards:** Setting standards that enable the organization to create consistent data that consistently meets quality expectations

- **Controls:** Putting in place auditable controls on data production and use
- **Protection:** Enforcing consistent protection of data to prevent misuse
- **Decision Making:** Enabling consistent decision-making processes for data and the processes that create and use data

Oversight should enable the organization to get more value from its data by reducing data redundancy, improving organizational understanding of data, and reducing the risks and costs associated with data use and misuse. Several structures have been proposed to address this need for oversight: the role of the CDO, the concept of data stewardship, and the concept of data governance. None of these has had the kind of impact that their originators envisioned. All have metamorphized over time. Each requires rethinking. Let's review these concepts and try to understand why they have not succeeded as promised.

The Chief Data Officer

The concept of a CDO is largely an outgrowth of the Sarbanes-Oxley Act, also known as SOX (2002), which itself was a US regulatory response to corporate corruption scandals at the beginning of the 21st century (Enron and WorldCom, to name the most infamous). Among other things, SOX mandated a high-level of transparency in financial reporting. Corporate executives (CEOs, CFOs) were required to ensure that financial statements were accurate and did not contain misrepresentations. They were made individually liable if the Securities and Exchange Commission were to find violations in a company's financial statements. Many quickly recognized the direct connection between their confidence in the organization's financials and the quality of the data on which these were based.

Capital One, a US-based financial services firm, appointed the first CDO in 2002. The concept was greeted with enthusiasm in data management circles. In addition to ensuring that the CEO does not wind up in jail, the purpose of a CDO is to oversee data management functions to help an organization get value from its data. As a business rather than technical position, it was thought that a CDO could bring focus to data at the upper management level and align data strategy with business strategy (Aiken & Gorman, 2013). The position can also be seen as an effort to take advantage of the recommendations from analyst firms like PriceWaterhouseCoopers (PwC) that business leaders should own the data (PwC, 2001) (See Chapter 1). The CDO role took on additional importance in the wake of the 2008 financial crisis as a means of establishing clear responsibility for data as an organizational asset. The concept has taken off. The Massachusetts Institute of Technology (MIT) established the International Association of Chief Data Officers and supports the organization's work with numerous webinars, articles, and an annual conference. As of 2018, well over 60% of senior Fortune 1000 business and technology decision makers said their organization had appointed a CDO (Zetlin, 2019).

Despite growth in the number of CDOs appointed, there is still no consensus on what the focus of the role should be. As *Forbes* reported in 2019, "No one agrees precisely on what the role entails, including CDOs." "Should the role be focused on defining data strategy or leveraging technology? Should it be focused on ensuring that data is protected or on defining how data should be governed? What is the optimal relationship between the CDO and the chief information officer (CIO)? To whom should the CDO report?" (Forbes Insights, 2019).

In the absence of consensus, the CDO role has morphed to include a range of responsibilities. Davenport and Bean (2020) describe seven different functions that a CDO might focus on. The first three of these represent what they characterize as *offensive data management*, the effort to get more value from an organization's data. The second four constitute *defensive data management*, that is, the effort to manage risks around data:

Chief data and analytics officer: Manage data science and analytics initiatives, including artificial intelligence.

Data entrepreneur: Monetize data, either by creating data products or by creating new businesses using data.

Data developer: Lead the creation of key applications or capabilities, such as data warehouses or data lakes, for the enterprise.

Data defender: Focus on data security, protecting the organization from fraud, breaches, and hacks and ensuring compliance with data protection regulation.

Data architect: Apply engineering to improve the data environment so consistently prepared data is available throughout the enterprise.

Data governor: Establish data governance programs and engage business managers to take responsibility for data domains.

Data ethicist: Focus on the ethics of how data is collected, safeguarded, and shared as well as who controls data.

As they rightly point out, it is not possible that one person can do all of these things, and in many organizations, responsibilities for some fall to others, such as the CIO, the chief analytics officer (CAO), enterprise architecture, the chief security officer (CSO), the data governance officer, or the chief data ethicist.[2]

The focus areas that are most familiar to many data management professionals are those of the data entrepreneur (monetizing data or leveraging data as an asset), the data governor (establishing data governance) and, to a lesser degree because it has a technical focus, the data architect (improving the data environment).[3] However, Davenport and Bean point out that there is limited appetite for these last two. About improving the data environment, they state, "[T]hese [improvement] programs tend to be expensive and time-consuming, and many business executives don't see sufficient value in them." They also report that in relation to data governance, a CDO told them, "I still try to get the business side involved, but I don't use the word 'governance'—it's become somewhat toxic."

Despite the lack of appetite for addressing these needs, the problems they represent are not going away by themselves. As Davenport and Bean point out in the Foreword to the 2020 NewVantage Survey on which their article draws: "We hear little about initiatives devoted to changing human attitudes and behaviors around data. Unless the focus shifts to these types of activities, we are likely to see the same problem areas in the future that we've observed year after year in this survey." Companies continue to focus on the supply side for data and technology, spending

---

[2]See also Deloitte (2016), which provides an overview of the evolution of the CDO role and a comparison to other C-level roles connected with data, IT, and analytics. And Zetlin (2020), also writing about the 2020 NewVantage Survey, who reports on high turnover rates for CDOs caused by lack of alignment on expectations between the organization and the CDO.

[3]See Aiken and Gorman (2013) for a full-length case for the establishment of the chief data officer position.

millions but not getting the return they expect on their investments. So, although there is hope that having a CDO can help an organization get more value from its data, including through improvement to data quality, it is no guarantee—at least not unless individual CDOs are able to establish a clear vision of the role within the context of their organizations. We are still in the "heroic" stage of maturity for CDOs.

Despite the mixed success of the CDO function, the idea itself still makes sense. The concept grew from the recognition that data is a resource that requires oversight at the highest levels if an organization is to get value from it. If an organization's finances are in disarray, their technology is not delivering expected benefits, or their workforce is underperforming, they will bring in leadership to address these problems. The idea of a data leader to address data problems makes sense. The difference is that there are well-defined, mature practices for managing and getting value from money, technology, and people. This is not the case with data, despite ongoing efforts to develop these practices.

Data Stewardship

The idea of data stewardship existed before that of the CDO. The concept of data stewardship is almost invariably linked to data governance, but the two concepts actually emerged at different times and for different reasons. Data quality pioneer Larry English discusses stewardship at length in *Improving Data Warehouse and Information Quality* (1999, pp. 401–419). English defines *information stewardship* as "the willingness to be accountable for a set of business information for the well-being of the larger organization by operating in service, rather than in control, of those around us."[4] In describing this concept to the data management world, English is very explicit that "steward" is not a title but a set of accountabilities[5]: "Everyone in the organization has a stewardship responsibility for their role in creating, defining, or using information" (English, 1999, p. 403).

He then describes different types of stewardship, providing a holistic vision of how individuals could come together for the good of the organization.[6] People who steward data can be knowledge workers, process owners, managers, or subject matter experts. They are accountable for the information they produce and use, for the integrity of the processes they execute, and for the definition of data rules for validity and other characteristics. These roles are part of de facto system of decision rights and accountabilities for data. However, English describes them in the context of information management, not as part of a data or information governance program or organization.[7]

---

[4]English is indebted to Peter Block's *Stewardship: Choosing Service over Self-Interest* (1993). Block's book, deeply steeped in the New Testament vision of stewardship, is a self-defined call to revolution that "promised fundamental change in the way we govern out institutions." Block describes stewardship, "to hold something in trust," as a form of "service over self-interest," and as a way of "achieving fundamental change in the way we govern our institutions" through "accountability without control or compliance."

[5]DAMA (2009, 2017), Seiner (2014), and Plotkin (2020) also all assert that "data steward" does not need to be a job title, but many organizations still seem to see it this way.

[6]Other discussions of data stewardship have been a little less idealistic (Plotkin, 2014; Seiner, 2014) but have retained the fundamental idea that stewards work for the common good by helping other people understand and use data.

[7]Similarly, Malcolm Chisholm (2001) describes the role and responsibilities of the reference data steward, again, before the term *data governance* was actually coined.

Stewarding data is a way of interacting with data. It implies taking care of data and acting with accountability and responsibility for data for the good of the organization. Data can be stewarded at different levels. As Robert Seiner puts it, "Being a data steward describes a relationship between a person and some data, whether these data are a data element, data set, subject area, application, database—however granular you want to get with your association of steward to data" (2014, p. 69). In Seiner's view, aspects of stewardship can be formalized as a means of recognizing work that stewards perform and helping them support the organization's effort to use data. This is largely a process of defining accountabilities for specific data (Seiner, 2014).

David Plotkin's definition of stewardship is more formal and is directly aligned with data governance and the data governance organization: "Data Stewardship is the operational aspect of Data Governance, where most of the day-to-day work of Data Governance gets done…. Data Stewardship consists of the people, organization, and processes to ensure that appropriately designated stewards are responsible for governed data" (Plotkin, 2020). Data stewardship is one of the means by which an organization moves from ungoverned to governed data, "data that is trusted and understood and for which someone is accountable for both the data itself and for addressing issues about the data" (Plotkin, 2020).

The concept of data stewardship has evolved since 1999, but like the idea of data governance, it seems more susceptible than other ideas to being misunderstood. The concept of data stewardship was introduced to help solve challenges with responsibility for data—based on the idea that anyone who creates or uses data has a responsibility to take care of it for the sake of the enterprise. Instead, it has produced new challenges. Stewardship has evolved from the idea that smart, well-intentioned people would "hold" organizational data "in trust" and help their colleagues use it to a formal role (a steward is part of the data governance organization) and a set of "extra" responsibilities (stewarding data is something different from doing your job in relation to data).

In some organizations, the goal has been to get all manner of stewards (business, technical, operational, domain, executive) in place in a steward matrix, as if dubbing people as stewards (rather than cultivating behaviors of stewardship) makes them stewards. In others, data stewardship has come to imply that only people with the words *data steward* in their job title are privy to data knowledge or capable of making decisions about data. In this sense, poorly cultivated data stewardship has had the opposite effect of what its originators intended, resulting in fewer people feeling a level of responsibility for data, rather than more people stewarding organizational data. Like the CDO (and as we will see in the next section "Data Governance"), the idea of stewardship has been saddled with a cornucopia of disparate responsibilities, essentially negating the possibility of a clear general definition of the concept.

Where organizations have implemented formal stewardship, the idea of stewardship as an attitude toward data (where many individuals in different roles "steward" data for the sake of the enterprise) has died away. Where organizations have not implemented formal stewardship, they look at models of stewardship that seem to require an "army of stewards" of all shapes and sizes and decide that the approach is too costly to be workable. They still struggle with many data management fundamentals and may blame this on "a lack of data stewards."

From a data quality management perspective, there has been another repercussion of the struggles to understand data stewardship. Although most lists of stewardship responsibilities include reference to enabling "data quality," few actually go beyond this association to describe what stewards are supposed to do to enable data quality.[8] Consequently, in some organizations, the concept of data stewardship has replaced the concept of data quality management. Very few organizations look at data quality management in the way I have described here, as a comprehensive set of processes intended to manage the quality of data over its life cycle.[9] In fact, the level of discourse about what is required for data quality management has deteriorated and tends to center around undercooked ideas about what it means to profile data. The ideas of defining standards, managing the data chain, designing for quality, or implementing statistical process controls have faded into the distance and have been replaced with a general assumption that somehow, stewards are responsible for the quality of data, without explaining exactly how they are supposed to do this, given the complexity of organizational data.

And yet, like the idea of the CDO, the idea of data stewardship makes sense. People who have deep knowledge of business processes and the data they use and create will help organizations succeed, especially if they are able to share their knowledge with others. Recognizing and rewarding people for this work also makes sense because it brings value to the organization. Where it makes sense, formalizing the role can bring additional value because it can raise overall awareness of how data works within the organization. However, making stewardship appear as if it is an extra responsibility undermines the whole process.

Data Governance

As noted earlier, the need for an enterprise perspective on data emerged with the advent of data warehousing, but the term *data governance* itself was coined in the early 2000s by Gwen Thomas, who founded the Data Governance Institute in 2003 and published the first book on data governance in 2006. The concept of data governance was originally focused on the need to make better decisions about data, with a goal to help improve and manage data quality. Very quickly there emerged an effort to formalize processes and professionalize activities related to governing data.[10] The concept received widespread attention with the publication of the first edition of DAMA's Data Management Body of Knowledge (DMBOK1) in 2009.

The financial crisis took place in 2008, shortly before the publication of the DMBOK1. With the introduction of legislation related to data privacy and data traceability, the focus of data governance

[8]The exception to this is Plotkin (2020). He describes in detail a number of activities that data stewards may engage in, including data quality rule definition, issue management, reference data management, and master data management. These activities, by definition, involve taking care of data for the sake of the enterprise, so they can be viewed as stewardship. They also can be viewed simply as other facets of data management.
[9]The vision of data quality management as a comprehensive set of practices is best understood through the six functional areas of the IQ International (IQint) framework, which include: IQ strategy and governance, IQ environment and culture, IQ value and business impact, information architecture quality, IQ measurement and improvement, and sustaining information quality. The fact that IQ International (formerly the International Association for Information and Data Quality [IAIDQ]) has been absorbed into the Business Analyst Professional Association and that data quality management practices are no longer viewed as a set distinct from other aspects of data stewardship is a symptom of what I am discussing here.
[10]For example, Information Quality International (IQint), DAMA International (the Data Management Association), and MIT Information Quality conferences.

efforts in many organizations hardly began before it shifted away from quality and toward questions of compliance, privacy, and security. Obviously, compliance, privacy, and security are critical to getting value from data. In some ways, this shift has allowed data governance to take hold. (Although it is fairly straightforward to impress upon employees that everyone has a responsibility to protect data and to put in place technical means of protecting data, it is more difficult to get people to understand that the data they create may not meet the quality requirements of their downstream colleagues.) But in other ways, the focus on these questions has also resulted in a command-and-control approach to data governance. Data governance is seen more as a police function or as a bureaucratic obstacle than as an enabler of or a strategic partner to efforts to get more value from organizational data.

The Data Governance Institute's short definition, "data governance is the exercise of decision-making and authority for data-related matters," succinctly summarizes the intention of data governance—to provide a level of oversight for data. Its longer definition unpacks what it would mean to govern data effectively: "Data Governance is a system of decision rights and accountabilities for information-related processes, executed according to agreed-upon models which describe who can take what actions with what information, and when, under what circumstances, using what methods."[11]

The idea of data governance is closely related to the general idea of corporate governance. BusinessDictionary.com defines corporate governance as:

> The framework of rules and practices by which a board of directors ensures accountability, fairness, and transparency in a company's relationship with all its stakeholders (financiers, customers, management, employees, government, and the community).

> The corporate governance framework consists of (1) explicit and implicit contracts between the company and the stakeholders for distribution of responsibilities, rights, and rewards, (2) procedures for reconciling the sometimes conflicting interests of stakeholders in accordance with their duties, privileges, and roles, and (3) procedures for proper supervision, control, and information-flows to serve as a system of checks-and-balances.

Corporate governance recognizes that key assets—people, financial, physical, intellectual, infrastructure, information technology (IT), information itself—require governance mechanisms, such as oversight committees, planning processes, policies, budgets, and measures of success. It also recognizes that people must be accountable for participating in these processes, following policies, and performing well in relation to success measurements. Data and other informational resources require a similar kind of oversight. Putting this oversight on data is challenging because data is both an asset in and of itself and a component of other assets, and it does not have the limitations of physical or financial assets or of human beings (e.g., it is not "used up" when used, it can be cheaply copied, shared, and manipulated).

Early discussions on data governance emphasized its structural role. As Elizabeth Pierce described it in 2007: "Data governance design lays out the decision-making structures, alignment

---

[11]The Data Governance Institute. This definition is also the basis of the DAMA Data Management Body of Knowledge (DMBOK) definition of *data governance*. See also Ladley (2019). Loshin (2011) incorporates the idea of data governance into the approach to a data quality program. For Loshin, reducing the business impact of poor-quality data is the goal of data quality strategy; data governance is one of the means to this end.

processes, and communication approaches that enable the strategic objectives for data quality to be implemented and to monitor how well these strategic objectives are being achieved." In clarifying who makes decisions and how decisions are made, the intention of data governance was to promote better behaviors around data—behaviors that recognized the interests of the overall enterprise and raised awareness of the ways in which the enterprise is connected through the data it produces, shares, and uses. These better behaviors are ultimately focused on improving the quality of data, that is, making data more fit for the purposes of data consumers. Early discussions on data governance also made a clear distinction between data governance, as the process for determining who makes decisions and how they are made, and data management, as the process of actually making and implementing the decisions (DAMA, 2009; Ladley, 2019; Pierce, 2007).

Unfortunately, data governance has not worked like this in many organizations. The first generation of data governance tended toward bureaucracy, formality, and *instruction* in the worst sense of the word and focused on following rules, rather than on meeting the goals the rules are intended to help the organization meet. When implementing data governance, some organizations focus only on "getting governance in place," sometimes simply for the sake of having governance in place (e.g., to prove to auditors that an organization is complying with a requirement to "govern data"), rather than on clarifying expectations about and improving practices and behaviors around data. In practice, this has resulted in the perception of data governance as something that only the data governance team does. Data governance teams are put in the uncomfortable position of being perceived simply as bureaucratic overhead and data governance processes being perceived as optional add-ons, rather than as a means to reduce confusion and improve efficiency around data. As quoted earlier in "The Chief Data Officer," people do not even want to use the word *governance* because it has become "somewhat toxic."

What's Wrong with Data Governance?

Although in theory the term *data governance* refers to the overall system of decision rights and accountabilities, including its rules and policies, accountabilities, decision-making bodies, and ways of enforcing particular behaviors, in practice, *data governance* usually refers to a team of people who are charged with "implementing" component pieces of this overall system.

Despite much thought being given to how to make data governance work, very few organizations have succeeded in establishing effective oversight for data. They lack clear policies on who is responsible for data often because they have not defined what "responsibility for data" entails. Several factors contribute to the difficulty in defining this responsibility, including those we have discussed in previous chapters; for example, the tendency to confuse managing data with managing IT systems and costs and the lack of awareness of the ways the organizations is connected through its data supply chain. Other factors have also contributed to this situation.

Bad Faith

Despite the proposed benefits of data governance, many data governance programs do not enjoy genuine leadership support. Because of government regulations in some places, organizations must have some level of data governance. However, data governance has become a checklist item, rather than a way to drive value. If the program is in place, that is enough, and the hard work of changing the organization does not take place. It does not need to be like that. But if it is, and there is no commitment to change how the organization behaves toward data, then data governance cannot be effective.

Too Much, Too Soon

This is not to say that data governance will succeed simply through leadership support. There are particular challenges to how organizations have attempted to implement data governance. These are largely connected to the effort to roll out fully fledged data governance programs using the pyramid model without first assessing the current state of the organization and defining the problems that data governance is intended to solve for the organization.

For example, experts (DAMA, 2017; Ladley, 2019) continually point out the following:

- **Data governance is a program, not a project:** Data governance cannot be implemented like a project, once and done. Data governance is a set of processes, each of which will have an initial implementation and a period of maturation. These must be rolled out over time so the organization can adjust to the changes brought about by new ways of behaving toward data. Organizations that attempt to implement multiple components of data governance all at once have little chance of success. An organization can only change so many processes at once.
- **Data governance is unique to the organization:** Data governance must work within the culture of the organization in which it is implemented. It must start with an understanding of the current state of the organization and especially the specific obstacles that limit its ability to get value from its data. It also must prioritize objectives based on the organization's business strategy.
- **Data governance requires cultural change management:** Adopting and formalizing data governance structures requires that people change how they work, behave, and act toward data. Therefore, data governance programs must include or be supported by a cultural change management process.

Nevertheless, many organizations essentially ignore these cautions and attempt to set up data governance based solely on the now-traditional data governance pyramid as published in the first edition of the DMBOK (2009). Data governance programs often fail not only because they try to impose a model that does not work for the organization, but also because they try to set up the program all at once without defining clear, specific goals and scope. They set up data governance councils and assign people as stewards but do not give them any real work do to. They do not take the time for the training and reinforcement required for real cultural change (Algmin, 2019). With data governance, as with many things, you must be able to walk before you can run. Even more importantly, given the lack of success many organizations have had with data governance, you must be able to lift your head and roll over before you can crawl.

Unclear Scope

Because data governance programs often do not set clear expectations, people who are not directly part of the data governance team are likely to misunderstand the role of data governance. They may "fill in the blanks" with their own expectations for data governance. They may, for example, expect the data governance team to have direct responsibility for all aspects of data management—to make every decision, to solve every data issue, to define every data element. These highly unrealistic expectations actually undermine efforts to govern data effectively across the enterprise because they imply that the only function responsible for data is the governance function, when the true purpose of data governance is to clarify the multiple accountabilities for data across the enterprise.

The Lure of Shiny Objects

Not surprisingly, when scope and process are unclear and the word *data* is mentioned, people are more susceptible to the dangers of technology hype. Data governance is fundamentally about people and process, rather than technology. The purpose is to define desired behaviors (accomplished largely through policies) and provide oversight of processes to ensure that these behaviors (policies) are followed. Tools can help. For example, they can be used to automate decisions within workflows, manage critical metadata, and enforce data usage policies. But if an organization has not yet defined its decision-making processes, then how can it automate workflows around them? If it does not know who is responsible for creating critical metadata, how can it manage this metadata? If it has not defined data usage policies, how can it automate their enforcement? The idea that a data governance tool, by itself, establishes or improves data governance is completely illogical. In fact, an organization that goes after data governance tooling without knowing what it wants to accomplish through data governance in the first place creates a distraction from which it may never recover.[12]

Failure to Achieve the Main Mission

Data governance is intended to establish a system of decision rights and accountabilities toward data. One of the first questions data governance programs try to address is that of data "ownership." This is because the question of accountability most often is figured as a question of "ownership." Data governance teams try to "find" data owners and put them on data governance councils, but once there, they often do not know what to do because no one has actually defined what they mean by ownership of data. This creates obstacles to data governance in two ways.

- First, data governance programs are likely to adopt a model data "ownership" at the data domain level or the business function level. This is how many data governance and data stewardship matrices are presented, but very few individuals or even teams have control over an entire domain of data. To assume that they do means they are charged with an impossible task from the outset.
- Secondly, most assumptions about data ownership do not account for the data chain. Data can be shared and used multiple times, so the lines of responsibility are murky. Unless the concept

---

[12]The same can be said about data quality. Some organizations start their data quality programs by "selecting a tool." The logical question is: A tool for what? Until you have defined some goals for data quality management and given it a focus, why invest in tools? Some people would say, "Well, you need a data-profiling tool." Maybe, if you have a use case for data profiling. But at the very beginning of a data quality management program, often the only tool you need is a query engine.

of data ownership recognizes that owners control data only for their links of the data chain, very few people will sign up to be owners.

Any data governance program must address these questions because they exist in every organization and are fundamental to the purpose of governance in the first place. Who gets to make decisions for data? Who is responsible for addressing data issues? Who is responsible for resolving conflicts about what makes data usable? However, few programs do so directly, probably because addressing these questions is difficult. Doing so requires the ability to look closely at the interactions among functional areas that produce and use data, to recognize risk, and to imagine better ways that these interactions could be handled.

The data ownership route is not working and not likely to work because data is fluid and moves rapidly within organizations. If the concept of data ownership were real (i.e., aligned with common organizational behavior), we would probably not have the challenges we have with data. Data is not "owned" by individual executives or by teams in the same way a budget or a set of computers is owned. Data moves horizontally, between verticals. It can be used multiple times without being used up. It gets replicated and transformed. The goal is not to stop data from moving around, but to get value from it because it is being used. Old fashioned "ownership," even if it could be established, would get in the way of deriving value from data.

There is a way forward, however. Although most organizations cannot solve for data ownership in the way envisioned in many governance models, they can solve for process ownership because most critical business processes already have owners. Instead of saddling people with accountability for whole data domains that they cannot control, data governance or data quality management organizations can work together with the people who are responsible for the processes that produce data and the people who consume data from these processes to ensure that data is complete and usable—as we would for any other product or business outcome.

Many data governance professionals are justly frustrated with the current state of data governance.[13] Data governance not only sounds like a good idea; it also seems clearly necessary to facilitate and sustain an enterprise perspective data. It is not clear by what other means this perspective could be gained. So, what has gone wrong? Several related factors get in the way of effective data governance:

---

[13]Numerous conference papers discuss the need for changes in data governance and call for "DG 2.0," and so on. For books, see Algmin (2019), Madsen (2019), and Edvinsson (2019). In a nice instance of technology hype, IBM has joined the fray with its blog: "RIP Data Governance." First by misstating the goal of data governance ("ensuring the quality of an organization's data across the data lifecycle")—this is the goal of data quality management. Data governance should support data quality management, but its focus is on defining decision rights and responsibilities for data), and then by introducing a new term, *data enablement*, which seems to be a new version of data governance without the nasty *g* word itself ("By building a program around data enablement, enterprises can ensure that the right data is delivered to the right resource at the right time. Data enablement requires innovative thinking, vision, people, processes and technologies."), but which apparently turns out to be a new set of tooling ("Data enablement is an active means of data management that relies on defined and enforced data policies. It provides the real-time ability to deploy automated and active data validation, classification and management, which comes with complete and visible data lineage and associated metadata. It incorporates a comprehensive and searchable data catalog (updated in real time), which enables self-service data access and data discovery.") that still requires data governance in some form ("None of this works, however, without assigning ownership and responsibility for the data to whoever creates it.") (Sutherland, 2019).

- **Unclear purpose:** People have lost track of the general problems that data governance was originally intended to solve; specifically, establishing decision rights and accountabilities for data from an enterprise perspective. And they have not taken the time to identify and understand the particular problems that they must address within their own organizations. Ironically, data governance was originally conceived as a way of clarifying decision rights and accountabilities, but data governance teams often face the challenge of having unclear responsibilities.
- **Unclear definitions of key concepts:** Directly connected to the lack of clear purpose is a fuzzy vocabulary. Many descriptions of data governance and nearly all of data stewardship emphasize the need to define data well. But few of them clearly define terminology related to data governance. For example, one goal of most data governance programs is to "identify data owners and make them accountable for data." But few actually define what they mean by "data ownership" or "accountability for data."
- **Lack of focus:** Organizations have become distracted by activities that do not solve important problems (and, with these, the tools that are supposed to "enable" data governance). For example:
  - Data stewards become caught up in a metric for defining a set number of terms, rather than solving problems related to the misunderstanding of data.
  - Data governance teams focus on choosing a tool to manage their policies, rather than defining policies that enable data uses.
  - Magical thinking about tools enables people to claim that they "have" governance because they have purchased a governance tool.
- **Sprawling scope:** A direct consequence of the lack of focus is unclear scope. Many definitions of *data governance* subsume other functions (stewardship, data quality management, master data management) in ways that limit the success of data governance generally and these other functions specifically.

These are similar to the conditions that have undermined the effectiveness of the CDO and of data stewardship. Organizations must develop a better understanding of how to focus activities that support their ability to get value from data.

Status of the Oversight Problem: Not Solved

Neither the CDO nor data stewardship nor data governance has had the effects that data management professionals anticipated they would. Although there are more CDOs than ever, organizations still do not treat their data as a strategic asset, and there has been limited success getting the board to pay attention to data strategy (Evans & Price, 2018). "Data steward" is now a job title, and, consequently, fewer people actually steward data. Also, data governance has become a part of embedded bureaucracy, rather than a means of removing obstacles to data value.

The problems CDOs, data stewardship, and data governance were intended to solve have not gone away. If anything, they have intensified as organizations create more data faster and as they try to leverage it to gain competitive advantage. If we think of data governance first as a set of activities and behaviors rather than as an organizational unit, then we can take a different approach to the problems that data governance is intended to solve. This is why I find the original definition of *data governance* powerful: "a *system* of decision rights and accountabilities for information-related processes," rather than merely an organizational function that is the sole responsibility of a single team.

As defined earlier, a *system* is an interconnected set of elements that is coherently organized to achieve a purpose (Meadows, 2008). Data governance activities exist within any organization that uses data. Even without a formal data governance program, people make decisions about data and take actions related to data (Seiner, 2014). But if this "system" is not explicitly defined and understood as such, it is unlikely to operate in ways that optimize the value of data. For example, unless someone is charged with defining and socializing an enterprise perspective on data, decisions about data will be made at the "local" level. The main purpose of an ad hoc system of decision rights and accountabilities is simply to enable day-to-day work to get done. Getting work done is important, but it does not change how an organization gets value from data.

Note that I am not saying that formal data governance can be implemented without a data governance team. On the contrary, changing an organization's relationship to its data requires work, and a team is required to drive the work. I am saying that data governance never starts with a green field, nor should it be viewed as completely new and an add-on. The starting point for data governance is understanding the organization and its goals. Existing practices may be cultivated, improved, or, in some cases, stopped. Data governance involves adding the element of intention to the system of decision rights and responsibilities, including for the data governance team itself. The team that helps establish formal data governance practices must therefore do the following:

- **Understand the organization and its data opportunities:** Understanding how the organization uses data, how it wants to use data, and what gets in the way of its opportunities to get value from data. The starting point of data governance is rooted in business strategy: to bring value, a data governance program should first understand the strategic role that data plays in the organization and then prioritize its governance goals based on their organization's specific challenges. Clarifying purpose is a prerequisite to bringing focus and defining a manageable scope. Data governance can address a wide range of issues and improvements. It should focus on those that are important to the organization.
- **Understand current state of governance practices:** Identifying "information-related processes" and describing the "decision rights and accountabilities" associated with them. This work involves understanding how the organization actually interacts with, defines expectations for, and makes decisions about data.
- **Define the desired future state:** Documenting and driving consensus on "who can take what actions with what information, and when, under what circumstances, using what methods." This work is focused on describing, in policies, guidelines, and standards, the expected/desired behaviors toward data for the organization. It also requires defining a framework for decision-making accountability. This may be implicit in policies or explicitly defined in a matrix. Defining the future state also includes defining the role and scope of the data governance team itself. This will differ depending on the problems the organization is trying to solve. It is hard work to formalize decision rights and accountabilities for data. It entails envisioning desired behaviors and putting them into words. But this is the one function that must be done by a data governance office or team because no one else in the organization is charged with doing this work.
- **Build consensus:** The work of defining the future state must go way beyond documentation of expectations. These concepts must be communicated, socialized, and refined so people understand not only what things they are supposed to do differently but also why they should do

them differently. That is, they should understand how proposed process changes, policies, and standards help them do their jobs and enable the organization to get more benefit from data. Changes also must be prioritized. Organizations cannot do everything at once, and not every governance activity is of equal importance to every organization. The effort to build consensus itself requires a type of governance organization that is different from what has evolved so far. Data governance cannot be successful if it is perceived as bureaucratic and top down. Consensus must be developed around the benefits of clearer decision rights, principles, responsibilities, policies, and standards.

- **Oversee process and policy compliance:** Ensuring that work is executed according to these models is the true "oversight" part of data governance. To know how the organization benefits from improved decision making and clear accountability, data governance must audit processes and measure results. Done poorly, this will create more bureaucracy. Done well, it will accomplish two goals:
  - Enable the organization to measure the benefits of process improvements, policies, and standards
  - Serve as a feedback mechanism to improve interactions within the "system of decision rights and accountabilities"
- **Act on findings:** Feedback is critical to the additional responsibility of the data governance team: evolving the models and processes to enable efficient work related to data. Data governance involves a set of ongoing processes that can and should be managed over time. This is why, as Ladley has stated repeatedly, "Data Governance is a program, not a project" (Ladley, 2019). These will not work perfectly the first time. Any data governance team must be able to evaluate its work, listen to its customers (the people who are creating and using organizational data), and respond to opportunities for improvement.

Notice that this list does not mention the CDO or data stewardship. Along with the structure, organization, and scope of the data governance work, stewardship and a CDO are part of the solution to the problems data governance is trying to solve. It should not be presupposed that every organization needs them or that they will be organized the same way in every enterprise.

If the organization has a CDO or is planning to hire one, this person is likely to drive the process of defining (or redefining) the approach to data governance. If the organization does not have a CDO, then the current state assessment may show the specific reasons why it would (or would not) benefit from having a CDO.

Formal data stewardship can be a component of data governance, depending on the problems that the organization is trying to solve. How stewardship is organized (full-time, part-time, ad hoc; domain level, process level, system level) and executed (the specific responsibilities of specific stewards) depends on these same problems, existing organizational culture, and the desired future state. I worked in one organization that had formal stewardship but unclear accountability for data; in another organization that had no formal stewardship but very clear accountability for data; and in another that had a small team of stewards to facilitate knowledge sharing among stakeholders and directly manage critical shared data sets. The organization with no named stewards but very clear accountability was the most successful at getting value from its data.

As with other possible components of data governance, the approach to stewardship should be defined based on organizational goals and requirements. It should also account for organizational culture—how people work together. If having named stewards helps the organization get data work done, then the organization should name them. If doing so makes people step back from responsibilities toward data, then the organization should find another way.

Meeting the Challenges: Improving Data Governance

Organizations are complex. They produce data through multiple processes. Even if each of these processes works well in isolation, they are unlikely to work well together unless they are intentionally made to do so. In the effort to manage this complexity, data management professionals have introduced the ideas of data governance, data stewardship, and the CDO, but they still appear to be in the "storming" stage of development.

To improve this situation, it helps to return to a fundamental question: What problems are we trying to solve? At its simplest, we want to enable organizations to get value from their data. Value is the difference between the cost and the benefit of a thing. To increase value, you must either lower costs or increase benefits. I see five ways that clarifying organizational accountability and responsibility for data can reduce cost and improve efficiency. If lessons learned from organizations that focus on quality can be applied to data management, these approaches may also create opportunities to increase revenue.

- **Oversight:** Provide enterprise oversight of data and data-related processes to enable consistency and reduce technical and process costs associated with data production, use, and management.
- **Accountability:** Define accountability for data quality to the people who own the processes that create and use data. This will reduce organizational friction and simplify decision making.
- **Knowledge sharing:** Enable knowledge sharing around data to enable more efficient data use.
- **Better data manners:** Encourage specific behaviors toward data that enable its use and prevent its misuse.
- **Focus on quality:** Ensure that data is of high quality to reduce the costs of poor-quality data.

This combination provides a way to clarify and simplify existing models of governance, stewardship, and data quality management.

Focus Data Governance on Oversight and Changing Behaviors Toward Data

The primary purpose of data governance is to provide oversight of data from an enterprise perspective. The data governance team should define policies, guidelines, frameworks, and standards that describe desired behavior and enable consistency of execution for data-related activities, including decision making. Their primary responsibility should be to facilitate and enforce the use of these policies and other guidelines. But this should not be done for its own sake. The goal is to cultivate the behaviors the organization needs to be successful with data.

Focus Data Governance on the Most Important Data

Scope also applies to the scope of data the governance team accounts for. Trying to govern every piece of data to the same degree is both unrealistic and unnecessary. Some data is simply more important than other data. Data governance professionals should identify the most important data and prioritize activities around it. Gartner analyst Andrew White made this argument in 2013 through a simple model, the three rings of information governance, which describes "the different degrees to which information is governed in support of improved business outcomes." The inner ring represents master data that is used by multiple processes. The outer ring represents data used by the fewest applications and processes. The middle ring, which represents data that is used by multiple processes but not so widely that it is considered "master data," is the gray area where people get stuck. The solution? Focus first on the inner ring. Figure out what works. Then extend to the middle ring, prioritizing based on what you learn as you go.

Align Accountability/Responsibility for Data with Process Ownership

One clear lesson learned from manufacturing is that supply chain management works. Expectations are clear, and all participants have a stake in the outcome. As will be discussed in Chapter 11, the data chain within an organization is analogous to the supply chain in manufacturing. Upstream business processes produce data that is used as input for downstream operations, reporting, and analytics. If each process owner knows the quality requirements of his or her downstream data consumers, then the chance of meeting these requirements increases substantially.

Put Process Before Tools

Tools do not solve governance challenges. The organization should start by defining the problems it is trying to solve through data governance. Once these challenges are defined, processes can be defined to solve them. These processes may generate requirements for tooling. Requirements can then be used to identify and implement appropriate tooling.

Focus Stewardship on the Organization's Data Requirements

Stewardship is about taking good care of things that belong to an organization. However, the particulars of what these things are and how they are best taken care of depends on the needs of the organization. Develop a stewardship model that meets your organization's requirements, rather than adopting a generic one that requires many people to start doing "stewardship stuff," such as defining business terms and putting them in a business glossary without a plan or a goal. There may be a need for different flavors of stewardship to address different challenges. Some stewards may be responsible for particular data sets. Others may facilitate working groups to address specific data questions. Some may have "data steward" in their job title. Others may not. Do what makes sense and what works.

Formally Cultivate Better Data Behavior

Transforming an organization from its current state to a state in which it effectively governs and manages the quality of its data in support of strategic goals will require changes in behavior. People will not change unless they see a reason to do so. Even if they want to change, they are likely to need help making changes. Efforts to govern data, clarify and enforce accountabilities, steward data, and manage data quality must be supported through a cultural change management program. Especially important is to reward work that demonstrates accountability for data and contributes to improved quality.

Formalize Data Quality Management Practices

This chapter has focused on governance and stewardship, rather than data quality management, but the three are closely connected. Data governance practices can contribute to data quality improvement by raising awareness, setting standards, enforcing policy, and most importantly, helping change behavior. Data stewardship enacts a set of these desired behaviors. Stewards build and share organizational knowledge about data and help their colleagues use data appropriately. Data quality practices can enable the success of data governance efforts by showing the impact of governance efforts on the quality and usability of the data. Data quality management may be embedded in a data governance program, or it may exist separately from a data governance program. In either case, the organization should clearly define the scope and focus of these data quality management practices along with their relation to data governance efforts.

Data Quality Management Practices 3

The purpose of Section 3 is to describe the capabilities an organization must develop to better manage its data and to show how these capabilities can be integrated into project and operational processes. Many organizational processes can have an impact on the quality of organizational data—in fact, any process that creates or uses data can influence its quality. Heightened awareness of these potential impacts can help an organization produce higher-quality, more reliable data. Core data quality management capabilities can help an organization raise awareness of these impacts, identify and mitigate risks associated with data, and improve its processes so they create higher-quality data. Data quality management is also necessary to sustain high levels of quality.

Chapter 9: Core Data Quality Management Capabilities *describes the functions required to build organizational capacity to manage data for quality over time, in the context of organizational data management. It reviews models for understanding data quality processes (DAMA's framework, ISO 8000's Data Quality Management Process Model, and Danette McGilvray's Ten Steps Process), each of which provides perspective on the capabilities themselves. The capabilities include the following:*

- **Data Quality Standards:** Describe what is meant by high-quality data; set standards and requirements for data quality.

- **Data Quality Assessment:** Observe and analyze characteristics of particular data to identify errors, risks, and obstacles to use and to quantify data quality levels.
- **Data Quality Monitoring:** Track quality levels within a system or process to detect unexpected conditions and to take action in response to them.
- **Data Quality Reporting:** Communicate information about the condition of data to data consumers and other stakeholders.
- **Data Quality Issue Management:** Identify, quantify, prioritize, and facilitate the remediation of root causes of data issues (obstacles to data consumers' uses of data).
- **Data Quality Improvement:** Identify and facilitate the implementation of process and technical changes to prevent data issues, enforce data quality standards, and improve the overall trustworthiness of organizational data.

Chapter 10: Dimensions of Data Quality provides an in-depth discussion of a core concept in data quality management: data quality dimensions. Dimensions provide a framework through which to understand the core capabilities. As the foundation for data quality rules and requirements, they play a critical role in helping answer the first and second fundamental questions about data quality: "What do we mean by high-quality data?" and "How do we detect low-quality data?" They also provide a basis for assessment, issue management, data quality monitoring and reporting, and quantifying data quality improvement so accountable people in the organization can answer the third question: "What action will we take when data does not meet quality standards?" The discussion about dimensions is organized in relation to four of the five challenges of data quality management (data, process, technology, people). It provides detail about how dimensions pertain to different levels of data (data set, column, relationship) and to data management capabilities that enable the production of high-quality data (data modeling, metadata management, system controls, data consumer support).

Chapter 11: Data Life Cycle Processes describes four processes that provide different perspectives on managing the quality of data: The data life cycle, the data supply chain, the data value chain, and the systems development life cycle. These cycles help put the core data quality management capabilities in the context of other work carried out within the enterprise. Each model offers a variation on how we can think about executing data quality management activities. In combination, they provide data quality practitioners, data producers, data consumers, data stewards, data modelers, application developers, process improvement teams, and other stakeholders a means of understanding their work in the context of the wider enterprise. They also show the intersection of processes that can influence the condition of data. These models help practitioners communicate across the enterprise because they depend on analogous processes that are executed by various business and technical teams (product management, supply chain management, value creation, project and program management).

Chapter 12: Tying It Together summarizes the arguments in the book as a whole and strongly encourages readers to apply the ideas and work to change their organizations for the better.

Core Data Quality Management Capabilities

"The winds and waves are always on the side of the ablest navigators."
Edward Gibbon, *The Decline and Fall of The Roman Empire*

Introduction

People often ask me to explain my "data quality process." I always want to respond by asking: "Which data quality process?" Data and information are vital to organizational success. They are elements in the system that is the organization and a means of binding the organization together and enabling it to accomplish its goals. So, ideally, any process that creates data accounts for its quality. Ideally, as data moves through an organization, every process that touches it helps ensure its quality (or at least not reduce its quality). Indeed, ideally, even processes that use data should contribute to the overall quality of data within an organization. Uses of data may result in the creation of new data and metadata. They are also a source of feedback to the owners of the processes that created their inputs. Ideally, if data were created with clear intention and moved in and through an organization via a well-managed supply chain, where process owners were accountable to each other to deliver data of required quality, then there would not be a need for data quality management per se. Quality would be built into each process and each step.

Alas, we do not live in an ideal world. Very few organizations manage their data by design. Most organizations operate using a mixture of older and newer systems and a combination of well-defined to haphazardly defined processes that are executed by people with differing degrees of skill, knowledge, insight, commitment, and awareness of the effects their work has on others. Teams struggle to integrate data produced under conditions that create differences in granularity, format, and meaning. The business and technical processes that touch data do not necessarily focus on ensuring its quality. They are more likely to treat data simply as the stuff that they are moving around or as a by-product of their processes than as an output that others require (i.e., as a usable product). Projects that focus on data movement focus on just that: getting the data from one place in the organization to another, not necessarily noticing if it gets banged up along the way. So, although organizations must recognize that the quality of data can be influenced by many people and processes, there is also a need to actively manage the quality of data. Without active management, an organization and its data can easily succumb to entropy.

Not only this, but when organizations do take up the mantle of data quality and start to see the interconnectedness of organizational data and the impact of every process on the quality of data, there is a risk that in their enthusiasm, they will consider everything that touches data to be part of data quality management, just as many now see everything that touches data to be part of data governance. In such cases, data quality management becomes top-heavy, burdened with unmanageable scope, and dies a painful death.

Meeting the Challenges of Data Quality Management. DOI: https://doi.org/10.1016/B978-0-12-821737-5.00009-2

This chapter defines the core capabilities required to actively manage the quality of data and to distinguish between these and other capabilities. Although high-quality data depends on many things, my argument is that data quality management must be an ongoing effort that focuses on the data itself. It should not be an information technology (IT) add-on or a minor piece of data stewardship. It requires a high degree of data literacy, a recognition of how the organization is bound together through data, and a relentlessly optimistic attitude toward the possibility of improvement.

Core data quality management functions include the following:

- **Defining data quality standards:** Describing what is meant by high-quality data; setting consistent standards and requirements for data quality
- **Assessing data quality:** Observing characteristics of particular data to identify errors, risks, and obstacles to use and to quantify data quality levels
- **Monitoring data quality:** Tracking quality levels within a system or process to detect unexpected conditions and to take action in response to them
- **Data quality reporting:** Communicating information about the condition of data to data consumers and other stakeholders
- **Managing data quality issues:** Identifying, quantifying, prioritizing, and facilitating the remediation of root causes of obstacles to data consumers' uses of data
- **Improving data quality:** Identifying and facilitating the implementation of process and technical changes to prevent data issues, enforce data quality standards, and improve the overall trustworthiness of organizational data

Together, these processes form an instance of the Shewhart cycle: Plan, Do, Check, Act (PDCA), which we discussed in Chapter 5 and will review again in Chapter 11. The relationships among these processes are illustrated in Fig. 25 and discussed in detail in the subsections that follow.

A working assumption is that building these capabilities and executing related activities requires a team dedicated to this purpose. How such a team operates will depend on the size and complexity of the organization itself as well as on the problems it is trying to solve. A data quality management team may operate at the enterprise level as a center of excellence, or the organization may have federated data quality management teams at the system or process level. Or both—an organization can have a center of excellence and a set of data quality management teams. There are two reasons for establishing a data quality management team or teams. First, data quality management requires specialized knowledge and skills. Second, data quality management activities are not likely to be executed consistently unless they are defined, standardized, and facilitated by a team trained in executing them and responsible for their adoption across the organization.

This chapter will first look at the core data quality management capabilities in relation to a range of other data management activities, as defined by DAMA International (an association for data management professionals). Then it will explore two overarching process models for data quality management (the ISO 8000 Process Reference Model and McGilvray's Ten Steps to Quality Data and Trusted Information). Each of these models presents a way of thinking holistically about data quality management as a set of interrelated processes and in relation to other organizational processes. Then, it will explore each of the individual capabilities in depth, discuss how they interact with each other, and propose how they can be applied to different levels of project and operational work.

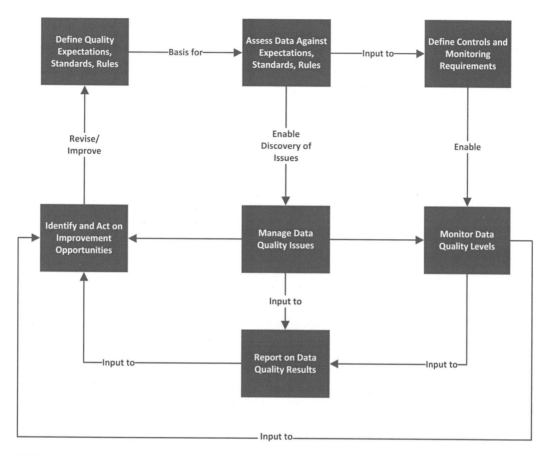

FIGURE 25

Core data quality management functions.

Data Quality in the Context of Data Management

Data quality management should not take place in a vacuum. It should be part of the overall effort of an organization to manage and govern its data. *Data management*, broadly defined by DAMA, "is the development, execution, and supervision of plans, policies, programs, and practices that deliver, control, protect, and enhance the value of data and information assets throughout their life-cycles" (DAMA, 2017). It includes a wide range of functions that, together, enable an organization to use and get value from its data. DAMA identifies 11 functional areas within data management: data architecture, data modeling and design, data storage and operations, data integration and inter-operability, data warehousing and business intelligence, document and content management, reference data management and master data management (MDM), data security, metadata management, data governance, and, of course, data quality management. These functional areas are intercon-nected and dependent on each other, but each has its own focus.

All data management functions, indeed all of the activities through which data is produced and used, have the potential to affect the quality of data. Let's review how these are defined by DAMA.

Data Architecture

Data architecture defines the blueprint for managing data assets. Data architects align data requirements with organizational strategy and design an approach to meeting these needs. Data architecture enables higher-quality data by clarifying requirements, planning for how components will work together, and accounting for quality within the design process. It also contributes to expectations for quality by helping clarify strategic requirements for data.

Data Modeling and Design

Data modeling is the process of representing and communicating data requirements via the data model. Data models, like architecture in general, help enable higher-quality data by clarifying expectations for data. Data models propose and refine how data will represent real-world entities and events (via the granularity of the entities themselves and the precision of the attributes selected to represent entities); they also specify the meaning and precision of individual attributes and clarify relationships between entities. Relational data models define fundamental data quality expectations by identifying optionality at the field level and by establishing foreign key relationships through which validity and referential integrity can be defined. In doing so, data models also define fundamental expectations about how data sets fit together. They are critical to defining data quality standards, rules, and expectations. The modeling process often uncovers differences among data from different parts of the organization. Consequently, modeling requires detailed discussions with stakeholders about their expectations for data. Resolving these differences can play an important role in standardizing data across the organization. As we will discuss in Chapter 10, choices in how to model have a direct impact on the perceived quality of data. In addition, the data modeling process is an important source of information about the meaning of data and expectations for data use. Data models themselves are a critical source of metadata.

Data Storage and Operations

Data storage and operations includes the design, implementation, and support of stored data. Choices about how data is stored can also have a direct impact on quality, especially with respect to the currency (how often and by what means data is maintained) and accessibility of data (what tools are used to access data, what kind of authentication is required). Operations teams not only ensure system availability and performance, but they are also responsible for monitoring functions that support basic data integrity (audit/balance/control).

Data Integration and Interoperability

Data integration and interoperability includes processes related to moving and consolidating data within and between applications. Critical to many uses of data, data integration has a direct impact on data usability. Because organizational data is often produced in silos, integration can be quite complex. Integrating data is likely to introduce risks and the concomitant need for controls on data. The concept of interoperability points to the desirability of planning for data to fit together—a kind of integration preparation by design. Good design and orchestration of data can considerably reduce technical complexity and the risks that technical complexity brings (Reeve, 2013). If technical and business requirements for data are better aligned, the result will be reduced complexity, less risk, and, consequently, data that is easier to manage.

Data Warehousing and Business Intelligence

Data warehousing includes management and control of decision support data used for analysis and reporting. *Business intelligence* (BI) is the term used to refer to this analysis and reporting. The goal of a data warehouse is to bring together data from different parts of the organization so it can be analyzed to get a clear picture of organizational performance. Because warehouses are charged with integrating heterogenous data, developing a warehouse often uncovers differences in meaning, granularity, and the details of representation. Because they represent risk, data warehouses are prime spots for the implementation of data quality controls. BI applications represent a critical use of data and therefore a critical lens through which to define quality expectations.

It is important to recognize that data storage and operations, data integration and interoperability, data warehousing and business intelligence, and data security all directly affect how the data supply chain operates. They all work better if data is created based on documented standards and if the people responsible for different links in the data chain understand and plan for each other's data quality requirements. We will discuss the data supply chain in more detail in Chapter 11.

Document and Content Management

Document and content management includes managing the life cycle of information in a range of unstructured media, especially documents that support legal and regulatory compliance requirements. Data quality with respect to document management includes ensuring that records can be located and that they are accurately classified with respect to their content and legal status. Content management refers to a range of practices that support the accessibility of various forms of content, usually on websites or knowledge-sharing applications. Both document and content management depend on the creation and maintenance of ontologies and other hierarchies through which information can be organized. These information management processes highlight the direct connection between managing the quality of data and information and managing the quality of metadata.

Reference Data and Master Data Management

Reference data and master data are both instances of critical shared data. The goal in managing each is to enable consistent access to the most accurate, timely, and relevant version of truth about essential business entities. Because master data and reference data are directly connected with transactional data, failure to manage them effectively can have direct and detrimental effects on the quality of other data as well as on business operations. The effort to manage them involves, in part, the application of data quality core processes to specific data management requirements.

Data Security

Data security is focused on ensuring that data is protected in terms of both its confidentiality and its physical accessibility. Higher-quality data and metadata both support the ability to secure data. For example, part of managing data includes knowing what data an organization has, where this data is located, and how it is accessed and used. This information has a direct effect on the ability to protect the data. Metadata is needed not only to identify and locate data that requires protection, but also to classify data based on protection and risk levels. When data is of high quality (e.g., clearly defined/correctly aligned with supporting metadata, complete, accurate, correctly formatted), then it is easier to secure. It is also easier to manage other risks related to data. Data protection laws, such as the General Data Protection Regulation (GDPR), directly make the connection between data quality and data security by requiring organizations that hold data to investigate and resolve inaccuracies or non-completeness of data (O Brien, 2021).

Metadata Management

Metadata management includes planning and control activities that enable access to definitions, models, data flow diagrams, and other information critical to understanding data and the systems through which it is created, maintained, and accessed. Understanding requirements for quality starts with understanding what data represents. Metadata provides this information. Well-defined, well-managed metadata reduces the time it takes to find and use data. It also reduces data-related risks. If data is well-defined, it is easier to classify and protect appropriately. There is less chance that it will be misunderstood or misused. The opposite is also true; poorly managed metadata can result in confusion about the data itself and can lead to mistakes in integrating, accessing, and using data.

Data Governance

Data governance provides direction and oversight for data management by establishing a system of decision rights over data that accounts for the needs of the enterprise. By setting policy and establishing accountability for data, data governance ensures that organizational structures are in place to set standards for data and to remediate data-related issues. When data governance also includes a stewardship component, stewards may be charged with activities that directly affect the quality of data. For example, stewards may be accountable for the quality of metadata or other shared data sets. Data quality management is sometimes viewed as a form of data stewardship. In some organizations, the data quality team may be part of the data governance organization.

Other Components of Data Management

The DAMA *Data Management Body of Knowledge* (DMBOK2) includes other topics in data management that are not defined as functional areas, but are nevertheless recognizably important. The DMBOK2 incudes chapters on:

- **Data ethics**, which describes how to ensure that data is managed in ethical ways across its life cycle
- **Big Data and data science**, which outlines and explains the management and use of data in Big Data environments, especially with respect to the creation of predictive models

- **Data management maturity assessment**, which describes the process of understanding the current state of the organization's data management capabilities in relation to a maturity model in order to improve them
- **Data management organization and role expectations**, which clarifies models for how to define responsibility for data and organize people and teams to execute data management activities
- **Data management and organizational change management**, which describes approaches for bringing about cultural change, specifically in support of data management goals

DAMA and Data Quality Management

Although each of DAMA's functional areas can affect the quality of data and all of them should be directed at enabling the organization to create, access, and use high-quality data, none of these areas is the same as data quality management itself.

In addition to intersecting and influencing other data management knowledge areas, data quality management is sometimes associated with activities such as quality assurance testing, system controls, data cleansing and de-duplication, and the specification of extract, transform, and load (ETL) processing rules. These activities also influence the quality of data. People who manage data quality must understand them and influence the standards by which this work is executed. However, these are not core data quality management functions. They will be executed as part of the development process and as part of data processing, regardless of whether the organization has a formal approach to data quality management and a team charged with facilitating it.

A word about data stewardship and data quality management. As described in Chapter 8, the concept of data stewardship is often defined very broadly. Any organization that adopts it must focus the responsibilities of stewards in ways that contribute to the organization's specific goals. Data quality management involves a core set of activities. Carrying out these activities is a form of data stewardship. It is a means of managing data assets on behalf of others for the good of the organization (McGilvray, 2021). However, data quality management is not the same thing as generalized data stewardship. Data quality management owes a great debt to practices for managing and improving the quality of products and services, as discussed in Chapter 5. It benefits from specialized knowledge of these practices and methodologies, in addition to knowledge of the organization's data.

DAMA's definition of data quality management as the "planning, implementation, and control of activities that apply quality management techniques to data in order to assure it is fit for consumption and meets the needs of data consumers" (DAMA, 2017) is very much aligned with what I have described in this book. DAMA's overall framework provides a great starting point for an overall understanding of the components of data management. However, because there is a lot to take in, the relationships among the pieces are not always clear.

Fig. 26 presents a framework that draws from and clarifies the DAMA framework, while accounting for additional components.

- **Data strategy:** Data strategy focuses on what the organization wants to accomplish with its data. For an organization to realize value from its data, its approach to data must be aligned with business strategy. Getting there takes a data strategy driven by business goals and priorities. These goals should drive capability and technical alignment. Data strategy must include an approach to changing culture because "getting out in front on data" (as Tom Redman would say)

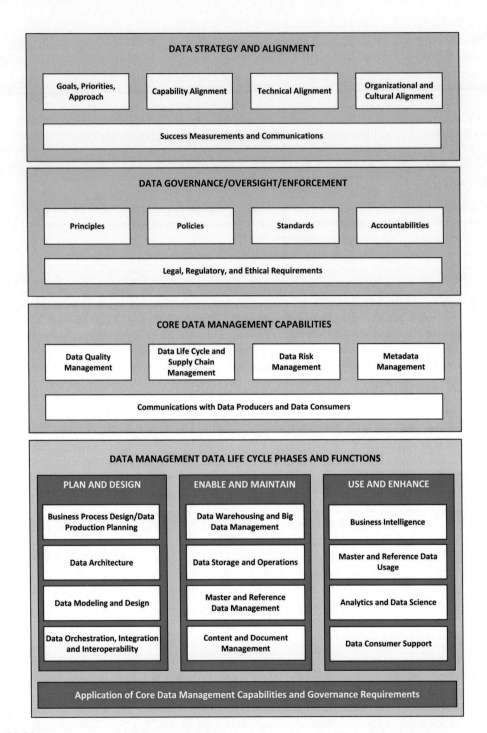

FIGURE 26

Data quality in the context of data management.

requires that people change how they work together. It must also include measures of success and active communication about the ways the data strategy contributes to the organization's goals.

- **Data governance/oversight/enforcement:** Data governance defines how people within the organization are expected to behave toward data. To get value from data, an organization must reduce costs and risks associated with data, while increasing opportunities to use data in support of organizational goals. As discussed in Chapter 8, data governance as it is currently being implemented in many organizations is not working as promised, largely because governance has been overburdened with responsibility for everything to do with data. The problems data governance was intended to solve are still with us. Governance programs must get back to the core function of governance: oversight for data. This comes in the form of principles, policies, standards, and defined accountabilities. As with data strategy, data governance must include a communications plan that emphasizes the importance of desired behaviors around data. Such a program also must "have teeth": data governance must be able to enforce desired behaviors around data.

- **Core data management capabilities:** Core data management capabilities focus on the activities an organization must execute consistently throughout the data life cycle if it is to reduce the waste and risk associated with data. Like data governance, the concept of data management is also overburdened. Early on, *data management* referred largely to technical practices. DBAs were the core of data management. To their credit, the people who were managing the data technically realized that non-technical people (businesspeople) expected technical people to do things with data that they could not do. Technical people could not make the data better simply through technology. And so the concept of what was meant by *data management* expanded to include things like metadata management and data quality management. When we think of the definition of *management* itself as "a process of planning, decision making, organizing, leading, motivation and controlling the human resources, financial, physical, and information resources of an organization to reach its goals efficiently and effectively" *(iEduNote)*, we can ask, "What are the aspects of data that must be organized and controlled for an organization to meet its goals?" I would answer, "The quality, the life cycle, the supply chain, and the risks around data (expanding the idea of data security to include a wider range of risks related to data) and the management of the information (metadata) required to create and use data."

- **Data management data life cycle phases and functions:** Data management life cycle processes are the ongoing activities through which an organization makes its data usable and accessible. Many activities associated with DAMA's functional areas are executed as part of the overall data life cycle (e.g., data architecture, data modeling and design, data integration and interoperability, data warehousing and business intelligence). Several of these functional areas focus on subsets or types of data that have particular life cycle requirements (e.g., documents and content, reference data, master data, metadata). The data management life cycle phases and functions part of the framework first accounts for the data life cycle abstractly. The data life cycle includes design functions, enablement, and maintenance as well as use and enhancement of data. The framework then parses out some additional detail related to the functional areas at different points in the overall life cycle (e.g., reference and master data usage as well as management). As will be discussed in Chapter 11, core data management capabilities and governance activities must be executed throughout the data life cycle.

This framework accounts for the DAMA model, organizes the pieces so it is easier to see the relationships among them, and adds components that are not explicitly called out in DAMA's functional areas.

- **Data strategy:** The first of these is data strategy, which in recent years has evolved as a part of business strategy. DAMA associates data strategy with data governance, but the two require separation. Data governance cannot provide oversight of data if it is also driving the strategy.

- **Life cycle management:** The second is life cycle management as a core data management capability. The DMBOK2 asserts that data should be managed throughout its life cycle but does not call out life cycle management as a function, although the practice of product life cycle management presents a model for doing so.
- **Business process design and customer support:** Next, business process design and customer support are recognized as data life cycle components. Business process design as a life cycle process calls attention to the need to build business processes so they produce a higher-quality data product. This represents the first critical phase in the data life cycle: data creation. Data consumer support is also a data life cycle function. Consumer support recognizes the second critical point in the life cycle: data use. Data consumer support is critical because data brings value only when it is used. Sometimes people need help using data. The data product requires support.
- **Data stewardship:** Notably absent from the framework is the "function" of data stewardship. This is because people who steward data (take care of it on behalf of the organization) may do so in conjunction with any of the processes included in the framework. In addition, anyone who is performing one of these functions should be doing so with the intent of ensuring that the data will meet the needs of data consumers. Some organizations will benefit from having people with the job title of data steward as part of their data governance or business teams. Other organizations will choose to clarify responsibilities toward data without including the job title of data steward. Still others may use a hybrid approach, with named stewards and clarification of responsibilities toward data in existing roles.

Fig. 27 turns this framework on its side for a moment to offer additional insight into the relationships between these functions and the core data quality management capabilities we will discuss in this chapter. Planning and design activities can be said to enable data quality management because these can be executed to build data quality into processes, models, and applications. Likewise, reliable quality management of reference data and metadata enable data quality management by providing the inputs needed to assess data and respond to data issues. Data quality management itself is focused on enabling data consumers to

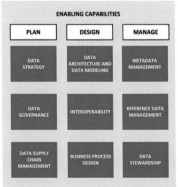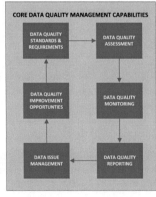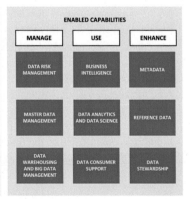

FIGURE 27

Capabilities that enable and are enabled by data quality management.

use data. Data stewardship is associated with both data creation and data use. The point in having different frameworks to describe these functions is to draw attention to the multiple ways that the functions themselves connect, interact, and depend on each other.

ISO 8000 Part 61: Data Quality Management: Process Reference Model

The International Organization for Standardization (ISO) Process Reference Model for data quality management (Fig. 28) provides a different perspective on executing core data quality management functions within

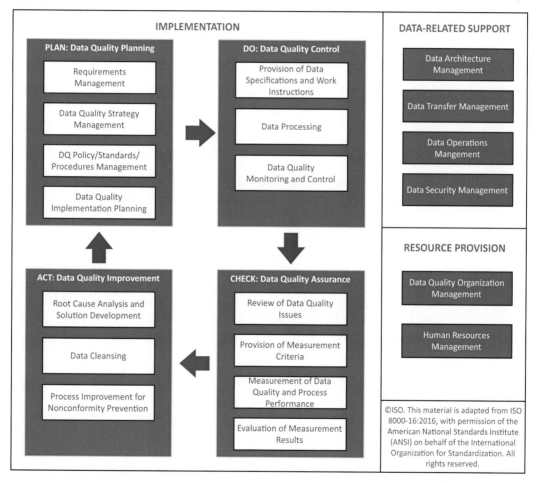

FIGURE 28

ISO Data Quality Management: Process Reference Model.

Copyright ISO. Adapted from ISO 8000-16:2016, with permission of the American National Standards Institute (ANSI) on behalf of the International Organization for Standardization. All rights reserved.

an organization. The reference model is a "framework for process-centric data quality management" focused on "improving underperforming processes" (ISO, 2016) based on the Shewhart cycle: PDCA, which is discussed in Chapter 5. As ISO describes the cycle in relation to data quality, it looks like this:

- **Plan:** Planning includes defining and managing requirements, setting strategy and governance (policies, standards, procedures), and planning for the implementation of processes to control and monitor data.
  - ISO's view of "plan" aligns closely with the core capability of defining data quality standards through documented expectations and rules.
- **Do:** Doing includes all aspects of quality control: creating specifications for data processing[1] and monitoring data that has been processed; evaluating and managing risks related to data processing; and communicating with stakeholders when results differ from requirements. The goal is to prevent issues from occurring.
  - ISO's definition of "do" aligns with data assessment, data quality monitoring, issue management, and data quality reporting.
- **Check:** Checking includes activities related to quality assurance: reviewing issues, defining measurement criteria, and evaluating measurement results. This includes not only the particulars of the data, but also the degree to which the data quality strategy is achieving its goals.
  - Some aspects of "do" include an aspect of "check." For example, monitoring data quality and managing issues.
- **Act:** Acting is taking advantage of opportunities for improvement, including developing solutions to address root causes and prevent errors. Even after root causes have been addressed, planning for monitoring and quality assurance continue. New issues will be discovered, stakeholders will provide feedback on existing data, and new requirements will emerge that will begin the cycle again.
  - For ISO, "act" is the improvement part of the improvement cycle: applying what is learned through the process.

ISO's model is useful not only because it provides a comprehensive, high-level picture of the processes required to manage data quality, but also because it connects these to other processes within the organization. Data quality management depends on technical processes (design/architecture, data movement, data operations, and data security management). It also depends on having people in place with the skills to get the work done (data quality organization management and, more generally, human resources management).

The Ten Steps Process: Accounting for Data Quality in Projects

Danette McGilvray's Ten Steps Process, as described in *Executing Data Quality Projects: Ten Steps to Quality Data and Trusted Information* (McGilvray, 2021), is the most detailed methodology I am aware of for bringing a data quality perspective to project work. I will summarize it

---

[1]My definition of *data quality management capabilities* differs somewhat from the ISO model as it does not include the definition of *data specifications and processing instructions* as a core data quality management capability. This is because, in my experience, business analysts, rather than data quality teams, develop these specifications. That said, ISO's placement of this process within the data quality management space serves as a reminder that the goal of such specifications (to define how data will be created, updated, and deleted to meet the goals of stakeholders) should always include expectations related to the quality of data. If a data quality team has defined quality requirements, standards, and policies, these should be used as input for the specification process, regardless of who writes the actual specification.

briefly here to make two points: First, there are many opportunities to bring a data quality perspective to any project, and second, there are well-defined ways of doing so. We will discuss these concepts in more detail in Chapter 11.

McGilvray defines *project* broadly to mean any work effort structured to address business needs. Data quality project work may be organized, managed, and accomplished in different ways. Some projects are focused on a specific data quality improvement. But data quality activities can also be executed as part of a larger project. And techniques that are part of the Ten Steps Process can be applied to operational processes and to programs (foundational aspects of data quality) as well as being used ad hoc.

Any use of the Ten Steps Process (Fig. 29) brings common sense to data projects.

- The critical first step is to determine the business needs that the project will address and the approach to addressing these needs. In a large development project, this means understanding the overall goal and the ways poor-quality data might become an obstacle to reaching that goal. In a data quality improvement project, it means understanding the goals businesspeople are trying to achieve and what obstacles they face. Data quality practitioners may see things in the data that seem wrong or anomalous, but before investing time and energy in addressing them, they should determine whether these characteristics of the data are important to the people using the data.
- Step 2 is assessing the "information environment—the settings, conditions, and situations that surround, may have created, or exacerbated, data quality problems." This includes reviewing documentation, understanding requirements, processes, and technology that affect the data; for example, understanding the data supply chain and the data life cycle. In this assessment, it is critical to talk with stakeholders. Doing so will provide insight into the context of the problems you are trying to help solve.

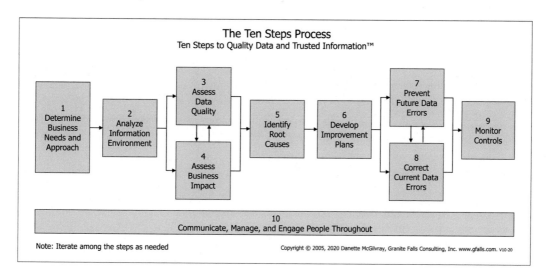

FIGURE 29

McGilvray's Ten Steps to Quality Data and Trusted Information.

From McGilvray, D. (2021). Executing Data Quality Projects: Ten Steps to Quality Data and Trusted Information (2nd ed.).
Burlington, MA: Morgan Kaufmann. Used with permission.

- Steps 3 and 4—assessing data quality and assessing business impact—work in harmony with each other. They involve clarifying, defining, and quantifying issues, obstacles, or requirements and determining their impact to business processes and stakeholder goals.
- Analysis of the data and business processes from steps 3 and 4 is necessary to determine the root causes of data issues (step 5) and how to address them (step 6).
- Steps 7 and 8 also work in harmony. Preventing future errors requires envisioning what can go wrong with data. Insight often comes from knowledge of root causes of existing errors. The process of correcting data problems provides insight on what kinds of controls will be most effective.
- Next, because data processes evolve, it is necessary to monitor data quality to ensure that it remains in range and to respond if it does not (step 9). This step recognizes that "monitor controls" can be monitoring the quality of a specific data set and sharing results via dashboards and reports. A control can also be built into a business process to help prevent data quality issues (step 7). Of course, if a preventive control is in place and data quality levels are also monitored and reported on, then the combination creates the opportunity to report on the effectiveness of the control itself. Controls that do not sustain or improve quality may not be the right controls.
- Step 10 is a first, continuous, and final step. It is necessary to "communicate, manage and engage people *throughout*" the project process (emphasis added). This means taking appropriate communications actions in every step of the process. No one does this work alone. In a large development project, communicating and engaging entails working with team members and stakeholders to increase the visibility of data quality requirements. In improvement projects, it means sharing findings and insights so decisions can be made about the priority of issues and concerns.

Core Data Quality Management Capabilities

DAMA's data management functional areas and ISO's and McGilvray's process models provide the big-picture backdrop for how data quality improvement takes place. Core data quality management capabilities are integral to this picture. They focus on understanding, improving, and sustaining the quality of organizational data to ensure that data is fit for the purposes of data consumers.

As described in this book's Introduction, three questions are at the heart of data quality management:

- What do we mean by high-quality data?
- How do we detect low-quality or poor-quality data?
- What action will we take when data does not meet quality standards?

Core data quality management capabilities (see Fig. 25) are the means through which an organization answers these questions by defining expectations, assessing data, and taking action, on an ongoing basis, as the organization and its data evolve. In support of these capabilities, a *data quality* program must also define templates, processes, and deliverables for executing the work related these capabilities. Core data quality management capabilities include the following[2]:

[2]Implementing data quality management almost always entails a level of cultural change and therefore strong communications and interpersonal skills. I have not called these out as core data quality management capabilities because they are not particular to data quality management. They are core to cultural change itself and very useful in almost any role. See McGilvray (2021), Ladley (2019), and Chapters 16 and 17 of DAMA (2017).

- **Data quality standards definition:** Describe what is meant by high-quality data; set clear, consistent expectations and requirements for data quality.
- **Data quality assessment:** Observe characteristics of particular data against data quality standards to identify errors, risks, and obstacles to use; quantify the results.
- **Data quality monitoring:** Track quality levels within a system or process to detect unexpected conditions and identify their causes in order to take action in response to them.
- **Data quality reporting:** Communicate information about the condition of data to data consumers and other stakeholders.
- **Data quality issue management:** Identify, quantify, prioritize, and remediate the root causes of obstacles to data consumers' uses of data.
- **Data quality improvement:** Identify and implement process and technical changes to prevent data issues, enforce data quality standards, and improve the overall reliability and trustworthiness of organizational data.

These capabilities can be applied to individual systems, data sets, entities, or attributes. They can be applied within business functional areas and across the data supply chain and the life cycle (see Chapter 11). They all have the same goal: to ensure that data is fit for purpose and fit for use by data consumers so the organization can deliver on its mission and serve its customers.

People with knowledge and experience in data quality management should facilitate these activities. Ideally, data quality management efforts should be coordinated and facilitated by a data quality management team focused on educating teams within the organization about how to improve data quality. Those system or process-based teams will focus directly managing the quality of data under their responsibility. Because they cover both project and operational responsibilities and intersect with development and data governance initiatives, these activities are not usually included as part of the direct responsibility of project teams or operational teams. They are not likely to be executed at all unless someone is accountable for ensuring that they are. They will bring more value if they are coordinated across the enterprise.

A Word of Caution: SAIL

When people hear words like *comprehensive, holistic*, or *enterprise-wide*, they become concerned that they are being asked to do everything possible and everything at once. They caution, "We should not try to boil the ocean." And they are right. Data quality improvement does not work this way.

Data quality management activities should focus on the organization's critical and at-risk data. It is neither possible nor necessary to "manage" every piece of data. Nor do the processes need to be carried out in a linear sequence. They inform each other. To keep focused, keep this simple acronym in mind: SAIL.

- **Start small, but keep the big picture in mind:** Getting an organization to think differently about its data (e.g., by focusing on the quality of data as a product of organizational processes) is a big change for most organizations. Do not try to do everything. Do not try to do it all at once. Instead, start small. Every small step toward the goal is a step in the right direction. So do not lose sight of the goal. Keep the bigger picture in mind.
- **Always prioritize:** Some data is simply more important than other data. When it is of low quality, it prevents people from doing their jobs, gets in the way of serving customers, and causes organizational friction. Or, if it is wrong, it will get the organization into trouble with

regulators. Data quality efforts should focus on the data that is most important to the organization and most at risk for being of low quality. Talk to data consumers and ask them their pain points. These are the best starting points for data quality improvement efforts. Prioritizing is about putting first things first; it is *not* about getting all of the lower-priority items in perfect order. Keep the list of priorities small and focused. Ensure that it is clear why they are priorities. Be able to articulate the impact on processes and their customers.

- **It is a circle for a reason:** Although almost any description of an improvement cycle starts by defining what is meant by quality, work on improvement can start anywhere in the circle (PDCA). Practically speaking, a lot of data quality improvement work starts not with a highfalutin enterprise perspective but from a boots-on-the-ground, stop-the-bleeding pain point. You can start at any point in the quality improvement process.

- **Learn from everything you do and from everyone you meet:** As you assess data, understand the root causes of issues, and work to improve processes through which data is created, managed, and used, you will be exposed to a lot of information about people, data, processes, and technology. Learn from these. Recognize that when people say, "Every situation is different," they are telling only half the story. Yes, particular data problems have specific characteristics, but many data issues have common root causes (e.g., process gaps, lack of understanding, technical limitations, typos). Understanding these in general and understanding your organization in particular will help you get better at doing this work. A variation on learning from everything you do is learning from everyone you work with. No one can know everything about an organization's data, so be prepared; many other people will know more than you do, especially about the particulars of data sets, technical applications, and business processes. Such people are part of the solution. Listen to them. Multiple perspectives provide important insight into data problems, their causes, and their effects.

Define Data Quality Standards

To achieve quality of any kind requires defining expectations for quality. For data, these may come in the form of existing process expectations and business rules, they may be documented in metadata (e.g., the data model, system specifications, business documentation), or they may need to be explicitly formulated as part of the data quality program. Once formulated, they may then be used as input to the data modeling and development processes, as well as data quality assessment.

Defining data quality standards includes describing and documenting the characteristics that data is expected to possess. Ideally standards should be measurable assertions and rules. This sounds technical, but data quality standards are a means of formalizing the common expectations of data consumers. Once defined, they provide important input to other core data quality management functions: assessment, monitoring, reporting, quantifying issues, and measuring improvement.

Some people shy away from standards. Standards may be perceived as a top-down imposition that will make it more difficult to get work done. ("We cannot finish our project on time because we now have to follow this new standard.") Or they are perceived as creating low-value work. ("Now we will need to change everything just to meet the standard.") It is too bad that people have these reactions. The intention of setting standards is to simplify work and enable it to be done more efficiently. In setting a standard, an organization makes a decision once and applies it many times. Having standards should reduce the amount of time people require to answer questions because the standards themselves should answer many of the questions people may have. The keys to getting value from standards include the following:

- **Taking advantage of existing standards or de facto standards:** For example, if the organization has a disciplined data modeling practice, then the modelers likely already have naming standards as well as standards for data types and other data characteristics.
- **Focusing standards definition where standards will do the most good:** There is little value in setting standards for non-controversial data elements. These are likely to be, de facto, standardized. There may still be value in documenting the de facto standards because doing so makes the assumptions and presuppositions transparent (e.g., that a Zip code will be stored as a five-digit code, rather than as an integer).
- **Engaging stakeholders appropriately to define them:** If standards are perceived as an imposition or a forced change rather than a solution to a problem, they are not likely to be adopted. If stakeholders are engaged in prioritizing and defining standards, then they will see the value in them and be more likely to adhere to them and ask others to adhere to them.

Data quality standards start with a definition of the data. Data can be defined at different levels:

- **Data set:** A collection of data from a given system or process (e.g., membership data, provider data, claim data, sales data, geographic data)
- **Entity:** The real-world things about which the organization wants to know something (e.g., members, providers, claims, customers, products)
- **Attribute:** A characteristic of the entity about which the organization wants to know (e.g., name, address, age, credential, time, date, procedure, price, color)
- **Relationship:** The expected connection between two data sets, two entities, or two attributes

A customer can be defined as a person who has purchased goods or services from an organization or as a person to whom the organization has attempted to sell goods or services. Both definitions work. But each will result in different standards for quality as well as in different attributes.

Data quality standards are generally based on dimensions of quality (which will be discussed in depth in Chapter 10). For example, the concept of completeness is considered a fundamental dimension of quality. Data is understood as complete if data consumers have all of the data they need. However, completeness can be understood at different levels, therefore standards for completeness can be defined at different levels:

- **Data set:** The claim data set is considered complete, for example, if it contains records for all transactions executed during a set period of time and if these transactions can be associated with records for members who received services and the doctors who provided services.
- **Entity:** If the organization defines *customer* as an individual with whom the organization has interacted on a sale or potential sale, then the customer entity is considered complete if it contains references to all individuals with whom the organization has had any form of contact regarding sales (in-person, phone, email) within a set period of time and if these references contain the minimum required attributes (e.g., name, address, phone number).
- **Attribute:** An attribute is considered complete if it is populated to the degree required to enable a business process to execute (e.g., customer given name and family name are required fields, but customer middle name is not required).
- **Relationship:** Every claim record is expected to have at least one service record, every sales record must contain a reference to at least one product, and so on.

Because data standards describe and enable documentation of data's expected characteristics, it is best to approach the process of developing data standards by creating a template that enables one to capture the attributes required to define a standard. For example, for data elements, each standard should include: name, definition, and general expectations for quality. These general expectations do not need to be formal. They can simply be observations about how people expect the data to behave. Once the data consumer perspective is documented, a data quality analyst can translate these expectations into measurable assertions (e.g., rules) about data quality. These assertions can then be reviewed with data consumers to ensure that they are correct, complete, and comprehensible.

Data quality standards may also include information related to how data is implemented, such as the standard name and data type for the physical column, and the standard default value to be populated when data is missing from the field. Some may say these are modeling standards or standard transformation rules. And they would be right! If it helps to call them *modeling standards* instead of *data quality standards*, then do so. It does not matter what they are called, as long as you can use them to come to consensus about what data is supposed to look like and to guide process and system development.

Let's walk through the process of building a standard for birth date. I use this relatively simple example to show the range of observations that can be translated into a standard. For birth date, general expectations can include the following:

- Every person is born on one specific day, so every person should have a birth date and only one birth date.
- Birth is a one-time event, so this date should not change, unless the change involves a correction to data.
- All records referring to the same individual should have the same birth date.
- Within a specific system, all dates, including birth date, should be formatted consistently.
- A birth date has three components—day, month, and year. It does not need to include the time (hour and minute) of birth.
- Birth dates cannot be future dates.[3]
- Depending on the population of people with whom the organization interacts, birth date may have reasonability limits. For example:
  - If your organization serves the elderly, you will set reasonability limits based on the age when services are available (in the United States, people become eligible for Medicare at 65 years of age, though younger people may be eligible if they have chronic conditions) and a reasonable expectation of life span (few people live to be more than 110 years of age).
  - If your organization works with schoolchildren, you can set reasonability limits based on both the minimum and the maximum age you expect these children to be.

These commonsense observations about birth date can be translated into a formal data quality standard, based on dimensions of quality, as illustrated in in Table 14.

As with data modeling, the process of defining standards can uncover new or implicit requirements that you can then explicitly define. For example:

---

[3]The only possible exception to this rule that I can think of is a birth by scheduled cesarean. If an expected delivery date is required, this should be captured in a separate field. Do not use a field for something other than what it is meant for. This is a frequent cause of data quality problems.

Table 14 Birth date: Example of a data quality standard.

Component	Component description
Attribute name	Birth date
Definition	The day, month, and year when an individual person was born, as recorded on their birth certificate.
General quality assertions	Every person should have a birth date. Birth date values should not change unless the change involves a correction to data. All records referring to the same individual should have the same birth date. Within a particular system, dates should be formatted consistently. A birth date cannot not be a future date. Birth dates that indicate really old people are questionable (e.g., >110 years of age).
Completeness	Birth date must be populated on all records that represent individual people and contain the attribute.
Format	Birth date must be formatted consistent with other dates in system X.
Precision	Birth date includes day, month, and year of birth.
Validity	The value of a birth date must be a valid calendar date (e.g., February 30 is not a valid calendar date).
Validity	A birth date cannot be a future date (based on when the record was created).
Reasonability	A birth date that indicates the person is more than 110 years of age is not expected.
Integrity	All instances of birth date recorded for the same individual should be the same value (unless corrections have been made to the data).
Data type	Birth date must be implemented as a data-type *date*.
Default value	When a valid birth date is missing from a record, the value of birth date should be set to 1900-01-01.

- The definition of *birth date* as the day, month, and year on which a person is born implies an expectation about precision (birth date does not require a timestamp) that can be explicitly defined as part of the standard, if making this explicit helps people understand the requirements.
- Recognizing that you do not expect birth dates to change but that they may change due to data capture errors can help you recognize that you may need a way to know if a record has been corrected (e.g., a flag, tag, or status).
- Stating that birth date is required for records related to individual people also implies that it is not required for records related to other entities (e.g., organizations, products). It also alerts you to the possibility of missing data, so you can account for how to handle these situations (e.g., designating a standard default value, rather than leaving the choice up to individual data processors).
- Defining a format standard based on the system in which the data resides may indicate that you need a clear modeling standard for all dates in that system.

Because they formalize expectations and provide a basis for comparison, standards can be used to assess the quality of data and to define requirements for data quality monitoring and reporting.

Assess Data Quality

Data quality standards provide a basis for data assessment, but data assessment can also be used to define standards. Assessing data quality is the process of systematically observing data characteristics via data analysis and inspection to draw conclusions about the data's quality. This can be done from two different perspectives, depending on your starting point in the data quality improvement cycle:

- By comparing characteristics of actual data and supporting metadata to documented expectations for data (rules, standards, or other artifacts that define its quality)
- By examining data to propose or refine standards and rules (and to capture these as metadata)

The most familiar form of data assessment is data profiling. Data profiling is a form of data analysis that produces high-level statistics at the column level (cardinality, percentage NULL, format analysis) along with a detailed distribution of values. Also called a *frequency distribution*, a distribution of values includes a count and a percentage for each value in each profiled column. (See Table 15 for an example using a frequency distribution of US state codes.) Profiling allows analysts to develop insight about data structure as well as column-level details. Profiling thus provides a means of quickly looking across a large data and identifying potential issues and risks. There are several use cases for data profiling.

- **Profiling for discovery:** Assess an unfamiliar data set to understand it and identify potential issues and risks. This use case is often executed as part of development projects or data quality improvement projects.
- **Periodic reassessment of data:** Compare a new profile of a data set previously profiled to identify and assess changes to distributions and other characteristics.
- **Selective profiling for monitoring:** Profile individual columns or related columns on an ongoing basis, and compare the results to past instances of the profile to detect unexpected changes in distributions.

In the following discussion, we will focus on profiling for discovery. This is the most comprehensive use case, and the analysis techniques used for discovery apply to all use cases.

Profiling provides a means not only to assess data, but also to assess metadata. In *Data Quality: The Accuracy Dimension*, Jack Olson describes the inputs and outputs of data profiling:

- **Inputs:** Accurate and inaccurate data and metadata
- **Outputs:** Accurate metadata and facts about inaccurate data

This simple formulation says a lot about how to plan and execute the process. Data should not be profiled blindly. Before starting the process, the analyst should learn as much as possible about the data being assessed. If data quality standards have been documented or if a data model exists, these can be used to assess the data. If standards have not been created, then profiling provides valuable input to this process. In all cases, when differences are found between documented knowledge and the actual data, these differences will need to be shared and resolved.

Profiling a table with a standard profiling tool produces two levels of output: high-level statistics about each of the columns and a detailed distribution of values of each of the columns. Many profiling engines also allow cross-table analysis, which can help discover or confirm relationships between tables.

High-level statistics can tell you a lot about the data and give you a basis for judging reasonability. For example:

- **Cardinality:** The distinct number of values present in the column for the sample can be used as a reasonability check. For a large health care payer that supports commercial clients, a birth date field that contains only a few hundred values would be questionable. If we assume that people work for 40−50 years of their lives, then approximately 18,250 birth date values would be represented in the commercially insured population.

- **Missing data:** The percentage of records with a NULL value also serves as a reasonability check. Not all fields are expected to be populated under all conditions. But mandatory fields are expected to be. If you know which fields are mandatory, you can quickly detect a problem. You may also identify fields that are not documented as mandatory but are always populated. This presents the opportunity to refine your expectations. Some related fields will have the same percentage of nulls. Identifying these can also help you refine rules. (When provider type = FACILITY, the birth date column should not be populated). In addition, a profiling engine that allows you to sort high-level results by the percentage of data missing will enable you very quickly to see which fields are completely unpopulated.
- **Format characteristics** (e.g., probable data type): Data is not always constrained by format. It can exist with a range of lengths (names, comments, descriptions), but other data is defined by strict format rules (dates, amounts) and may be invalid if it does not conform to these rules. Some data falls in between.

After reviewing the high-level statistics, a review of the detailed distributions of values (counts and percentages of all the values in a column) can reveal additional data characteristics. For example:

- **Cardinality:** If a column has 100 distinct values but 95% of the data is associated with only two of them, then you will want to understand why the other 98 are present at all.
- **Missing data:** A column can have no NULL values and still be missing a lot of data. SPACE and default values like 0 are not the same as NULL and therefore will not show up in the high-level statistics. (It is important to know how the profiling tool identifies "missing" data in the first place.)
- **Format characteristics:** High-level statistics may show that a column has multiple formats, but if these are associated with just a few records, then the data quality expectation may indeed be for a single format.
- **Validity:** If you have access to a full list of domain values for a column and you can see all of the values in the distribution, then you can identify whether any values are invalid and know what percentage of the sample these represent.
- **Reasonability:** Even for columns with large sets of values, it is possible to identify potential errors and anomalies. For example, the percentage of records in which customer first name = INVALID or DO NOT USE.
- **Differences from metadata:** Profiling will uncover instances of data that do not align with documentation about that data. For example, column names and definitions may not reflect what is actually in the data set.

Let's look at the example shown in Table 15, the profile of a column of US state codes on a customer address table showed 74 distinct values. This seemed surprising because the United States has only 50 states, along with a dozen or so territories. Inspection of the values showed not only US state codes and US territories, but also Canadian provinces and territories. In addition, there were records with a default value used for non-US, non-Canadian addresses, and there was one record in which the state code was a space.

The information discovered simply by looking at the values in the column can be shared with data consumers so they are not surprised by missing data or unfamiliar code values. It can also be used to update metadata and reference data, for example, by updating the definition of state code to make clear that it includes more than just the 50 US states and ensuring that reference data contains names of each valid value.

Any column profile can be used to check for completeness (presence of NULL, space, default). Many can be used to check validity (against a defined domain of values). With a concept like state code, it is also possible to do a reasonability check based on data from external sources, such as US Census data. Table 15 presents a frequency distribution of the top 10 state code values for customer address records by state code in a database for a US company and compares this with population counts by state from the World Population Review website. Not surprisingly, there is close alignment between the number of customers in the company's top 10 states and the most populous US states. But there is not complete alignment. California, the state with the largest population, ranks seventh in the top 10 list for the company. This may reflect missing data or a characteristic of the business the company does in California.

Data profiling can provide insight into the structure and content of data, the relationship between columns, the relationship between tables, and the differences between data and documentation about data. For data that is unfamiliar, it provides a quick way to learn a lot and serves as a foundation for asking questions and doing further analysis.

Like other data quality activities, it should be done with intention and planning. Profiling is usually done to assess data for use in a development project or to assess a data set that has been identified as having problems. Before looking at data, clarify goals and scope. In addition, develop a template or other means to capture observations and manage findings related to data structure, metadata, and details of individual columns. Plan a deliverable that includes a summary of findings, a list of risks and action items, and any detailed analysis required to meet the goals of the work (e.g., proposed updates to definitions, rules and standards, recommendations for monitoring).

Data assessment may surface data errors (e.g., missing or invalid values, a lack of integrity between related tables) or other obstacles to the use of the data. Errors and issues should be

State code	Record count	% of records	State	Population	Rank in US population	% of US population
NY	45,254	8.8	New York	19,299,981	4	5.7
TX	44,286	8.6	Texas	29,730,311	2	8.9
OH	39,373	7.7	Ohio	11,714,618	7	3.5
IL	36,021	7.1	Illinois	12,569,321	6	3.7
NJ	35,469	6.9	New Jersey	8,874,520	11	2.7
FL	34,879	6.8	Florida	21,944,577	3	6.6
CA	33,016	6.5	California	39,613,493	1	11.8
PA	25,069	4.9	Pennsylvania	12,804,123	5	3.8
VA	22,173	4.3	Virginia	8,603,985	12	2.6
GA	15,993	3.1	Georgia	10,830,007	8	3.2

Table 15 Percentages of state codes in a database compared with population figures[4].

[4]Source: https://worldpopulationreview.com/states, May 2021.

managed through an issue management process (discussed later in this chapter) that includes a more in-depth analysis to identify and propose remediation of root cause analysis (RCA).

An issue management process that "has teeth" and can quantify the business impact of issues is important to getting the best resolution to issues. For example:

- It is important to report errors because doing so raises awareness of their existence, which will help in assessing their impact. However, simply reporting issues back to the owners of the system that supplied the data is not likely to result in significant change (e.g., implementation of controls or other means to prevent errors) unless the errors affect the use of that system.
  - "Having teeth" means that the issue management process can influence changes in systems and processes for the benefit of data consumers (regardless of whether the owners of these systems and processes directly benefit).
- In the case of a warehouse or other integrated data store, understanding the root causes of errors may require analysis of the data supply chain. Because RCA takes time and expertise, some organizations do not commit to it and do not get the benefits of it.
  - "Having teeth" means that the issue management process enables resources to do real RCA and can escalate issues whose root causes are several links away from the symptoms that affect data consumers.

Although the need to address errors is obviously critical, another important output from a data assessment is the identification of risks to data. Risks are conditions of the data that are not yet issues (obstacles to use) but may become issues depending on how data is used. For example, differences in data structure (e.g., granularity, level of detail, format) among systems represent risks to integrating data and, because of this, to using data. The lack of edits and controls in an originating system also represents risk. Data may be free from errors at the time of the assessment, but without controls, errors can be introduced, and data quality can deteriorate.

Within the data quality improvement cycle, data assessment is critical to defining requirements for ongoing data quality monitoring. Through assessment, one can identify instances of critical data and relationships and home in on data that appears to have issues or be at risk. This information provides the basis for determining which data to monitor and how to monitor it.

Monitor Data Quality

Monitoring data quality is the ability, through measurements and other controls, to track levels of quality within a system or process and to detect potential issues so action can be taken in response to them. Monitoring is just what it sounds like: paying attention to the shape of data over time, whether shape is defined by specific rules, the distribution of values in particular columns, or other data characteristics (e.g., file sizes, averages of numeric fields). It includes reviewing the results of data quality measurements, responding to threshold breaches, and reviewing trends to detect changes in data patterns for emergent issues. Data quality monitoring is necessary to sustain quality levels as well as to improve quality. Data quality assessment provides the basis for defining data quality monitoring requirements—identifying what data and relationships should be monitored, by what methods, and how frequently. Monitoring results provide a primary input for data quality reporting through which information about quality levels is shared with data consumers.

Monitoring serves two purposes:

- **Risk mitigation:** It is a means to detect potential issues and respond to data problems before data consumers experience issues.
- **Transparency:** It is the basis for data quality reporting, the goal of which is to build trust with data consumers by making data quality levels known to them.

Both purposes are important. Risk mitigation reduces the impact of data issues and their associated costs. Transparency creates a feedback loop that contributes to formal organizational knowledge of data and creates trust in data and the people managing the data.

But data quality monitoring does not come for free. There is a cost to setting up monitoring rules and to reviewing and reporting on the results. Not every piece of data can or should be monitored. Data quality monitoring should focus on critical data and data relationships associated with business or technical processes that present risk. For example, if assessment shows that data is sound for claims that are adjudicated fully and, in contrast, that data is frequently missing from claims that are manually adjusted, then it may make sense to focus data quality monitoring on adjustments, rather than on all claims. Or, if customer data captured through a web application appears sound, and the same application has controls and validations in place to prevent data errors, then it is likely less important to monitor this data than to monitor customer address data that is manually entered by employees in a call center.

Data Quality Monitoring Principles

The following principles apply to data quality monitoring

- **Error prevention comes first:** Preventing errors in the first place is better than monitoring data to detect errors. Put another way, there are ways of preventing input data from being wrong in the first place (e.g., validating credit card numbers and address components; ensuring that all required fields are populated with valid values before a record can be created). These should be implemented before data monitoring is put in place. Error prevention that eliminates known risks also removes the need to monitor data for those risks.
- **Focus monitoring on risks:** The highest value data quality monitoring focuses on high-risk processes with multiple inputs (e.g., points where data is integrated or derived). However well-designed such processes are, they may still have gaps in logic. In addition, data evolves. Changes in the production of any of the inputs may result in conditions that are not accounted for in the integration code or derivation logic.
- **Take action when issues are detected:** Monitoring should be in place at the earliest point in the data chain where the issue might appear. For example, if the output from an integration or derivation process is to be monitored, the measurement should be taken in conjunction with the process or as soon as possible after the process is executed so appropriate action can be taken. For example:
  - **If no errors or changes are detected**, data proceeds along the data chain. Data consumers, including owners of downstream processes, should be informed that the data is consistent with the

expectation. Keeping them informed not only builds trust, but it also creates the opportunity for them to provide feedback and to communicate whether their requirements have changed.

- **If errors or changes are detected within tolerance**, data proceeds along the data chain, but data consumers are informed that there are errors and what these errors are. Exception records may be inspected for patterns related to the characteristics being monitored.
- **If errors or changes are detected that exceed tolerance**, then data processing may be stopped altogether until the root causes of the errors are found and addressed. If data is allowed to proceed along the data chain, then data consumers and owners of downstream processes must be informed about the issue.

- **Automation:** Monitoring should be as automated as possible. Monitoring is, by definition, focused on measuring defined characteristics or features of the data. Measurements will be executed more consistently if they are automated. Without automation, the monitoring process is simply not scalable for most data sets. Automation should include not only the collection of data and execution of calculations that make the data comprehensible (e.g., calculation of the percentage of records that meet/do not meet a requirement), but it should also include capture of measurement results for reporting and analysis and notifications when measurements have crossed thresholds. Automated monitoring collects data quality measurement results and performs first level "triage" based on thresholds. When automated monitoring identifies errors, people need to take action on the results.

Just as data quality assessment can uncover issues, so can data quality monitoring. These findings must be made known to data consumers through data quality reporting and addressed through an issue management process. Data consumers can provide feedback on the priority of issues, including information about the impact of issues on specific processes and about options for addressing these issues. Monitoring and reporting help identify opportunities to learn from and improve the processes through which data is created and used.

Report on Data Quality

At its simplest, data quality reporting is formally sharing information about quality levels with data consumers (analysts and other people who directly use the data) and other stakeholders (people who manage teams of analysts; process and system owners; and upper management, such as the chief data officer). Often this includes sharing aggregated results from the monitoring process. It can also include sharing information about the discovery and remediation of issues as well as about the impact of improvement efforts. The transparency brought about by data quality reporting builds trust in the data and the systems and processes that supply it. Reporting draws on assessment, monitoring, and issue management activities and outputs.

Because the goal of data quality reporting is to inform data consumers about the condition of data, the best starting point to developing reports is to ask them what they want to know. At least, this is what it would appear on the surface. From asking this question directly, I have learned a lot about what data consumers do and do not care about. For example, they have no interest in abstract dimensions of quality, but if they are educated in how the dimensions work, they recognize them as useful categories through which to understand data issues. Also, they do not really care about the technical details of how data quality measurements are taken, though they want to understand how the issues they care about are quantified. Most importantly, they want to know about anything that can affect or get in the way of their ability to use the data. Conversations about data quality reporting requirements will often surface important information about the impact of data quality issues on business intelligence and other forms of reporting. In doing so, these conversations can be helpful in prioritizing what to monitor in the first place.

Any organization's data quality reporting will evolve over time, but a good starting point includes the following:

- Time period for the report
- Data domain, system, or data set being reported on
- An overview of report contents (e.g., summary results from data quality monitoring, counts and status of issues, highlights of specific reports or trends)
- Basic information about the monitoring process. For example, how many monitoring rules are in place, what type of data they measure, and what characteristics they measure. This can be expressed in relation to the dimensions of quality if these are presented in business terms, as in Tables 16 and 17. Some of this contextual information will be virtually static. It is still important to include it because it enables people who are new to the report to understand what is being shared. Also, when new issues emerge, it provides a foundation for discussing them.
- Summarized/aggregated results about the rules that are being monitored, by data domain, system, or data set and dimension of quality

Table 16 Summary of data quality dimension purpose and number of rules monitored.

Dimension	Definition	Purpose	Number of rules
Completeness	Completeness rules measure whether a column is fully populated, based on defined conditions (e.g., record type, record status).	Detect when required source data is missing or when derivations have resulted in a default value.	60
Validity	Validity rules measure whether a column contains valid values based on a list, code table, or range.	Detect new or incorrect values in columns. Alert the data quality team to inspect reference data sets.	30
Reasonability	Reasonability rules measure the distribution of critical values based on past instances of the data. (Note: These rules do not detect errors.)	Detect unexpected changes in the distribution of values so data quality team can alert stakeholders	10

Table 17 Implemented data quality rules by dimensions across subject areas.

Data domain	Completeness	Validity	Reasonability	Total
Claim	20	15	4	39
Membership	25	10	5	40
Provider	15	5	1	21
Total	60	30	10	100

- Summarized information about issues, such as the number, severity, and status of issues within each data domain, system, or data set
- Specific detailed results and other information about rules that are of most interest to data consumers. These may be of interest because of past performance or simply because the data itself is important to many people.

Practices Around Summarized/Aggregated Results

The goal of summarizing results is to present a high-level picture of findings during the report period. This can be done in a number of ways. It is tempting to describe findings in terms of dimensions of quality (Table 18; Fig. 30), but as will be illustrated in a moment, this is not always the best approach.

Table 18 Percentage of data quality rules without errors by dimension of quality.			
Report date	**Completeness**	**Validity**	**Reasonability**
1/1/2022	97	80	88
2/1/2022	97	92	88
3/1/2022	100	88	100
4/1/2022	94	93	92
5/1/2022	100	93	94
6/1/2022	98	94	100

FIGURE 30

Data quality results summarized by data quality dimension.

Table 19 Percentage of data quality rules without errors by data domain.

Report date	Claim	Membership	Provider
1/1/2022	99	95	85
2/1/2022	99	93	86
3/1/2022	98	91	82
4/1/2022	95	94	90
5/1/2022	93	93	94
6/1/2022	90	93	86

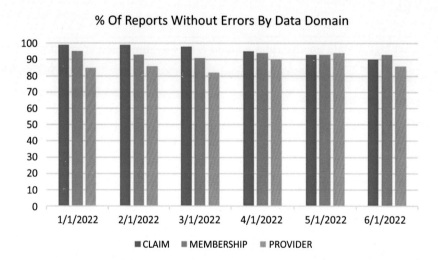

FIGURE 31

Data quality results summarized by data domain.

Your business stakeholders are not likely to care about this level of information unless they are well-educated in the dimensions of quality and are highly familiar with data quality reports themselves. Dimensions of quality help data quality and data governance teams define rules and characterize issues. When all is going well, they provide a quick way to communicate this fact to stakeholders. However, when there are issues, dimensions are too abstract for data consumers. They may not even be sure how to ask questions about a graph like this. It is better to present this information in terms of what data is impacted (Table 19; Fig. 31).

Fig. 31 shows data consumers information in terms they care about. For example, they can see that claim data appears to be doing pretty well during the first quarter, but it has deteriorated a bit in the second quarter; they also can see that provider data is consistently measured at lower quality than claim data.

Fig. 31 also points to the need to define goals for your data visualizations so they will be as effective as possible. Because one goal of data quality reporting is to build trust in the data, it is usually a good idea to present the positive picture—how much of the data meets expectations. However, it is hard to see trends in such data because, in this case, well over 90% of the data meets defined expectations. Reversing how this data is presented and showing the percentage of rules that did detect errors (Table 20; Fig. 32) paints a different picture—one that is less positive but that also makes it easier for people to see where there are issues or risks.

Fig. 32 makes it easier to see differences in performance in the three data domains. In doing so, it makes the job of the data quality analyst easier. However, it may not be the best way to present information to data consumers because it requires that they learn to read the chart in a way that is slightly unconventional. (Usually, bigger is better. In this case, bigger is worse.)

If the data quality monitoring process is fully automated and the measurement result data is captured in a way that supports reporting, then creating summary data can be done relatively easily in

Table 20 Percentage of data quality rules with errors by data domain.

Report date	Claim	Membership	Provider
1/1/2022	1	5	15
2/1/2022	1	7	14
3/1/2022	2	9	18
4/1/2022	5	6	10
5/1/2022	7	7	6
6/1/2022	10	7	14

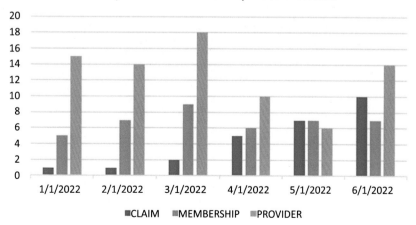

FIGURE 32

Data quality results summarized to show the presence of errors.

a basic data visualization tool. But the visualization itself is only the beginning of the story. Data consumers may be happy to hear that, in general, the data is okay. But what they really want to know is: Is the data I need to use measuring up to the standards I require? Can I use it to do my job? That means the high-level summary data must be supplemented with information about individual rules, especially if the monitoring process has detected issues or risks.

A data quality report may include fuller detail (e.g., total records and number of and percentage of records that did not meet the rule) on highly critical measurements. Table 21 shows counts and percentages for a single data quality rule that is monitored on a daily basis. The rule measures the records that are not fully integrated during the claim-to-member match process. It calculates the percentage against the total number of records in the load file. The graph in Fig. 33 makes it easier to see the results, including the spike near the end of the month.

Table 21 Counts and percentages for non-integration claims.

Load date	Non-integrated count	Total record count	Non-integrated percent
9/1/2022	349	402,908	0.0866
9/2/2022	395	446,093	0.0885
9/3/2022	3,131	796,663	0.3930
9/4/2022	1,571	509,742	0.3082
9/5/2022	149	38,085	0.3911
9/6/2022	31	7,545	0.4156
9/7/2022	379	839,212	0.0452
9/8/2022	568	848,455	0.0670
9/9/2022	219	479,956	0.0455
9/10/2022	145	987,517	0.0147
9/11/2022	143	973,866	0.0147
9/12/2022	306	782,469	0.0391
9/13/2022	20	8,725	0.2246
9/14/2022	15	20,840	0.0705
9/15/2022	415	781,851	0.0530
9/16/2022	254	694,275	0.0366
9/17/2022	190	844,500	0.0225
9/18/2022	304	538,410	0.0564
9/19/2022	1,127	388,553	0.2901
9/20/2022	13	22,028	0.0578
9/21/2022	580	489,416	0.1185
9/22/2022	908	567,148	0.1602
9/23/2022	163	921,639	0.0177
9/24/2022	448	945,425	0.0474
9/25/2022	1,771	1,125,999	0.1573
9/26/2022	735	21,761	3.3776
9/27/2022	8	5,565	0.1409
9/28/2022	350	1,658,709	0.0211
9/29/2022	463	493,640	0.0937
9/30/2022	417	670,554	0.0621

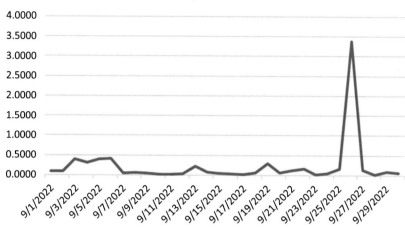

Non-Integrated Percent

FIGURE 33

Trend on percentage of non-integration claims.

Presenting Summarized Issue Management Data

Data around issues will take a form similar to data derived from the data quality monitoring process. As will be discussed later, issues will need to be categorized along several axes:

- Data domain or data set affected
- Status
- Age/time between discovery and remediation
- Factors that influence priority
  - Severity based on business impact
  - Severity based on data impact
  - Work effort to remediate
  - Root cause

If the issue management process includes collecting data about these characteristics, then they can serve as categories through which to summarize information by the status and priority of the issues (Table 22; Fig. 34). As with data about monitoring results, this information can also be captured in an

Table 22 Data issues by data domain and priority.				
Data domain	**High priority**	**Medium**	**Low**	**Total**
Claim	3	8	1	12
Membership	4	6	5	15
Provider	2	5	10	17
Total	9	19	16	44

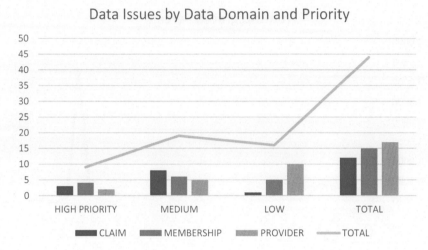

FIGURE 34

Data issues summarized by data domain and priority.

application in ways that enable quick and easy visualization. However, also like aggregated monitoring results, this information in and of itself is not of great interest to stakeholders. They will want to know about the specific conditions that affect their uses of the data. So the report itself must contain information about specific issues, and members of the data quality team must be able to explain the nature and status of specific findings, issues, and risks.

Presenting the Data Quality Report

But data quality reports should not simply be sent out to stakeholders in the hope that they will look at and understand the findings. Data quality reports are a communications tool. As such, they present the opportunity for communications to go in both directions (following McGilvray's Step 10: "communicate, manage and engage people *throughout*"). Not only do they keep stakeholders informed about the condition of data, they also provide a way to get feedback from anyone using the report. Feedback can be used to improve the reporting itself; for example, it helps the data quality team ensure that they are measuring characteristics that stakeholders care about in ways that are meaningful to stakeholders. Feedback is also needed to understand the impact of issues so they can be effectively prioritized.

Sharing this information is best done in a regularly scheduled meeting, usually monthly, with a standing agenda focused on sharing findings, clarifying impacts, and setting priorities. Meeting regularly helps build trust by establishing open lines of communication. It contributes to building a common vocabulary around data and data issues, and it is a way to get direct feedback on data quality reporting. Such a meeting can be augmented by ad hoc meetings with individuals and teams of stakeholders to address high priority, time sensitive issues.

Data Quality Issue Management Overview

Data quality issue management is the process of identifying, analyzing, quantifying, prioritizing, and remediating the root causes of obstacles to data consumers' uses of data. The goal of data quality issue management is to remove or reduce the impact of obstacles to the use of data by data consumers (people, processes, and systems). Issue management is both a phase in the data quality improvement cycle and a stand-alone process. When well-executed and focused on eliminating the root causes of issues, it represents a microcosm of the overall data quality improvement cycle.

A data quality issue is any obstacle to a data consumer's use of the data, regardless of why it is an obstacle; what its root causes are; who discovered the issue; when, where, or how it was discovered; or how it may be remediated. Managing data quality issues requires the ability to detect them, prioritize them, analyze their root causes, and remediate those causes. Learning from this process, an organization can make process and technical changes that prevent issues and reduce risks associated with data creation, maintenance, and use.

Data quality issues are not limited to incorrect and missing values. They include *any* obstacles to the use of data. They can be thought of as gaps between what a person or process expects data to look like and what the actual data looks like. If metadata is absent or poorly written and data consumers do not know which data to use because they do not have reliable information about the choices, then that is a data quality issue. The fact that the issue can be addressed by providing the required information does not make it any less of an obstacle to use.

Data that has been mangled by a technical process is poor-quality data. A common response to these situations is to say, "That's not really a data quality issue. It's more of a technical issue." This is an excuse that prevents problems from being addressed. Incomplete or incorrectly executed data processing logic creates bad data. If one wants to improve data quality, it is not acceptable to ignore bad logic or dismiss things like data gaps and unclear models as "not data quality." These structural and technical obstacles are generally larger impediments to data use than are missing and incorrect values (see Fig. 15 in Chapter 5).

The Issue Management Elephant in the Room

Let's be candid. Anyone who has ever tried to make the issue management process work knows that it is one of the most painful parts of data quality management and data governance. Resolving issues should be the place where all of the pieces come together: taking an enterprise view of data; ensuring accountability along the data chain; getting to the root causes of problems; taking actions that result in measurable, long-term improvements; and working for one's team and for the greater good. Instead, issue management often illustrates all that is wrong with the current state. No one wants to admit there are issues. Then no one has the time or funding to do real RCA. Instead, people jump to conclusions about causes and point fingers. Or, worse yet, issues become hot potatoes, and no one does any real analysis because they fear being the messenger who will be shot. Even when analysis is done and root causes are clearly identified, the results may not be acted on because the people who must make the changes do not benefit from the work.

This is why improving the quality of data takes leadership commitment and cultural change. If the leaders of the organization do not commit resources to the process and if they do not establish ways to make actual improvements to business and technical processes, then the quality of data will not improve, and the organization will continue to waste time and effort on the direct and hidden costs of poor-quality data.

On the other hand, if leadership is committed and establishes an issue management process with teeth, based on accountability along the data supply chain, then it will reap the benefits of higher-quality data—not only improved efficiency, but also improved employee satisfaction and with it, if the history of quality improvement is a guide, improved customer satisfaction.

Issue Management Principles

Issues with data can originate at any point along the data chain because any process that touches data has the potential to affect the quality of data. To address this risk, data quality issue management should follow a set of guiding principles:

- **Prevent issues by design:** Prevention of data issues starts at the beginning of the data life cycle by ensuring that data is created based on clear expectations of what it represents and how data is structured. Prevention is not limited to the initial creation of data. Issues can be introduced at any time data is moved, processed, accessed, or transformed. Prevention is about ensuring that the data chain itself is well designed and that hand-offs within the data chain are executed in ways that do not negatively affect the quality of the data. The data chain should clear the path for data usage; data processing should not create obstacles to use.
- **Metadata is a form of issue prevention:** If data values are incorrect, then that is a data quality issue. But it is also an issue if a person does not understand the data. Lack of knowledge is not only an obstacle to data use; it is also a risk. A person who does not understand the data is more likely to misuse it. To reduce the risk of misunderstanding the data, to describe appropriate uses, and to clarify quality expectations related to the data, information about data (metadata) should be created when the data is created. This requirement for metadata holds true not only for data created in transactional systems, but also for data that is derived or aggregated for reporting and analysis.
- **Remediate issues at their root causes:** A root cause of an issue is a factor in a process that sets in motion causes and effects that result in the undesirable condition (the issue). RCA is the process of understanding the factors that contribute to an issue and the ways that they contribute. Knowledge of root causes can be used to improve process results by eliminating conditions that cause issues. RCA is critical to improving the quality of data and to reducing the costs of poor-quality data. When issues are discovered, their root causes should be identified and addressed. Addressing root causes is a form of issue prevention. True RCA requires more time than does applying a bandage that addresses only the symptoms of an issue. But the amount of time is small compared with the costs involved in dealing with recurring problems if root causes are not addressed.[5]
- **All issues are not created equal:** Although any obstacle to data use is, by definition, a data issue, not every issue requires the same amount of attention. Issues become issues only when a person or process cannot use the data. If issues are discovered in data that no one is using, such as very old records (as sometimes happens when data is comprehensively profiled and assessed for quality), then it is the responsibility of the data quality team to recognize that these

---

[5]At least, if the bandage is a true bandage, simply slapped on. Organizations can waste a lot of time arguing about "tactical" versus "strategic" solutions to issues while forgoing the actual RCA. Time would be better spent addressing the root causes one time, rather than failing to address them multiple times.

conditions exist and to inform data consumers about them so they do not need to be rediscovered, but it does not mean that there is value in remediating them. Two critical components of data issue management are quantification and prioritization. All issues should be prioritized and evaluated via a cost-benefit analysis (CBA). The most important issues—those that have the largest impact on the most important data—should be addressed first. High-priority issues may be the only ones that are addressed. Some issues may never be remediated.[6]

- **Information about data quality issues should be shared with data consumers:** A critical component of data issue management is transparency. Issue management includes reporting. Hiding data issues is detrimental to the success of the organization. Data consumers should be well-informed about any risks or limitations to the data they are using. They also should drive prioritization of issues.

Issue Management Phases

Like other cyclical processes, issue management can be described as a set of phases that represent the beginning, middle, and end of the process. These phases may go by different names in different organizations. Some people see definition, analysis, and quantification as one phase. The phases described here include identification, definition, RCA, quantification, prioritization, and remediation (Fig. 35). The overall process should be supported by tracking and reporting. It is important to be able to share with data consumers both the status of individual issues and the success of the process in resolving the most important issues in a timely manner.

Identification

The first step in managing issues is identifying that they exist. Issues can be identified through the following:

- Data analysis, such as profiling
- Reports from data consumers
- Failure of technical processes
- Data quality monitoring

For tracking purposes, it is important to capture details about where, when, how, and by whom the issue was identified as this information can be valuable to all phases of the process.

Definition

The definition of an issue equals the "what" of it. Issues are often identified through their symptoms—signs that something about the data is not right. It takes analysis to figure out what the issue is and how it should be addressed. Analysis is the process of taking something apart, looking at the pieces, and putting them back together again with a greater understanding of what they represent. Analysis of an issue should result in a written description, with supplementary visuals and data examples, if necessary, that allows people to understand what is wrong with the data.

---

[6]Some people think that the goal of data quality management is to ensure that every piece of data is perfect. I am not one of those people. Most of us work in organizations in which we have to make choices about where to spend organizational time and money. This is true within data quality management as well. Unless an issue has a negative impact on the organization and its customers, it should not be addressed.

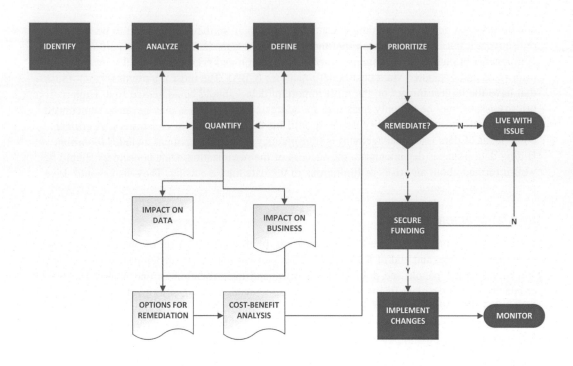

FIGURE 35

The issue management cycle.

Defining an issue is often an iterative process. The person who discovers the issue sees a symptom, but the original observation or characterization of the symptom may not accurately describe the actual problem. For example, an issue was reported that there were invalid values in a US state code field. Instead of the usual two-letter abbreviations, a set of records included the values "201" and "202." Additional analysis of the data showed that not only were the state codes incorrect, but other data associated with the address was incorrect as well (county code, Zip code). The problem was caused by a technical process hiccup that caused data to be displaced within the file (the technical team did not get to the true root cause—what caused the hiccup). Date data (the years 2018−2020) had landed in the State Code field. Calling this issue "invalid state codes" made it sound like a data entry issue that affected only one field, when it actually was a technical issue that affected several fields.

Each issue should be clearly defined, following standards for clear writing. The description should contain enough information about the issue that stakeholders can help with prioritizing it. This is not always easy because issues are generally reported based on first impressions. As the issue is analyzed, the definition should be clarified and updated to reflect the true nature of the issue. Because knowledge about an issue changes through the analysis process, it is also best to have a numeric identifier for the issue so it can be tracked despite changes in name and description.

Not only are the name and definition of the issue important, so are other characteristics, such as the data and processes affected. This information will help analysts see connections among issues. It will also help stakeholders prioritize sets of issues that affect a data domain or a specific business process.

Root Cause Analysis

As described earlier, RCA is the process of understanding the factors that contributed to the issue. RCA is critical not only to resolving the issue but preventing recurrence. In other words, it is critical to improvement. RCA is also simply good practice. In the absence of knowledge and the ability to take action on root causes, issues are likely to recur, which means any investment in quick fixes is not likely to pay off. RCA should account for factors related to technical and business processes as well as the data itself. The process of analyzing the causes of an issue should result in a set of options for how to address the issue along with the relative costs of each option. For tracking purposes and, more importantly, for improvement efforts, there should be a way to document and categorize the root causes and contributing factors of issues.

Quantification

Quantifying data issues is a form of analysis critical to understanding and defining the issues themselves. Quantification will have two focal points:

- **Quantifying the impact to the data:** How many fields, rows, tables, or systems are affected by the issue? When did the issue start and stop? Or is it still ongoing?
- **Quantifying the business impact of the issue:** How many customers are affected? How much revenue is affected? What reporting functions are affected?

Often, through the process of quantification, an analyst will get a clearer understanding of the nature of the issue itself, including its root causes, dependencies and impacts that may influence prioritization, and potential risks associated with not addressing the issue. This understanding can be used to ensure that the issue is clearly defined and that stakeholders have the information they need to prioritize it. Combined with RCA and issue definition work, quantification contributes to an assessment of options for remediation. Once root causes are identified and remediation options are defined, these options must also be quantified so the costs and benefits of each option can be understood.

Quantification is central to issue management. It is a direct input to prioritization because it allows issues to be categorized in terms of their relative severity. Because the relative impact of an issue is also directly related to the value in remediating it, quantification is critical to decision making within the process. Quantification should be included in tracking and reporting on issues.

Prioritization

Because all data is not created equal, all data issues are not created equal. Organizations must make decisions about which issues to address, how to address them, and when to address them. (Always prioritize!) Prioritization depends on the following:

- **Definition:** A clear understanding of what a given issue is
- **RCA:** What caused the issue
- **Quantification:** The quantified business impact of the issue, including any risks associated with not addressing it, and the options for remediation. If the cost of remediation outweighs the benefits, then an organization may decide to accept the risks associated with living with an issue.

Prioritization is important to tracking and reporting on issues because it describes the relative importance of an issue and speaks to the benefit side of the cost-benefit analysis. It is possible to have an issue that affects a lot of data but has limited business impact. Addressing such an issue would be a lower priority than addressing an issue that affects a small data set but has a high business impact.

Remediation

Resolving a problem means finding and implementing a solution and bringing it to closure. Remediation includes deciding on the best option for resolving an issue and then implementing the process and technical changes required to fix the issue and, hopefully, prevent it from recurring. This usually requires obtaining funding or using funding set aside for the purpose of addressing issues. Ideally, remediation includes implementing controls that will either prevent the issue or alert teams to any recurrence.

Tracking and Reporting

Tracking issues serves many purposes. First, tracking is a necessary part of managing issues. At the very least, a tracking mechanism enables the data quality team to know how many issues exist and what their status is. As described briefly in the "Presenting the Data Quality Report" section, a well-designed approach to tracking helps stakeholders understand the types of issues, the data they affect, the decisions that have been made about them, and the rate at which they are addressed. Analysis of tracking data can be used to identify improvement opportunities and estimate their impact. Importantly, a tracking mechanism is a communications tool. It allows you to inform stakeholders about the existence of issues and risks as well as the status of remediation, and to get their input and feedback on approaches to remediating them.

Improve Data Quality

Core data quality management capabilities depend on and interact with each other to comprise an improvement cycle based on the Shewhart cycle (PDCA). As illustrated in Fig. 36, the interactions depend on feedback loops among the core functions.

Although the diagram begins with defining expectations, this is not the only starting point for data quality improvement. (It's a circle for a reason!) One can begin the process anywhere in the cycle: through the discovery of an issue, through data quality monitoring, through the effort to begin reporting, or by responding to known opportunities for improvement. In addition, although the cycle progresses in a logical order (issues cannot be managed until they have been identified), there are also feedback loops among the different capabilities. Assessment of data may result in new standards or refinement of standards. Reporting may result in feedback from customers that identifies additional risks to be monitored. And so on. Assessment and measurement are critical to the overall process. To show improvement, one must know what the starting point was.

These capabilities can be applied to particular kinds of data, for example, master data. MDM ensures that master data is complete and current and that identifiers for different entity instances are correctly associated. The process of entity resolution determines the correct association of records and contributes to the quality of master data. Much of this can be done via well-designed

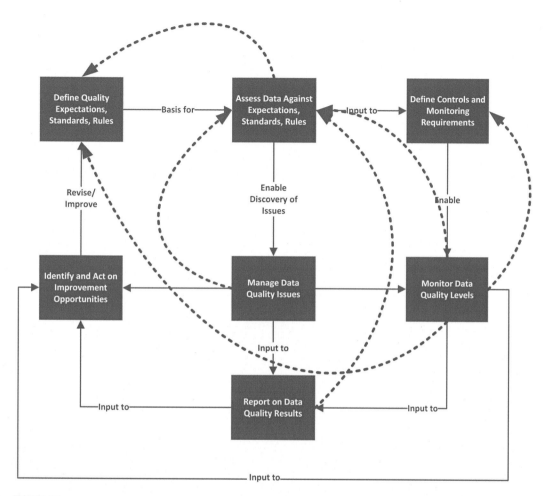

FIGURE 36

The data quality improvement cycle: core data quality management capabilities with feedback loops.

automation. But there is always a certain amount of fallout that must be addressed. The overall process requires setting standards for the data, assessing its condition, monitoring it, managing issues, reporting, and looking for ways to improve its quality. When thought of this way, MDM is the application of data quality processes to a particular kind of data with specific quality requirements. Because it also involves specialized domain knowledge, MDM is more often executed as its own specialized function, rather than as part of a data quality program. But the principles are the same.

Reference data management is another such application. The goal of reference data management is to ensure that the organization has access to a complete and current set of domain values, with

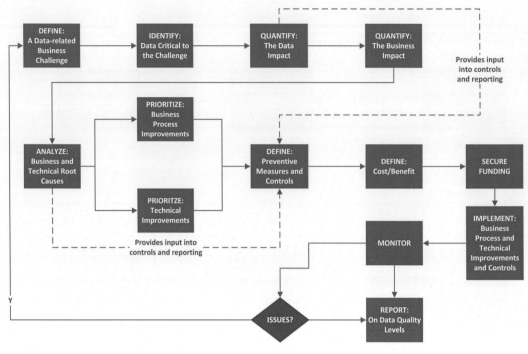

FIGURE 37

Data quality improvement cycle initiated by a data-related business challenge.

accurate definitions, for all codified data. To get there, reference data must be assessed and monitored. Reference data management is more likely to be included in a data quality program because reference data often serves as the standard for the validity of other data. For example, measuring the validity of Zip codes on customer address records requires a complete and current listing of Zip codes from the US Postal Service.

A second way to look at data quality improvement is illustrated in Fig. 37, which takes as its starting point the identification of a data-related business challenge; defines the data related to this challenge; quantifies and prioritizes the issues, impacts, and controls required to prevent the issues from reemerging; and implements improvements.

Applying Core Data Quality Management Capabilities

Because of the many ways in which data is created and used in organizations, data quality management processes can be applied at different levels and with different focal points. For example, as discussed earlier, MDM and Reference Data Management can be seen as specific applications of the ideas of data quality management. More generically, these processes can be applied to the following:

- **An individual data quality issue:** Data missing from a report, inability to balance between two data sets, missing claim data, inaccurate sales data
- **A data set within a single system:** Address data within a customer or membership system, inaccurate product data within an inventory system
- **All data within a system:** A customer relationship management system, claim adjudication system, an enrollment system, a sales system
- **The interaction between different data sets within a single system:** Provider and membership data as used by the claim adjudication system; product inventory data used in a sales system
- **A specific data set across systems:** Product data across sales, marketing, and inventory systems; membership data across eligibility, claims, and financial systems; master customer data; reference data
- **Data that supports a single process:** Customer relationship management, direct marketing, member counting, month-end close
- **The integration of data sets from different processes and systems within a warehouse or data mart:** Membership data integrated with claim data, sales data integrated with customer data
- **A data quality improvement effort:** Integration of geospatial data into a marketing system, improvement of an MDM system through data purchased from a data broker, reduction of reprocessed claims resulting from missing or incorrect provider data

Core data quality management capabilities may be executed as part of projects, as part of the ongoing operations of an organization, or as part of a focused improvement effort to address specific issues or support the strategic needs of the organization. They can also be understood with respect to how they contribute to the organization's overall data quality management capability as either foundational, project-oriented, or operational. To understand how these pieces interact in different settings, we must understand these settings, each of which provides a different perspective on how to execute the data quality functions:

- **Foundational:** Activities that define the approach/strategy and enable the initial setup of information, standards, processes, and tooling to be used by projects and as part of operational data quality management. Through these activities, deliverables are created (i.e., standards, templates, and process-definition documents) that are used in projects and operations.
- **Project:** Activities executed to meet project goals and deliverables by applying the foundational processes and standards within development work. Assessing data and defining requirements for data monitoring are generally executed as a part of projects. (They may even be executed as a data quality improvement project.) However, they are time-bound work efforts focused on achieving particular goals.
- **Operations:** Activities focused on managing the systems that support business processes and ensuring that the data that these processes create is of high quality and is usable. Data monitoring is largely an operational activity (although setting up automation for monitoring is likely to be part of project work).

Each of these capabilities should be defined within the organization. Project-based activities should be integrated into the organization's project methodology. Operational processes should be supported by standard operating procedures, as illustrated in Fig. 38.

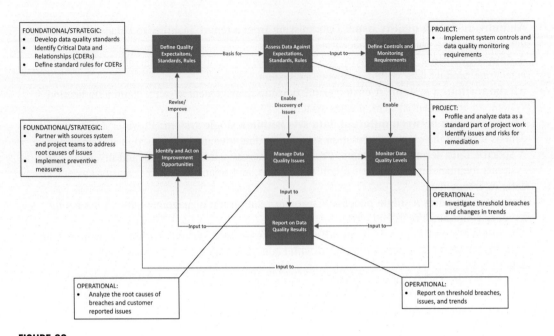

FIGURE 38

Core data quality management capabilities associated with organizational activities.

Conclusion

Many organizations do not necessarily have a clear picture of what they mean by data quality management. For people who have not been directly engaged in the work, it can be talked about as a jumble of good intentions mixed in with technical mumbo jumbo. For me, the core capabilities presented in this chapter are at the heart of the work. To execute these effectively requires specialized knowledge, training, and experience as well as support from leadership and engagement from stakeholders.

Within a complex organization, data quality management intersects with many other processes that can influence its outcomes. In working to improve the quality of data, it is important to know how these intersections take place and to work with people who are responsible for these other processes for mutual success. Doing so requires aligning data quality management priorities with other organizational priorities and executing on data quality priorities as effectively as possible, so the organization gets the benefit of improved data. In Chapter 11, we will discuss how core data quality capabilities can be aligned with and, to a degree, integrated into other life cycle processes (e.g., the systems development life cycle). But first, in Chapter 10, we will dive into one of the key conceptual tools in data quality management—dimensions of data quality.

Dimensions of Data Quality

"A mind that is stretched by new experiences can never go back to its old dimensions."

Oliver Wendell Holmes, Jr.

Introduction

We introduced the concept of data quality dimensions in relation to product quality in Chapter 5. A dimension of data quality is an aspect of data that can be measured and through which its quality can be understood, assessed, and quantified (Sebastian-Coleman, 2013). Dimensions of quality help answer the first and second questions that are fundamental to data quality management: "What do we mean by high-quality data?" and "How do we detect low-quality data?" They also provide a basis for assessment, issue management, data quality monitoring and reporting, and quantifying data quality improvement. As such, dimensions help accountable people in the organization answer the third question: "What action will we take when data does not meet quality standards?"

In both product quality and data quality management, the term *dimension* works by analogy to physical dimensions (height, length, width, weight, density) and reminds us that although data is not a physical product, it does possess measurable characteristics. Dimensions provide a way to understand quality in relation to a scale and, through this, in relation to other data measured using the same scale. When used to define data quality measurements, dimensions provide information about why we measure. That is, often the dimension is the basis for the question a measurement answers (e.g., How complete is this data? How valid is it? To what degree does it possess integrity?).

That said, many lists of dimensions go beyond what can clearly be measured (objective characteristics of data, such as completeness, validity, timeliness) and include more subjective features, such as believability, interpretability, and trustworthiness, as well as expectations related to data use (e.g., accessibility, security). Some dimensions of data quality depend on information that is not directly accessible through the data itself but is part of the data environment. For example, the existence of a data model and other metadata; the existence of governance policies and data standards; the reliability of systems that process data; and the usability of tools to access and analyze data.

This chapter will begin with a brief overview of dimensions of quality published by data quality thought leaders. These sets of dimensions illustrate that quality expectations are related not only to the structure and content of the data itself, but also to the metadata, systems, and tools through which we understand and use data as well as through the knowledge and perspective of individual data consumers. It will then present a more fully defined set of data quality dimensions that pertain

Meeting the Challenges of Data Quality Management. DOI: https://doi.org/10.1016/B978-0-12-821737-5.00010-9

to four of the five challenges of data quality management as introduced in Chapter 2 and discussed in detail in Chapters 4 to 7:

- **The meaning challenge** related to data's representational function and the choices people make in creating data
- **The process challenge** related to defining quality based on documented knowledge of data and the processes that produce it
- **The technical challenge** related to how data is instantiated and used through information technology systems
- **The people challenge** related to how people understand and use organizational data and to their perceptions of quality

The discussion of dimensions does not specifically call out the culture challenge because with respect to organizational data, it is present in the other challenges. An organization's data is specific to itself. Any given organization's processes and technical applications differ from those of other organizations, even within the same industry. These differences mean each organization encodes meaning in ways that are specific to itself. Employees of an organization must understand the specifics of how the organization works if they are to create, understand, and use organizational data.

The dimensions presented here can be applied to assess data at different levels (column, record, file/table, data set, system, metadata, processing) and at different points in the data life cycle (data creation, data processing, data use). These dimensions will provide a basis for standard rules, examples of which will be provided throughout the chapter.

Perspectives on the Dimensions of Quality

Let's start with existing knowledge. Leading thinkers have developed sets of dimensions that help data quality practitioners focus on aspects of data that relate directly to an organization's ability to understand and assess the quality of its data and make decisions about how to improve this quality.[1]

---

[1] As discussed here, Wang and Strong (1996), Redman (1997, 2001), Loshin (2001, 2011), McGilvray (2021). See also Sebastian-Coleman (2013) for detailed definition of the dimensions that form the foundation of the Data Quality Assessment Framework (DQAF). For the DQAF, I specifically limited the dimensions to an objective set, which I saw as fundamental to basic management of data (knowing the condition of data, almost irrespective of whether that condition would be considered good or bad quality). The discussion that follows is informed by numerous papers from the International Conference on Information Quality (ICIQ) [https://ualr.edu/informationquality/iciq-proceedings/]. There have also been efforts to create a standardized set of data quality dimension names and definitions (Black & van Nederpelt, 2020; DAMA UK, as documented in DAMA 2017; Myers, 2017). The discussion here draws on those standardization efforts. It is not my goal, however, to propose a standard. Rather, I simply want people to understand the wide range of data quality dimensions and how they can be used. No matter what, organizations implementing data quality assessment and monitoring processes will need to focus measurements on problems they are trying to solve. As with other data quality tools, dimensions are a means to an end, not an end in themselves.

Wang and Strong

Wang and Strong (1996), whose categories of dimensions we discussed in Chapter 5 (intrinsic, contextual, representational, accessibility), focus their dimensions on the question of how to ensure "data … are fit for use by data consumers." They define 15 data quality dimensions, each of which describes "a single aspect or construct of data quality." They recognize accuracy and believability as intrinsic dimensions; relevance, timeliness, and completeness as contextual; interpretability, ease of understanding, and structural and semantic consistency as part of representational data quality; along with security and accessibility as part of accessibility data quality.

Redman

Redman (1997) begins his discussion on dimensions with a definition of data rooted in data structure. A data item is a "representable triple": data represents entities, which have attributes, which have values. (Or, in reverse, a data value exists in the domain of an attribute within an entity.) From here, he describes a set of 27 dimensions related to the data model, data values, and data's representational functions. For Redman, high-quality data must be relevant, obtainable, clearly defined, and modeled at the right level of grain with the right degree of precision. Importantly, data should be semantically and structurally consistent. Values should be accurate, complete, current, and consistent. Data should be interpretable and physically instantiated according to standards.

English

English (1999) uses the term *characteristic* to describe what others have called *dimensions*. His nine Inherent characteristics are static features of the data itself, independent of its uses. These include things like conformance to definitions, completeness of field population, conformance to business rules, and accuracy to both a surrogate source and to reality. Inherent characteristics also include non-duplication and equivalence and concurrency of redundant or distributed data. English's six Pragmatic characteristics are associated with the amount and kind of work that can be done with data. Pragmatic characteristics are dynamic; their importance can change, depending on the uses of data. They include accessibility and timeliness as well as clarity and usability. Although he does not call it a dimension of quality, English also accounts for characteristics of the information environment (the overall context in which the organization creates, manages, and uses data) to support the use of data.

Loshin

Loshin (2001) points out that defining a set of dimensions is the first step to classifying requirements and measurement goals for data. The dimensions he presents draw heavily on both Wang and Strong as well as Redman. He focuses first on data structure and describes characteristics of high-quality data models (clarity of definition, comprehensiveness, flexibility, robustness, essentialness, attribute granularity, precision of domains, homogeneity, naturalness, identifiability, obtainability, relevance, simplicity, semantic and structural consistency). He then addresses characteristics of data values (accuracy, treatment of nulls, completeness, consistency, currency/timeliness).

Loshin's approach adds a new facet to the discussion when he addresses the quality of data domains. He recognizes that enterprise agreements on usage, the level of stewardship, and the degree to which different departments share data (ubiquity) all influence the quality of data. These dimensions are characteristics of the data environment rather than the data itself, but they are still dimensions of quality. He also addresses presentation quality, which includes aspects related to things like the clarity of labels and the choices in design (e.g., layout, color, use of graphics). Ideally, appropriate choices in design will lead to correct interpretation of the data. However, with the exception of representational consistency, the dimensions that Loshin associates with presentation quality (flexibility, format precision, portability, representation of null values, use of storage) do not seem directly connected with presentation but with structure and values.

Loshin revisited the dimensions of quality in 2011. There, his definition of dimensions is again focused on measurement: "A dimension of data quality describes a context and a frame of reference for measurement, along with suggested units of measurement" (Loshin, 2011, p. 130). But like McGilvray's (discussed next), his 16 data quality dimensions encompass not only the data itself, but also the context in which people understand and use data. In addition to objective characteristics like accuracy, completeness, consistency, currency, and identifiability, he identifies specific metadata as dimensions of quality: lineage, quality indicators, status of the data source as authoritative, and the existence and enforcement of processes, policies, and standards.

McGilvray

McGilvray's (2021) 13 broad and fully articulated dimensions provide a lens through which to view the whole of her Ten Steps methodology. She defines data quality dimensions as "characteristics, aspects, or features of data. ... [that] provide a way to classify information and data quality needs. Dimensions are used to define, measure, and manage the quality of data and information." People who are trying to solve data quality problems can use the dimensions that are most applicable to the problem to be solved. McGilvray includes suggestions about where to start and how to use the dimensions.

McGilvray organizes the dimensions around the methods for assessing them. She begins with the perception of relevance and trust as a core dimension. Within data integrity fundamentals, she includes many of the objective characteristics of data: completeness, validity, and structural and content consistency. She accounts for data decay as a separate dimension. She describes the specific approaches to assessing accuracy, timeliness, synchronization, uniqueness and deduplication, data coverage, and data decay. She also accounts for the need for metadata (data specifications) and for controls for access and security, along with presentation quality and usability.

ISO 8000

The ISO Standard for Data Quality, ISO 8000, uses as its starting point ISO's definition of data as "the reinterpretable representation of information in a formalized manner suitable for communication, interpretation, or processing." In describing ISO's approach, Benson (2019a) separates dimensions related to information from those related to data. The information represented in data is associated with trust, relevance, representation, and timeliness. The data itself is characterized by its format (syntax) and its encoding (semantics). ISO's definition of quality characteristics for data are that it is portable (not only is it system-agnostic, it also carries with it metadata about its content), it meets requirements, its provenance is known, it is accurate (conforms to facts), and it is complete (all required parts of the data set are present) (Benson, 2019a).

Common Threads

These quick summaries of approaches to dimensions of data quality make it clear that the concept of dimensions of data quality extends beyond the structure and content of data itself. Dimensions also encompass characteristics associated with the following:

- The existence and quality of fundamental metadata required to understand and use data
- The execution of related data management processes, such as metadata and reference data management
- Knowledge of business processes that create data
- The existence and enforcement of data governance standards and policies
- Knowledge of data risks and a risk management process for data
- Assumptions about the quality of system architecture and implementation

There is much to be learned from these sets of dimensions. One thing that stands out is that dimensions do not always describe "a single aspect or construct of data quality." Some dimensions, such as completeness, imply multiple aspects. For example, some can be applied to data at various levels (e.g., file, record, column, data model), and others can be understood through a range of lenses. For example, trustworthiness, a dimension in and of itself, is influenced by a number other dimensions, including the perceived reasonability of the data, the source of the data, the reliability of the systems in which it is created and managed, and the usability of tools for accessing, analyzing, and interpreting data. This means some dimensions can be measured in relatively direct ways, largely through comparisons to rules or other standards, and others must be assessed using a composite approach that depends on knowledge of expected patterns in the data, rather than just rules.

Categorizing Dimensions of Quality

Dimensions of quality can be applied to define specific characteristics of data. In doing so, they allow us to ask specific questions about the condition of the data and formulate specific assertions about what makes data of high quality. For example, what criteria must be met for a data set to be complete? What makes an individual value valid or invalid in a specific context? Why does a data set seem questionable or unreasonable?

The dimensions outlined in the previous sections begin with reference to **the quality of data structure and values**. That is, they refer to the following:

- The choices made in creating and organizing the data
- The degree of standardization in the data model
- How consistently the data model is implemented
- Whether recorded data values are correct or incorrect

These ideas will be covered in the section entitled "The Meaning Challenge: Choices about Representation" later in this chapter.

Dimensions also extend beyond the data and recognize characteristics of the data environment that directly affect both measurable data quality characteristics and the perception of quality. These include the following:

- **Metadata and support for data use**, including the existence of specific types of metadata (e.g., data definitions, data classification, data standards, data lineage) and governance structures (designation of systems of record or authoritative sources, access and security policies, controls). These will be discussed in the section called "The Process Challenge: Capturing Metadata."
- **System and data process design**, including the design of the systems where data is created, the existence and application of system controls, and service level agreements (SLAs). These will be discussed in the section called "The Technical Challenge: Technical Processes affect the Quality of Data."
- **The knowledge and skills of individual data consumers**, including their experience with the systems and tools used to access data and the degree to which the presentation of data follows familiar practices. These will be discussed in the section called "The People Challenge: Data Consumers are the Arbiters of Quality."
- **Governance processes** around data creation, metadata management, reference data management, systems management, and data access and usage. These will be discussed in the section called "Data Governance Policies and Metadata."

Dimensions can also be understood in relation to combinations of these things because these concepts are interconnected and dependent on one another. It is hard to use data if you do not know where to find it or cannot determine whether the data represents the entities you expect it to represent; it is yet more difficult if you cannot get access to the system in which it resides.

For example, some people include data lineage as a dimension of quality. I do not see it this way. To me, lineage is a type of metadata. However, the existence of data lineage (documentation of the movement of and changes to data as it passes through systems and is adopted for different uses) is extremely helpful in understanding the quality of data. Lineage ideally tells you the provenance of data (i.e., the system or process that created it) as well as the ways in which data has been transformed as it has been moved between systems and processes. Thus, lineage provides knowledge about the data and context for use. Given that, designing a data model so it contains attributes that reflect the lineage of the data (e.g., source system name, file name) and designing a system so it captures data related to its own processing (create date, update date, record statuses, results of validations) not only enables data quality management (especially root cause analysis), but also supports the overall auditability of a system and its data (a data governance requirement). Equally important, data consumers may also require these attributes to query and prepare data.

In almost any list, there are a lot of dimensions, so it helps to categorize them in ways that allow better understanding of their relationships. As noted earlier, to bring greater clarity to the dimensions themselves and to the goals of this book, I will discuss them in relation to four of the five challenges of managing data quality discussed in Chapter 2 and discussed in detail in Chapters 4 to 7.

The Meaning Challenge: Choices About Representation

The meaning challenge provides a lens through which to view the dimensions related to data structure, data values, and the quality of the data model as well as how consistently the data model is implemented. Data is created based on choices about how to represent objects, concepts, and events in the real world. Data structure (how data is organized into entities with attributes) and data values (the ways the meaning of individual attributes is encoded) result from these choices. A data model is a means of organizing, documenting, and explaining these choices. One of the primary purposes of a data model is to clarify and precisely define data requirements, including rules about relationships between the entities and attributes represented in the data, which themselves can serve as criteria for quality.

Many of the objectively measurable dimensions of data quality pertain directly to how data is defined, structured, and maintained over time. Quality dimensions related to data structure ask how well and, importantly, how consistently the model represents what it purports to represent. Quality dimensions related to values of individual attributes focus on the degree to which these values correspond to what is known about the attributes of objects, concepts, and events that they represent (Are measurements accurate? Are concepts categorized consistently? Are dates correct?).

Data Modeling Terminology

In summarizing thought leaders' collections of dimensions of data quality, I associated data structure with a "data model." Before going into detail on quality dimensions associated with an organization's data model, it is important to understand what a data model is and how it influences the quality of data.[2]

A model is a representation of something, usually in miniature form and often created in order to understand that thing better. For example, anatomical models allow medical students to understand how the human body works. Models have historically been associated with the process of designing physical objects. Architects build models to show what their building designs will look like in three dimensions and in the context of a particular landscape. The more abstract idea of a model as "a standard for imitation or comparison, thing or person that serves or may serve as a pattern or type" has also been around for several centuries (etymonline.com).

A data model uses symbols and text formally and precisely to represent an organization's data, its data requirements, or a combination of these things. Models serve many purposes, including supporting application development. But for purposes of data quality management, they document unambiguous expectations about data and through this, enable communication and education of those expectations.

Data modeling, the process of developing a data model, includes analyzing and often discovering an organization's data requirements so they can be represented in the model. Although there

---

[2]This discussion draws heavily on Hoberman (2009). The vocabulary is drawn largely from relational data models. Relational models are often developed through three stages: conceptual, logical, and physical. There are other kinds of data models (again, see Hoberman, 2009), but for the goals of this book, I will focus on relational to illustrate my points about the connection between data quality and the data model.

are many different approaches to data modeling (e.g., relational, dimensional, object oriented), data models share common characteristics.

- **Models describe entities:** An entity is an object, event, or concept about which an organization collects information. Referred to as the "nouns of the organization," entities answer fundamental questions: who, what, when, where, how, and how many. For example, an organization has customers, products, and sales transactions.
- **Entities contain attributes:** An attribute is a characteristic or property of an entity. It may describe, measure, or simply identify an entity. For example, customers have names and addresses; products have product numbers, colors, and sizes; sales transactions have times, dates, and locations.
- **Attributes have domains:** A domain is the complete set of values that may be assigned to an attribute. A domain may be defined as a list of values, as a range of values, through a rule or a calculation, or it may consist only of a format constraint. For example, US customer addresses have Zip codes; these codes are defined by the US Postal Service as five-digit numbers. Any Zip code with fewer or more than five digits cannot be valid.
- **Domains have values:** A value is the meaningful piece of information that describes the attribute of an entity instance. For example, the Zip code associated with a specific street address is a value.
- **Entities relate in specific ways to other entities:** Entities interact in defined ways with other entities, and these interactions allow us to understand attributes of both entities. For example, a customer buys one or more products via one or more sales transactions. Multiple customers can buy a product at different times. A sales transaction can include one or more products. But each sales transaction is associated with only one customer and takes place at only one time.

Even though this vocabulary sounds a bit technical, it is useful in describing data because it is precise. It is important to understand it. The vocabulary here pertains to what is known as a *logical data model*. A logical data model is a technology-independent representation of an organization's data (or a subset of that data). A logical model can be translated into a physical model, which will need to account for system requirements. For example, format constraints come into play when a logical data model is physically implemented. These constraints depend on the technology of the system in which it is implemented.

In the discussion on data structure later in this chapter, entities are essentially equivalent to tables or files—data structures that contain records representing entity instances. I will use the term *entity instance* to refer to a record of the thing represented. For example, when we say a data set should contain only one entity instance for each customer, we are saying there should not be multiple (i.e., duplicate) records for the same customer. Attributes refer to characteristics of entities, which makes them essentially equivalent to columns or fields in tables. So, we can say a customer has a US address and that this address has a street name and number, a city, a state, and a Zip code. The term *value* refers to the actual data populated in a given field. If the customer is located in the state of Massachusetts, the value in the state code field should be "MA." A value is valid if it is part of the domain for the attribute. The US Postal Service abbreviations for the 50 US states and US territories make up the domain of valid US state codes. A value is considered invalid if it is not recognized as part of the domain. Looking back at the example in Chapter 9, an organization doing business in both the United States and Canada is likely to include Canadian province and territory codes in its domain of valid state codes, even though Canadian provinces and territories are not "states."

A note on the difference between "a data model" and "the data model." A data model is a model produced for a purpose, usually as part of a development project. When we talk about "the data model," we are referring to a more abstract idea: the enterprise data model (EDM), "a holistic, enterprise-level, implementation-independent conceptual or logical data model providing a common, consistent view of data across the enterprise" (DAMA, 2017). Few organizations actually produce an EDM and enforce enterprise-wide data modeling standards. However, the idea that these standards should exist and that enterprise data should be consistent in ways that an EDM would demand is nevertheless embedded in many assertions about data quality.

If an organization could start with a green field, create its EDM, and base its applications on the EDM, then there would not be disparate or heterogenous data because the organization would have already imagined how all of the pieces fit together. Also, it would achieve a level of data coherence that others not only dream of but also use as the basis of assertions about data quality.

The Quality of Data Structure: Data Model Quality

Dimensions associated with the quality of the data model are focused on characteristics that make the data as complete, consistent, and comprehensible as possible. Because data models document not only names and definitions but also the relationships between entities, they provide a way to clarify expectations about data quality. Models provide a means to overcome disparity in organizational data by defining expectations for correctness and consistency with respect to how data is structured, formatted, and aligned with other data. By standardizing data structure and values, a data model can help an organization reduce differences in the ways that its existing systems represent objects, events, and concepts. To the degree that data is modeled consistently and that models are implemented consistently, other quality characteristics can be achieved. For example, when data is modeled consistently, it is easier to associate records that refer to the same entity instance, such as all records that represent the same customer. Loshin (2011) calls this dimension *identifiability*, and Daas et al. (2010) call it *linkability*. This capability is at the heart of master data management (MDM). Indeed, if an organization could implement an enterprise data model with the characteristics described in the following sections, MDM would almost become unnecessary because any data that complied with the standards would be "mastered" simply through this compliance.

In the listing here and the ones that follow, I will include the dimension itself and the details of the dimension. Each sub-bullet includes an assertion that describes an expectation related to quality. In some cases, I have elaborated on the implications of these assertions.

Dimensions of data quality related to the data model include the following[3]:

- **Completeness**
  - **Comprehensiveness:** The data model includes all entities about which the enterprise requires information.
  - **Level of detail/granularity:** Each entity in the data model includes all attributes about which the enterprise requires information for that entity.

---

[3]Dimensions outlined here focus on characteristics most important to the quality of data. For more in-depth studies of data model quality itself, see Hoberman (2015) and West (2011).

- **Cardinality relationships:** The relationships between entities are completely documented (all relationships are documented).
  - **Optionality (mandatory/optional):** All mandatory attributes are identified. Rules are documented for when optional attributes are expected to be populated.
- **Correctness**
  - **Correctness of names:** The names of entities and attributes reflect the organization's understanding of what these things represent.
  - **Correctness of definitions:** The definitions of entities and attributes are accurate and reflect the organization's understanding of the meaning of each.
  - **Correctness of data types/format constraints:** Columns are associated with the correct data type, based on the meaning of the field and any requirements connected to industry standards or interoperability.
  - **Cardinality relationships:** The relationships between entities are correctly defined and reflect the organization's processes for creating data.
- **Uniqueness/Non-duplication**
  - **Uniqueness of entities and attributes:** In a normalized data model, there should be only one instance of each entity and each attribute. Normalization reduces the risk of discrepancies among multiple representations of the same entity instance or the same attributes.
  - **Distinctness of attributes:** Each attribute should represent a single characteristic of the entity. Attributes should be mutually exclusive/non-overlapping.
- **Consistency**
  - **Semantic consistency—Entity and attribute names and definitions:** The same logical concepts are named and defined the same way throughout the model and consequentially throughout the enterprise.
  - **Semantic consistency—Attribute values:** Attribute values for the same logical concepts are expressed and defined the same way throughout a system and consequentially throughout the enterprise. This includes a consistent means of defaulting values in a column (expressing the absence of a value [missing value] or the inapplicability of a value).
  - **Structural consistency—Level of detail/granularity:** The same logical concepts are implemented to the same level of detail within a system and consequentially throughout the enterprise.
  - **Structural consistency—Field format:** The same logical concepts are implemented using the same data types within a system and consequentially throughout the enterprise. Technology-dependent differences in format are known and accounted for along the data chain.

These dimensions for data model quality imply a lot about expectations for the quality of data housed in the model. Data consumers want complete data that consistently reflects the level of detail they need to understand the processes that the data represents. In reviewing the characteristics of a high-quality data model, it should be clear that creating such a model depends on other factors that are part of the data environment and that also support data quality management:

- Knowledge of the entities that are important to the organization
- Knowledge of business processes that create data—what attributes are required, captured, and used by the organization as well as how they are captured and used
- Knowledge of the technology and systems that create, store, and maintain data

- The existence and use of data modeling standards that define expectations for consistency within the model
- The choice of modeling tools; although the conventions of data modeling are common across tools, there are differences in how modeling tools enable validation and enforce modeling standards as well as how they capture metadata

Because the modeling process itself is focused on defining and understanding data, in most organizations, data models are a primary source of data dictionary level metadata (names and definitions of tables and columns in databases along with data types of columns), which is essential to understanding data quality. The quality of the data model greatly influences not only the quality of the data, but also the ability of people in the organization to establish criteria for data quality. Whether or not there is a data model, it is relatively easy to see missing data, to find inconsistencies in formatting of columns with similar data, and even to identify clearly invalid values. However, it is difficult to determine whether a column is correctly formatted if there is no standard for how it should be formatted; to determine whether it is expected to be populated if there are no documented rules related to population; or to know if a value is actually valid if there is no reference data set to confirm validity. The same goes for more complex questions.

That said, few organizations have a comprehensive, standardized, well-maintained enterprise data model because few perceive the benefit of creating one, and no one wants to retro-fit an existing application portfolio to an enterprise data model. Fortunately, most organizations model their data at least to some degree. In fact, rather than referring to "the data model," it is more realistic to refer to a data model for a given system and to the set of models that represent the enterprise. Existing models provide a starting point for assessing data quality at the system or application level. This use of data models is also a source of feedback about these models themselves and can be used to bring a greater degree of consistency to enterprise data. And over time, the enterprise data model itself becomes a standard through which to assess data quality.

A Note About Unstructured Data

I have been using the term *data structure* as a synonym for the data model and also as a substitute for the idea that data, by its very nature as a representation, has a level of inherent organization. That said, some readers are undoubtedly thinking, "Yeah, but what about unstructured data?" Structured data is defined as data that adheres to a predefined data model. As noted, a data model not only provides a way of organizing data, but also defines expectations related to data quality.

Data created in applications is not always modeled. In fact, unless there is a conscious effort to design the output from the process that the application supports, data is often seen as a by-product of the process. (In this sense, when data is taken from an application and put into a data warehouse, the data model imposes a particular kind of structure on data.) However, data produced by an application used to execute a business processes has an inherent structure related to the processes itself.

Unstructured data is defined as data that does not adhere to a predefined model. This means the breadth of information that falls under the umbrella of "unstructured data" is very wide. It includes the following:

- Data that has a clear inherent structure, such as machine-generated streaming sensor data, where data structure and format are defined by the design of the collection device

- Information that is captured in standardized documents and on websites (semi-structured data), where data structure is defined by the format of the document or the page
- Social media posts that are constrained only by the application interface, the number of characters allowed, and the language and typing skills of the people posting

At one end of the "unstructured" spectrum (machine-generated sensor data), the expectations for quality are based on the process being measured and the purpose of the measurement. The actual quality of data can be understood in relation to the process and the device. Completeness would be that the data stream has no interruptions in the expected interval of sensing (whether continuous or periodic); format is constrained through the device; validity depends on the calibration of the device; and integrity depends on consistent calibration across a collection of devices. In the middle, where we have semi-structured data, the expectations for completeness are connected to legal requirements for documents. Other aspects of quality are directly related to the quality of the presentation of the information as well as its factuality. At the other end of the spectrum, such as Twitter feeds, there is no definition of completeness (when will we be finished with tweeting?) and no requirement for format correctness, validity, integrity, or consistency, so the question of quality is moot.

The bottom line is that although unstructured data does not adhere to a predefined data model by definition, in many instances the inherent structure of data provides a means by which to compare expectations for data with the data as collected. The key is to explicitly define this structure in order to define the associated expectations. Unstructured data only becomes functional as data when the user imposes structure (Kenett & Redman, 2019).

Example: Uniqueness and Provider Data Granularity

The problem of uniqueness and duplication is directly connected to how an organization defines its entities. For example, a health care company had two systems for managing data related to medical providers. Data about providers can be complex because it includes references to both people (e.g., doctors, nurses, technicians) and facilities (e.g., hospitals, outpatient clinics). A provider can be an individual person, an organization, or a facility. Leaving aside this challenge, these two systems had different ways of defining what constituted an instance of an "individual" provider—a person who provides medical services.

The first system assigned one identifier to each person represented in the system (this was referred to as "Doc on the Nose"). The other system assigned an identifier to each combination of a person and a location where services were provided. The system contains multiple records for each individual doctor who worked out of multiple offices or who was affiliated with multiple hospitals.

This meant that the data in the two systems looked quite different, as illustrated in Tables 23 and 24. System A contained one record for each person. System B contained multiple records for each person. To

Table 23 Provider granularity example 1: One identifier/individual provider.

System A		
Provider ID	**First name**	**Last name**
10000	Cho	Chang
20000	Padma	Patel
30000	Fred	Weasley

Table 24 Provider granularity example 2: One identifier/individual provider and location.			
System B			
Provider ID	**Location ID**	**First name**	**Last name**
525	10	Cho	Chang
432	11	Cho	Chang
167	15	Cho	Chang
649	11	Padma	Patel
782	12	Padma	Patel
256	15	Fred	Weasley
190	19	Fred	Weasley

complicate matters, the Provider ID in System B did not get reused from location to location, making it hard to tie together records for one person within that system as well as between systems.

The challenge of integrating the data from the two systems involved assigning the Provider ID from System A to each record in System B. Doing so worked in most, but not all, cases. When it did not work, the fundamental difference introduced a level of complexity that sometimes got in the way of data use. Data consumers were confused or frustrated, and responding to their questions took time. It is important to note that, even if the data in each system were perfect within that system (all records in System A are complete and accurate; all records in System B are complete and accurate), there is still risk that using the data from both systems could introduce misalignment and, with it, inaccuracies and gaps.

The Quality of Data Values

The desire for completeness (including its relationship to uniqueness/non-duplication), accuracy, format correctness, consistency, and standardization is also inherent in the dimensions of quality commonly associated with data values. These dimensions are expressed based on the assumption that a data model exists to define the structures in which the values are captured. As noted, they can also be applied to unstructured data, once expectations about inherent structure of that data are explicitly articulated.

Dimensions related to the quality of data values include the following:

- **Completeness**
  - **Data set completeness:** A data set should contain all of the records required by a data consumer (person, system, or process). Requirements for completeness can be defined in different ways, including: all records from a system, all records related to a specific population (all customers, all products; a subset of customers, a subset of products), or all records generated in a defined timeframe.
  - **Record/row completeness:** For a record to be complete, all mandatory fields must be populated.
  - **Field/column population completeness:** If a field is mandatory, then it should be fully populated (it should not contain any NULL or default values). If a field is optional, then it should be populated based on rules that define the conditions under which its population is required or under which its population is not required.

- **Uniqueness/non-duplication**
  - A data set should include only one record for each entity instance.
    - o Note: Meeting this requirement means having a clear definition of what constitutes an entity instance and what constitutes a unique record. Having a definition of each is critical to understanding the completeness of a data set. The presence of duplicate records creates noise in the data that can directly interfere with the assessment of completeness.
- **Accuracy**
  - **Field/column data value accuracy:** Data values correctly represent characteristics of their real-world counterparts.
  - **Accuracy of derived data values:** Transformation logic used to derive a data value must result in the correct value.
    - o Note: Accuracy of derived values is a specific instance of data values correctly representing the attributes of their real-world counterparts, in which the derivation itself creates the representation. If the logic of the derivation is incorrect or incomplete, then it will produce incorrect results.
- **Format correctness**
  - **Field/column format correctness:** The data type and length of the field must align with the physical definition as documented in the data model or other metadata, such as a defined standard.
    - o Note: There are different degrees of format correctness. Where a unique format is expected (e.g., US state code), all values must be the same length as well as data type. Where length can vary (e.g., product price, paid amount), values must be expressed as numbers and cannot exceed the length constraint, but they do not have to all be the same length.
- **Field/column data value precision:** Numeric data values include the required degree of precision (number of places beyond the decimal point). Numeric precision is a specific example of format correctness and is also directly related to accuracy when accuracy requires a specific level of precision.
- **Currency**
  - **Record/row currency:** Within a system that does not maintain historical data (i.e., that keeps only one record for each entity instance and updates that record as values change), each field of each record should contain the most recent value for the attribute. Within a system that maintains historical data, each record should be clearly associated with the timeframe during which it was the current record (e.g., through the use of record start and end dates), and each field for each record should contain the value that was associated with the attribute during that timeframe.
  - **Field/column currency:** Within a system that does not maintain historical data, the value in a given field is the most recent value for that attribute. Within a system that maintains historical data, the value in the field should contain the value that was associated with the attribute for the timeframe during which that record was the current record.
- **Validity**
  - **Field/column data value validity:** Populated values must be part of the domain of accepted values for the field. Acceptable values may be defined as a range, a distinct set, or output generated via a rule or calculation.
  - **Validity of related values:** Values populated in related fields within a record must be in a valid relationship with each other (e.g., US Zip code must be associated with the US state code to which it is related).

- **Integrity**
  - **Data domain integrity:** The domain of valid values is the same for all instances of a logical attribute across different data sets.
  - **Data value integrity:** The populated values for all instances of the same attribute for the same entity instance at a given time are the same exact value across data sets.
  - **Integrity of related fields:** The populated values in related fields between data sets are in a valid relationship with each other (e.g., US Zip code and US state code)
  - **Parent/child referential integrity:** Where there is a foreign key relationship, each record in the "child" table should have a corresponding record in the "parent" table (i.e., no "orphan" records exist). For example, in health care, there should not be a claim service line record without a claim header record.
  - **Child/parent referential integrity:** Where there is a foreign key relationship and a population rule that requires a "child" record, each record in the "parent" table should have a corresponding record in the "child" table (i.e., no "childless parent" records exist). For example, every claim header record should have at least one corresponding service line record.
  - **System reconciliation:** Data within a downstream system is expected to reconcile to its direct sources and/or to the systems of record for the data. Reconciliation can be defined in different ways and will differ, depending on the structure of the data in the two systems: number of records, number of represented entities, and reconciliation between amount fields. In cases where records that are excluded as part of data processing, reconciliation logic will need to account for these records.
- **Consistency**
  - **Field/column definitional consistency:** The data in the field must be consistent with the logical definition as documented in the data model or other metadata.
  - **Field/column default value consistency:** The values in the field reflect a consistent use of NULL or another value to indicate the absence of data or the non-applicability of the field to the record.
  - **Field/column consistency of population over time:** For processes that are expected to produce consistent output between increments of data, the column profile/frequency distribution for the population of the field at different times should be statistically consistent. Consistency may be assessed based on record counts or data in numeric fields.
  - **Equivalence of related data sets:** Two or more data sets that are purported to be equivalent should be measurably similar. For example, if they are said to represent the same population of customers, they should contain records representing the same set of distinct customers for a given time period. Depending on structural differences between the systems, they may not have the same number of records. Note: Exact reconciliation between systems is described under "integrity."
  - **Consistency with benchmark:** A data set that purports to reflect a population similar to that of an industry or organizational benchmark should be measurably similar. For example, the medical claims for a given health care payer will have a similar distribution of hospitalizations as a benchmark set of claims for the same geographic area during the same time period.
- **Reasonability**
  - **Correspondence with known facts:** Data that purports to represent a specific population should correspond in meaningful ways to what is already known about that population. For example, the established number of customers in a market or the population of a geographic area.

These dimensions reflect fundamental expectations about what makes data of high quality. When people use data, they want to make sure they have all of the data they need (completeness) and that the data correctly reflects the real-world entities and attributes it purports to represent (accuracy, correctness, and validity) during the timeframe that these are represented (currency). Because data use always involves manipulation and presentation of data, they want as little interference as possible in these activities. If data is structurally and semantically consistent, then it is easier to use. A high level of consistency enables all of the pieces to fit together (integrity). There should not be any extra data (duplication, redundancy) that can interfere with data uses.

All of this sounds like common sense, and to a large degree, it is. However, organizations create data through disparate processes, defined at different times, using different standards, applied with different degrees of discipline. So organizational data is disparate and heterogenous. It is not always easy to determine what makes a data set complete, never mind determining whether it is equivalent to another data set. Doing these things requires additional information connected to the data environment, and this is the job of data management.

Dimensions provide a way of thinking about both expected and unexpected data characteristics. The purpose in describing these aspects of data that can be measured is to identify ways to assess and measure the quality of data. Using dimensions of quality, data quality standards can be formulated using a consistent approach to syntax, as illustrated in Table 25. These abstract assertions (Data Quality Mad-Libs) can quickly be applied to create rules for specific attributes. The following are some examples:

- Zip code must be populated for US addresses; the default value "00000" is acceptable only for non-US addresses.
- Birth date must be populated for individual provider records.
- Birth date must NOT be populated for facility provider records.

Table 25 Syntax for standard data quality rules.

Quality assertion name	Quality assertion	Standard rule
Field completeness— mandatory field	If a field is mandatory, then it should be fully populated with no NULL or default values.	[Field Name] must be populated. NULL, Blank/Space or other default values are not expected and not acceptable.
Field completeness— mandatory field, default allowed	If a field is mandatory, then it should be fully populated with a default value only under conditions defined as acceptable.	[Field Name] must be populated. The [Standard Default Value—VALUE] is allowed.
Field completeness— optional field— positive condition	If a field is optional, then it should be populated based on documented optionality rules.	[Field Name] must be populated when [Stipulate the condition that requires the field be populated].
Field completeness— optional field— negative condition	If a field is optional, then it should be populated based on documented optionality rules.	[Field Name] must be NOT be populated when [Stipulate the condition that prevents the field from being populated].

The Process Challenge: Capturing Metadata

The knowledge challenge is the driver for dimensions of quality that depend as much on the data environment as on how the data is structured and how values are assigned. While some data may be obviously wrong or unquestionably correct (e.g., birth dates in the 1800s cannot be correct for people purchasing health insurance in 2022), assessing the condition of other data often requires additional information that sheds light on quality expectations. To determine whether organizational data meets quality requirements, it often must be compared to documented knowledge and standards. More simply put, people need process information, metadata, and reference data to understand the quality of other data.

Metadata provides criteria for quality—if nothing else, basic definitions of tables and fields tell the data consumer what the data is intended to represent. Well-managed metadata will include much more, for example, information about how data is created, the systems in which it was created, how it is stored, how it should relate to other data, and what its levels of quality are. Metadata is required as input for all forms of assessment, from basic conformance to definitions to the ability to determine the degree of measurable similarity between conceptually equivalent data sets.

The quality of data depends on both the quality of the data model and the quality of fundamental business metadata (table and column names and definitions) because both include and imply commonsense criteria for data quality. Assessing data quality is also made simpler if specific metadata assets (e.g., security classifications, data lineage, and data standards) are available and if governance processes are in place that help people understand which data to use to meet their goals (e.g., designation of systems of record or authoritative sources of data).

Metadata Requirements to Support Data Quality

Metadata is a broad category. As defined in Chapter 2, metadata is explicit (i.e., documented) knowledge about data that enables data to be created, understood, and used. A wide range of information is included under the umbrella of metadata, including definitions of what the data represents and the processes by which it is created and stored. Some metadata is critical to assessing and managing the quality of data:

- **Names and definitions of entities and attributes:** Names and definitions of data elements are the most basic form of business metadata. They allow data consumers to understand what the data is intended to represent. In addition, clear definitions allow data quality analysts to assess whether data represents what it purports to represent.
- **Data structure/data model:** A data model will depict which columns are part of which tables. This information is required for people to query data. It is also very helpful simply to understand data. For example, knowing that address data is stored separately from data describing individual customers (because a customer can have more than one address) helps in making decisions about which address data is needed for a customer outreach program.
- **Business process descriptions:** Names and definitions do not tell the whole story of what data represents. People also require knowledge of the process represented by the data. Business process knowledge is critical to understanding data quality because it describes expected relationships within a data set as well as how a given data set (e.g., a list of customers) is expected to fit together with other data sets (e.g., a list of products, vendors, or locations).

Business process descriptions provide the basis for population rules. These include rules about which fields are mandatory and the conditions under which optional fields are populated.

- **Data lineage:** Data moves horizontally through organizations, sometimes in multiple directions at once. As it moves, it may be cleansed, augmented, aggregated, or otherwise transformed. Data lineage is a form of metadata that describes the movement of data through systems from its origin or provenance to its use in a particular application. Lineage is related to both the data chain and the information life cycle. It can be depicted at different levels of detail, from high-level architectural flows that describe how data moves among systems to detailed transformation rules within a specific system or process. Most people concerned with the lineage of data want to understand two aspects of it: the data's origin and the ways in which the data has changed since it was originally created. Change can take place within one system or among systems. Lineage is critical to understanding data quality because it allows people to see why there are differences between data as it was originally created and data as it is instantiated in a particular downstream context (a system or a report). Different types of lineage are defined in Table 26.
- **Data standards:** Data standards are assertions about how data should be created, presented, transformed, or conformed for purposes of consistency in presentation and meaning and to enable more efficient use. Data standards can be defined in relation to data structure or values. They have an impact on technical processing and storage of data as well as on data consumer access to and use of data. The most fundamental standard for a data element is its definition, but standards go beyond this.
  - Data modeling standards focus on entity and attribute names, classifications, data types, and formats.
  - Data quality standards describe expectations in terms of data quality dimensions: what it means for data to be complete, valid, consistent, and so on.
  - Presentation standards describe expectations for data visualization and other aspects of data presentation.

Table 26 Types of data lineage.

Artifact	Purpose	Type of lineage	Level of detail
Architectural drawing—multisystem	Shows the relationship among systems, including how data moves between systems	System-to-system	Depends on purpose
Architectural drawing—single system	Shows the relationship among component parts of a system, including how data moves within the system	Intrasystem	Depends on purpose
Architectural data flow—multisystem	Focuses on how data moves among systems	System-to-system	Depends on purpose
Architectural data flow—single system	Focuses on how data moves within a system	Intrasystem	Depends on purpose
Data mapping specification (Source to target mapping)—file/table level	Describes the relationship between one or more source tables/files and one or more target tables/files. At the file level, a data mapping specification will describe what equals a record in the source and target data as well as how source records must be combined or separated to fit in the target table/file	File/table to file/table (usually at the record level)	File/table level

Table 26 Types of data lineage. *Continued*

Artifact	Purpose	Type of lineage	Level of detail
Data mapping specification—column level	Describes the relationship between columns in one or more source tables/files and columns in one or more target tables/files. A data mapping specification will contain the rules that describe data movement and any associated changes in the data. The simplest kind of mapping rule is a direct move with no formatting changes to data. More complex rules include concatenations, translations of data values (If "A" in source, populate "1" in target), or complex derivations (use a set of inputs and logic to generate outputs)	File/table to file/table at the column level	Column level
ETL specification	Describes the technical processes that will move and transform data within a system	Intrasystem (except for extract description)	Job level
ETL code	Executes the movement and transformation of data within a system	Intrasystem (except for extract process)	Job level
Tool-generated based on managed metadata	Visual depiction of the technical processes that will move and transform data within a system, based on a tool extracting metadata from ETL code, using the conventions of the ETL tool from which it is sourced	Intersystem or intrasystem, depending on the tool	Many lineage tools allow drill up/down to different levels of detail

Data standards are important to data quality management because they describe formal expectations related to data creation, storage, and use.

- **Data quality metadata:** Data quality metadata is critical to overall data quality management. Metric definitions quantify data quality expectations. These definitions include the rules and conditions that are measured, where within the data chain measurements are taken, and the thresholds (tolerances) at which notifications and alerts will be sent, along with the details of the measurements themselves (e.g., date taken, counts, percentages). The results of measurements allow data consumers to compare quality among data sets and over time. Data quality metrics themselves depend on other forms of metadata (definitions, lineage, data standards, policies, data classifications) and contribute to refining these metadata assets.

Metadata Quality

Metadata not only must exist to support data quality management, but the metadata itself must be of high quality. For technical and operational metadata that is structured and stored as data, the dimensions related to the quality of the data model and the quality of data values apply directly. However, for descriptive metadata, such as definitions, critical dimensions of metadata quality include completeness, clarity, and currency:

- **Completeness**
  - **Metadata comprehensiveness:** The organization's metadata assets should include all of the types of metadata the organization requires to use the data, including those required to define and assess the quality of data and to support data inspection, assessment, and audit (e.g., data lineage, quality metrics).
  - **Definition completeness:** All entities and attributes, standards, rules, and policies should be defined.
- **Clarity**
  - **Writing clarity:** All entity and attribute definitions, standards, rules, and policies should follow standards for good writing (Clark, 2008; King, 2010; Strunk & Poff, 2018; Zissner, 2016).
  - **Correctness of individual definitions:** Each definition must correctly define the data described.
- **Currency**
  - **Currency of definitions:** Entity and attribute definitions should be maintained so that they contain the most current version of the definition. Historical definitions should be clearly associated with the timeframe during which they were current.
  - **Currency of standards, rules, and policies:** Standards, rules, and policies should be reviewed on a scheduled basis to ensure that they remain aligned with organizational needs and external requirements.

Dimensions of quality that address metadata, including the clarity of definitions, and the existence and application of standards related to business processes, data collection, security, and compliance help data consumers understand and assess the impact of contextual factors that influence data structure and of data use. Metadata-related dimensions also help identify discrepancies between data as created and data as it ideally should exist if it were designed to build quality in. Knowledge of this gap is the first step to closing the gap.

A Note About Unstructured Data

Many of the assertions about metadata quality pre-supposed the existence of a data model from which names and definitions of entities and attributes can be harvested. However, as noted earlier, unstructured data, by definition, does not have a predefined data model. Because there is no formal process to define a model for unstructured data, there is also generally no formal process to create the metadata that will support the use of unstructured data.

That said, like all forms of data, most unstructured data has some inherent structure. If we take, for example, the idea that "Big Data" is "big" in part because of its variety, then Big Data can come in a range of formats. One aspect of the structure of any given data set, then, is its format. Another aspect is its content. The data has been created. It contains some kind of information. This information can be described, even if its description consists merely of the process that created it and the time at which it was created (e.g., Trump Tweet, 2021−01−06). In addition, any data object that is brought into a Big Data environment has a name, even if the name is highly technical and may not even be translatable, and it has been brought into the Big Data environment from a source at a point in time. This information can also be captured as metadata.

As noted in Chapter 5, data is different from other resources with respect to how it is produced, inventoried, stored, and used.

- **Production:** Data is created in many places, often as a by-product of other processes; there may be very little control over the inputs.
- **Inventory:** Organizations do not know what data they have, what condition it is in, what relation it has to the processes that created it, and so on.
- **Storage:** Data can be easily stored, and the ways that we store data have an impact on its quality.
- **Usage:** We do not always know how data will be used. Although there is often a direct connection between data production and data uses, data can be used multiple times without being used up. It also lasts for a long time, so data created for one purpose can often be used in unanticipated ways for other purposes.

If data in general is different from other resources, unstructured data is even "more differenter." It is produced through a wider range of processes, ingested into large platforms that often lack a formal means to inventory data, and used as input for what are essentially experiments. For these reasons, metadata is as important—perhaps even more important—to managing the quality of Big Data as it is for traditional data, but it also has a different focus.

When thinking through metadata quality for Big Data, it is best to define and focus on foundational metadata requirements. The first of these is simply ensuring that the process for ingesting data into a Big Data platform includes capturing an inventory of what data is ingested, from where, when, by whom, and for what initial purpose. Minimum requirements will focus on the basics:

- **Production and Lineage:** Know where data comes from and who requested that it be ingested; do not allow data to be ingested without basic metadata.
- **Inventory:** Track what comes into the platform though an automated data catalog or other tool; prevent ingestion of duplicative data.
- **Storage:** Understand how ingest and storage processes affect the data itself and the ability of data consumers to find, access, and use the data they need.
- **Usage:** Consumers must know what the data represents, how it was produced, and how it is stored so they can determine whether it meets their requirements, but it is also important for people managing the system and the data to understand how data consumers are using the data. Information about data usage is critical to managing risk around data.

Depending on how much data is coming into the Big Data environment, where it comes from, and who will use it, it may not be possible to define every field as is expected with traditional data that is modeled, but it is possible to know basic information. This level of data cataloging creates a foundation from which other questions about quality can be addressed. Without this foundational information, individual data sets in a Big Data platform or data lake can quickly become the proverbial, unusable data swamp.

Reference Data Quality

Most people think of reference data as codes and descriptions. This is not incorrect, but a more abstract definition is helpful because reference data goes beyond just code tables and includes hierarchies and other information needed to understand core data. Reference data is data used to characterize other data in an organization or to relate data to information beyond the bounds of an organization (Chisholm, 2001). For example, status codes are used to characterize the state of a record (e.g., active/inactive). Geolocation codes are used to associate records with a standard way of identifying places. Some people consider reference data a form of master data, while others think of it as a form of metadata. Though it has characteristics of both, I prefer to treat it as a distinct kind of data because this allows for specific criteria to be defined for reference data quality.

Reference data quality is critical to data quality generally because reference data sets are often the standard for measuring the validity of core data. If reference data is not complete and current, it is not possible to confirm whether data values in core tables are valid. The dimensions of reference data quality are the same as those for metadata (completeness, clarity, currency), but the assertions for quality have some differences.

- **Completeness**
  - **Existence of reference data sets:** Reference data sets should exist for all attributes that require them. These sets can take different forms (e.g., stored in tables, presented in views, or incorporated into data dictionary listings).
  - **Completeness of reference data values:** Reference data sets should contain a full set of values and their definitions. For example, a Zip code table should include all Zip codes and the city/state combinations that they represent.
- **Precision**
  - **Reference data values:** Values include the required degree of exactitude for the attribute. For example, if the use of Zip code data requires not only the five-digit Zip code, but also the four-digit Zip code extension, then the granularity of the Zip code reference data should be at the level of the Zip code/Zip code extension.
- **Clarity**
  - **Writing clarity:** Descriptions of codes should follow standards for good writing.
  - **Uniqueness of reference data values:** Each reference data value should have one and only one meaning.
  - **Distinctiveness of reference data values:** Reference data values should be mutually exclusive. Meaning should not overlap among values.
- **Currency**
  - **Reference data currency:** Reference data sets should be maintained so they contain the most recent values and definitions. Historical values and definitions should be clearly associated with the timeframe during which they were current.
- **Accessibility**
  - Data consumers should have appropriate access to the reference data they require to use and interpret data.

Data Governance Policies and Metadata

Data governance processes are not themselves dimensions of quality, but they are part of the data environment. Their presence can support behaviors that enable the enterprise to produce high-quality data. Their absence can increase the risk that the enterprise will not do so. Data governance policies provide guidance on data creation, protection, and use in order to ensure that the organization can comply with laws, regulations, contractual obligations, and implied or stated promises to stakeholders, including its ability to serve its customers and employees. Governance policies guide both the legal and ethical aspects of data use. To support legal compliance, organizations establish policies related to data protection (security and privacy), data access (who can access which data for which purposes), and data use (how data can be used, how it cannot be used). Particularly in the realm of compliance, policies must be supported by metadata that enables appropriate uses and helps prevent inappropriate uses of data, for example by classifying data by security and confidentiality levels. Data governance policies can also be put in place to enforce the use of data standards that support data management and help meet requirements around interoperability.

Among the processes that can help are the following:

- **Authorized data sources:** Identifying systems of record for specific data sets and authoritative sources of data for designated uses.
- **Data protection:** Ensuring that security and privacy policies are defined and enforced.
- **Standards:** Ensuring that data standards, data modeling standards, and metadata standards are developed and followed.
- **Oversight of critical metadata:** Ensuring that key metadata, such as classification metadata, is created and maintained so the data can be kept in compliance with laws and regulations.
- **Oversight of critical reference data:** Ensuring that critical reference data is appropriately maintained. This can include data such as industry standard codes, but more importantly for many organizations, it includes things like general ledger codes and other proprietary hierarchies that are used to measure business success.
- **Supporting auditability:** Defining data modeling, metadata, and system processing requirements to ensure that data is auditable.
- **Oversight of key processes connected to shared data:** Providing oversight of metadata management, issue management, data change management, and reference data management.
- **Stewardship and support:** Ensuring that adequate support is in place for data consumers through support of production systems, data stewardship, and other forms of knowledge sharing.
- **Communications:** Well-managed metadata, data governance policies, and data standards are all communications tools. They describe expectations for data. One role of a data governance team is to ensure that these tools are created, used, and maintained. Doing so requires building awareness and providing training. A data governance communications process helps ensure the following:
  - Data producers are aware of and follow standards for data, data modeling, data security, and interoperability so they can create data and metadata that meets requirements, including requirements for quality. Data consumers know and contribute to the standards that data producers follow.
  - Data consumers are aware of issues that may affect their use of data; are aware of controls and restrictions on data; know how to access and use current metadata and reference data; and can provide feedback when they identify issues or opportunities for improvement.

The Technical Challenge: Technical Processes Affect the Quality of Data

We would not have the data we have without the technology to create, maintain, store, manage, and enable the use of it. However, poorly designed systems (those that do not account for the quality of the data they create or manage) are often the source of data quality issues. They can also exacerbate data quality issues rooted elsewhere. In contrast, well-designed systems can and should include features that enforce requirements for data quality as well as for other risky aspects of data management, such as privacy and security. Systems not only make data available; the design of transactional systems also influences what data is created in the first place. Systems can also be designed to enforce data quality requirements at the point of creation.

At the very least, systems should have controls in place that confirm that data is fully processed and that no data is lost in processing. Systems can bring about more consistent data through cleansing, standardizing format, and enhancing content. They can systematically enforce quality rules and should include controls that prevent some issues from happening. Data processing systems also produce metadata about their processes that can help assure the availability and timeliness of data. Systems can make data more auditable by storing attributes about the maintenance process (source system name, input file name, creator name, create date, updated by, update date, update process name).

System Reliability Characteristics

Characteristics of reliable systems are directly connected to their transparency and their predictability. They include the existence and application of controls that help build the confidence of data consumers in the reliability and consistency of data, which support the dimensions completeness, accessibility, and timeliness/availability. Although they are not directly about the quality of data, these characteristics contribute to an environment that builds trust and confidence in data. They include the following:

- **Documented:** System specifications are documented so people understand the purpose and design of the system.
- **Scheduled:** A data delivery schedule is in place, and data delivery is monitored to ensure that schedule requirements are met.
- **Accountable**
  - SLAs are in place to define when the system will make data available to data consumers.
  - When system events take place that break SLAs, data consumers are informed about data availability status.
- **Controlled**
  - System edits are in place to prevent the creation of low-quality data.
  - Automated controls are in place, and system processes are monitored to ensure performance and availability.
- **Transparent/auditable:** The system captures information about its own processes (operational metadata) so overall system performance can be monitored and so system processes and data can be audited.
- **Secure:** Controls are in place to
  - Enable legitimate access and prevent inappropriate access to the system.
  - Prevent unauthorized uses of specific data sets.
  - Prevent unauthorized changes to data.

- **Supported by metadata:** Data within the system is classified based on risk (data's potential value to bad actors), regulation (who is allowed to see the data), and confidentiality (who needs to see the data) levels.
- **Responsive to change:**
  - Processes are in place to respond to data consumer questions and to accept feedback from data consumers, including feedback about the quality of the data.
  - Resources are in place to manage required changes in the system in response to customer feedback.
  - Platform and software upgrades are implemented in a timely manner to ensure vendor support.

System characteristics contribute to an organization's ability to create, maintain, and use high-quality data. They ensure that the performance and outputs from the system are reliable and predictable. They also ensure that if something goes wrong with the system, it will be identified quickly and responded to. These types of characteristics are used by some organizations to identify authoritative systems of record.

Data Quality Dimensions Dependent on System Reliability

Although system reliability characteristics are not themselves dimensions of quality, they have a direct impact on data availability and accessibility. Also, system controls can be put in place to ensure that data is completely processed (no data is lost during processing).

- **Timeliness**
  - **Scheduled availability:** The system should make data available to data consumers based on timeframes documented in SLAs. Scheduled availability depends on both the timely delivery of data from source systems and the predictability of data processing within a target system.
- **Completeness**
  - **Completeness of inputs for processing:** All data (i.e., the full set of files) needed for processing is accounted for before processing starts.
  - **Processing controls:** Processing is monitored through controls that ensure that data is not lost as part of processing. Controls may be applied at the record count level or to other features of data (e.g., balancing numeric fields, through distinct counts of entities within a data set).
  - **Complete processing of data:** The outcome of processing is confirmed through audit/balance controls.
- **Validity**
  - **Validity controls:** Controls are in place to detect invalid conditions (missing data, incompletely populated data, unusable records) and alert system owners to these conditions.
- **Accessibility**
  - **System accessibility:** Data consumers should have appropriate access to the data. Inappropriate access is prevented.
  - **Access controls:** Only authorized people and processes can change data.

These characteristics describe expectations for traditional systems such as warehouses and data marts that deliver data. While there have been claims that data warehousing is dead, a lot of it is still going on, and warehousing is likely to continue into the foreseeable future. Also, these characteristics are pretty fundamental, regardless of the type of system in place. Whether it is processing traditional or Big Data, a system must be comprehensible and reliable.

The People Challenge: Data Consumers Are the Arbiters of Quality

Meeting the people challenge is about enabling people to use and understand data to meet their goals. The experience of people using data is dependent on the dimensions referred to in the other three categories: those that define expectations for data structure and values, set expectations for quality metadata and other aspects of the data environment, and establish technical and system controls to prevent data issues and make data accessible. When an organization designs its data well—by modeling it and by controlling the processes through which it is created, managed, and stored—it has a better chance of getting value from it because these processes reduce the risks associated with the ability of people to understand disparate data. Getting value also depends on ensuring that people have the tools, information, and support they need to access and understand data. They require knowledge of what a specific data set represents in order to determine the kinds of questions the data may be able to answer.

The dimensions of quality related to the people challenge include characteristics like relevance, ease of understanding, interpretability, objectivity, believability, credibility, reasonability, reliability, and reputation. These can be understood through three broad dimensions:

- **Relevance:** The importance and applicability of the data to the goals of data consumers: whether they think the data will meet their needs.
- **Usability:** Whether data consumers can actually use the data to answer questions, complete analyses, and present conclusions.
- **Trustworthiness:** Whether data consumers have confidence that the data represents reality in an accurate and reliable way.

It is easy to characterize these dimensions as "subjective," but there are ways to measure and assess how well data conforms to expectations implied by them, especially be seeing them in relation to characteristics that can be measured more objectively.

- **Relevance:** With complete and accurate metadata, including information about the original purpose of the data, the conditions of data creation, the population represented in the data, and the known limitations of the data, data consumers should be able to determine whether a data set is relevant for their purposes.
- **Usability:** Usability depends on metadata and on numerous factors associated with data structure and values, including semantic and structural consistency and the availability of reference data. It also depends on other aspects of the data environment, such as what tools, training, and support are available to data consumers. Importantly, usability depends on the data consumer's knowledge and skills—their level of data literacy. A data consumer who can use a range of analytic tools and is familiar with best practices for data visualization and other standards related to presentation quality will be better able to interpret data than those who are less familiar with these things.

- **Trustworthiness:** Data consumers ultimately decide whether data is trustworthy. Trust starts with a commonsense correspondence between what data purports to represent and the experience of individuals and the organization with previous instances of a data set. Sudden changes in data will reduce trust. At the very least, they require investigation. Trust can be built by defining quality and proving through data quality monitoring that data meets standards. Trust should also be supported by other processes and activities that are not directly about the quality of data, but that nevertheless influence people's perceptions of data. For example:
  - The existence of governance processes around changes to data
  - Maintenance processes for data
  - The level of data protection and security
  - The types of metadata and their quality
  - The level of customer support provided for data use
  - The reliability of the systems from which data consumers access data
  - The specific tools they use for their analyses

  Trustworthiness can also be directly connected to the presence of specific metadata, for example, data lineage information and audit fields that indicate when and by what process records were updated. In contrast, obstacles to data use (e.g., inability to access data, difficulty understanding data, issues with missing or incorrect data) will reduce people's trust in the data.

As noted under usability, people must have the skills to use data. Individuals will have different perceptions of quality because they have different levels and kinds of knowledge, different perspectives and opinions, and different incentives in using data. These differences can actually benefit an organization because they represent the potential to see data in a range of ways. All individuals will get more out of data if they have data literacy skills that enable them to do the following:

- Understand data structure and relationships
- Query and manipulate data
- Use tools to visualize and present data
- Make appropriate choices about how to present data
- Use interpretive skills that develop through exposure to multiple uses of data

Relevance, usability, and trust can be measured through instruments like surveys. Surveys can also measure the effectiveness of the activities and practices intended to build trust.

Concluding Thoughts

Dimensions of quality are a critical tool in data quality management. They allow an organization to define what it means by high-quality data and to assess data against this definition. Dimensions should be used in the way any good tool is used: appropriately to the task at hand. (The goal of having a socket wrench set with 100 sockets is not to use each of them, but to have one of the right size when you need it.) The same is true of the dimensions of quality. Understanding the characteristics the dimensions describe helps analysts define expectations for data and detect issues with data. When determining what data to monitor, organizations should apply the dimensions in ways that meaningfully inform data consumers about the condition of the data. When using the dimensions, keep in mind the first two assertions of the SAIL acronym: Start Small, and Always Prioritize.

Importantly, dimensions of data quality help build knowledge of data by creating a vocabulary through which to communicate about data quality expectations and issues. This allows data quality practitioners to work with other teams to integrate data quality assessment into other organizational life cycle processes with the goals of reducing risk, improving efficiency, and building quality into data production and use by design.

Data Life Cycle Processes

"In measuring a circle, one begins anywhere."

Charles Fort

Introduction

A life cycle is a series of stages through which an organism progresses from its conception to its death. Each stage is marked by a new level of development as an organism changes from an egg or seed to an adult able to produce offspring and then eventually dies. Some life cycles are complex (caterpillars completely change form when they become butterflies), while others are simpler and involve only growth and development rather than metamorphosis (a puppy looks like a small dog, with disproportionately large eyes). The life cycle phase and the characteristics of each phase for a particular species provide insight into the similarities among individuals of that species and the species' differences from other species. This is probably why the life cycle is a useful metaphor to describe other things, such as the conception, development, maturity, and obsolescence of products and the process of creating and managing data to realize value from it within an organization.

This chapter will examine several organizational processes that depend on the life cycle metaphor—the asset life cycle, the supply chain, the value chain, and the systems development life cycle (SDLC)—and show how they can be applied to data. The goal of the chapter is to demonstrate how knowledge of these cycles can be applied to build data quality into their supporting processes. My goal in presenting these cycles is to show how they inform each other. Multiple models show multiple perspectives and point to the reasons for complexity in a system like an organization. But just like a diagram of body systems (see Fig. 1), models also simplify complex systems and allow us to actually seem more than we can when we are trying to comprehend everything at once (Page, 2018).

The Data Life Cycle and the Asset/Resource Life Cycle

The data life cycle strongly resembles Juran's quality trilogy (planning, design, control) and the product life cycle that is the basis for it. As discussed in Chapter 5, data is a product of the processes that create,

Meeting the Challenges of Data Quality Management. DOI: https://doi.org/10.1016/B978-0-12-821737-5.00011-0

collect, and organize it. Life cycle management is an extension of the idea of quality control to all aspects of creating a product. Juran's *Quality by Design: The New Steps for Planning Quality into Goods and Services* is an extended explanation of how this works for physical products and services (Juran, 1992).[1]

Data can also be viewed as an asset that brings value through use, or, more generally, as a resource used to accomplish organizational goals. It has characteristics of both of these as well as some qualities that are distinctive to itself. If an organization is looking to improve overall data management and implement data quality by design in order to get more value from its data as an asset, then it helps to look at data from a higher level of abstraction: the data life cycle.

The phases of the data life cycle resemble those of other resources, such as equipment, finances, or even people (English, 1999). Acquiring and using resources requires planning. These resources then must be created, purchased, or hired. Often, work is required to prepare the asset to be used. People must be trained. Equipment must be set up and installed. To bring value, resources must be used. As English points out, "Idle resources produce negative value" (English, 1999, p. 201), meaning, of course, that they cost money. Many require maintenance, ongoing management, or tending to while they are being used. And, at the end of their useful lives, they must be appropriately disposed of; for people, we hope this means a happy retirement. Certain data must be destroyed when it is no longer legal or feasible to retain it. Economic value comes when the benefit from a resource's application is greater than the costs incurred from its planning, acquisition, maintenance, and disposition (English, 1999).

In addition to these standard phases of planning/preparation, creation, maintenance, use, and disposal, data also requires a level of design and enablement. It must be understood and its meaning documented if it is to be used by new people over time.[2] It also must be stored in a system where it can be both understood and accessed. The uses of data often result in the discovery of data issues (obstacles to the use of data), the creation of new data, or the identification of new data requirements. These situations mean there is a need to remediate or enhance data or to improve the processes by which it is created, maintained, stored, and shared. Data enhancement starts the life cycle again because enhancements require planning and preparation as well as data design and creation.

---

[1]This section relies on and draws significantly from McGilvray's *Executing Data Quality Projects: Ten Steps to Quality Data and Trusted Information* (McGilvray, 2021) and on English's *Improving Data Warehouse and Business Information Quality: Methods for Reducing Costs and Increasing Profits* (English, 1999). McGilvray's formulation of the data life cycle, POSMAD (Plan, Obtain, Store and Share, Maintain, Apply, Dispose) draws on English's work and expands it in significant ways. POSMAD describes and depicts the alignment of data with the universal resource life cycle. Using POSMAD as the basis for a life cycle model, I have added phases that are particular to data—Design, Enable, and Enhance—in part to more closely align it with Juran's trilogy. Like McGilvray's Store and Share, which recognizes that data must be made accessible to data consumers, these additional phases acknowledge conditions that are especially important for data. Especially when compiled from multiple sources, data is rarely in the exact form we need it to be in. It requires a level of design, along with the capture of explicit knowledge. It also must be set up in a system that makes it accessible. Loshin also describes an information life cycle: Create, Distribute, Access, Update, Retire (Loshin, 2011).

[2]See Joshik (n.d.), who points out that because "Many organizations spend 60 to 70 percent of their IS budgets on systems maintenance. . . . it is desirable that the documentation necessary for system operation and maintenance be produced as the by-product of the development process." I wish he had said "product," but I think the intention is there. Joshik includes data flow diagrams and data dictionaries as part of the documentation that should be produced by the SDLC.

Data life cycle phases include the following:

- **Plan/prepare:** Planning for data includes planning for each phase of the life cycle. Determine what data is needed as well as how it will be created, sourced, or acquired. Planning for known uses and ongoing support of use (e.g., training, customer support), access and security requirements, maintenance requirements, and archiving and disposal requirements. Planning should also include understanding and documenting the costs and anticipated value of the data.
- **Create/obtain:** Get the required data, either by obtaining it through an existing process, purchasing it, or establishing a process to create it.
- **Design and enable:** Define and design the technical and business processes to ensure that data can be accessed and kept current and complete. If there is a need to create new data, then design will be part of the create/obtain phase. If an organization will use data produced through operational processes, then design will be a separate phase.
- **Store and share:** Put data into a system that is secure and accessible to those who are authorized to see it and use it.
- **Maintain:** Implement operational processes that keep data current and complete and the monitoring functions that will alert production support teams and data users when unexpected conditions are detected.
- **Use/apply:** Use data in operational processes and reporting, analyze data to identify trends and business opportunities, incorporate the data into models and other applications, and, potentially, sell the data as a product.
- **Enhance and improve:** Recognize gaps and potential improvements, report issues and unexpected behavior in the data, and formulate proposals for improving data content and structure.
- **Dispose of:** Ensure that data is removed from systems and processes when it has reached the end of its useful life. Archive data that must be kept for legal or other reasons. Dispose of data that must be destroyed. Disposal schedules may be driven by regulation, contractual obligations, business requirements, or a combination of these things.

Having a picture of the data life cycle allows us to see that the activities required to manage data and ensure its quality differ from phase to phase (Fig. 39). In terms of quality, the most important points in the data life cycle are when data is created and when data is used or applied.[3] Creation provides the best and most obvious opportunity to ensure that data is complete and accurate. However, quality characteristics must also be defined when data is enhanced as this is a new moment of creation. In addition, as will become clear when we look at the data supply chain, data is often changed as it moves through the organization. A "moment of creation" can occur multiple times within the supply chain if data is aggregated, calculated, or transformed. The only time data brings value is when it is used, and if it is not of high quality at that point, its use may result in incorrect conclusions, bad decisions, or negative interactions with customers or other stakeholders. In such cases, data ceases to be an asset and functions as a liability. An organization actually loses value if its data leads to mistakes that negatively affect its stakeholders.

---

[3]This insight comes from Tom Redman, who discusses the importance of data creators and data customers in the overall management of data quality, and from Danette McGilvray, who observes that although all phases of the life cycle involve cost, benefit is created only when data is used (McGilvray, 2021, p. 38).

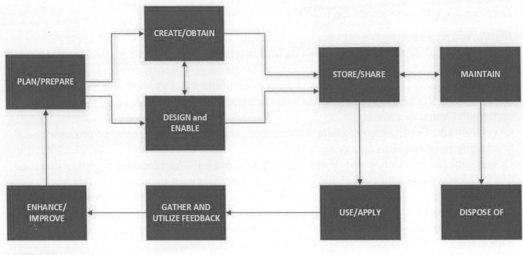

FIGURE 39

Data resource life cycle.

Managing Quality Throughout the Data Life Cycle

Although creation and use are the most important points in the data life cycle, the quality of data can be influenced at any point in the life cycle. This is related to the fact that, while we refer to a data "life" cycle and understand that certain characteristics of data are similar to organic materials (e.g., grows over time, takes on new meaning, "reproduces itself"), data is not actually organic. It is created by people or by machines designed by people, which means we have a lot more control over its creation than we give ourselves credit for. It is worth taking another look at the life cycle phases with this observation in mind. Doing so allows us to see how quality can be managed throughout the data life cycle.

Plan/Prepare

Planning includes defining expectations and requirements for quality and putting in motion the activities required to use the data over time.

- **Clear criteria for quality:** If expectations for data quality are unclear or undefined, then data will not be created consistently or correctly. If controls are not put in place to reduce the chance of errors, then more errors will occur. If processes do not account for how data will change over time and maintenance is not built in, then quality will deteriorate over time. If data creators do not know how the data is used and who uses it, then they will not understand the purpose or importance of the data they create, and quality will deteriorate over time. For these reasons, planning for data should include explicitly defining requirements for quality. These may be based on data standards, dimensions of quality, process requirements, data consumer requirements, or a combination of these things.

- **Supported by metadata:** Planning and preparing must account not only for data, but also for the information required to use the data—the metadata. Documented knowledge about data is essentially for its use. Without comprehensible definitions of data sets and data elements and without information about the processes that create data, data consumers will perceive data to be of low quality, regardless of the data's intrinsic "correctness." The limits of their own understanding will influence the level of trust they have in the data.
- **Account for the costs of poor planning:** The need for metadata increases as the ability of organizations to produce and use data increases. There is simply less time to learn, so if data is not documented, knowledge about it disappears into the ether. In the absence of usable definitions, models, specifications, and data flow diagrams, every data consumer must recreate the knowledge on his or her own. This extra work, repeated multiple times, diminishes the potential value an organization can get from its data. It increases costs (people must recreate knowledge about data) and risks (in recreating this knowledge, they will make mistakes and create discrepancies) while reducing the time spent using and thus deriving benefit from data.

Create/Obtain

Data can be obtained from an existing process or establishing a process through which it can be created. In organizations focused on using analytics to improve their performance, the most important source of data will be its own operational or transactional processes. Many organizations will augment this internal data with data from external sources that may provide, for example, additional demographic information about customers. In such cases, obtaining data requires finding a source or broker who can supply it. Because its quality will depend on the supplier, it is important to have explicit quality requirements when selecting a supplier.

Except for organizations that directly monetize data, it would be rare to create a new process simply to produce data. However, when new products or services are introduced, it makes sense at the beginning of the process to account not only for the data that will be created but for how data will be collected as these decisions have a direct impact on data quality. The create/obtain phase should include documenting the following:

- **Clear criteria for quality:** In creating a new process through which to obtain data, an organization has the opportunity to build quality into the process itself. This includes defining quality expectations up front and defining controls within the process to ensure that these expectations are met.
- **Knowledge of the creation process:** When obtaining data from an existing process, start with the assumption that the data may not yet be fit for purpose. Understand how that process works, including the conditions under which data is created and the incentives for particular outcomes. For example, if a claim adjudication process is focused on the speed at which claims are processed, it will produce one type of outcome; if it is focused on the accuracy of claims or on reducing the risk of reversals, it will produce another type of outcome. If it is focused on the accuracy of clinical information rather than the accuracy of contractual information, it may produce yet a different outcome. Understanding the purpose and drivers of the creation process will guide the creation of controls or other requirements.
- **Specifications for data suppliers:** When purchasing data, define quality requirements. Even if these cannot be met, having them documented is a vital step in selecting a supplier. It will also allow for the identification of risks and gaps.

Design and Enable

Design and enablement includes planning for the business and technical processes that ensure quality. These can take place at the application level to support the execution of the process, or they can take place at the level of the data store to support analytics and reporting. Design must account for both the technology through which data is created or shared and the business processes the data supports. Design directly affects usability, which affects both measurable quality characteristics and data consumers' perception of quality.

- **Enforce quality:** Designing an application to support a business process that produces high-quality data requires understanding the desired outcomes and putting in place the technical controls and validations that support those outcomes. Design can help prevent errors, for example, by restricting a domain of possible values (through drop-down lists or lookups), implementing logic based on business rules (birth date cannot be a future date), or preventing a process from moving forward if input data represents an invalid condition (a Zip code that is not correctly associated with a city; an invalid credit card number).
- **Enforce an enterprise perspective:** Enabling data for storage and use in analytics includes understanding how data will be brought together, often from different sources, and resolving problems of integration (granularity, differences in meaning, gaps at the attribute level across different data sets) and orchestration (timing and coordination of data delivery and processing) before they happen. An enterprise perspective includes setting standards for architecture, modeling, and development work to ensure that data is created, stored, and maintained consistently across applications. These processes can have a large impact on the quality of data. The enterprise perspective should include system controls to ensure that data sets are complete as they are brought into a warehouse, mart, or other storage platform. It should also include data quality monitoring routines that validate data against rules and patterns, including measuring referential integrity.

Store and Share

Storing and sharing are the equivalent of a physical distribution method, but for data. They are the means by which authorized data consumers access data and put it to use. How data is stored can have a direct impact on quality because it has a direct impact on the people and processes that access data. The ability to share data affects the value an organization can realize from data because it can influence the work associated with data use.

- **Standardize data storage:** If data across the enterprise is created based on consistent standards (ideally, through an enterprise data model), it is easier to store and share. If data is not created consistently, it should be standardized as part of data storage to make it easier to use across the enterprise. If data is difficult to access or share, then it will require additional work to use it, thus reducing its value to the organization.
- **Enable appropriate access/prevent inappropriate access:** Data brings value only when it is used, so enabling people to access data is critical to an organization's ability to leverage data. At the same time, inappropriate access to data represents risk. Planning for data storage should

also include planning for access controls that prevent data misuse by internal data consumers, and data security architecture that prevents access by external agents.

- **Support data sharing through appropriate metadata:** All stored data should be supported by metadata that enables it to be understood and efficiently accessed. This metadata should include information about data quality conditions, measurements, and issues.
- **Help data consumers understand data structure:** The way that data is physically stored has an impact on how it is accessed and shared. Few data consumers will understand the finer points of data modeling or physical storage, and they do not have to. But they will need foundational metadata to find and query the data they want to use.
- **Recognize the impact of access tools on the perception of data quality:** The sharing part of store and share is also important. Different access tools can affect the quality of data. For example, different tools may present numeric data at different levels or precision or have different methods for rounding numbers. These differences can influence people's perception of data quality, especially when different tools that make the same data set appear to have different characteristics.

Maintain

Maintenance processes also influence quality. Data currency is directly dependent on the method and frequency through which data is updated. Some maintenance processes may make data less usable. For example, fully refreshing a data set when a data consumer requires detailed history will make data unfit for purpose. The history will be lost. Similarly, data with complex history can be hard to use if a data consumer must focus only on the most current version of the data set.

- **Define maintenance requirements as part of quality requirements:** Data consumers will want to understand how historical data is maintained: are existing rows updated or fully replaced, or are new rows added with updated information? They will need to know what actions result in a row being updated versus a new row being created. Also, they will want to know the timing between when data is created via its originating process versus when it will be available for use.
- **Include metadata about maintenance processes:** Among the metadata required to support the use of stored data is information about its maintenance processes, including the maintenance schedule and the approach by which data is maintained (e.g., fully refreshed versus incrementally updated, versus a combination). These details enable data consumers to understand whether data is current enough to meet their needs as well as whether data contains the level of historical detail required for their analyses. Stored data should also include audit columns that timestamp when rows were created and updated.

Use/Apply

As noted earlier, the only phase in the life cycle during which an organization gets value from data is when data is used. All other phases should support the use of data. Data use is also the most important source of feedback about data quality because data consumers are the customers of the processes that create and manage data.

- **Support data use with metadata:** Using data requires knowledge of what the data represents and how it represents its concepts (e.g., knowledge of the process by which it is created and often knowledge of the system in which the data is stored and maintained). This knowledge comes in the form of metadata—documented information about the meaning and structure of the data. If metadata is not stored with the data or made accessible to enable use and sharing, then the costs of usage increase, diminishing the value that can be gained from data. The level of knowledge needed to use data corresponds to the usage task at hand. A person who is running a canned report needs a lot less data knowledge than a person creating a new report, using data in reporting, or analyzing data to identify trends and business opportunities.
- **Improve metadata quality through data use:** As noted under "Plan/Prepare," managing the data life cycle also includes managing the metadata life cycle. Metadata required for data use should be created/obtained as part of the development process. It should also be maintained as data uses evolve. Metadata improvement can include information about the ways data can be accessed and used as well as on the quality expectations related to the data.

Gather and Utilize Feedback

Feedback is critical to the improvement of any system, especially a system for managing data. Because the goal of data is to represent people, objects, events, and concepts in the real world, data that is disconnected from the reality it represents quickly deteriorates in quality. Systems theorist Ken Orr put this very directly:

> The principal role of most information systems is to present views of the real-world so that people in the organization can create products or make decisions. If those views do not agree with the real-world for any extended period of time, then the system is a poor one, and, ultimately, like a delusional psychotic, the organization will begin to act irrationally (Orr, 1996, p. 2).

The data life cycle can be viewed as a system for managing data. Its subcomponents include the business processes and systems through which data is created, enabled, maintained, stored, accessed, and used. Such a system is likely to generate feedback about the meaning of the data, its quality, and the ability of data consumers to use the data. Feedback represents the opportunity for improvement of the following:

- **The meaning of the data:** Questions about the meaning of the data represent opportunities to improve metadata.
- **The quality of the data:** Feedback about the quality of the data may also represent an opportunity to improve metadata. Such feedback may identify issues that require remediation, requirements for new data, or other improvement opportunities.
- **The ability to use the data:** Feedback on data use may reflect limitations of data structure, tools, or the data itself.

Correct, Enhance, and Improve

When people use data, they see gaps and issues and identify opportunities for enhancement or other improvements. Even if individual data consumers do not propose changes, business processes and

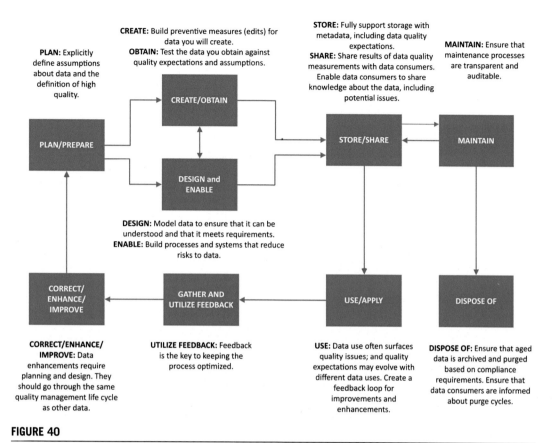

PLAN: Explicitly define assumptions about data and the definition of high quality.

CREATE: Build preventive measures (edits) for data you will create.
OBTAIN: Test the data you obtain against quality expectations and assumptions.

STORE: Fully support storage with metadata, including data quality expectations.
SHARE: Share results of data quality measurements with data consumers. Enable data consumers to share knowledge about the data, including potential issues.

MAINTAIN: Ensure that maintenance processes are transparent and auditable.

DESIGN: Model data to ensure that it can be understood and that it meets requirements.
ENABLE: Build processes and systems that reduce risks to data.

CORRECT/ENHANCE/ IMPROVE: Data enhancements require planning and design. They should go through the same quality management life cycle as other data.

UTILIZE FEEDBACK: Feedback is the key to keeping the process optimized.

USE: Data use often surfaces quality issues; and quality expectations may evolve with different data uses. Create a feedback loop for improvements and enhancements.

DISPOSE OF: Ensure that aged data is archived and purged based on compliance requirements. Ensure that data consumers are informed about purge cycles.

FIGURE 40

Data life cycle annotated with data quality considerations.

compliance requirements evolve over time. Data creation processes and data storage applications change over time through remediation and enhancement. The process of improving data restarts the life cycle process (Fig. 40). Improvements require planning, obtaining data, and so on. They require evolving metadata along with the data itself.

Dispose Of

When data reaches the end of its life cycle, it must be properly disposed of. While, in theory, data could last forever, in practice, a lot of data is not allowed to last forever. For some data, retention periods are regulated, and organizations are required to purge data from their systems and securely dispose of it. Likewise, for legal or regulatory reasons, organizations may be required to keep other data for a set period of time, even after the organization itself no longer uses the data. Disposal is often a two-step process that includes first archiving data (storing it in a largely inaccessible environment) and then actually destroying it. Managing the retention and disposal of data is part of overall life cycle management and should be accounted for up front as part of planning because data at different phases of its life cycle may be stored and managed differently. These differences can affect the costs of storing, sharing, and accessing data. Planning for storage and retention should include accounting for audit fields (e.g., record status codes, create and update dates, record begin and end dates, user IDs, and process IDs) that might be required to ensure data meets archiving requirements.

Benefits of Understanding the Data Life Cycle

There are multiple benefits to understanding the data life cycle. Obviously, doing so allows an organization to plan for the overall management of the data and its associated metadata. This planning has direct effects on the organization's ability to manage the quality of data as well as to meet legal and regulatory requirements. In addition, as will be discussed in the next section, understanding the life cycle of individual data sets also enables the organization to develop a clearer picture of the data supply chain, and from that its value chain. Knowledge of the data life cycle enables an organization to evaluate the costs and benefits associated with a data set during its lifetime. If, for example, an organization wants to understand whether it is getting value from its customer data, it can determine the costs of obtaining, storing, and maintaining customer data against the value brought by using that data. Knowledge of these costs and benefits can help answer questions about how long the data should be retained before it is disposed of and whether there is value in enhancing the data.

The Data Supply Chain: Moving Data Into and Within an Organization

The data life cycle focuses on how different data sets will be managed over time to bring value to an organization, but it is a relatively abstract, system-agnostic concept. The data supply chain focuses on the details of how particular data moves into and through the processes and systems in an organization. The supply chain highlights the relationships among functions that create and use data. In doing so, it allows the organization to see where data is expected to fit together and interact with other data. It allows planners to identify data quality requirements related to data exchange and interoperability. This knowledge, important for internal processes, is even more critical for organizations that obtain data from external entities (hence ISO's definition of quality data as "portable" data).

People who are familiar with data management terminology may be asking, "Aren't you talking about data lineage?" I would respond, "Yes and no." The concept of lineage—descent from a common ancestor—provides an important lens for understanding data within an organization. Data lineage is a form of metadata that describes where data originates, how it moves through an organization's systems and processes, and, importantly, how it is transformed as it moves. As described in Chapter 10, lineage can be depicted at a high level (architectural diagrams are a form of data lineage), or it can be very detailed (as code that describes the input to and output from specific transformation rules under specific conditions). A documented data supply chain diagram is a form of lineage, but not the only form.

The data supply chain is focused on who creates and uses data and for what purposes. Thus, it provides an excellent pathway into discussions about data quality expectations as well as about the costs and benefits of the organization of the chain. Documented knowledge of both lineage and the data supply chain are also critical when data quality issues arise. They provide important input to root cause analysis as well as the business impact of data issues.

Supply Chain Management Defined

A simple definition of the supply chain in manufacturing is the set of processes involved in the production and distribution of a product or commodity. A more elaborate definition acknowledges the complexity involved with getting a product to market:

> A supply chain is the network of all the individuals, organizations, resources, activities and technology involved in the creation and sale of a product, from the delivery of source materials from the supplier to the manufacturer, through to its eventual delivery to the end user. The supply chain segment involved with getting the finished product from the manufacturer to the consumer is known as the distribution channel (Tech Target, n.d.).

> Supply chain management is oversight, coordination, and integration of the flow of materials, information, and finances as they move in a process from supplier to manufacturer to wholesaler to retailer to consumer (Tech Target, n.d.).

> A well-managed supply chain enables efficiencies. Manufacturers create and ship only as much product as can be sold. This helps suppliers, manufacturers, and retailers manage inventory. Supply chain management also helps build working relationships because managing a supply chain requires setting clear expectations related to timing, quality, and communications necessary to delivering products on time, to specification, and to the right locations (Perkins & Wailgum, 2017).

Data Movement as a Supply Chain

The concept of a supply chain provides a useful metaphor for how data moves within an organization. It acknowledges that there is a beginning point to data (data provenance)—its creation or purchase—and that data can move through a series of processes and activities before it is used by a data consumer. The idea of a "chain" helpfully implies that these processes are linked together and dependent on one another. It also reminds us that a weak link endangers the whole chain.

The recognition that a supply chain includes not only the flow of materials, but also of finances and information is instructive. Data is not free. It costs something to create data or bring data into an organization and to share it. Information—various forms of metadata, a knowledge of technical and business processes, an architectural approach—is required to move data and, ultimately, to enable people and processes to use data. Because in many organizations data producers may not be aware of their customers, internal data consumers, the supply chain model can raise awareness of how data moves within an organization, and of the resources and channels required to move data from its origin to its multiple uses.

Depicting this chain also provides a way to rationalize and simplify data movement. Anyone who has ever seen a "spaghetti" chart of an organization's systems architecture will admit that in many organizations, data is moved among systems more often and in more complex ways than most of us would guess. Having a visual of these relationships is a first step to reducing this complexity.

Fig. 41 presents a very simplified diagram of a data supply chain for a health care insurance company. Data about clients (commercial entities that provide health care benefits to their employees), members (the employees who receive these benefits), and products (the benefits themselves) all combine to identify who is eligible for which benefits at which time. Data about health care providers, their contracts, and the networks they are part of is used in combination with eligibility data to pay claims. Claim experience of a given client is used by underwriting to determine the premium the clients must pay. The clinical results of treatments are used to rate providers. These ratings influence provider contracts. Much of this data then is used in financial reporting. This simple depiction of a supply chain nevertheless shows that there are complex relationships between data producers and data consumers, with most systems and processes playing both roles.

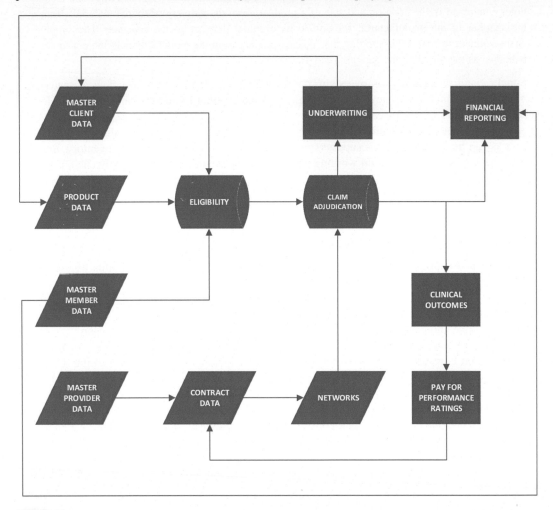

FIGURE 41

Conceptual data supply chain for a health care insurance company.

The Supplier/Purchaser Relationship

In manufacturing, successful supply chain management requires a mutually beneficial relationship between suppliers and purchasers. This mutual benefit depends on clear expectations, including expectations for quality. If a purchaser cannot meet a price, the supplier does not deliver the goods. If a supplier cannot meet expectations for quality or timely delivery, a purchaser can go elsewhere for materials. If the parts they supply do not meet specifications for the inputs, suppliers can, in some cases, be held responsible for the quality of finished products.

A successful supply chain depends on a level of balance and equality. If there is a lack of balance, the process may not support quality outcomes. For example, if there is only one supplier for a given input, then the purchaser is put in a position of having to accept the inputs regardless of timing or quality. If there is only a single purchaser for an input or if the market is dominated by a very large purchaser, then suppliers may not get the price they need for their goods and may be forced out of business. Manufacturers must manage their supply chains to make a profit.

Organizations may not even think about their data as part of a supply chain. The first step to improving the data supply chain is recognizing that it exists. The next steps are assessing how well it works and identifying opportunities to make it work more smoothly. In looking at their data supply chain for the first time, organizations are likely to recognize some common characteristics:

- **Data "suppliers" do not always think of themselves that way**. They see their data more as a by-product of their operational processes than a product to be used by others in the organization. Because of this, they are not likely to think of people and processes who use the data as "customers" whom they are trying to please. Yet, case studies show that when data suppliers become aware of their customers, even minor changes can help improve data quality (Kenett & Redman, 2019).
- **Internal data supply chains are often out of balance**. The option of finding a new source of data, a new supplier for organizational data, rarely exists. When a project requires membership data within a health care insurance company, the data must come from the eligibility system. There is no other option. However, once the people managing eligibility information understand their role as a supplier, again, even minor changes can help make their data more usable downstream.
- **Like data itself, the data supply chain has an organic nature**. It is not as linear as the manufacturing supply chain. In many organizations, data moves in patterns that more closely resemble a web or a data mesh (see Fig. 41). Once supplied, data can be used for new and evolving purposes, without the suppliers even being aware of these uses.

These risks, however, are among the most important reasons why it is useful to envision data moving in a supply chain. If people within an organization understand how and by whom data is created and used, then they will be better able to manage data. Knowledge of downstream data uses enables the establishment of clearer expectations. Knowledge of business processes that create data can be used to improve those processes and enable higher-quality data. Known gaps can be identified and, in some cases, filled if the data producers are aware of requirements. For example, if the quality of customer address data is poor, an organization can improve it by purchasing reliable address data from an external source—to which they can and should state clear data quality expectations.

Knowledge of the supply chain amounts to a specialized form of knowledge about the organization. The handoffs of data from one process or system to another will work better if the supplier understands the quality requirements of the process being supplied with data. Knowledge of the supply chain also introduces the opportunity to put in place controls to identify the extent to which quality expectations are met. Improving the supply chain starts with seeing it. The goal is not necessarily to make it perfect, but to clarify the connections and, where possible, to simplify it so as to reduce risks and redundancies.

The Value Chain: Finding Efficiencies and Adding Value

If the supply chain model allows us to picture how materials move through a set of processes to become products or services, the value chain allows us to evaluate the costs and benefits of the activities and purposes associated with this movement—a kind of lens through which to view supply chain activities. The value chain envisions an organization as a system (a set of things working together as part of a mechanism, network, or method, according to which something gets done) that uses resources (inputs) and transformation processes (subsystems) to create products and services (outputs) (Porter, 2008).[4] Resources include money, people, materials, equipment, information, and other processes (e.g., management, administration).

Each activity in the value chain has costs and may add value to the end-product. The overall value chain represents the costs of creating a product and shows where value is added to the product by each step of the process. Economic value is produced when the benefit from a resource's application is greater than the costs incurred from its planning, acquisition, maintenance, and disposition.

The primary activities in a value chain—those that add value directly—include the following:

- **Inbound logistics:** Activities required to receive, store, and disseminate inputs
- **Operations:** Activities required to transform inputs into outputs (products and services)
- **Outbound logistics:** Activities required to collect, store, and distribute products and services
- **Marketing and sales:** Activities required to inform potential customers about products and services
- **Service:** Activities required to keep the product or service working after purchase

These are supported by secondary activities, which add value indirectly (e.g., procurement, human resources management, technological development, and infrastructure)

Value chain analysis is a form of process analysis that considers each step in a value chain to determine whether it adds to competitive advantage. In doing so, the analysis can identify process points that may be disadvantageous or "low value-add." Value chain analysis creates knowledge about an organization's operational activities, including the cost drivers for each activity and the

---

[4]Porter's definition of a system is similar to Meadows's: a system is "a set of elements or parts that is coherently organized and interconnected in a pattern or structure that produces a characteristic set of behaviors often classified as its 'function' or 'purpose'" (Porter, 2008) and Deming's: a system is "a network of interdependent components that work together to try to accomplish the aim of the system. A system must have an aim. Without an aim there is no system" (Deming, 1994).

relationship among activities. Recognizing how activities depend on one another can help an organization identify opportunities for reducing both cost and risk. Value chain analysis can also be used to improve products by recognizing activities that create features that customers value most and finding opportunities for an organization to differentiate its products and services from those of its competitors.

From the perspective of data quality management, the value chain model implies a set of questions that can be asked about the processes that enable movement along the data supply chain.

- **Inbound logistics:** What costs are associated with creating or purchasing data and moving it from where it is created to where it will be used? What subprocesses can enable data to be better prepared so it is easier to use and can be used multiple times?
- **Operations:** What work is required to make data secure, accessible, current, and prepared for use? What processes are in place to enable data to be used multiple times? How is metadata maintained to simplify the use of data?
- **Outbound logistics:** What costs are associated with distributing data within the organization? Where are there redundancies in data storage? How is data reuse incentivized and data replication discouraged? How can access be simplified? How does the organization track the value of its uses of data?
- **Marketing and sales:** What are the costs of making data consumers aware of what data is available? What information is available to encourage data consumers to use data sources that are designated "authoritative sources," "systems of record," or "sources of truth"?
  - Note: Unfortunately, the marketing and sales aspects of the data value chain are often ignored, resulting in reduced value to the organization. Investing in making data consumers aware of existing sources of data can add value by reducing data redundancy. Redundant data reduces value directly (it costs time and money to create and store redundant data) and increases risk (redundant copies of data are more likely to get out of synch with their sources and with each other). Again, reliable metadata (e.g., a comprehensive data catalog) adds value and reduces risk.
- **Service:** What are the costs of maintaining data and supporting data use? How are data consumers informed about changes and updates to data? How are they informed about data quality levels? How are they made aware of issues that may affect their use of data?

The organic nature of data complicates the value chain and the supply chain. Neither one is linear. They can be hard to depict. Nevertheless, insight into the current state of the overall process can help identify ways to reduce waste and improve value.

The formal process of defining a data value chain can be accomplished through the use of information product maps that depict the transformation of a data unit into an information product that can be used by a data consumer (Fig. 42). The associated costs, value, and quality requirements can be mapped so the overall value of the data unit can be calculated (Heien, 2012). For example, if it costs $5 each to produce data in two sources and $5 to process the data, the total cost would be $15 for the information product. If the product is worth $10 each to the two consumers who use it, then its total value ($20) is greater than the cost of producing it, and the organization realizes $5 in added value (Fig. 43).

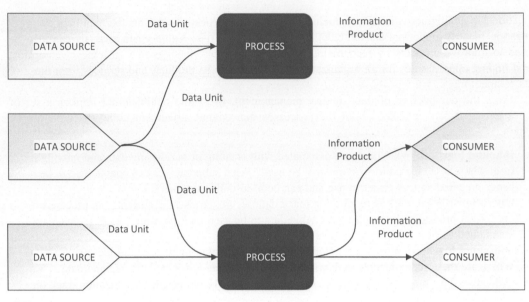

FIGURE 42

The basic components of information product maps.

From Heien, C. H. (2012). Modeling and Analysis of Information Product Maps (Ph.D. Thesis). University of Arkansas at Little Rock.

Used with permission.

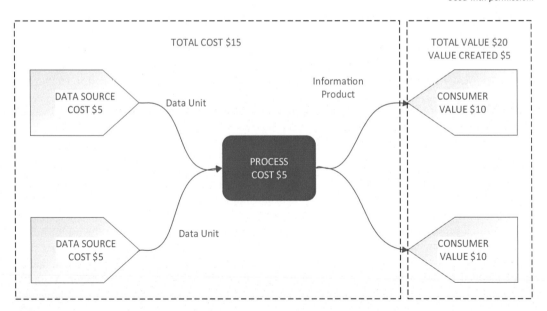

FIGURE 43

Basic usage of metadata in information product maps.

From Heien, C. H. (2012). Modeling and Analysis of Information Product Maps (Ph.D. Thesis). University of Arkansas at Little Rock.

Used with permission.

These models are simplified to illustrate how cost and benefits, and thus, value, can be understood within the process of data creation and use. Such depictions have multiple uses:

- Mapping data sources to information products to consumers of those products raises awareness of the data connections within the organization and improves understanding of the data supply chain.
- This knowledge can be used directly and indirectly to improve data quality because stakeholders along the data chain can see their relationships and define their requirements for quality.
- Overlaying the costs of the processes and the value to data consumers allows for the calculation of value to the enterprise.
- Knowledge of how data is used can be applied to identify potential reuses of data to derive additional value.
- Analysis of information product maps can be extended over time and across data consumers to get a clearer picture of the value of data to the organization.

This knowledge can inform a range of processes, including identifying which information products to invest in and ways to direct data consumers to existing information products to get more value from them. This is because each additional use of the same information product creates more value at a significantly reduced cost. For example, in Fig. 43, if a third data consumer were to use the same information product and benefit to a value of $10, the organization would get a total benefit of $15, provided the costs are fixed.

Information product maps can also be used to understand the overall costs of managing a data set. As noted, value is the difference between the benefit gained through the use of an asset and the costs associated with all of the other life cycle phases. When the benefits outweigh the costs, value is created. When the costs outweigh the benefits, value is lost. If data is designed to be of high quality, then it is relatively easy to measure the costs associated with each life cycle phase (because there are not a lot of hidden costs), to determine the benefits gained by data use, and to compare the two to see how much value the data brings.

Because data can be used without being consumed, each additional use of data can add value, with limited additional cost. If an organization has a complete and current list of customers, with correct addresses, phone numbers, contact names, and email addresses, and if the process to maintain the data has reliable controls, the sales department can use it to contact customers, the marketing department can use it to communicate about new products, the shipping department can use it to ship products, and management can use it in reporting.

If data is not of high quality, then an organization will incur unexpected costs related to poor quality, for example, scrap and rework, combined with the risk and inefficiency of multiple users cleansing or preparing data that they thought was ready for use. These activities reduce the value by creating more cost. The costs themselves may be harder to measure because they are usually hidden. (No salesperson wants to tell their boss that they spent the day cleansing data, rather than connecting with customers.) But whatever they amount to, we know that with each use of the data, they will increase. Fig. 44 depicts this situation, showing the impact of data quality remediation on the value created in Fig. 43. Just as value increases with each use of a high-quality information product, cost and risk increases with each use of a poor-quality information product.

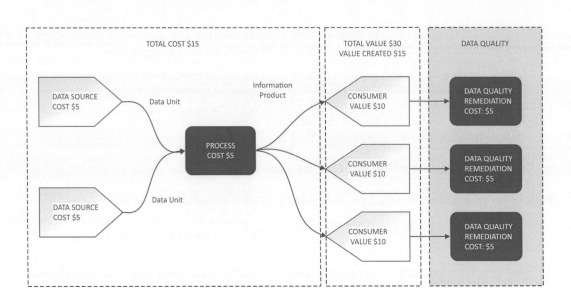

FIGURE 44

Poor-quality data reduces the value of information products.

Modified from Heien, C. H. (2012). Modeling and Analysis of Information Product Maps (Ph.D. Thesis). University of Arkansas at
Little Rock. Used with permission.

These hidden costs add risk to the use of the data, which may further reduce its value. The sales department may change the data one way, while underwriting makes a different set of changes, and marketing makes yet a third set. Soon "the same" data set becomes multiple data sets that data consumers assume are "the same." If they are aware of these differences, they may pay to get the data "fixed." If they are not aware, they may use it and confuse their customers with conflicting information.

It costs organizations money to create and share data, but few organizations programmatically recognize the costs of creating data as such. And yet, the benefits of this kind of analysis are clear. It can identify opportunities for efficiency with data production, management, and distribution; encourage reuse; and fuel conversations about quality. A better understanding of the value chain can inform data strategy, solution design principles, and architecture standards. Better consumption and use models can be implemented for shared data assets.

The Systems Development Life Cycle

Most people will recognize a similarity among the asset management life cycle, the supply chain, and the SDLC.[5] Indeed, each describes a methodology for managing a complex process through

---

[5]The SDLC is also sometimes referred to as the *project life cycle* because the development phases must be managed to schedule and to budget. I have tried to focus on the system part of the concept, but I have slipped between the two on occasion.

well-defined phases. However, they focus on different things. The data life cycle is about planning for data to meet organizational needs and enabling the use of that data over time as data is stored, shared, maintained, and applied within an organization. The data supply chain describes the connections between data producers and data consumers and how they rely on each other. The value chain describes the costs and benefits of producing and using information products. The SDLC is about implementing technical functionality to meet the range of organizational goals that are dependent on data. That technical functionality enables the internal data supply chain. (It should be noted that the technologies implemented via the SDLC also have a life cycle outside of the projects through which they are implemented [DAMA, 2011; English, 1999]).

There are risks in confusing these, though, especially because most SDLC methodologies do not require that teams pay specific attention to the quality of the data itself. To the extent that SDLC methodologies recognize data as an input (and they do), they do not account well for the work of data quality assessment or for the possibility that available data may fail to meet either stated requirements or implicit expectations for quality.

A lot of work to ensure that an organization has high-quality data could be accomplished via information technology (IT) projects. It is true that some IT projects are purely technical, such as those that focus on implementing new infrastructure or improving the performance of a system or platform. However, most focus on one or a combination of the following:

- **Application development:** Creating or implementing new applications to execute operational business processes or support analytics
- **Application enhancement:** Improving the functionality of existing applications for operations or analytics
- **Data integration:** Integrating data from multiple sources into data stores for use in operations or analytics

These have a common thread: the goal, from a business perspective, is either to create or use data and information. These projects extend or enhance the data supply chain. But they rarely account for the data.

This point is often missing in discussions about IT projects. For example, when Wikipedia observes "a system can be composed of hardware only, software only, or a combination of both," someone seems to have forgotten that information systems contain, well, information. The Business Dictionary tries harder, defining an information system as "a combination of hardware, software, infrastructure and trained personnel organized to facilitate planning, control, coordination, and decision making in an organization." This includes a lot more than Wikipedia's hardware and software, but an essential ingredient—data or information itself—is still missing.

Fortunately, one does not have to go back too far to find a definition of information systems that emphasizes information: "An information system ... [is] a set of interrelated components that collect (or retrieve), process, store, and distribute information to support decision making, coordination, and control in an organization" (Laudon & Laudon, 2001, p. 7). In this definition, an information system performs four activities that bear a very strong resemblance to Juran's definition of creating a product ("a product is the output from any process" [Juran, 1992]):

- **Input:** Collect or capture data from the organization or its environment.
- **Processing:** Organize it into a more meaningful form.

- **Output:** Transfer the processed information to the people who will use it to make decisions, control operations, analyze problems, or create new products and services.
- **Feedback:** Output that is used to evaluate or correct the input or processing stage.

An SDLC is a process for creating or enhancing an information system. Like an asset/resource life cycle, an SDLC provides a lens through which to think about data and data quality. If we can focus this lens on data, we can improve the quality of data a system creates.

A well-defined SDLC is designed to manage schedule and budget (the project management goals) and to ensure a level of quality for the system that is developed (the development and quality assurance [QA] goal). An SDLC consists of a set of phases, each of which is associated with milestones that mark the progress of the work and deliverables that are work products (designs, code, test cases, and test results) or are used to manage the delivery of work products (project plans). The process is governed by a series of gates—or checkpoints—at which deliverables are reviewed to ensure that they are meeting project goals. The phases themselves may be called by different names, depending on the methodology, but they represent, essentially, a beginning, middle, and end of a project.

A comprehensive SDLC accounts for the true beginning of the system—its conception and feasibility—and the end of a system—its maintenance and obsolescence (Fig. 45). However, because

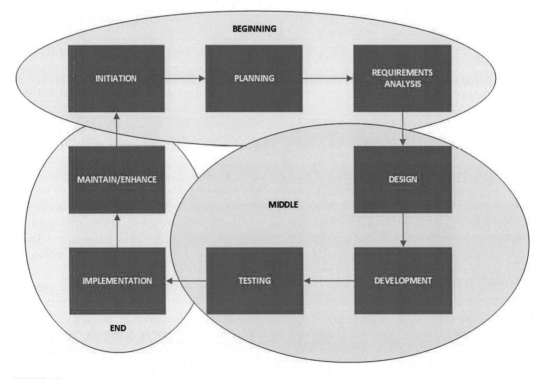

FIGURE 45

The fundamental narrative structure of the systems development life cycle.

the usual use of an SDLC is to manage project activities and deliverables, these end points are often off-stage for most people developing a system. The project has been conceived before development work starts. The project team disbands, and an operational team takes over when a system is put into a production environment. The phases most project team members are familiar with look something like this:

- **Initiation:** Getting the project started, getting funding, getting resources
- **Planning:** Determining the project schedule and dependencies
- **Requirements analysis and definition:** Clarifying and documenting the business needs that the project must fulfill
- **Design:** Defining the solution that will meet the business needs
- **Development:** Building the solution, assembling and configuring the hardware, writing the software
- **Testing:** Ensuring that the functionality described in the specification works the way the specification says it should
- **Implementation:** Putting the hardware and software into an environment where it can be accessed and used by end users, and confirming that the system has been implemented correctly
- **Maintenance:** Handing off the work to a production support team who will be responsible for ensuring the continued functioning of the system

The beginning (initiation, planning, requirements analysis) and middle (design, development, and testing) phases closely resemble the early phases of the asset/resource life cycle. The end phase—implementation—makes the data asset ready for use.[6] Based on this, it is easy to imagine accounting for data as part of the SDLC. Unfortunately, many IT projects focus only on the system and its functionality, and they do not account for the data itself.[7] This failure can result in building technology that simply moves bad data around the organization or that turns good data into bad data and then moves it around the organization.

An example may illustrate the point. When I first started working in IT, as a data quality analyst in an enterprise data warehouse, the data quality section of the specification template included a disclaimer along these lines: "The quality of the data in the warehouse depends on the quality of the source data." This was just a polite way of saying, "We have no control over the quality of data here. 'Garbage In/Garbage Out.'" However, a review of help desk tickets showed that more than three fourths of the issues reported by end users of the warehouse were not rooted in source system data errors. Many were, instead, connected to the ways that data had been stored or maintained in the warehouse. In some cases, this meant that the technical decisions by the development team had created undesired characteristics in the data. The root cause of some of these issues was that the implementation team did not under-

---

[6]I put this in terms of beginning, middle, and end to make my point that there is a narrative implicit in any SDLC. Someone will probably scratch his or her head and ask: What about Agile? To which I would say (though it may sound like anathema to compare Agile to other methodologies), "Agile is an SDLC, with a beginning, middle, and end. Each program increment is a mini-SDLC (plan, design, develop, test, release, repeat) as is each sprint."

[7]This assertion is based on analysis of the mention of data in the PMBOK *(Project Management Body of Knowledge)*. Thanks for Bob Furce for this analysis.

stand or account for differences in data from different sources when that data was integrated in the warehouse. The data was fine from the perspective of the different source systems, but because the data was structured differently in the sources, it could not be fully integrated unless the warehouse development team recognized these differences when it integrated the data. Instead of "Garbage In/Garbage Out," we had a case of "Pretty Good Data In/Garbage Out."

This is not to imply that software development ignores quality. It does not. The principles of total quality management have been applied to software development itself because software is a product that can have different levels of quality and because "Information systems are a necessary component of the feedback loop in managing an enterprise" (Joshik, n.d.). Software has recognizable and recognized quality characteristics (e.g., usability, reliability, modifiability). Also, the process for developing software often includes techniques focused on ensuring quality as defined by the customer/end user. For example, in traditional software development, customer input can be obtained through joint application development (JAD) sessions. In Agile software development, demos of functionality allow stakeholders to provide feedback on what is being developed before it is completely developed, so the Agile team can respond and better meet requirements. The QA function within the SDLC is focused on ensuring that software meets defined specifications and requirements.

However, the requirements themselves do not specifically focus on the quality of the data being presented to end users by the system. They describe what the system will do. Requirements include what inputs the system will need and what outputs it will produce (both of which are data) as well as how data may need to be stored and maintained in the system and what volume of data the system will be able to process. Some SDLC descriptions even include data analysis and the documentation of data flow within the system, but none directly acknowledge the possibility that the data may not be available or the need to define quality requirements for the data itself.

As discussed in Chapter 6, there is some basis for IT disowning responsibility for data. Making data reliable depends first and foremost on well-defined, reliably executed business processes. In this sense, "the business" should "own" the quality of the data. However, most business processes are executed via IT applications, so these too should be designed to produce reliable data. Also, because data moves through the organization through IT systems, each of which leaves its imprint on the data, IT has a responsibility to ensure that data moves correctly and completely and that it is usable by consumers along the data chain. Doing so requires understanding data structure, identifying and managing data-related risks, implementing controls to prevent damaging or losing the data, and monitoring data in order to inform data consumers of any known limitations of the data. These activities themselves depend on specifying data quality requirements as part of the development or enhancement of a system.

In fact, most SDLC methodologies hardly acknowledge that the purpose of any information system is the information itself. If they did, a lot of the pain and suffering associated with IT development projects would be reduced (Keizer, 2004; Snaplogic, 2021). Given the depth of experience most organizations have with data not meeting expectations, it is hard to sympathize when project teams choose to assume that the data must be okay, rather than checking to see what it looks like. This observation raises the question: What would it look like if data were not only accounted for during development work, but if it were viewed as

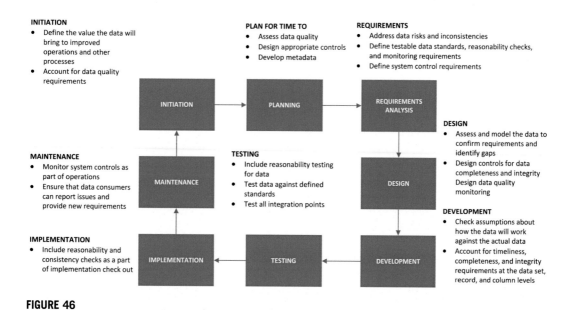

INITIATION
- Define the value the data will bring to improved operations and other processes
- Account for data quality requirements

PLAN FOR TIME TO
- Assess data quality
- Design appropriate controls
- Develop metadata

REQUIREMENTS
- Address data risks and inconsistencies
- Define testable data standards, reasonability checks, and monitoring requirements
- Define system control requirements

DESIGN
- Assess and model the data to confirm requirements and identify gaps
- Design controls for data completeness and integrity Design data quality monitoring

DEVELOPMENT
- Check assumptions about how the data will work against the actual data
- Account for timeliness, completeness, and integrity requirements at the data set, record, and column levels

MAINTENANCE
- Monitor system controls as part of operations
- Ensure that data consumers can report issues and provide new requirements

TESTING
- Include reasonability testing for data
- Test data against defined standards
- Test all integration points

IMPLEMENTATION
- Include reasonability and consistency checks as a part of implementation check out

FIGURE 46

Building data quality processes into the SDLC.

the most critical part of the system being developed, the end product of the development cycle? (See Fig. 46.)

- **Initiation**
  - Define the value of the project in terms of the value the data will bring to improved operations and other processes.
  - Identify resources who can define data quality requirements.
- **Planning:** Account for the time needed to
  - Assess data quality and manage any identified risks
  - Design and put in place appropriate data quality controls
  - Develop and groom semantic metadata required to use the data
- **Requirements analysis**
  - Resolve conflicts identified through data risks, including unexpected granularity, invalid values, unknown or inconsistently applied business rules, and unclear or inadequate metadata.
  - Define testable data standards, reasonability and consistency checks, and monitoring requirements.
- **Design**
  - Assess and model the data to confirm requirements and identify gaps.
  - Design controls that will ensure data completeness and integrity and alert production support teams to unexpected system events that affect the data.
  - Design data quality monitoring functionality that will alert data consumers to unexpected characteristics of the data.

- **Development**
  - Check assumptions about data against the actual data.
  - Account for timeliness, completeness, and integrity at the data set, record, and column levels.
- **Testing**
  - Include reasonability testing for data, in addition to testing system functionality
  - Test data against defined standards.
  - Test the completeness of all integration points.
- **Implementation**
  - Include data reasonability and consistency checks a part of the implementation check out.
- **Maintenance**
  - Monitor system controls as part of operations.
  - Ensure that data consumers can get their questions answered, report issues, and provide feedback, including new requirements.

Concluding Thoughts

Data has characteristics of a resource or asset that organizations use to generate value. In this way, data can be understood as similar to equipment, financial resources, or even human resources (people with particular knowledge and skills needed by the organization). If an organization is looking to improve overall data management and implement data quality by design, it helps to look at data from the perspective of the data life cycle and identify the points in that life cycle where it can define its quality requirements. The supply chain, as a means of understanding the movement of data within an organization, presents the opportunity to clarify expectations for the quality of data supplied to a range of organizational processes and to provide feedback if the data does not meet these requirements. The value chain allows us to ask questions about the uses of data, the costs associated with it, and the ways it may bring value.

Importantly, value chain analysis can be used to stop costly processes if they are not adding value. These two complementary models work best when organizations are looking at their products or services. The idea of the data supply chain shows features of how data is created by data producers and used by data consumers within a particular organization or in support of a specific goal. It is useful to know these details, whether one is trying to improve the organization's processes or address a specific data quality issue, because they remind us that we can produce higher-quality data by controlling the processes that create data.

Ultimately, data creation and development processes are implemented through projects. Including data quality management components as part of the SDLC improves the chances of delivering and maintaining reliable data.

These multiple models of data management show us the ways in which data is integral to all of an organization's activities. Data binds organizations together in complex ways. In revealing these connections and complexities, the models also show us a way forward. There are many opportunities to improve the quality of organizational data. Being aware of these is the first step to making better data. Purposefully connecting them to core data quality and data management practices is the next step.

Tying It Together

"Observe good faith and justice toward all nations. Cultivate peace and harmony with all."
George Washington, US President

It is fairly easy to summarize the ideas in this book:
High-quality data is

- Well defined and comprehensible
- Created through processes that are intentional, understood, and executed consistently
- Accurate in representing characteristics of the people, objects, concepts, and events it is intended to represent
- In conformance with rules, conventions, and structural requirements
- Accessible and usable
- Protected against misuse
- Supported by
  - Clear, comprehensible documentation
  - People who understand its content and structure

Creating high-quality data is challenging, but there are ways to address the challenges associated with the process:

- To address the data challenge, organizations must implement better data management practices, especially formal data quality management.
- To address the process challenge, they must recognize the relationship between their data production and data use and improve management of both the data life cycle and the data supply chain.
- Addressing the technology challenge requires accounting for data before technology so as to better leverage technology to meet the organization's strategic goals. This can be achieved, in part, by integrating data quality requirements into the SDLC.
- Addressing the people challenge means helping people within the organization educate themselves about data so they can understand and use data more effectively.
- Addressing the culture challenge requires clearly defining and enforcing accountability and responsibility for data, up and down the data chain, and actively changing organizational culture to focus on quality.

Meeting the Challenges of Data Quality Management. DOI: https://doi.org/10.1016/B978-0-12-821737-5.00012-2

It sounds easy when it is all reduced to five bullet points. But it is not easy. The biggest challenge by far is the culture challenge. Many efforts to improve how organizations get value from data have failed because they have not been supported in good faith by organizational leadership. The way to address the culture challenge is to demand that leadership act in good faith.

When I started working on this book, I believed that the biggest problem we needed to solve with respect to data quality management was that of education. If people better understood the core functions of a data quality program and could see these in relation to other organizational activities, such as business process improvement and systems development, then they would uncover multiple opportunities to create better data, improve efficiencies, and act on opportunities. Ideas about data quality management would cease to be focused on free-range data profiling and setting thresholds; instead, they would be part of the effort to enable organizations to have trust and confidence in their data. This would bring direct value to the organization.

I also thought that the main challenge with implementing data governance was a lack of clarity of purpose. Governance programs overburdened with scope not only have trouble getting out of the gate, but they have also become counterproductive because many people who should be stepping up and "stewarding" data assume that it is the role of data governance to do all of that. If governance programs could reduce their scope and help other teams and individuals in the organization recognize their roles in creating and using data, then they could reduce risks, become more efficient, and improve quality. In other words, I thought the governance and stewardship problem could also be solved through education.

Education is important, and it always will be. People need to understand organizational data in order to get value from it. But the more I read, the more people I talked with, the more seminars and webinars I listened to, and the more I tried to implement change at work, the more I realized that the problem is not, per se, a lack of education or a lack understanding. The concepts of quality improvement and governance are not particularly difficult to comprehend. But they are difficult to implement, unless people act in good faith. And that is the problem. Many organizations have only paid lip service to data quality improvement and data governance, just as many only paid lip service to product and service quality improvement in the decades following World War II, despite the fact that examples of the value of focusing on quality (e.g., the Japanese economic miracle, the success of the US space program) were staring them in the face.

In *Out of the Crisis* (first published in 1982), W. Edwards Deming called for a transformation of the style of Western management. He saw the existing approach as diseased, wasteful, and counterproductive. He recognized its negative effects on both organizational success and society as a whole. He placed the cause of this failure squarely on a lack of leadership, or, as he put it, "the failure of top management to manage" (Deming, 1986). The full elucidation of his 14 Points (Chapter 2, Principles for Transformation) and his analysis of the patterns and habits that prevent success (Chapter 3, Diseases and Obstacles) ring true to this day. Yet we seem to be in the same place in relation to data that we were in relation to manufacturing when he published the book. Poor-quality data is tolerated because organizational leadership allows toleration of poor-quality data.

People who call for digital transformation without recognizing the profound need for cultural transformation use his words but miss his point. To use data to its fullest potential requires genuine change. We cannot continue to manage data the way we have been doing—wasting at least 20%–30% of analysts' time just trying to find and prepare data—and expect to get more value from it. We cannot create reliable and trustworthy data if we continue to focus on tools for "correcting flaws" in data (Chien & Ankush, 2021) while ignoring the opportunity to prevent errors and improve processes. We cannot automate accountability for data.

Without accountability for data, real change cannot take place. But when leadership commits to being data driven and to changing the organization to improve data quality, manage the data supply chain, support data literacy, and leverage technology more effectively, not for the sake of technology but to meet organizational goals—when leadership makes itself accountable for data as an organizational asset—then real change can take place and organizations can unlock data's potential.

Glossary

"Words are not as satisfactory as we should like them to be, but, like our neighbors, we have got to live with them and must make the best and not the worst of them."

Samuel Butler

ABC Controls Audit/balance/control (ABC) processes govern the movement of data within and between systems. Also referred to as *system controls* or *control reports*. These controls involve counting or summing records at different points during data processing to ensure that data has not been lost or "dropped" as part of processing. These work on traditional formats (e.g., tables, files) in which the data itself is static, rather than dynamic.

Access Metadata A type of operational metadata that describes what people, processes, and systems accessed which data sets at what time, and for what data. It includes details like access IDs, SQL code, and execution time of queries. It can be mined for access and usage patterns.

Accessibility A dimension of quality that measures the degree to which data consumers can obtain data from an appropriate source and in a form that allows them to use it.

Accountability To be accountable means to be answerable, literally "liable to be called to account" (Online Etymological Dictionary). Accountability means a person is expected to act in a defined manner and must be able to explain their actions. To have accountability for data means having overall responsibility for a data set and defining clear responsibilities for those that produce the data; people accountable for data also ensure that data is in its expected condition and are able to explain the condition of data under their control.

Accuracy A dimension of quality. The degree to which data correctly represents attributes of a real-world object, concept, or event.

Asset A useful or valuable thing; a kind of property available to meet debts and other commitments.

Attribute In logical data modeling, an attribute represents a characteristic of an entity. Because of this use, *attribute* is sometimes understood as a data element (a piece of data used to represent a characteristic of an entity), a field (part of a system used to display or intake data), or a column (a place in a table to store a defined characteristic of a represented entity, i.e., to store values associated with data elements).

Authorized Data Source A system or process that has been designated by a data governance team as the place from which to obtain data for specific uses. For example, the customer relationship management system may be designated as the authorized data source for obtaining data for email campaigns. Synonyms include: *authoritative data source* and *system of record*.

Basel Accords A voluntary regulatory framework for the financial services industry created in response to the global financial crisis of 2008. The accords provide a means to test bank capital adequacy, stress testing, and market liquidity risk. They have important effects on how financial institutions handle their data.

Baseline Measurement A baseline measurement is taken to serve as a point of comparison for subsequent measurement. ASQ defines it as "The beginning point, based on an evaluation of output over a period of time, used to determine the process parameters prior to any improvement effort; the basis against which change is measured." (Source: ASQ.)

Big Data Data characterized by large volume (large amounts of data created), variety (a range of formats), and velocity (data created and made accessible very quickly). For processing and storage, Big Data requires different technologies than does traditional data.

Business Glossary A system used to document and manage terms and definitions needed to understand an organization's business concepts and to describe the relationship among concepts. In a complex organization, business glossaries are needed to ensure that people understand each other. Business glossaries play a critical role in data management because they enable data consumers to make connections at the conceptual or logical level among data elements that may have different names and different structures in different systems. A business glossary is intended to supply system-agnostic information related to data (as opposed to a data dictionary, which describes data that has been instantiated in a system).

Business Metadata Business metadata focuses largely on the content and condition of the data and includes details related to data governance. Business metadata includes the non-technical names and definitions of concepts, subject areas, entities, and attributes; attribute data types and other attribute properties; range descriptions; calculations; algorithms and business rules; and valid domain values and their definitions. (Source: DMBOK2.)

Business Process Owner A person who is accountable for execution of a business process that produces data. Ideally the business process owner should be accountable for the quality of the outputs from the process, one of which is data.

Business Rule A defined constraint on a business process. Business rules describe what must happen or what cannot happen within a process. Business rules can be used as requirements for technical processes or to establish data quality expectations.

Business Strategy A plan for an organization to achieve its goals. This includes aligning the people, processes, technology, and information required to meet these goals.

Business Terminology The words an organization uses to describe itself and its processes. The concept of business terminology recognizes that each organization has its own vocabulary for its business processes and that there is often a difference between how concepts are defined in business processes and how they are named when they are defined as data in systems. There are also differences in naming conventions among systems. Business terminology provides a means by which data can be understood in relation to business processes and in relation to other data. In doing so, it helps people recognize when instances of the same data are named differently as well as when instances of different data have the same name.

California Consumer Privacy Act (CCPA) Data privacy and protection legislation enacted by the state of California in 2018.

Certified Data Data that has passed certification requirements. These requirements may include a range of criteria, such as: data is populated completely, data reconciles to a defined standard, data has passed all data quality rules, data is supported by metadata. Criteria will differ, depending on the data set, but certification requirements must clearly state what the criteria are for a data set.

Clarity A dimension of quality. The degree to which data values are unambiguous, distinct, non-overlapping, and comprehensible.

Codified Data Information that is represented by code values. To codify a thing is to reduce it to a code. For example, an ICD-10 code provides a short-hand way to refer to a medical diagnosis. A US Zip code refers to an area where mail is delivered.

Column Column/field/attribute. A column is a component part of a table in a database. Tables are made up of rows, each representing one instance of an entity represented by the table, and columns, containing characteristics of the represented entity. *Field* and *attribute* are usually understood as synonyms for *columns* because they also contain characteristics of a represented entity. But columns are specific to tables.

Column Profile See *Distribution of Values*.

Commerce-based Organizational Data See *Organizational Data*.

Completeness A dimension of quality that answers the question: Do I have all of the data I need or expect to have? Completeness describes the degree to which a data set contains all required data. It can be understood at the data set level (Does the data set cover the population required?); the record level (Does the data set contain all of the fields needed for the analysis of the population?); the field level (Are all mandatory fields populated? Are optional fields populated according to population rules?). Completeness can also be seen through the lens of other requirements: all the data for a population, from a system, for a time period.

Consistency A dimension of quality that answers the question: Does the data conform to patterns defined through other instances of the same data set? The degree to which data exhibits expected patterns.

Consumer Data Rights (CDR) Data privacy and protection legislation enacted by the state of the Federal Australian Government in 2019.

Control A means of providing feedback within a system. A data control can be set up as binary; the data either meets the conditions of the control, or it does not. If the data does not meet the conditions of the control, then the feedback to the system is to stop the process. A control can also provide feedback through a tolerance level or threshold (e.g., $x\%$ of data met the condition of the control; $100\% - x\%$ did not). (Source: Sebastian-Coleman, 2013.)

Correctness A dimension of quality that answers the question: Does this data accurately represent what it purports to represent? Correctness can be understood in terms of format (Is the data formatted correctly?), definition (Does the definition accurately describe the data?), or data values (Is the value in the column the right value for this entity instance?). Correctness is a synonym for *accuracy*.

Cost of Poor Quality (COPQ) The cost associated with providing poor-quality products or services. There are four categories: internal failure costs (costs associated with defects found before the customer receives the product or service), external failure costs (costs associated with defects found after the customer receives the product or service), appraisal costs (costs incurred to determine the degree of conformance to quality requirements), and prevention costs (costs incurred to keep failure and appraisal costs to a minimum). (Source: ASQ.)

Cost-Benefit Analysis (CBA) A comparison of the costs of implementing a change and the expected benefits of implementing the change. Also called *benefit-cost analysis*. A CBA accounts for hard numbers (direct measurable costs) and soft numbers (expected effects on people's behavior and attitudes). Data quality improvement efforts should include a CBA.

Critical Data Element (CDE) Data that is required by the business to execute is processes and must be of high quality for those processes to execute successfully. Critical data includes data required to serve customers; meet strategic goals; ensure compliance with laws, regulations, and contractual obligations; and measure its own success, CDEs are the focus of data quality monitoring and improvement efforts. (Source: Jugulum, 2014.)

Critical Data Elements and Relationships (CDERs) The R added to CDE emphasizes the fact that many data quality challenges are not limited to isolated data elements but to the relationship among component pieces of data.

Currency A dimension of quality. The degree to which data is maintained and values correctly reflect their real-world counterparts within a given timeframe.

Data A means of encoding and sharing knowledge and information about the real world. Data is the representation of selected characteristics of objects, events, and concepts, expressed and understood through explicitly defined conventions related to their meaning, collection, and storage. Since the introduction of the computer in the mid-20th century, the word *data* has also been used to refer to any information captured in or processed by a computer or other information technology system.

Data as an Asset An organization's data is an asset in that it can be used by the organization to create value. Data is often compared to other organizational assets: people, equipment, money, and intellectual property. When talked about as an asset, data is considered a broad category. The totality of an organization's data is an asset to that organization. (Source: DMBOK2.)

Data as Data An understanding of how data functions in a semiotic system; how it is created or collected, structured, and organized for use; and how it may change over time and have different uses in different circumstances (e.g., knowledge of the data life cycle).

Data Asset The recognition of data as an asset has led to the idea of a data asset. A data asset it a set of data that brings value to the organization in particular ways that can be recognized as distinct from those of other data sets. A data asset can be large or small, formally or informally defined. The ability to distinguish individual data assets within the entirety of an organization's data is useful because different data sets have different value to the organization (just as different financial instruments or investments may have different value to the organization). Being able to identify and recognize the value of individual data sets helps an organization prioritize work related to managing different data sets. For example, it may be far more important to get customer data correct than to get vendor data correct. Taken together, these individual data assets comprise the overall data assets of the organization.

Data Catalog A list or inventory of objects in a database or other system/platform, with basic metadata about them (e.g., name, definition, origin, business purpose, subject area, format, categories, tags of data, and other attributes about the data object that may be important to its use by people, processes, or systems). A data catalog can contain references to data at different object levels (e.g., files, tables, and views), and it is organized in a way that allows it to be associated with finer levels of grains (e.g., fields, relationships). Data catalogs support data discovery. They enable people to bring together sets of data for different purposes (e.g., via tagging or categorization). Data catalogs can be created manually or generated by running a program against a database, or through a combination of both.

Data Certification The process of measuring data against defined certification criteria (certification requirements) and determining the degree to which it adheres to the criteria. Criteria may include standards for data quality, conditions for management, level of security/protection, quality of metadata and other supporting information, or a combination of these things. Standards for certification may be based on requirements external to the organization that wants its data certified (e.g., data is "certified" if it meets requirements for BASEL or SOX), or standards may be internally defined (Critical Data Elements are certified based on business defined requirements). Different levels of data may be certified (e.g., system, data set, data relationship, data element). Data certification is not a one-time event. After initial certification, data must be periodically re-audited for certification requirements. Different standards for certification may also be defined and measured (e.g., "Gold" standard certification means data has passed all requirements; "Silver" may mean it has passed 95% of requirements; "Bronze" may mean it has passed 90%, and so on.)

Data Chain See *Data Supply Chain*.

Data Consumer Any person, process, or system that uses data. The term is used to distinguish between data producers (who create data) and those who use data. A data consumer for one process may be a data producer for another process. Synonyms include *data customer, end user*, and *target system*.

Data Democratization The process of enabling a wider group of people to access and use data. It involves removing obstacles to data usage and encouraging more people to become data literate. It is also associated with reduced reliance on IT resources to use data.

Data Dictionary A data dictionary contains table and column names and definitions along with other information that helps data consumers use data. Data dictionaries often contain details about the physical structure of data (e.g., the key structure for a table and the data type and field lengths for columns). A comprehensive data dictionary for a relational database will include information on standard joins between tables. It may even include filter criteria for particular kinds of reports. A data dictionary is usually set to support the use of a particular system. See also *Business Glossary*.

Data Discovery The exploration and assessment of data that is conducted to understand its structure, content, and potential for use. Discovery often includes data preparation. It also may use data visualization techniques to identify patterns and outliers (thus going beyond basic data profiling). Discovery can be used to understand what data exists in a system and to determine whether data can be used for a particular purpose. It can be conducted against an existing data store or against candidate data for a project. It can be focused on multiple sources and the relationship among them, on a single data source, or even on an individual data set.

Data Element A data element is a part of a data set. It is usually understood as a column or field, but a data element can include multiple attributes (e.g., "address" with all of its attributes can be thought of as a single data element).

Data Environment A broad term for the collection of factors that influence the creation and use of data: the business processes through which data is produced, the technical systems through which it is produced and stored, the data itself, metadata (including data standards, definitions, and specifications), technical architecture (including data access tools), and data uses. All of these have implications for understanding data quality. The data environment includes the people, processes, and technology involved in creating and using data. (See English, 1999; McGilvray, 2021.)

Data Governance Organizational oversight of data and data-related processes. The Data Governance Institute describes it as "a system of decision rights and accountabilities for information-related processes, executed according to agreed-upon models which describe who can take what actions with what information, and when, under what circumstances, using what methods." (See The Data Governance Institute, Datagovernance.com.)

Data Governance Organization A team formally assigned to implement and manage a data governance program.

Data Governance Program A set of projects and processes put together to define responsibilities for data, establish and execute processes for making decisions about data and ensuring that responsibilities for managing data are executed consistently. Data governance programs may include multiple components that focus on aspects of data management, such as data policy, data security, metadata management, data quality management, reference data management, and master data management.

Data Governance Strategy A data governance strategy describes how an organization will implement, execute, and derive benefit from data governance functions. For example, such a strategy will state how the organization will define decision rights and accountabilities for data as well as the behaviors that the organization will adopt and enforce to ensure that data is used to benefit the organization and not used to the detriment of the organization.

Data Issue See *Data Quality Issue*.

Data Life Cycle A set of high-level phases related to how data is created, changes over time, and is disposed of. Based on the product development life cycle, this set of phases has been described differently by different experts, but all versions contain the idea that data is created or obtained, stored, used, and disposed of. The data life cycle is critical to data management because there are different management requirements at the different phases of the life cycle. The data life cycle differs from both the system development life cycle (SDLC), which describes how projects are executed, and the data chain, which describes how data moves within and between systems to meet the needs of a particular organization. (Source: Sebastian-Coleman, 2013.)

Data Lineage Data lineage is a form of metadata that describes the movement of and changes to data as it passes through systems and is adopted for different uses. Lineage can be described at different levels of detail (process-to-process, system-to-system, table-to-table, column to column). A documented data chain for an organization is a version of data lineage. Data lineage refers to a set of identifiable points that can be used to understand details of data movement and transformation (e.g., transactional source field names, file names, data processing job names, programming rules, target table fields). Most people who are concerned with the lineage of data want to understand two aspects of it: the data's origin and the ways in which the data has changed since it was originally created. Change can take place within one system or among systems. (Source: Sebastian-Coleman, 2013.)

Data Literacy The ability to read, understand, interpret, and learn from data in different contexts and the ability to communicate about data to other people.

Data Management Strategy A data management strategy defines how the organization will manage and support the data it needs over time. Data management includes a range of functional areas, each of which may have its own strategy. All component pieces of a data management strategy must support the business strategy.

Data Mapping Specification A data mapping specification documents the rules associated with moving data point-to-point along the data supply chain. A mapping specification may describe movement at the file/table level or at the column/field level. Also called a *source-to-target map* (STM or STTM).

Data Mart A data collection put together to serve specific purposes.

Data Model A visual representation of data content and the relationships between data entities and attributes, created for purposes of understanding how data can be (or actually is) organized or structured. Data models include entities (understood as tables), attributes (understood as columns containing characteristics about represented entities), relationships between entities, and integrity rules along with definitions of all of these pieces. Logical data models and physical data models have different attributes and are related to each other. A data model contains a set of symbols with text labels that attempts visually to represent data requirements as communicated to the data modeler, for a specific set of data that can range in size from small (for a project) to large (for an organization). The model is a form of documentation for data requirements and data definitions resulting from the modeling process. Data models are the main medium used to communicate data requirements from business to IT and within IT, from analysts, modelers, and architects, to database designers and developers. (Sources: DAMA, 2017; Hoberman 2009; Sebastian-Coleman, 2013.)

Data Modeling The process of discovering, analyzing, and scoping data requirements and then representing and communicating these data requirements in a precise form called the *data model*. Data models depict and enable an organization to understand its data assets. (Source: Hoberman, 2009.)

Data Monetization The process of deriving economic value from money, either directly (by selling data or incorporating data into other products) or indirectly (by using data to support the exchange of other goods and services). (Source: Laney, 2018.)

Data Owner A person who is accountable for the quality of data in the widest sense of the term *quality*. *Ownership* can be defined at the process, system, domain, or data set level. Ownership must be defined not only in relation the scope of data, but also within the data chain and the data life cycle. Ownership of data may change at different points in the data chain or at different phases within the data life cycle, or one person may be accountable for data throughout the data chain or across the data life cycle.

Data Pipeline A term used to describe data coming into a data lake or other large unstructured data storage system.

Data Processing Metadata A type of operational metadata collected via the execution of programs that move data between and within systems, often transforming it as part of this movement. It includes the history of extracts and results; details of the timing, size, and success of ETL processes; data captured via ETL logs and audit/balance/control processes; and error logs. This metadata can be mined to identify schedule anomalies, patterns in files sizes, and the consistency of data delivery and processing. Data processing metadata is supported by metadata that describes SLA requirements, processing schedules, and source system contact information. It can also be used to aggregate volume metrics.

Data Producer Any person, process, or system that creates data. The term is used to distinguish between data consumers (who use data) and data creators (who make data). A data consumer for one process may be a data producer for another process.

Data Profiling A form of data analysis used to inspect data and assess the quality of data and metadata. Using statistical techniques to discover data structure and content, profiling enables analysts to determine how closely data aligns with the expectations of data consumers. Profiling provides a picture of data structure, content, rules, and relationships by applying statistical methodologies to return a set of standard characteristics about data: data types; field lengths; cardinality of columns; granularity; value sets; format patterns; content patterns; implied rules; cross-column and cross-file data relationships; and cardinality of these relationships. There are benefits to profiling data in different contexts. For example, comprehensive profiling of data at the beginning of the project life cycle can be used to test assumptions about data in order to reduce project risks. Profiling of data within a system can also be used in quality improvement efforts to identify data issues, improve metadata, define data quality measurements, set thresholds, and so on. (Sources: Olson, 2003; Sebastian-Coleman, 2013.)

Data Profiling Results The detailed data values returned when data is run through a profiling process. For example, profiling results for columns usually include minimum and maximum values, implied format and data type, along with a frequency distribution of the set of values.

Data Provenance The origin of the data, usually understood as the system or process through which data is created.

Data Quality A measure of the degree to which data meets the expectations and requirements of data consumers. This idea is sometimes expressed as the degree to which data is "fit for a purpose." The term *data quality* is also sometimes used to refer to the activities and tools used to manage the quality of data (See *Data Quality Management.*)

Data Quality Dimension A characteristic of data that can be measured and through which its quality can be quantified. There are many frameworks that define data quality dimensions. There is no agreed-to set. However, all account for similar concepts that have a common sense meaning.

Data Quality Issue Any condition of data that presents an obstacle or a risk to a data consumer's use of that data regardless of who discovered the issue, where/when it was discovered, what its root causes are, or what the options are for remediation.

Data Quality Issue Management The process of removing or reducing the impact of obstacles to the use of data by data consumers (people, processes, and systems) by identifying, analyzing, quantifying, prioritizing, and remediating the root causes of obstacles to data consumers' uses of data. (Source: Sebastian-Coleman, 2013.)

Data Quality Management A set of activities intended to ensure that data is fit for the purposes of data consumers; it includes the core activities required to assess, measure, and report on the condition of data as well as those required to manage data issues, prevent problems, and improve the quality of data.

Data Quality Management Strategy A plan that defines the core data quality management capabilities the organization will implement, what data sets they will be applied to, what tools will be used, who will be responsible for executing them, and what the expected benefits will be to the organization.

Data Quality Measurement Results The detailed data values returned when data quality rules or reasonability tests are executed. For example, the result of measuring the completeness of a column will return the count of records with a NULL, count of total records, percentage of records violating the rule, and potentially other calculations that put the individual measurement result in context (e.g., threshold value, mean of past results). (Source: Sebastian-Coleman, 2013.)

Data Quality Monitoring The ability, through measurements and other controls, to track levels of quality within a system or process to ensure that it continues to meet requirements and to detect unexpected changes in patterns of size, composition, or other characteristics of population, and to detect potential issues so action can be taken in response to them.

Data Quality Rule A constraint defined on a quality dimension for a data set, a data element, or the relationship between data elements. Data quality rules can be used to validate or measure data as well as to monitor data. Data quality rules can be the basis of transformation rules to cleanse data.

Data Quality Standard An assertion about the expected condition of data, usually related directly to a quality dimension: how complete the data is; how well it conforms to defined rules for validity, integrity, and consistency; and how it adheres to defined expectations for presentation. A standard may be expressed as a simple rule ("First Name must be populated on Member records") or may describe a set of conditions that must be met ("Address data must conform to USPS standards"). Data quality standards should be measurable. Determining whether data meets a set of conditions may involve multiple measurements.

Data Set A collection of data brought together for a purpose. The definition of *set* may be simple with a clear purpose; for example, a table is a data set put together to represent attributes associated with a specific entity. Or it may be more complicated and serve multiple purposes; for example, data domain may comprise multiple tables from multiple systems and be used for billing and interacting with customers as well as analysis and reporting.

Data Standards Assertions about how data should be created, presented, transformed, or conformed for purposes of consistency in presentation and meaning and to enable more efficient use. Data standards can be defined at the process (describing the required inputs or expected outputs), value (column/field), structure (table), or database levels. They have an impact on technical processing and storage of data as well as on data consumer access to and use of data.

Data Steward A steward is a person whose job is to manage the property of another person. Data stewards manage data assets on behalf of others in the best interests of the organization (McGilvray, 2021). Informally, a subject matter expert in a data domain, data set, process, or data element who acts accountably toward data and on whom others rely for information and expertise. Formally, as a job title, a person who has specifically defined responsibilities related to helping the organization create, manage, govern, use, and derive value from its data.

Data Stewardship Stewarding data is a way of interacting with data; specifically, acting with accountability for data for the good of the organization. Data can be "stewarded" at different levels, using informal and formal approaches. Stewardship is required of every individual who creates or uses organizational data. *Data stewardship* is the most common label to describe accountability and responsibility for data and processes that ensure effective control and use of data assets. (Sources: DMBOK2; Seiner, 2014.)

Data Store A generic name for a database, data warehouse, mart, lake, fabric or other system that holds data for analytics, operations, or other purposes.

Data Strategy A plan that describes how the organization intends to get value from its data. A data strategy requires that the organization has the data it needs to support business goals and that the organization can use the data effectively. A data strategy must account for the data itself (how the organization will obtain or create the data it needs and how this data will be managed for value over its life cycle) and for the ability of the organization to use the data (accessibility and tooling, metadata, and other explicit knowledge required for use, skills, knowledge, and experience—data literacy—of data consumers).

Data Supply Chain The set of processes through which data is created and distributed within an organization or among organizations.

Data Validation A process of executing tests against data to determine whether it is usable or not. Validation can include a range of functions, from checking received data against control files to interrogating specific fields and rules. Different actions can be defined based on the results of the validation tests.

Data Valuation Data asset valuation is the process of understanding and calculating the economic value of data to an organization.

Data Warehouse An integrated, centralized decision support database and the related software programs used to collect, cleanse, transform, and store data from a variety of operational sources to support business intelligence. A data warehouse may also include dependent data marts. (Source: DAMA, 2011.)

Default Value A value populated in a column or field to indicate that a meaningful value is not available or does not pertain to the attribute in the context of the record.

Derived Data Data created within a system from other data, for example, through a complex transformation rule or calculation.

Designed Data Data that has been created through processes that account for its quality in relation to its potential uses. Designed data includes characteristics that help enable its use; for example, it is supported by high-quality metadata, and it meets identified standards for interoperability.

Dimension of Quality See *Data Quality Dimension.*

Distribution of Values A synonym for a *column profile of values.* It includes both the count of each distinct value in a column and the percentage of records associated with that value. In many cases, a distribution of values provides a quick way of assessing the reasonability of data content. A distribution for a data set or increment can be compared with other data sets (such as a benchmark or a previous instance of the same data set) to identify whether there are differences that may indicate a problem with the data.

Edit A control on data input. Edits constrain what data can be input to a system. Some edits are simple (e.g., using a drop-down list of options to preventing an invalid value from being entered in a field). Others are can be more complex (e.g., preventing a record from being inserted if an instance of the record already exists in the system).

Enterprise Data Model (EDM) A holistic, enterprise-level, implementation-independent conceptual or logical data model that provides a common consistent view of data across the enterprise. It is common to use the term to mean a high-level, simplified data model, but this is a question of abstraction for presentation. An EDM includes key enterprise data entities (i.e., business concepts), their relationships, critical guiding business rules, and some critical attributes. It sets forth the foundation for all data and data-related projects. (Source: DMBOK2.)

Entity In the process of entity resolution, an entity is "a real-world person, place, or thing that has a unique identity that distinguishes it from all other entities of the same type" (Talburt, 2011, p. 205). In the process of modeling, an entity is a concept being modeled and is sometimes used as a synonym for *table.*

Extract, Transform, Load (ETL) The process of pulling data from a source system, preparing it for use in a target system, and then loading it to that target system. ETL is the standard process for populating data in data warehouses and marts. In Big Data environments, an ELT (extract, load, transform) process is sometimes adopted. ELT speeds up the process of making data available by removing the need to transform data to load it.

Field See *Column.*

File A set of data that has not been put into a data structure (e.g., a table).

Foreign Key Relationship A foreign key in a table is a reference back to another table. For example, a diagnosis code in a claim table will join to the diagnosis code table and connect with descriptions and other information about the meaning of the code.

Format Conformity A dimension of data quality that answers the question of whether data is in the expected form, usually defined via data type and length. Format conformity refers to the adherence of data to a defined physical format. For example, US Zip codes are five digits long. A Zip code that contains fewer or more than five digits does not conform to the expected length of a Zip code. A US Zip code that contains letters does not conform to the expected format of a Zip code. Some data elements have strict format requirements that are enforced via data type constraint (e.g., dates). Others have very broad requirements that may not be worth measuring (e.g., first name must be made up of letters, but can be of almost any length).

Frequency Distribution See *Distribution of Values.*

General Data Protection Regulation (GDRP) A European Union data protection legislation implemented in 2018.

Health Insurance Portability and Accountability Act (HIPAA) Legislation enacted by the US federal government in 1996; contains provisions that affect the use of protected health information.

Integrity A dimension of data quality that answers the question: Do the pieces of a data set relate to each other (fit together) in expected ways? Integrity refers to the state of being whole and undivided or the condition of being unified. Integrity is the degree to which data conform to data relationship rules (usually as defined by the data model) that are intended to ensure the complete, consistent, and valid presentation of data representing the same concepts. Integrity represents the internal consistency of a data set.

Issue Management See *Data Quality Issue Management*.

Management The process of controlling people, activities, or things to meet a set of goals.

Master Data Master data objects are core business objects used in different applications across an organization, along with their associated metadata, attributes, definitions, roles, connections, and taxonomies. Master data objects represent the "things" that matter most to an organization—those that are logged in transactions, reported on, measured, and analyzed. (Source: Loshin, 2008.)

Metadata Explicit (i.e., documented) knowledge about data that enables data to be created, understood, and used. Metadata is required for the use of data. The absence of metadata is a data quality issue because lack of information about data is an obstacle to the use of data. A wide range of information is included under the umbrella of metadata. Metadata includes information about technical and business processes, data rules and constraints, and logical and physical data structures. It describes the data itself (e.g., databases, data elements, data models), the concepts the data represents (e.g., business processes, applications systems, software code, technology infrastructure), and the connections/relationships between data and concepts. (Source: DMBOK2.)

Metadata Asset A set of metadata that is used for particular purposes that bring value to the organization. For example, a data dictionary for a particular system is a metadata asset. Metadata assets are sets of metadata that, taken all together, constitute the metadata assets of the organization.

Metadata Management A specialized form of data management that focuses on managing metadata throughout its life cycle. Metadata management encompasses planning, implementation, and control activities to enable access to high-quality, integrated metadata. Metadata management activities focus on ensuring that high-quality metadata is widely accessible throughout the enterprise. (Source: DMBOK2.)

Metadata Model A data model that defines the attributes of and relationships among different types of metadata assets (e.g., business glossary, catalog, data dictionary, data quality standards, data processing metadata). As with other data models, it describes the attributes associated with each entity. For example, metadata attributes for each table in a database include things like: Table Business Name, Table Physical Name, Table Subject Area, Originating system for the table, and so on. It can be used to define requirements and to support overall metadata management.

MIN/MAX In a column profile, the minimum (lowest) and maximum (highest) values in a distribution of values, based either numerically, alphabetically, or through a combination.

Normalization The process of structuring relational data so it follows the standards for normal form as defined by E.F. Codd. In less technical language, it means reducing multiple instances of an attribute to one instance so there is less redundancy and one and only one source for each value.

Operational Metadata Operational Metadata describes details of the processing and accessing of data.

Optionality As part of data modeling, defining whether the population of a column is mandatory/required or optional (populated only under particular circumstances).

Organizational Culture "The pattern of beliefs, values and learned ways of coping with experience that have developed during the course of an organization's history, and which tend to be manifested in its material arrangements and in the behaviors of its members" (Brown, 1998). More simply put, culture describes the way people work within an organization, with some reflection on why they work the way they do. The culture of an organization may be described through characteristics such as the attitude toward work itself, leadership style, and so on.

Organizational Data Data created and captured as part of the process of exchanging goods and services. Commercial organizations, governments, educational institutions, and non-profits all create data that reflects the operational practices of those organizations as well as the people and other organizations with which a given organization interacts.

Originating Source System A system that creates data. Used to signify where a particular data set, or even a single data element, was first created. The term is used to describe the role a system plays in the data life cycle for a particular subset of data. Systems can play multiple roles.

Parent-Child Relationship In a referential relationship, the entity that must "come first" is referred to as the *parent entity*. The entity that depends on the first entity is the *child entity*. For example, for an organization to sell products, it must first have a listing of its products. "Product" would be a parent entity to "Sales." The use of *parent/child* as a metaphor for these relationships allows for other assertions; for example, orphan records are records on a child table for which references are not present on the parent table.

Personal Information Protection and Electronic Documents Act (PIPEDA) Canadian Privacy protection legislation passed in 2000.

Precision A dimension of quality that describes the degree to which data meets a requirement for exactitude.

Process A series of steps that turns inputs into outputs.

Product The output from a process.

Reasonability A dimension of data quality that answers the question: Does this data conform to general expectations based on the population it represents?

Reference Data Reference data, sometimes referred to as *look-up data* or *code and description data*, associates codified data values with their meanings. It is used "to characterize other data in an organization or to relate data to information beyond the boundaries of an organization" (Chisholm, 2001). Reference data is critical to the use of other data. Without reference data, other data is often incomprehensible.

Referential Integrity (RI) The degree to which data in two or more tables related through a foreign key relationship is complete. Referential integrity is often explained through parent/child table relationships. Within a database, all values that are present in a child table should also be present in its parent table. If a child table has values that are not in its parent table (orphan values), it does not have referential integrity with the parent table. The concept of referential integrity can also be applied at the record level.

Relevance A dimension of quality that answers the question: Will this data meet my needs? Relevance measures the applicability of the data to the goals of data consumers.

Risk The possibility that something unpleasant or unwelcome will happen. Risk to data is the possibility that something will negatively affect its quality and make it less fit for use or that it will be misused, either intentionally or unintentionally.

Risk Management Using managerial resources to integrate risk identification, risk assessment, risk prioritization, development of risk-handling strategies, and mitigation of risk to acceptable levels. (Source: ASQ.)

Root Cause The root cause of a problem is the fundamental reason the problem exists.

Service Level Agreement (SLA) A formal commitment between a team that provides services and the users of those services to meet specific levels of performance, for example, to provide services within a defined timeframe. Production support teams for IT systems often have SLAs to define expected delivery of data and availability of the system.

Single Source of Truth A term used to describe an aspirational goal of some data management processes: to establish one system or data set that will contain the highest-quality data in the organization and that all data consumers will use this as their source of data. The concept of a single source of truth is also contrasted with the idea of "multiple versions of the truth"—multiple data sets that may represent the same people, objects, or events, but that may have variation based on how data is collected, structured, processed, or maintained.

Source System An application or database from which a person, process, or other system obtains data. The data may originate in the source system, or it may simply be stored there for usage.

Source-to-Target Mapping (STTM) See *Data Mapping Specifications*.

Standard Something considered by an authority or by general consent as a basis of comparison; an approved model. Or it is a rule or principle that is used as a basis for judgment. Standards embody expectations in a formal manner. To standardize something means to cause it to conform to a standard or to choose or establish a standard for something. ASQ defines *standard* as "the metric, specification, gauge, statement, category, segment, grouping, behavior, event or physical product sample against which the outputs of a process are compared and declared acceptable or unacceptable." (Source: ASQ.)

Standardization To standardize data is to make it conform to a standard, however that standard is defined (Note: In data management, *standardization* is different from *normalization*.)

Structured Data Data that is defined through a data model.

System An interconnected set of elements that is coherently organized to achieve a purpose. (Source: Meadows, 2008).

System/Application An information technology (IT) system is an application designed to enable users of the system to execute processes and meet goals, whether these are business oriented (sell products) or have other ends (play a game). Information systems include hardware, software, peripheral equipment, and data.

System Constraint A condition in a system that prevents or minimizes actions that the system can perform.

System Control A means of providing feedback about automated activities carried out by an automated process or system. Controls may be put in place to stop a process or send an alert if conditions of the control are met. See *ABC Controls*.

System of Record A system that is designated as the place where the best copy of a data set or even a single data element exists.

Table A data-based structure comprising rows and columns that organize data about a defined entity.

Target System A system or application to which data is brought in order to be stored and used. For example, a data warehouse is a target system that is populated with data from disparate applications and databases.

Technical Data Skills The ability to query data, organize it, aggregate it, and present it for purposes of communicating about the data.

Technical Metadata Technical metadata provides information about the technical details of data, the systems that store data, and the processes that move it within and among systems.

Technology Strategy A technology strategy describes how the organization will improve and leverage technology in support of business goals. It will include the future state technical architecture the organization intends to build, how the organization will make decisions about technology, and what strategic drivers will influence these decisions.

Threshold See *Tolerance*.

Timeliness A dimension of quality. The degree to which data is available for use within a required timeframe.

Tolerance The level of rule violation, error, or unexpected condition that is acceptable. May be expressed as a raw number or as a percentage of records or variance from a set number. May be calculated in different ways, depending on what is being measured and how measurements are executed.

Traditional Data With the emergence of the term *Big Data*, the term *traditional data* has emerged to refer to data created in older technology. It is worth noting that even traditional data can be "big."

Transformation Rule A transformation rule describes how data should be changed as it is brought from a source system into a target system. Transformation rules can be simple (directly moving a value; reformatting a field) or complex (combining a set of records to a single record).

Trustworthiness A dimension of data quality that measures the perceived reasonability of the data itself, confidence in the source of the data, and the reliability of the systems in which it is created and managed.

Uniqueness/non-duplication A dimension of quality; refers to the degree to which redundant data is present within a system or data structure. Uniqueness can be understood at the entity instance level (Does the master data contain multiple representations of the same customer?), at the record level (Does the sales data contain multiple instances of the same transaction?), and, in reference data, at the value level (Does the value set contain values with meanings that overlap?).

Unstructured Data Data that is not defined through a data model.

Usability A dimension of data quality that measures the degree to which data consumers can actually use the data (e.g., they have the metadata they need to understand data content and structure, they have the tools they need to access the data, and the data content includes the required population of entity instances and the characteristics of the population they want to study).

Validity A dimension of data quality. Expresses the relationship between values populated in a field and values defined in a domain of valid values. A domain may be defined through a list of values stored in a data dictionary (gender code = M, F, U) *or* in a reference data table (e.g., all of the diagnosis codes in the diagnosis code table), *or* it may be defined through a range of values (e.g., amount paid must be between $0 and $1 million) through a defined logic rule (e.g., birth date cannot be before today's date minus 100 years) *or* through a description of values that are *not* valid (first name cannot contain numbers. First name cannot = DO NOT USE, and so on) *or* through a combination of these methods. Note: A value may be valid but not necessarily correct in a given context.

Value Chain The set of processes and activities through which the creation and use of data contributes value to an organization's products and services.

Volatility The degree of change that data will be subject to over time. Highly volatile data will change frequently. Static data will not change at all.

Volume Metrics Measurements of the amount of data brought into or used by the system along with measurements of the relationship between data usage, processing, and system performance.

Bibliography

"If you tell the truth, you won't have to remember anything."

Mark Twain

Ackoff, R. (1967). Management misinformation systems. *Management Science, 14*(4), B147−B156.

Ahlstrom, R. (2019). The Role of Data in the Age of Digital Transformation. *Forbes*, January 17, 2019. https://www.forbes.com/sites/forbestechcouncil/2019/01/17/the-role-of-data-in-the-age-of-digital-transformation/#4c1b4ac94509.

Aiken, P. (1995). *Data Reverse Engineering: Slaying the Legacy Dragon*. McGraw-Hill.

Aiken, P., & Billings, J. (2013). *Monetizing Data Management: Finding the Value in Your Organization's Most Important Asset*. Technics Publications.

Aiken, P., & Gorman, M. (2013). *The Case for the Chief Data Officer: Recasting the C-Suite to Leverage Your Most Valuable Asset*. Morgan Kaufmann.

Algmin, A. (2019). *Data Leadership: Stop Talking and Start Making an Impact!* Dataversity Press.

Allen, G., & Chan, T. (2017). Artificial Intelligence and National Security. (Website). Belfer Center for Science and International Affairs, Cambridge, MA. https://www.belfercenter.org/sites/default/files/files/publication/AI%20NatSec%20-%20final.pdf.

Alter, S. (2014). Theory of workarounds. *Communications of the Association for Information Systems, 34*(55), 1041−1066.

Anodot. (n.d.). The Price You Pay for Poor Data Quality. (Blog). https://www.anodot.com/blog/price-pay-poor-data-quality/.

ASQ. Website for the ASQ (formerly the American Society for Quality). https://asq.org/.

Australian Curriculum, Assessment and Reporting Authority (ACARA). (n.d.). F-10 Curriculum, General Capabilities, Literacy. (Website). https://www.australiancurriculum.edu.au/media/3596/general-capabilities-literacy-learning-continuum.pdf.

Batini, C., Cappiello, C., Francalanci, C., & Maurino, A. (2009). Methodologies for data quality assessment and improvement. *ACM Computing Surveys, 41*(3), Article 16, 1−52.

Benson, P. (2019a). ISO 8000 Data Quality Principles. (White Paper). January 19, 2019. https://eccma.org/private/download_library.php?mm_id=22.

Benson, P. (2019b). The Guide to ISO 8000. (White Paper). February 13, 2019. https://eccma.org/private/download_library.php?mm_id=22.

Black, A., & van Nederpelt, P. (2020). Dimensions of Data Quality (DDQ) 2020: Definitions, Extended Version. (White Paper developed in conjunction with DAMA Netherlands). June 2020.

Brackett, M. (2012). *Data Resource Design*. Technics Publications.

Brown, A. (1998). *Organizational Culture*. Financial Times.

Brumfiel, G. (2021). Anti-Vaccine Activists Use a Federal Database to Spread Fear About COVID Vaccines. NPR (National Public Radio). June 14, 2021. https://www.npr.org/sections/health-shots/2021/06/14/1004757554/anti-vaccine-activists-use-a-federal-database-to-spread-fear-about-covid-vaccine.

Burke, P. (2000). *A Social History of Knowledge: From Gutenberg to Diderot*. Polity.

Business Dictionary. (n.d.). Definitions of *Corporate Governance* and *Information System*. (Website). https://www.facebook.com/businessdictionary.

Cairo, A. (2016). *The Truthful Art: Data, Charts, and Maps for Communication*. New Riders.

Canic, M. (2019). The Cost of Quality: The 1:10:100 Rule. Making Strategy Happen. (Blog). https://www.makingstrategyhappen.com/the-cost-of-quality-the-1-10-100-rule/.

Centers for Disease Control and Prevention (CDC). (2020a). Guidance for Certifying Deaths Due to Coronavirus Disease 2019 (COVID-19). Clinical Outreach and Communications Activity (COCA). (Webinar). April 16, 2020. https://emergency.cdc.gov/coca/ppt/2020/Final_COCA_Call_Slides_04_16_2020.pdf.

Centers for Disease Control and Prevention (CDC). (2020b). Health Equity Considerations and Racial and Ethnic Minority Groups. July 24, 2020. https://www.cdc.gov/coronavirus/2019-ncov/community/health-equity/race-ethnicity.html.

Centers for Disease Control and Prevention (CDC). (2020c). ICD-10-CM Official Coding and Reporting Guidelines, April 1, 2020 through September 30, 2020. (Guidelines for Covid 19.) *International Classification of Diseases, Tenth Revision, Clinical Modification* (ICD-10-CM). https://www.cdc.gov/nchs/covid19/icd-10-cm-coding-guidelines.htm.

Chien, M. (2019). Drive Data Quality Improvement from a Foundation of Metrics. Gartner Research Note. ID G00378494. (PDF). July 22, 2019.

Chien, M., & Ankush, J. (2021). Magic Quadrant for Data Quality Solutions. Gartner Research Note. ID G00389794. (PDF). March 15, 2021.

Chien, M., Judah, S., & Ankush, J. (2020). Build a Data Quality Operating Model to Drive Data Quality Assurance. Gartner Research Note. ID G00466307. (PDF). January 29, 2021.

Chisholm, M. (2001). *Managing Reference Data in Enterprise Databases. Binding Corporate Data to the Wider World.* Morgan Kaufmann.

Chisholm, M. (2010). *Definitions in Information Management.* Design Media.

Chisholm, M. (2012). Data Quality Is Not Fitness for Use. *Information Management*, August 16, 2012. https://www.facebook.com/InfoMgmt.

Chisholm, M. (2015). Just What Is Data Quality? TDAN. (Website). November 1, 2015. https://tdan.com/just-what-is-data-quality/19124.

Chisholm, M. (2017). Fundamental Concepts of Data Quality. First San Francisco Partners. (Website). July 10, 2017. https://www.firstsanfranciscopartners.com/blog/fundamental-concepts-data-quality/?cn-reloaded=1.

Clark, R. P. (2008). *Writing Tools: 55 Essential Strategies for Every Writer.* Little, Brown Spark.

Codd, E. F. (1970). A relational model of data for large shared data banks. *Communications of the ACM, 13* (6), 377–387.

Codd, E. F. (1979). Extending the database relational model to capture more meaning. *ACM Transactions on Database Systems, 4*(4), 379–434.

Codd, E. F. (1982). Relational database: A practical foundation for productivity. *Communications of the ACM, 25*(2), 109–117.

Cramer, J. J. (2019). Why You Need a Data Steward and Best Practices to Do It Right. Dun and Bradstreet Perspectives. (Website/blog). March 15, 2019. https://www.dnb.com/perspectives/master-data/6-key-responsibilities-of-data-stewards.html.

Crosby, P. (n.d.). Quality Is Free—If You Understand It. (Website). http://archive.wppl.org/wphistory/PhilipCrosby/QualityIsFreeIfYouUnderstandIt.pdf.

Daas, P. J. H., Ossen, S. J. L., & Tennekes, M. (2010). Determination of Administrative Data Quality: Recent Results and New Developments. (Session Paper). https://q2010.stat.fi/media/presentations/special-session-34/daas_ossen_tennekes_q2010_paper_session34_piet_daas_paper.pdf.

DalleMule, L., & Davenport, T. H. (2017). What's Your Data Strategy? The Key Is to Balance Offense and Defense. *Harvard Business Review*, May–June 2017. https://hbr.org/2017/05/whats-your-data-strategy.

DAMA. (2009). *The Data Management Body of Knowledge.* Technics Publications, [DMBOK1].

DAMA. (2011). *The DAMA Dictionary of Data Management* (2nd ed.), Susan Earley (Ed.), Technics Publications.

DAMA. (2017). *The Data Management Body of Knowledge* (2nd ed.). Technics Publications, [DMBOK2].

Daston, L., & Galison, P. (2010). *Objectivity*. Zone Books.

Data Leaders. (2017). The Leader's Data Manifesto. https://dataleaders.org/.

Davenport, T. H., & Bean, R. (2020). Are You Asking Too Much of Your Chief Data Officer? *Harvard Business Review*, February 07, 2020. https://hbr.org/2020/02/are-you-asking-too-much-of-your-chief-data-officer.

Davidson, B., Lee, Y. W., & Wang, R. (2004). Developing data production maps: Meeting patient discharge data submission requirements. *International Journal of Healthcare Technology and Management*, 6(2), 223–240.

De Saulles, M. (2020). Data Poisoning: A Ticking Time Bomb. *Information Matters*, July 31, 2020. https://informationmatters.net/data-poisoning-ai/.

Dedeke, A. (2005). Building quality into the information supply chain. In R. Wang, E. Pierce, S. Madnick, & C. W. Fisher (Eds.), *Advances in Management Information Systems—Information Quality Monograph (AMIS-IQ)*. Monograph.

DeFeo, J. A., & Juran, J. M. (2014). *Juran's Quality Essentials for Leaders*. McGraw-Hill.

Deloitte. (2016). The Evolving Role of the Chief Data Officer in Financial Services: From Marshal and Steward to Business Strategist. (White Paper). https://www2.deloitte.com/content/dam/Deloitte/uy/Documents/strategy/gx-fsi-evolving-role-of-chief-data-officer.pdf.

Deming, W. E. (1986). *Out of the Crisis* (2nd ed.). MIT Press.

Deming, W. E. (1994). *The New Economics for Industry, Government, Education* (2nd ed.). MIT Press.

Derman, E. (2011). *Models. Behaving. Badly: Why Confusing Illusion with Reality Can Lead to Disaster on Wall Street and in Life*. Free Press.

Dodds, L. (2020). Do Data Scientists Spend 80% of Their Time Cleaning Data? Turns Out, No? (Lost Boy: The Blog of @ldodds). January 31, 2020. https://blog.ldodds.com/2020/01/31/do-data-scientists-spend-80-of-their-time-cleaning-data-turns-out-no/#:~:text=variant%20of%20it%3A-,Data%20scientists%20spend%2080%25%20of%20their%20time,data%20rather%20than%20creating%20insights.&text=Data%20scientists%20only%20spend%2020,data%20quality%2C%20standards%2C%20access.

Domo. (2018). Data Never Sleeps 6.0. (Website). https://www.domo.com/solution/data-never-sleeps-6.

Eckerson, W. W. (2002). Data Warehousing Special Report: Data Quality and the Bottom Line. (ADTmag.com). May 1, 2002. https://web.archive.org/web/20050405233600/http://www.adtmag.com/article.asp?id=6321.

Edvinsson, H. (2019). *Data Diplomacy: Keeping Peace and Avoiding Data Governance Bureaucracy*. Technics Publications.

Eltis, D. (2001). The volume and structure of the transatlantic slave trade: A reassessment. *The William and Mary Quarterly*, 58(1), 17–46.

English, L. (1999). *Improving Data Warehouse and Business Information Quality: Methods for Reducing Costs and Increasing Profits*. Wiley.

English, L. (2009). *Information Quality Applied: Best Practices for Improving Business Information, Process, and Systems*. Wiley.

Enterprise Data Management Council (EDM). (2014). Data Management Capability Assessment Model (DCAM). https://dgpo.org/wp-content/uploads/2016/06/EDMC_DCAM_-_WORKING_DRAFT_VERSION_0.7.pdf.

European Commission. (n.d.). Protection of Personal Data. (Website). https://ec.europa.eu/info/aid-development-cooperation-fundamental-rights/your-rights-eu/know-your-rights/freedoms/protection-personal-data_en.

European Commission. (2016). Regulation (EU) 2016/679 of the European Parliament and of the Council of 27 April 2016 on the protection of natural persons with regard to the processing of personal data and on the free movement of such data, and repealing Directive 95/46/EC (General Data Protection Regulation) (Text with EEA relevance). (Website). https://eur-lex.europa.eu/legal-content/EN/TXT/?uri=celex%3A32016R0679.

Evans, N., & Price, J. (2012). Barriers to the effective deployment of information assets: An executive management perspective. *Interdisciplinary Journal of Information, Knowledge, and Management*, 7, 177–199.

Evans, N., & Price, J. (2018). Death by a thousand cuts: Behaviour and attitudes that inhibit enterprise information asset management. *Information Research*, 23(1), paper 779.

Evans, N., & Price, J. (2020). Development of a holistic model for the management of an enterprise's information assets. *International Journal of Information Management, 54*, 102193.

Evernden, R., & Evernden, E. (2003). *Information First: Integrating Knowledge and Information Architecture for Business Advantage*. Elsevier.

EWSolutions. (n.d.). Data Management University: Definition of *Data Literacy*. (Website.) https://www.ewsolutions.com/services/data-literacy/.

Farlex. The Free Dictionary by Farlex. Definition of *Statistics*. (Website). https://www.thefreedictionary.com/Statistical+data.

Feigenbaum, A. (1991). *Total Quality Control* (3rd ed., revised). McGraw-Hill.

Fenn, J., & Blosch, M. (2018). Understanding Gartner's Hype Cycles. Gartner Research. ID: G00370163. August 20, 2018. https://www.gartner.com/en/documents/3887767.

Few, S. (2015a). *The Data Loom: Weaving Understanding by Thinking Critically and Scientifically with Data*. Analytics Press.

Few, S. (2015b). *Signal: Understanding What Matters in a World of Noise*. Analytics Press.

Fisher, T. (2017). Validating Data in the Data Lake. DZone. (Website). January 9, 2017. https://dzone.com/articles/validating-data-in-the-data-lake.

Forbes Insights. (2019). Rethinking the Role of the Chief Data Officer. May 22, 2019. https://www.forbes.com/sites/insights-intelai/2019/05/22/rethinking-the-role-of-the-chief-data-officer/#1cb3dcf31bf9.

Funk, J. (2019). What's behind technological hype? *Issues in Science and Technology, 36*(1), 36–42.

Gartner. (2014). Gartner Says Beware of the Data Lake Fallacy. (Website). July 28, 2014. https://www.gartner.com/en/newsroom/press-releases/2014-07-28-gartner-says-beware-of-the-data-lake-fallacy#:~:text=%22The%20fundamental%20issue%20with%20the,of%20information%2C%22%20said%20Mr.&text=More%20detailed%20analysis%20is%20available,.com%2Fdocument%2F2805917.

Gartner Glossary. (n.d.). Definition of *Data Literacy*. https://www.gartner.com/en/information-technology/glossary/data-literacy.

Gartner Glossary. (n.d.). Definition of *Data Strategy*. https://www.gartner.com/en/information-technology/glossary/data-strategy.

Garvey, J. (2008). *The Ethics of Climate Change: Right and Wrong in a Warming World*. Continuum.

Garvin, D. A. (1987). Competing on the Eight Dimensions of Quality. *Harvard Business Review*, November 1987. https://hbr.org/1987/11/competing-on-the-eight-dimensions-of-quality.

Ghosh, A. (2017). *The Great Derangement: Climate Change and the Unthinkable*. University of Chicago Press.

Gitelman, L. (Ed). (2013). *Raw Data Is an Oxymoron*. MIT Press.

Goodman, M., Finnegan, R., Mohadjer, L., Krenzke, T., & Hogan, J. (2013). Literacy, numeracy, and problem solving in technology-rich environments among U.S. adults: Results from the Program for the International Assessment of Adult Competencies 2012: First Look (NCES 2014-008). U.S. Department of Education. Washington, DC: National Center for Education Statistics. https://nces.ed.gov/pubs2014/2014008.pdf.

Google. Google Books Ngram Viewer. (Website). http://books.google.com/ngrams. Search included: *data literacy, numeracy, data fluency, literacy*.

Gould, S. J. (1996). *The Mismeasure of Man*. W.W. Norton & Company.

Gummer, E., & Mandinach, E. B. (2015). Building a Conceptual Framework for Data Literacy. Teachers College Record. (Website). https://www.tcrecord.org/Content.asp?ContentId=17856.

Hainey, S., & Van Hove, N. (2016). S&OP, Current State and a Vision for the Future: An Interview with Steven Hainey. Supply Chain Trend. December 13, 2016. https://supplychaintrend.com/2016/12/13/sop-a-vision-for-the-future-the-expert-interview-series-7/.

Harris, J. (2015). Big Data Quality—Part 1. (SAS Blogs). https://blogs.sas.com/content/datamanagement/2015/10/07/big-data-quality-part-1/.

Heien, C. H. (2012). Modeling and Analysis of Information Product Maps (Ph.D. Thesis). University of Arkansas at Little Rock, 2012. https://library.ualr.edu/record=b1775281~S4 [Accessed via a PDF from C.H. Heien].

Hillard, R. (2010). *Information-Driven Business. How to Manage Data and Information for Maximum Advantage*. Wiley.

Hippe, R. (2012). How to measure human capital? The relationship between numeracy and literacy. *Économies et Sociétés, 46*(8).

Hoberman, S. (2009). *Data Modeling Made Simple* (2nd ed.). Technics Publications.

Hoberman, S. (2015). *Data Model Score Card: Applying the Industry Standard on Data Model Quality*. Technics Publications.

Holland, J. H. (1992). Complex adaptive systems. *Daedalus, 121*(1), 17−30.

Huff, D. (1954). *How to Lie with Statistics*. W.W. Norton.

iEdunote. (n.d.). Definition of *Management*. (Website). https://www.iedunote.com/management.

Information Is Beautiful. (2021). World's Biggest Data Breaches & Hacks. Information Is Beautiful. (Website). Updated April 2021. https://informationisbeautiful.net/visualizations/worlds-biggest-data-breaches-hacks/.

International Data Group. (2018). The State of Digital Business Transformation, 2018. (White Paper). April 22, 2018. https://www.idg.com/news/the-state-of-digital-business-transformation-2018/.

International Data Group. (2019). Is Digital Transformation Dead? The Experts at IDC Say Absolutely Not. https://www.idg.com/is-digital-transformation-dead-the-experts-at-idc-say-absolutely-not/.

International Data Group. (2020). 2020 State of the CIO. January 23, 2020. https://www.idg.com/tools-for-marketers/2020-state-of-the-cio/.

International Organization for Standardization (ISO). (2016). ISO 8000-61:2016 Data Quality—Part 61: Data Quality Management: Process Reference Model. [PDF].

Ivanov, K. (1972). Quality-control of information: On the concept of accuracy of information in data-banks and in management information systems. Stockholm, Sweden: The Royal Institute of Technology and the University of Stockholm Sweden. https://www8.informatik.umu.se/~kivanov/diss-avh.html.

Jewell, N. (2018). Study Reveals How Much Time Is Wasted on Unsuccessful or Repeated Data Tasks. IT Pro Portal. (Website). June 08, 2018. https://www.itproportal.com/features/study-reveals-how-much-time-is-wasted-on-unsuccessful-or-repeated-data-tasks/.

Jones, B. (2020a). *Data Literacy Fundamentals: Understanding the Power & Value of Data*. Data Literacy Press.

Jones, B. (2020b). *Learning to See Data: How to Interpret the Visual Language of Charts*. Data Literacy Press.

Joshik, K. (n.d.). Chapter 15: Development Life Cycle and Systems Analysis. Online course: Database Management Systems. University of Missouri St Louis; Information Systems and Technology Department. http://www.umsl.edu/~joshik/msis480/chapt15.htm.

Jugulum, R. (2014). *Competing with High Quality Data: Concepts, Tools, and Techniques for Building a Successful Approach to Data Quality*. Wiley.

Juran, J. M. (1992). *Juran on Quality by Design: The New Steps for Planning Quality into Goods and Services*. Free Press.

Juran, J. M. (Ed.). (1995). *A History of Managing for Quality*. ASQ Press.

Jurevicius, O. (2013). Value Chain Analysis. Strategic Management Insight. (Website). April 25, 2013. https://strategicmanagementinsight.com/tools/value-chain-analysis.html.

Kahneman, D. (2013). *Thinking, Fast and Slow*. Farrar, Straus and Giroux.

Keizer, G. (2004). Gartner: Poor Data Quality Dooms Many IT Projects. CRN. (Website). May 17, 2004. https://www.crn.com/news/channel-programs/18841781/gartner-poor-data-quality-dooms-many-it-projects.htm.

Keller, S., Korkmaz, G., Orr, M., Schroeder, A., & Shipp, S. (2017). The evolution of data quality: Understanding the transdisciplinary origins of data quality concepts and approaches. *Annual Review of Statistics and Its Application, 4*, 85−108.

Kenett, R. S., & Redman, T. (2019). *The Real Work of Data Science: Turning Data into Information, Better Decisions, and Stronger Organizations*. Wiley.

Kent, W. (2000). *Data and Reality*. 1st Books Library, First edition published in 1978.

King, S. (2010). *On Writing: A Memoir of the Craft* (Classic edition). Scribner.

Kite-Powell, J. (2020). Here's How 2020 Created a Tipping Point in Trust and Digital Privacy. *Forbes*, October 27, 2020. https://www.forbes.com/sites/jenniferhicks/2020/10/27/heres-how-2020-created-a-tipping-point-in-trust-and-digital-privacy/?sh=132ae2254fc5.

Klein, A., Do, H.-H., Karnstedt, M., Lehner, W., Hackenbroich, G., & Lehner, W. (2007). Representing Data Quality for Streaming and Static Data. Data Engineering Workshop, 2007 IEEE 23rd International. https://www.researchgate.net/publication/4297383_Representing_Data_Quality_for_Streaming_and_Static_Data.

Knaflic, C. N. (2015). *Storytelling with Data: A Data Visualization Guide for Business Professionals*. Wiley.

Koerth, M. (2020). The Uncounted Dead: Why Some People Who Likely Died from COVID-19 Aren't Included in the Final Numbers. FiveThirtyEight. (Website). https://fivethirtyeight.com/features/coronavirus-deaths/?cid=referral_taboola_feed.

Kolesar, P. J. (1994). What Deming told the Japanese in 1950. *Quality Management Journal, 2*(1), 9−24.

Kumar, V. (2019). Solving Data Quality in Streaming Data Flows. (Blog). March 13, 2019. https://streamsets.com/blog/solving-data-quality-streaming-data-flows/.

Ladley, J. (2010). *EIM: Enterprise Information Management*. Morgan Kaufmann.

Ladley, J. (2019). *Data Governance: How to Design, Deploy and Sustain an Effective Data Governance Program* (2nd ed.). Morgan Kaufmann, First edition published in 2012.

Lanata, S., & Miller, B. L. (2021). A Vaccination Against the Pandemic of Misinformation: False Beliefs, Similar to Those Seen in Alzheimer's Patients, May Result from a Lack of Science Literacy. *Scientific American*, February 22, 2021. https://www.scientificamerican.com/article/a-vaccination-against-the-pandemic-of-misinformation/.

Laney, D. (2017). *Infonomics: How to Montetize, Manage, and Measure Information as an Asset for Competitive Advantage*. Bibliomotion.

Laudon, K. C., & Laudon, J. P. (2001). *Essentials of Management Information Systems: Organization and Technology in the Networked Enterprise* (4th ed.). Prentice Hall.

Lohr, S. (2014). For Big-Data Scientists, "Janitor Work" Is Key Hurdle to Insights. *New York Times*, August 17, 2014. https://www.nytimes.com/2014/08/18/technology/for-big-data-scientists-hurdle-to-insights-is-janitor-work.html.

Loshin, D. (2001). *Enterprise Knowledge Management: The Data Quality Approach*. Morgan Kaufmann.

Loshin, D. (2008). *Master Data Management*. Morgan Kaufmann.

Loshin, D. (2011). *The Practitioner's Guide to Data Quality Improvement*. Morgan Kaufmann.

Lynch, M. (2019). What Are the Five Stages of Reading Development? The Edvocate. (Website). March 13, 2019. https://www.theedadvocate.org/what-are-the-five-stages-of-reading-development/.

Madsen, L. B. (2019). *Disrupting Data Governance*. Technics Publications.

Mahanti, R. (2019). *Data Quality: Dimensions, Measurement, Strategy, Management, and Governance*. ASQ Quality Press.

Marr, B. (2017). *Data Strategy: How to Profit from a World of Big Data, Analytics and the Internet of Things*. Kogan Page.

Marr, B. (2018). How Much Data Do We Create Every Day? The Mind-Blowing Stats Everyone Should Read. *Forbes*, May 21, 2018. https://www.forbes.com/sites/bernardmarr/2018/05/21/how-much-data-do-we-create-every-day-the-mind-blowing-stats-everyone-should-read/?sh=5dd4fad260ba.

Marr, B. (2019). 13 Mind-Blowing Things Artificial Intelligence Can Already Do Today. *Forbes*, November 11, 2019. https://www.forbes.com/sites/bernardmarr/2019/11/11/13-mind-blowing-things-artificial-intelligence-can-already-do-today/#3c68972b6502.

Marsh, R. (2005). Drowning in dirty data? It's time to sink or swim: A four-stage methodology for total data quality management. *Journal of Database Marketing & Customer Strategy Management, 12*, 105−112.

Massachusetts Institute of Technology (MIT). Center for Information Systems Research. Definition for *Data Strategy*. https://cisr.mit.edu/content/classic-topics-data.

Mayer-Schönberger, V., & Cukier, K. (2014). *Big Data: A Revolution That Will Transform How We Live, Work, and Think*. Mariner Books.

McGilvray, D. (2021). *Executing Data Quality Projects: Ten Steps to Quality Data and Trusted Information* (2nd ed.). Morgan Kaufmann, First edition published in 2008.

McGilvray, D., Price, J., & Redman, T. (2016). Barriers that slow/hinder/prevent companies from managing their information as a business asset: Most commonly observed root causes. *Data Leaders*, October 2016. https://dataleaders.org/tools/root-cause-analysis/.

McKendrick, J. (2018). Overcoming Digital's Fragmented Funding Model. *Forbes*, January 16, 2018. https://www.forbes.com/sites/joemckendrick/2018/01/16/overcoming-digitals-fragmented-funding-model/#427fe2fa15b5.

Meadows, D. (2008). *Thinking in Systems: A Primer*. Chelsea Green Publishing.

Mecca, B. (2019). How can we reduce Bitcoin pollution? *Yale Environment Review*, April 30, 2019. https://environment-review.yale.edu/how-can-we-reduce-bitcoin-pollution-0.

Montoya, S. (2018). Defining Literacy. GML Fifth Meeting. October 17 to October 18, 2018. (Conference Presentation). http://gaml.uis.unesco.org/wp-content/uploads/sites/2/2018/12/4.6.1_07_4.6-defining-literacy.pdf.

Moody, D., & Walsh, P. (1999). Measuring the Value of Information: An Asset Valuation Approach. European Conference on Information Systems (ECIS 1999). https://www.semanticscholar.org/paper/Measuring-the-Value-Of-Information-An-Asset-Moody-Walsh/bc8ee8f7e8509db17e85f8108d41ef3bed5f13cc.

Moore, S. (2018). How to Create a Business Case for Data Quality Improvement. Smarter with Gartner. June 19, 2018. https://www.gartner.com/smarterwithgartner/how-to-create-a-business-case-for-data-quality-improvement.

Morrow, J. (2021). *Be Data Literate: The Data Literacy Skills Everyone Needs to Succeed*. Kogan Page.

Myers, D. (2017). List of Conformed Dimensions of Data Quality (r4.3). http://dimensionsofdataquality.com/alldimensions.

Myers, D. (n.d.). Research on the Dimensions of Data Quality. (Blog). http://dimensionsofdataquality.com/research.

Myers, J. (2016). How to answer the top three objections to a data lake. *Info World*, September 6, 2016. https://www.infoworld.com/article/3095232/how-to-answer-the-top-three-objections-to-a-data-lake.html.

New Oxford American Dictionary (NOAD). (2005). 2nd ed. Oxford University Press.

NewVantage Partners. (2020). Big Data and AI Executive Survey 2020: Executive Summary of Findings. Foreword by Thomas Davenport and Randy Bean. https://www.newvantage.com/thoughtleadership.

Nunberg, G. (1996). Farewell to the information age. In G. Nunberg (Ed.), *The Future of the Book*. University of California Press. https://pdfs.semanticscholar.org/dee7/d152532896141e15505ef08126b2fe4387e2.pdf.

O Brien, D. (2020a). The Role of Data Management in "The New Normal". (Blog). May 8, 2020. https://castlebridge.ie/2020/05/08/the-role-of-data-management-in-the-new-normal/.

O Brien, D. (2020b). Email to the author. December 20, 2020.

O Brien, D. (2021). Email to the author. June 8, 2021.

O'Keefe, K., & O Brien, D. (2018). *Ethical Data and Information Management: Concepts, Tools and Methods*. Kogan Page.

O'Neil, C. (2016). *Weapons of Math Destruction: How Big Data Increases Inequality and Threatens Democracy*. Broadway Books.

Ogbuji, U. (2017a). Pay attention to the data to get the most out of artificial intelligence, machine learning, and cognitive computing: Learn the importance of data to the creation of artificial intelligence and cognitive applications. *IBM Developer*, September 27, 2017. https://developer.ibm.com/articles/cc-cognitive-big-brained-data-pt1/.

Ogbuji, U. (2017b). Apply the software development lifecycle to the data that feeds AI applications: Learn how to handle AI data with the same discipline as you do the code. *IBM Developer*, October 2, 2017. https://developer.ibm.com/technologies/artificial-intelligence/articles/cc-cognitive-big-brained-data-pt2/.

Olson, J. (2003). *Data Quality: The Accuracy Dimension*. Boston, MA: Morgan Kaufmann.

Online Etymological Dictionary. Definitions for *Data, Accountable*, and *Responsible*. https://www.etymonline. com/search?q=data; https://www.etymonline.com/search?q=accountable; https://www.etymonline.com/ search?q=responsible.

Orr, K. (1996). Data Quality and Systems Theory. Proceedings of the 1996 MIT International Conference on Information Quality. https://drive.google.com/file/d/0B81NXHLVoIS3N3hacmhvZ1c3V1k/view?resource-key=0-C2Ku2c0OL2ucFCEkzPpBcA.

Oxford English Dictionary. (1989). Clarendon Press.

Page, S. E. (2018). *The Model Thinker: What You Need to Know to Make Data Work for You*. Basic Books.

Panetta, K. (2019). Champion Data Literacy and Teach Data as a Second Language to Enable Data-Driven Business. Smarter with Gartner. (Website). February 6, 2019. https://www.gartner.com/smarterwithgartner/ a-data-and-analytics-leaders-guide-to-data-literacy/.

Paulos, J. A. (2001). *Innumeracy: Mathematical Illiteracy and Its Consequences*. Holt McDougal.

Perez, C. C. (2019). *Invisible Women: Data Bias in a World Designed for Men*. Abrams Press.

Perkins, B., & Wailgum, T. (2017). What Is Supply Chain Management (SCM)? Mastering Logistics End to End. *CIO*, August 27, 2017. https://www.cio.com/article/2439493/what-is-supply-chain-management-scm-mastering-logistics-end-to-end.html.

Pierce, E. (2007). Designing a Data Governance Framework to Enable and Influence IQ Strategy. Proceedings of the MIT 2007 Information Quality Industry Symposium. http://mitiq.mit.edu/IQIS/Documents/ CDOIQS_200777/Papers/01_08_1C.pdf.

Plotkin, D. (2020). *Data Stewardship: An Actionable Guide to Effective Data Management and Data Governance*. Academic Press, First edition published in 2014.

Poovey, M. (1998). *A History of the Modern Fact: Problems of Knowledge in the Sciences of Wealth and Society*. University of Chicago Press.

Popper, K. (1963). Science as Falsification. (Excerpted from Conjectures and Refutations). https://web.archive. org/web/20180502201044/http://www.stephenjaygould.org/ctrl/popper_falsification.html.

Porter, M. (2008). *Competitive Strategy: Techniques for Analyzing Industries and Competitors*. Free Press, First edition published in 1985.

Porter, T. (1986). *The Rise of Statistical Thinking*. Princeton University Press.

Press, G. (2016). Cleaning Big Data: Most Time-Consuming, Least Enjoyable Data Science Task, Survey Says. *Forbes*, March 23, 2016. https://www.forbes.com/sites/gilpress/2016/03/23/data-preparation-most-time-consuming-least-enjoyable-data-science-task-survey-says/#30a7c57a6f63.

Price, J. (2021). Email to the author. July 1, 2021.

PriceWaterhouseCoopers (PwC). (2019). Navigating the Rising Tide of Uncertainty: Key Findings from PwC's 23rd Annual CEO Survey. https://www.pwc.pt/en/issues/ceosurvey.html.

PriceWaterhouseCoopers (PwC). (2001). Global Data Management Survey 2001. [PDF—Hard Copy Printed].

PriceWaterhouseCoopers (PwC). (2004). Global Data Management Survey 2004. [Summary]. http://dssre-sources.com/news/383.php.

PriceWaterhouseCoopers (PwC). (2015). Seizing the Information Advantage—Executive Summary. How Organizations Can Unlock Value and Insight from the Information They Hold. (White Paper in conjunction with Iron Mountain). https://www.ironmountain.com/resources/whitepapers/s/seizing-the-information-advantage-executive-summary.aspx.

Radhakrishnan, D., Judah, S., & Chien M. (2021). 12 Actions to Improve Your Data Quality. Gartner Research Note. (PDF). April 1, 2021. https://www.gartner.com/en.

Redman, T. C. (1997). *Data Quality for the Information Age*. Artech House Publishers.

Redman, T. C. (2001). *Data Quality: The Field Guide*. Digital Press.

Redman, T. C. (2008). *Data Driven: Profiting from Your Most Important Business Asset*. Harvard Business Review Press.

Redman, T. C. (2016a). Bad Data Quality Costs the US $3 trillion per year. *Harvard Business Review*, September 22, 2016. https://hbr.org/2016/09/bad-data-costs-the-u-s-3-trillion-per-year.

Redman, T. C. (2016b). *Getting in Front on Data: Who Does What.* Technics Publications.

Redman, T. C. (2017). Seizing opportunity in data quality: The cost of bad data is an astonishing 15% to 25% of revenue for most companies. *MIT Sloan Management Review*, November 27, 2017. https://sloanreview.mit.edu/article/seizing-opportunity-in-data-quality/.

Redman, T. C. (2018). If Your Data Is Bad, Your Machine Learning Tools Are Useless. *Harvard Business Review*, April 1, 2018. https://hbr.org/2018/04/if-your-data-is-bad-your-machine-learning-tools-are-useless.

Reeve, A. (2013). *Managing Data in Motion: Data Integration Best Practice Techniques and Technologies.* Morgan Kaufmann.

Rosenberg, D., & Williams, T. D. (2013). Data before the fact. In L. Gitelman (Ed.), *Raw Data Is an Oxymoron.* MIT Press.

Ross, R. (2003). *Principles of the Business Rule Approach.* Addison-Wesley Professional.

Russell, A. L. (n.d.). Standardization in History: A Review Essay with an Eye to the Future. http://www.arussell.org/papers/futuregeneration-russell.pdf.

Saey, T. H. (2015a). Is redoing scientific research the best way to find truth? *Science News*, January 13, 2015. https://www.sciencenews.org/article/redoing-scientific-research-best-way-find-truth.

Saey, T. H. (2015b). Big data studies come with replication challenges. *Science News*, January 26, 2015. https://www.sciencenews.org/article/big-data-studies-come-replication-challenges.

Schneier, B. (2015). *Data and Goliath: Hidden Battles to Collect Your Data and Control Your World.* W.W. Norton & Company.

Schryvers, P. (2020). *Bad Data: Why We Measure the Wrong Things and Often Miss the Metrics That Matter.* Prometheus.

Schultz, J. (2019). How Much Data Is Created on the Internet Each Day? (Micro Focus Blog). https://blog.microfocus.com/how-much-data-is-created-on-the-internet-each-day/.

Schwab, K. (2017). *The Fourth Industrial Revolution.* World Economic Forum.

Sebastian-Coleman, L. (2013). *Measuring Data Quality for Ongoing Improvement: A Data Quality Assessment Framework.* Morgan Kaufmann. https://booksite.elsevier.com/9780123970336/appendices.php.

Sebastian-Coleman, L. (2018). *Navigating the Labyrinth: An Executive Guide to Data Management.* Technics Publications.

Seiner, R. (2014). *Non-Invasive Data Governance: The Path of Least Resistance and Greatest Success.* Technics Publications.

Shannon, C. E. (1948). A mathematical theory of communication. *The Bell System Technical Journal*, *27*(3), 379−423, 623−656.

Shannon, C., & Weaver, W. (1949). Recent Contributions to the Mathematical Theory of Communication. September 1949. http://waste.informatik.hu-berlin.de/Lehre/ss11/SE_Kybernetik/reader/weaver.pdf.

Shapiro, B. (2003). *A Culture of Fact: England 1550−1720.* Cornell University Press.

Shear, M. D., Perlroth, N., & Krauss, C. (2021). Colonial Pipeline Paid Roughly $5 Million in Ransom to Hackers. *New York Times*, May 13, 2021; updated June 7, 2021. https://www.nytimes.com/2021/05/13/us/politics/biden-colonial-pipeline-ransomware.html.

Snaplogic. (2021). The State of Data Management—The Impact of Data Distrust. Snaplogic (Website). https://www.snaplogic.com/resources/research/state-of-data-management-impact-of-data-distrust.

Soares, S. (2012). Big Data Governance over Streaming Data. Dataversity. (Website). https://www.dataversity.net/big-data-governance-over-streaming-data/#.

Standish Group. (2014). The Rule of Ten. (PDF). https://www.standishgroup.com/sample_research_files/RuleTen.pdf.

Stein, B., & Morrison, A. (2014). The Enterprise Data Lake: Better Integration and Deeper Analytics. PwC Technology Forecast: Rethinking Integration. (PDF). https://www.pwc.com/us/en/technology-forecast/2014/cloud-computing/assets/pdf/pwc-technology-forecast-data-lakes.pdf.

Stephens-Davidowitz, S. (2017). *Everybody Lies: Big Data, New Data, and What the Internet Can Tell Us About Who We Really Are*. HarperCollins.

Strunk, W., Jr., & Poff, M. (2018). *The Elements of Style Workbook: Writing Strategies with Grammar Book*. Tip Top Education.

Sutherland, D. (2019). R.I.P. data governance: Data enablement is the clear path forward. (Blog). *IBM Smarter Business Review*, September 11, 2019. https://www.ibm.com/blogs/services/2019/09/11/r-i-p-data-governance-data-enablement-is-the-clear-path-forward/#: ~ :text=Data%20enablement%20is%20an%20active, data%20lineage%20and%20associated%20metadata.

Talburt, J. R. (2011). *Entity Resolution and Information Quality*. Morgan Kaufmann.

Tarnoff, B. (2018). Data is the new lifeblood of capitalism—don't hand corporate America control. *The Guardian* (US ed.), February 1, 2018. https://www.theguardian.com/technology/2018/jan/31/data-laws-corporate-america-capitalism.

Taylor, S. (2020). *Telling Your Data Story: Data Storytelling for Data Management*. Technics Publications.

Tech Target. (n.d.). Definitions for *Supply Chain, Supply Chain Management, and Unstructured Data*. What Is (Website). https://whatis.techtarget.com/definition/supply-chain; https://whatis.techtarget.com/search/query?q=supply+chain++management; https://whatis.techtarget.com/search/query?q=unstructured+data+.

Technopedia Dictionary. (n.d.). Definition for *Data Lake*. https://www.techopedia.com/definition/30172/data-lake.

Temming, M. (2021). The most ancient supermassive black hole is bafflingly big: The black hole doesn't fit theories of how the cosmic beasts grow so massive. *Science News* (Website). January 18, 2021. https://www.sciencenews.org/article/most-ancient-supermassive-black-hole-quasar-bafflingly-big.

The Data Governance Institute. http://www.datagovernance.com/ (Website). https://datagovernance.com/the-data-governance-basics/definitions-of-data-governance/.

The Literacy Cooperative. (n.d.). Literacy Levels. (Website). https://www.literacycooperative.org/literacy-facts/literacy-levels/.

Thomas, G. (2008). Data Governance with a Focus on Information Quality. The MIT 2008 Information Quality Industry Symposium. (PDF). http://mitiq.mit.edu/IQIS/Documents/CDOIQS_200877/Papers/12_02_4C-2.pdf.

Thomas, M. (2019). The Future of Artificial Intelligence: 7 ways AI can change the world for better…or worse. Built-in. https://builtin.com/artificial-intelligence/artificial-intelligence-future (This 2019 article was updated on September 16, 2021).

Thomas, R., & McSharry, P. (2015). *Big Data Revolution: What Farmers, Doctors and Insurance Agents Teach Us About Discovering Big Data Patterns*. Wiley.

Tufte, E. (1983). *The Visual Display of Quantitative Information*. Graphics Press.

University of Cambridge. (n.d.). Porter's Value Chain. Research—Decision Support Tools. https://www.ifm.eng.cam.ac.uk/research/dstools/value-chain-/.

US Department of Defense. (1965). A Guide to Zero Defects. (PDF). https://apps.dtic.mil/dtic/tr/fulltext/u2/a950061.pdf.

US Federal Government. (2020). Improving Agency Data Skills Playbook. Federal Data Strategy. https://resources.data.gov/assets/documents/assessing-data-skills-playbook.pdf.

US Federal Reserve. (2011). SR 11-7: Guidance on Model Risk Management. Supervision and Regulation Letters. April 4, 2011. https://www.federalreserve.gov/supervisionreg/srletters/sr1107.htm.

Video Coin. (2018). The 5 Most Important Metrics to Measure the Performance of Video Streaming. (Website). July 18, 2018. https://medium.com/videocoin/the-5-most-important-metrics-to-measure-the-performance-of-video-streaming-ab41f4eb9d99.

Wand, Y., & Wang, R. (1996). Anchoring data quality dimensions in ontological foundations. *Communications of the ACM*, *39*(11), 86−95.

Wang, R. (1998). A product perspective on total data quality management. *Communications of the ACM*, *41*(2), 58−65.

Wang, R., & Strong, D. (1996). Beyond accuracy: What data quality means to customers. *Journal of Management Information Systems*, *12*(4), 5−33.

Wang, R. Y., Lee, Y. W., Pipino, L. L., & Strong D. M. (1998). Manage your information as a product. *MIT Sloan Management Review*, July 15, 1998, pp. 95−105. https://sloanreview.mit.edu/article/manage-your-information-as-a-product/.

Warner, J. (2018). Innovative, Unheard of Use Cases of Streaming Analytics. Tech Target. IoT Agenda. (Blog). April 4, 2018. https://internetofthingsagenda.techtarget.com/blog/IoT-Agenda/Innovative-unheard-of-use-cases-of-streaming-analytics.

West, M. (2011). *Developing High Quality Data Models*. Morgan Kaufmann.

Westerman, G., Bonnet, D., & McAfee, A. (2014). *Leading Digital: Turning Technology into Business Transformation*. Harvard Business Review Press.

White, A. (2013). The Three Rings of Information Governance. (Gartner Blog). June 11, 2013. https://blogs.gartner.com/andrew_white/2013/06/11/the-three-rings-of-information-governance/.

Wikipedia. Systems Development Life Cycle. https://en.wikipedia.org/wiki/Systems_development_life_cycle#cite_note-2.

Wilder-James, E. (2016). Breaking Down Data Silos. *Harvard Business Review*, December 05, 2016. https://hbr.org/2016/12/breaking-down-data-silos?autocomplete=true.

Witze, A. (2021). How to detect, resist and counter the flood of fake news. *Science News* (Website). May 6, 2021. https://www.sciencenews.org/article/fake-news-misinformation-covid-vaccines-conspiracy.

Wolf, M. (2016). *Tales of Literacy for the 21st Century: The Literary Agenda*. Oxford University Press.

Woods, D. (2009). Why Data Quality Matters. *Forbes*, September 1, 2009. https://www.forbes.com/2009/08/31/software-engineers-enterprise-technology-cio-network-data.html#5d0101ac5859.

Worldometer. (n.d.). (Website). https://www.worldometers.info/world-population/population-by-country/.

Zetlin, M., & Olavsrud, T. (2019). What Is a Chief Data Officer? A Leader Who Creates Business Value from Data. *CIO*, September 28, 2020. https://www.cio.com/article/3234884/what-is-a-chief-data-officer.html.

Zissner, W. (2016). *On Writing Well: The Classic Guide to Writing Nonfiction* (30th anniversary ed.). Harper Perennial.

Zuboff, S. (2019). *The Age of Surveillance Capitalism: The Fight for a Human Future at the New Frontier of Power*. PublicAffairs.

Index